Dismantling Contemporary Deficit Thinking

Deficit thinking is a pseudoscience founded on racial and class bias. It "blames the victim" for school failure instead of examining how schools are structured to prevent poor students and students of color from learning. *Dismantling Contemporary Deficit Thinking* provides comprehensive critiques and anti-deficit thinking alternatives to this oppressive theory by framing the linkages between prevailing theoretical perspectives and contemporary practices within the complex historical development of deficit thinking.

Dismantling Contemporary Deficit Thinking examines the ongoing social construction of deficit thinking in three aspects of current discourse—the genetic pathology model, the culture of poverty model, and the "at-risk" model in which poor students, students of color, and their families are pathologized and marginalized. Richard R. Valencia challenges these three contemporary components of the deficit thinking theory by providing incisive critiques and discussing competing explanations for the pervasive school failure of many students in the nation's public schools. Valencia also discusses a number of proactive, anti-deficit thinking suggestions from the fields of teacher education, educational leadership, and educational ethnography that are intended to provide a more equitable and democratic schooling for all students.

Richard R. Valencia is Professor of Educational Psychology and Faculty Associate of the Center for Mexican American Studies at The University of Texas, Austin.

The Critical Educator
Edited by Richard Delgado and Jean Stefancic

American Indian Education: Counternarratives in Racism, Struggle, and the Law
Matthew L.M. Fletcher

Foundations of Critical Race Theory in Education
Ed Taylor, David Gillborn, and Gloria Ladson-Billings

Persistent Inequality: Contemporary Realities in the Education of Undocumented Latina/o Students
Maria Pabon Lopez and Gerardo R. Lopez

Dismantling Contemporary Deficit Thinking: Educational Thought and Practice
Richard R. Valencia

Dismantling Contemporary Deficit Thinking
Educational Thought and Practice

Richard R. Valencia

Routledge
Taylor & Francis Group

NEW YORK AND LONDON

First published 2010
by Routledge
711 Third Avenue, New York, NY 10017

Simultaneously published in the UK
by Routledge
2 Park Square, Milton Park, Abingdon, Oxon OX14 4RN

Routledge is an imprint of the Taylor & Francis Group, an informa business

© 2010 Taylor & Francis

Typeset in Minion by
RefineCatch Limited, Bungay, Suffolk

Library of Congress Cataloging in Publication Data
Valencia, Richard R.
Dismantling contemporary deficit thinking : educational thought and
practice / Richard R. Valencia.
p. cm.—(The critical educator)
1. Education—Philosophy.   2. School management and organization.
3. Racism in education.   I. Title.
LB14.7.V27 2010
370.1—dc22

                                                        2010005311

ISBN10: 0–415–87709–1 (hbk)
ISBN10: 0–415–87710–5 (pbk)
ISBN10: 0–203–85321–0 (ebk)

ISBN13: 978–0–415–87709–1 (hbk)
ISBN13: 978–0–415–87710–7 (pbk)
ISBN13: 978–0–203–85321–4 (ebk)

This book is dedicated to all progressive scholars and educators—of color and White alike—for challenging the ubiquity of deficit thinking in our nation's schools and in society.

To all students and their families who have been pathologized and marginalized by deficit thinkers, may you hold your heads high as you engage in your own struggles against such oppression.
—**Richard R. Valencia**

Contents

List of Figures and Tables

Figures

Tables

Series Editor's Foreword

Where does deficit thinking—the idea that minority students labor under intellectual handicaps because of their family structure, linguistic background, and culture—originate? And what are the consequences of this form of thinking? This impressive volume by Richard Valencia shows the ubiquity of this idea in the field of education. Indeed, once you begin looking for it, you see evidence of it everywhere, including in the writing of liberal social scientists like Daniel Moynihan and Oscar Lewis. You see it in works of educational theory and praxis. You get more than a whiff of it in judicial opinions such as *Grutter v. Bollinger*, which upheld affirmative action at the University of Michigan on the ground that it could benefit Whites to become familiar with nonwhites and their distinctive cultures.

One even sees it in professional education. Once, early in my career, I accepted an invitation to spend two weeks at a famous law school. As the holder of a short-term chair, my duties were light—a couple of talks—and thoroughly enjoyable. I met a few students and some of the faculty. With an office of my own and paid lodging near the university, I was even able to get a bit of my own work done.

In the middle of the visit, the dean's secretary invited me to a small dinner in my honor. Hosted by the dean himself, the meal turned out to be an intimate, convivial affair, attended by a group of perhaps a dozen of the faculty, the dean, and myself. It took place in a well-appointed conference room just outside the dean's inner sanctum and was catered by a first-rate restaurant.

Located in the Southwest, the law school where I was visiting is ranked among the nation's best. The state contains a very large Latino population, most of them Mexican Americans like me. So I was not surprised when, after making small talk about legal education and mutual friends, the dean, who was seated opposite me, asked about my family.

I explained that I was the son of a Mexican immigrant father, probably undocumented, and that we had moved around a lot when I was young. I told him that my dad had held a series of industrial jobs during the war years and that by 1950 he had saved enough money to buy a small house. I had barely sketched these details, when the dean, an elegant man with a patrician background and education, burst out: "But, Delgado, what enabled you to break the cycle?"

It turned out that he meant the cycle of poverty and educational underachievement. I explained that my family did not seem, to me, at the time, poor.

Although money must have been tight, we always had enough to eat and clothes to keep us warm. And the many moves made me bookish. With few long-term friends, I found solace in books, often checking out a dozen or more from the local library and poring over them in my room.

My dinner companion was not at all satisfied. For him, my rise from working-class origins seemed so improbable as to require an explanation more persuasive than the one—a love of books—I had given. Here I was, a product of a blue-collar, immigrant family, and doing the same things that he did for a living—writing law review articles, teaching classes, and engaging in intellectual conversation in the conference room of a law school.

He and I spent a few moments in one of those discursive disconnects that one sometimes finds oneself trapped in that end up going nowhere. I did not see myself as having been mired in a culture of poverty. He did. We eventually changed the subject, but I doubt I changed his mind.

Why did it matter that my host assumed that I started life weighed down with a nearly insuperable set of handicaps? For one thing, he probably treated my accomplishments—the very ones that brought me to his school's attention—as atypical and abnormal. But they are not. Many Chicanos have the same abilities and achievement orientation that I did, if not more. I doubt that exposure to me sparked the dean to search them out; his faculty to this day contains very few Latinos or Latinas. Might it be that the presuppositions that surfaced that evening played a part in suppressing the chances of promising Chicano candidates over the years? After all, if high-achieving students or faculty of color are rare, it might be impossible to find them. So, why bother to look?

Richard Valencia shows how deficit thinking plays out in a host of educational settings, mainly in the early grades. But what is its source? I believe that my dinner companion was entirely well meaning. After all, his school had singled me out for an opportunity, even if attitudes like those of its dean may have limited my chances of landing a permanent appointment there. Was that attitude a product of the dean's own elite background? Did he internalize it through conversations with his colleagues, almost all of whom were White? Whatever its source, is it a genteel form of racism?

Is it reversible? Controllable through effort? Through lawsuits and official sanctions? Richard Valencia's fine book shows its contours and extent. Educators interested in understanding and countering its pernicious influence should read this volume to understand the magnitude of the task that awaits them.

Preface

More than a decade has passed since the publication of my 1997 edited volume, *The Evolution of Deficit Thinking: Educational Thought and Practice* (Valencia, 1997a). I am pleased to report that the book as a whole, and the various chapters by the contributing authors, have attracted considerable attention over the years by scholars, both domestic and foreign (i.e., Australia; Belgium; Bulgaria; Canada; England; Ireland; Israel; Mexico; the Netherlands; New Zealand; Spain; Taiwan). From mid–2007 to early 2009, I undertook a comprehensive computerized literature search using "deficit thinking" as the primary descriptor and numerous secondary descriptors (e.g., "deficit thinking paradigm"), and I received 436 hits of scholarly writings (e.g., books, book chapters, journal articles, and doctoral dissertations) in which authors cite the 1997 volume, as a whole or its chapters. In light of the substantial attention *The Evolution of Deficit Thinking* has garnered, and the fact that deficit thinking in education injuriously continues, I decided to write a new, comprehensive edition—*Dismantling Contemporary Deficit Thinking: Educational Thought and Practice*—in which I serve as sole author. I thought it would be fitting to introduce the notion of deficit thinking by retelling two anecdotes I shared in *The Evolution of Deficit Thinking* (see Valencia, 1997b). I also relate a very recent encounter worth communicating. These events are useful in helping to understand the core structure of the construct of deficit thinking.

Shortly after my wife and I moved to Austin, Texas in 1989, I purchased a pair of prescription eyeglasses, a routine of upgrading my lenses for a long-standing, commonplace vision problem.[1] The new frames looked attractive, the stronger lenses provided better acuity, and all seemed well. A week later, however, problems with the glasses arose. Upon taking them off my face and gently placing them on my desk, the right lens popped out (in the absence of any external force). I took the glasses back to the optometrist's office, and upon close inspection, the salesperson from whom I initially purchased the glasses informed me that the optician had cut the lens too small for the frame, resulting in a poor structural fit.

After receiving the repaired glasses a couple of days later, I wore them and went on with my daily schedule. Lo and behold, a week later, the right side lens popped out again—as if it had an energy source of its own! Again, I returned to the optometrist's office and spoke to the same salesperson about the obstinate little lens that was refusing to stay put. Having been employed in retail business many years ago while I worked my way through college, I was well aware of the business maxim, "The customer is always right." Thus, I was expecting an honest and complete resolution to the problem at hand. Apparently, the salesperson with whom I had been dealing did not embrace the above code of business conduct. Much to my amazement and chagrin, she, in a hostile tone, *blamed me* for causing the problem! She more than suggested that I handled my glasses too roughly by placing excessive pressure on the lens during my regular handling of the glasses, causing it to become displaced. She also informed me that the glasses, since repaired, were structurally fit (a point she underscored the optometrist would confirm, if need be). After denying her ludicrous accusations—and seeing I was not going to receive satisfaction—I stormed out, stuck with defective eyeglasses. Suffice it to say, for the next pair of prescription glasses I went to a reputable business.

I wish to share a related account with the reader. In early December 1995, I viewed the weekly television news program, *Dateline*, which contained an interesting segment on the dangers of escalators (Grassie, 1995), those power-driven moving stairs that make our travel less arduous in large, spread-out buildings. To my surprise, I learned from the *Dateline* story that approximately 16,000 people, most of whom are children, get injured on escalators each year. The injuries, which involve mangled toes and ankles, typically occur when the space between the side of the escalator wall and the moving belt of stairs gradually widens over time due to normal wear and tear, and thus limbs (caught by clothes) can enter and get entrapped. The *Dateline* theme examined two opposing perspectives on the cause of the injuries—one view representing escalator manufacturers, the other representing people who were injured.

The manufacturers absolved themselves of blame, claiming that those injured individuals were at fault because they stood too close to the side of the escalator wall or they wore shoes or leg clothing that placed them at risk for entanglement. The injured, on the other hand, vociferously voiced that they were not at fault, pointing to the disrepair of the escalators as the cause of the bodily injury. Based on my analysis of the evidence provided—especially that of an expert on escalators—one could make a very strong case that the gradual and normal wearing down of the escalator belt and the subsequent failure of the manufacturers or owners to repair the mechanical defects caused the thousands of injuries yearly.

In June 2008, I had an experience that ties in with the first two anecdotes. I am an avid movie buff, particularly of the science fiction, horror, and drama genres. For me, viewing films in the comfort of my home relaxes me—freeing my mind for a welcome respite from writing. In early June, I rented four DVDs (digital video discs) from the nearby Hollywood Video store. Over a period of a few days, I viewed the first three films. On the evening before the DVDs were due, I put the last film in my DVD player and proceeded to watch the movie. As I viewed the movie trailers, the quality of the DVD looked fine. When the movie started, however, a problem with the picture occurred. On the top part of the film—displayed in letterbox—broken, moving, horizontal lines in the black band appeared. I had never seen such lines before and thought perhaps they were just part of the movie. But, after viewing the film a few more minutes, and then fast-forwarding it the lines remained. So, I concluded that the DVD was defective.

The next day, I returned the four DVDs to the Hollywood Video store, and explained the problem to the clerk. She, in turn, consulted with a co-worker, a male. Upon visual inspection of the DVD, they noted that it had a very small dent. At that point, I assumed they were in agreement with me that the DVD was defective. So, I started to walk away, informing them that I was going to find a substitute movie. About two minutes later, she approached me as I was looking for a film. The clerk, in a rather calm and deliberate manner, informed me that based on the DVD's rental history, *I had damaged the DVD!* That is, given that I was the first person to have rented the film, I had to be the source of the damage. Feeling my blood pressure rise, I told her that blaming me was absolutely ridiculous. I informed her that the first time I removed the DVD from its hard plastic protective case was last evening when I gently placed the DVD in the machine. I also asked her if she had considered alternative explanations for the cause of the damage. Perhaps the DVD was damaged at the factory during the production phase. Maybe it was damaged during transit. Perhaps the damage occurred during the stocking of shelves at the store. She did not respond to my rival possibilities. Rather, the clerk underscored that I was responsible for the damage. She informed me, however, that Hollywood Video would "eat" the cost of the DVD ($21.99)—but (and this is what further infuriated me) with one condition. On all my future DVD rentals, I would have to pay a 25¢ damage waiver ("Play Guard"), which appears to be some kind of insurance. I told her that her condition was insulting and wrong, punishing me for something I did not do. I further informed her that I would not agree with her ridiculous stipulation, and then asked for the name and phone number of the regional manager so I could register a complaint. I left two phone messages, but to no avail. I then tracked down and called customer service at Hollywood Video's corporate headquarters. I explained to the agent that I believed the clerk had violated my rights as a customer, then she devised an insulting and punitive solution to the issue. The agent agreed that the clerk was wrong and had violated company policy. That is, there was no hard evidence for the clerk to conclude that I had caused the damage to the DVD. Furthermore, the agent said that the clerk's demand that I pay the 25¢ damage waiver on future rentals was against policy. The agent apologized to me and informed me that she would pass this matter on to the regional manager, who in turn, would speak to the clerk. In sum, it felt good for justice to have prevailed. On top of all this, Hollywood Video corporate headquarters gave me two free movie rentals!

So, what do a defective pair of eyeglasses, an escalator in disrepair, and a flawed DVD have in common, and what do they have to do with "deficit thinking"—the construct under study in this book? Well, a lot. In the three instances, the more powerful party locates the blame for the problem or injury in the individual person, the victim, rather than in the structural problems of the unit. In the three cases above, *the blame shifts from structural defects* (i.e., a poor fit between lens and frame of the eyeglasses; worn, moving parts in disrepair in the escalator; a defect in the DVD) to *the alleged disregard, faults, and carelessness of the wronged party.*

Although the units of analysis described in the three examples are inorganic (i.e., the eyeglasses and the DVD) and mechanical (i.e., the escalator), I trust they provide mundane and commonsense illustrations for the reader unfamiliar with the notion of deficit thinking. If I were to compress the construct of deficit thinking into its most condensed meaning, it would be this: *Deficit thinking is tantamount to the process of "blaming the victim." It is a model founded on imputation, not documentation.*

Regarding the term itself, "deficit thinking," it appears that a small cadre of activist scholars in the early 1960s constructed this brilliant two-word phrase. These heterodox scholars launched an assault on the prevailing view that asserted the poor and people of color caused their own social, economic, and educational problems (A. Pearl, personal communication, August 8, 1991). Thus, the term deficit thinking appears to have its origin as a social construction stemming from the rising tide of nonconformist thought of the 1960s, a period in which deficit thinking discourse utilized its own socially constructed terms, such as, the "culturally disadvantaged child" (Black, 1966), "socialization of apathy and underachievement" (Hess, 1970), "cultural deprivation" (Edwards, 1967), and "accumulated environmental deficits" (Hess & Shipman, 1965).

Dismantling Contemporary Deficit Thinking focuses on how scholars, educators, and policymakers have advanced the deficit thinking model to explain school failure, particularly among low-socioeconomic status (SES) students of color (such as African American; Mexican American; Puerto Rican). These students have suffered, and continue to suffer, substantial overrepresentation among those who experience academic problems and school failure (e.g., reading below grade level; dropping out of high school),[2] and such students are prime and easy targets of the deficit thinking intellectual discourse that blames them, their cultures, and their families for diminished academic success.

Of the various conceptual frameworks that scholars and others have advanced to explain school failure among low-SES student groups of color, the deficit thinking paradigm has held the longest currency (Menchaca, 1997). Although the deficit thinking model contains several explanatory variants (to be discussed in chapters 2, 3, and 4), this model, as a whole, posits that students who fail in school do so because of alleged internal deficiencies (such as cognitive and/or motivational limitations) or shortcomings socially linked to the youngster—such as putative familial deficits and dysfunctions. Given the endogenous nature of the deficit model, deficit thinkers hold blameless systemic factors (e.g., school segregation; inequalities in school financing; curriculum differentiation) in explaining why some students fail in school. By sharp contrast, anti-deficit thinkers assert that systemic and structural aspects strongly influence school failure among many low-SES students of color. Structural inequality models focus on how the powerful (e.g., legislators; school boards) organize schools to exclude students of color from optimal learning by not making available equal educational opportunities.[3] I must underscore, however, that students who are failing in school must—along with their parents—muster every effort they can in achieving school success (e.g., the development of good study habits; parental participation in education; political involvement and action). Of course, such endeavors are difficult to mount in alienating, inequitable learning environments. Although deficit thinking overwhelmingly locates the bases of school failure in students, their cultures, and their families, failing students and their significant others must assert themselves in their quest for school success, given that deficit thinking theory and practice certainly do not work for their best interests. As I and coauthor Art Pearl discuss in the concluding chapter of this book, connecting political action and education can result in workable school reform.

My general plan of this book is to update what is known about the notion of deficit thinking, with an emphasis on dismantling contemporary deficit thinking in regard to educational thought and practice. Deficit thinking, an endogenous theory, "blames the victim" for school failure rather than examining how schools are structured to prevent poor students and students of color from learning. *Dismantling Contemporary Deficit Thinking* frames the linkages between prevailing theoretical perspectives and contemporary practices within the complex historical development of deficit thinking. The mindset of deficit thinking, which stems from the confluence of ideology and science, continues to make a volatile and egregious union in trying to understand the many educational problems and needs of economically disadvantaged and socially segregated student groups of color. A major objective of *Dismantling Contemporary Deficit Thinking* is to examine the ongoing social construction of deficit thinking as seen in the three endogenous variants of the paradigm—the genetic pathology model, the culture of poverty model, and the marginalization of poor students and students of color—and their families—as viewed through the "at-risk" discourse. In this book, I challenge these three contemporary variants of the deficit thinking theory and discuss competing explanations for the pervasive school failure of many students in the nation's public schools. Also, I discuss a number of suggestions from the fields of teacher education, educational leadership, and educational ethnography that aim to provide a more equitable and democratic schooling for all students.

Dismantling Contemporary Deficit Thinking contains six chapters. In chapter 1, "The Construct of Deficit Thinking," I unpack the complexities and characteristics of deficit thinking. I do so by first discussing the notion of school failure among students of color, underscoring that *racialized opportunity structures lead to racialized achievement patterns*. Next, I outline the features of several theoretical perspectives that scholars have offered to explain school failure (i.e., communication process; caste; social reproduction and resistance; deficit thinking). Last, I discuss a number of characteristics of deficit thinking in six specific settings (i.e., victim blaming; oppression; pseudoscience; temporal changes; educability; heterodoxy). A major point I develop here is that rationality has a lot to do with the attraction of deficit thinking. Based on the "law of parsimony," deficit thinking *is a type of cognition that is a relatively simple and efficient form of attributing the "cause" of human behavior*.

"Neohereditarianism: Pseudoscientific Explanations for Racial Differences in Intelligence" is the subject of chapter 2. Here, I focus on the resurgence of hereditarianism. My discussion of neohereditarianism centers on three temporal waves: wave I (1958–1982), wave II (1987–1997), and wave III (2000–2008). Wave III carries particular significance because contemporary scientific racists (e.g., John Philippe Rushton; Richard Lynn) focus on *international comparisons* of racial differences in intelligence, in which these authors draw genetic conclusions. A highlight of this chapter is coverage of the Pioneer Fund, an organization that for many decades has financially supported the work of numerous scientific racists. The chapter concludes with a close look at scientific investigations that explore indirect and direct evidence against a genetic hypothesis of racial differences in intelligence (e.g., a critique of the concept of heritability of intelligence; a critique of the racial admixture hypothesis.

In chapter 3, I provide an analysis of "Ruby Payne's Mindsets of Poverty, Middle Class, and Wealth: A Resurrection of the Culture of Poverty Concept." Payne, who proclaims herself "the leading U.S. expert of the mindsets" of social classes, is a major national force in providing guidance about the education of poor students—via her workshops and publications—to thousands of teachers and administrators in numerous school districts across the country and abroad. The chapter begins with a brief overview of historical attitudes toward the demonization of the poor. I follow by discussing and critiquing the "culture of poverty" notion, first popularized by anthropologist Oscar Lewis and then subsequently appropriated by many scholars who assert that the poor are the makers of their own problems. Next, I introduce and then provide a critique of Payne's best-selling book, *A Framework for Understanding Poverty* (2005). In my comprehensive critique of Payne (2005), based on 13 publications, I identified five themes that emerge across this corpus of literature: (a) culture of poverty; (b) stereotyping; (c) nonscientific research base; (d) deficit thinking; (e) no consideration of alternative explanations. I close this chapter with an Epilogue, briefly noting how Payne responds to some of her critics. I enter this fray by providing a published response to Payne's response.

In chapter 4, "At-Risk Students or At-Risk Schools?," I examine the historical and contemporary discourse on the "at-risk" notion. Popularized in the

1980s, policymakers—and later researchers—utilized the term in a predictive scheme to identify students (generally low-SES pupils of color) who were prone to experience school failure, particularly dropping out of school. I assert that deficit thinking permeates the term at-risk, as it overlooks any strengths and promise of the student so labeled, while drawing attention to the presumed personal and familial shortcomings of the individual. As such, at-risk has become a person-centered explanation of school failure. The at-risk notion fits under the rubric of deficit thinking in that the construct pays little, if any, attention to how schools are institutionally implicated in ways that exclude students from optimal learning. The chapter starts with a discussion of the historical origins of the at-risk notion (e.g., ties to medical and public health), followed by a coverage of the 1980s excellence movement (framers and critics) in which the term "at-risk" was co-opted by the proponents of the excellence movement. Next, I discuss the early and later at-risk literature (i.e., 1983 to 2008 range) based on representative studies of the "Early At-Risk Discourse" and "Contemporary At-Risk Discourse" periods. I close the chapter by discussing the characteristics of schools that place students at high risk for failure. I examine the nature of at-risk schools by discussing inequities in the distribution of teacher quality characteristics and inequities in the distribution of economic resources for schooling.

The subject of chapter 5 is "Deconstructing Deficit Thinking: Practical Solutions for Teacher Educators, Educational Leaders, and Educational Ethnographers." In light of the pervasiveness of deficit thinking in schools, it is important to discuss how some critical theorists have attempted to eliminate the pathologization of poor students and students of color. In this chapter, I provide examples of a number of means by which readers can utilize to help promote a more equitable and democratic schooling for all students. In particular, I draw from the literature that speaks to deconstructing deficit thinking in the following areas: (a) preservice teacher education; (b) parental engagement in education; (c) educational leadership; (d) social justice; (e) ethnography of schools.

The final chapter (6), coauthored with Arthur Pearl, presents a discussion of "Conclusion: (A) The Bankruptcy of the Standards-Based School Reform Movement; (B) Toward the Construction of Workable School Reform: Democratic Education." Here, we argue that deficit thinking is deeply embedded in every aspect of modern American life. Because it is so ubiquitous it saturates the entire political spectrum; what are advertised as campaigns against deficit thinking become instead substitutions of different forms of the deficit paradigm. Deficit thinking constitutes a fundamental canon of conservative thought, and, we contend, the model is inevitable without a countervailing theory that explains differences in alternative terms. In this chapter, we cover two key topics. First, we describe and critique the major type of school amelioration in the U.S.—the standards-based school reform movement, whose driving force is high-stakes testing. Among several critiques, we assert that this movement is structurally misdirected, hence deficit driven, because it treats the symptoms (i.e., poor student achievement), not the root cause (i.e., inferior schooling). Second, we offer an alternative to deficit thinking in education, namely "democratic education." We warn that unless schooling can meet the requirements of democratic education, deficit thinking will continue to exist and if anything, grow. We propose four requirements of democratic education: (a) providing that kind of knowledge that will enable every student to engage equally in an informed debate on every generally recognized important social and personal issue; (b) guaranteeing everyone equally the particular rights of freedom of expression (which includes the right to express unpopular political beliefs, and to disagree with constituted authority, including the teacher), specified rights of privacy, due process that includes presumption of innocence, trial by independent tribunal, and protection from cruel and unusual punishment, and freedom of movement; (c) providing everyone the opportunity and the skill to participate with equal power in all the decisions that effect one's life; (d) providing everyone equal encouragement in all of society's legitimate activities. Each of these four features of democratic education (knowledge; rights; participation; encouragement) has specific relevance to different aspects of deficit thinking, which we examine closely.

Acknowledgments

The completion of this book would not have been possible without the support and contributions of a number of individuals. I gratefully thank Catherine Bernard, Publisher, and Georgette Enríquez, Editorial Assistant of the Education list of Routledge, for their support throughout this project. Appreciation is also extended to Richard Delgado and Jean Stefancic, coeditors of the Critical Educator Series, for their encouragement and support from the beginning to completion of writing this book. My sincere appreciation goes to the University of Texas Co-operative Society for awarding me a Subvention Grant to assist with the underwriting of this book. Very special thanks go to Dr. Bruno J. Villarreal for his outstanding work as my research assistant. His bibliographic searches and typing of the manuscript text were of stellar quality.

I extend my affection and gratitude to my wonderful wife Marta. Thank you, dear, for your unwavering and thoughtful support while I cloistered myself in my home office for many hours during the writing of this book. To my pride and joy—my twin boys, Juan and Carlos—thanks, *mijos*, for being so patient while Dad did his writing.

1
The Construct of Deficit Thinking

School Failure

Widespread and intractable school failure among millions of students in kindergarten through grade 12 (K–12) education in the U.S. is deplorable. Unfortunately, many African Americans, Mexican Americans, Puerto Ricans, some other Latinos, and American Indians—especially those students of color from economically poor and working-class backgrounds—experience such failure (e.g., disproportionately high dropout rates from secondary school). School failure is the persistently, pervasively, and disproportionately low academic achievement among a substantial proportion of low-SES students of color (Valencia, 2002). Indeed, this pattern of low academic achievement of many students of color is long-standing. As a case in point, let us examine the 1927 master's thesis by Rollen Drake.[1]

A Comparative Study of the Mentality and Achievement of Mexican and White Children reports one of the earliest comparative investigations of academic achievement of Mexican American and White students. Seventh- and eighth-grade students attending a public school in Tucson, Arizona, participated in Drake's (1927) study. Table 1.1 presents comparative descriptive statistics for this investigation undertaken more than eight decades ago. For the Mexican American sample, I present, on the bottom half of Table 1.1, characteristics that describe the group's performance on the Stanford Achievement Test. As the data show, the Mexican American students, compared to their White peers, as a group demonstrated a depressed mean, restriction in variability, and a positively skewed distribution.

I must underscore that the Mexican American group also demonstrated overlap, meaning that some Mexican American students in Drake's study performed higher in achievement than some of their White peers (i.e., 15.4% of the Mexican American students exceeded the median score for the White students). It is important to emphasize that these four characteristics of Mexican American achievement test performance seen in this 1927 study became a recurring pattern for Mexican American students, as well as other Latino and African American students, for decades to come (Valencia, 2002). In addition to the features of a depressed mean, restricted variability, and positive skew in test scores—which signal trouble—we also need to be mindful of the overlap feature. To disregard or ignore overlap demeans students

1

Table 1.1 Descriptive Statistics for Stanford Achievement Test (Form A) for Mexican and White Students

Descriptive Statistic	Race/Ethnicity	
	Mexican (*n* = 95)	*White* (*n* = 108)
Mode (most frequent interval)	60–64	65–69
Range	44 (max. = 79; min. = 35)	54 (max. = 94; min. = 40)
Median	60.5	68.9
Mean	60.2	69.4
Standard Deviation	8.9	10.2

Characteristics of Mexican American Academic Achievement Performance
- Mean: Depressed
- Variability: Restricted
- Skew: Positive
- Overlap: Present

Source: Adapted from Drake (1927, Tables IV and V).

of color as it may lead to a stereotype that all such students are low achievers.

School failure among numerous low-SES students of color manifests in various ways. Once again, let us take Mexican American students as a case in point—who share much in common with K–12 Puerto Rican and African American students regarding school failure. In a previous publication (Valencia, 2002), I discuss *nine schooling conditions* that play a significant role in shaping and reproducing school failure among numerous Mexican American students (i.e., school segregation, language/cultural exclusion, school financing, teacher–student interactions, teacher certification, curriculum differentiation, special education, gifted/talented education, and the Mexican American teaching force). For example, school segregation continues as a ubiquitous contemporary schooling reality for these students. Historically, the school failure of Mexican American students in the Southwest region of the U.S. originated and intensified in the crucible of forced segregation (Valencia, 2008, chapter 1; Valencia, Menchaca, & Donato, 2002). Segregated schooling of Mexican Americans and other students of color frequently led, and still leads, to inferior schooling, hence school failure (San Miguel & Valencia, 1998; Valencia, 2005; Valencia, 2008, chapter 1; Valencia et al., 2002). Another influential schooling condition, inequities in public school financing, also contributes to the school failure of students of color, particularly Mexican Americans and African Americans. For example, historically in Texas property-rich White school districts, in comparison to property-poor Mexican American school districts, regularly provided considerably broader and superior educational experiences for their students (e.g., better equipped libraries; lower teacher–pupil ratios; higher paid teachers; see Valencia, 2008, chapter 2).

In Valencia (2002), I also discuss *six schooling outcomes* (i.e., school failure) that characterize the educational reality of a substantial segment of the K–12 Mexican American public school enrollment. Mexican American students—in comparison to their White peers—perform, on average, at lower levels on various academic achievement tests, have higher rates of grade retention, and drop out of high school at higher rates (the three other schooling outcomes concern college enrollment, high-stakes testing, and school stress). In summary, the structural inequality perspective contends that strong and predictable linkages exist between schooling conditions and schooling outcomes: *Racialized opportunity structures lead to racialized academic achievement patterns.*

Theoretical Perspectives Proffered to Explain School Failure

What accounts for school failure experienced by a sizeable proportion of low-SES students of color?[2] To be sure, scholars have not kept silent on this issue. They have offered many contrasting explanations, and we should best think of them as "families" of explanatory paradigms. In brief, these models focus on:

Communication Process

The earliest variant of this family of models is the "cultural difference" framework, which has its roots in the early 1970s (Baratz & Baratz, 1970; Labov, 1970; Valentine, 1971). This perspective, launched as a reactive, but serious critique of the 1960s deficit thinking models (see Pearl, 1997b), asserted that one should view the alleged *deficits* among children and families of color (particularly of low-SES background) more accurately as *differences*. Proponents of the cultural difference framework contended that the basis of the discontinuity between student and school often lay in a mismatch between the home culture and the school culture (e.g., regarding children's mother tongue; children's learning styles) that leads to learning problems for culturally diverse students (e.g., Hale-Benson, 1986; Ramírez & Castañeda, 1974). Regarding the early culturally shaped learning styles viewpoint, scholars have critiqued this viewpoint for its unsupported generalizations, and even stereotypes (see Irvine & York, 1995).

As scholarly discourse of the cultural difference model evolved, one variant focused on possible misunderstandings between student and teacher in verbal and nonverbal communication styles (Erickson, 1987). Such misunderstandings from these marked boundaries often result in teachers labeling students as unmotivated to learn. In short, such linguistic differences may lead to trouble, conflict, and school failure. An insightful analysis of this communication process perspective is seen in Lisa Delpit's 1995 book, *Other People's Children: Cultural Conflict in the Classroom*. Drawing from her experiences as a school teacher, graduate student, and a professor of teacher education (i.e., preprofessional teacher training), Delpit delves deeply into communication blocks between students of color and teachers (predominantly White). One of the major themes Delpit focuses on is what she refers to as "the culture of power" (p. 24). She proposes that five premises need to be considered in regard to understanding how teachers have power over students. To wit:

1. Issues of power are enacted in the classroom.
2. There are codes or rules for participating in power; that is, there is a "culture of power."
3. The rules of the culture of power are a reflection of the rules of the culture of those who have power.
4. If you are not already a participant in the culture of power, being told explicitly the rules of that culture makes acquiring power easier.
5. Those with power are frequently least aware of—or least willing to acknowledge—its existence. Those with less power are often most aware of its existence. (pp. 24–26)

With these premises in mind, Delpit contends that instructional methodology, centering on different perspectives concerning the disagreements over "skill" versus "process" methods of teaching, can lead to an awareness of student detachment and miscommunication, and thus to a comprehension of what she refers to as the "silenced dialogue" (p. 24). Rather than a "skill" versus "process" instructional pedagogy, Delpit contends that "the actual practice of good teachers of all colors typically incorporates a range of pedagogical orientations" (p. 24). In summary, Delpit (p. 45) suggests that in order to optimize the teaching/learning of children of color and of low-SES background, these students

> must be *taught* the codes needed to participate fully in the mainstream of American life, not by being forced to attend to hollow, inane, decontextualized subskills, but rather within the context of meaningful communicative endeavors; that they must be allowed the resource of the teacher's expert knowledge, while being helped to acknowledge their own "expertness" as well; and that even while students are assisted in learning the culture of power, they must also be helped to learn about the arbitrariness of those codes and about the power relationships they represent.

The communication process framework certainly has theoretical import in advancing our understanding of school failure, as well as success, for low-SES students of color. Researchers in this area, however, have raised issues about the dearth of empirical inquiry that has been advanced to demonstrate the nature, presence, and academic effects of cultural discontinuity between home and schools. Such concerns have existed for at least two decades (see Kagan, 1990; Tyler et al., 2008), and have led researchers to design methodological approaches to investigate, quantitatively, cultural discontinuity (e.g., Tyler et al., 2008). Notwithstanding that scholars have conducted extremely little empirical research in this area, the communication process family of models has considerable potential to further our understanding of academic performance variability among students of color.

Caste

Another explanation of school failure lay in "caste theory," a model advanced by the late educational anthropologist John Ogbu (see, e.g., Ogbu, 1978, 1986, 1987, 1991, 1994). In his numerous writings, Ogbu classifies racial/ ethnic minority groups in the United States as either "immigrant minorities" (e.g., some Latinos from Central America; Koreans; Japanese) or nonimmigrant or "involuntary minorities" whose current societal status is rooted in slavery (e.g., African Americans), conquest (e.g., American Indians), or conquest and colonization (e.g., Mexican Americans; Puerto Ricans). Sometimes referring to these involuntary minorities as "caste-like," Ogbu (1991) asserts that members of these groups "resent the loss of their former freedom, and they perceive the social, political, and economic barriers against them as part of their undeserved oppression" (p. 9). Ogbu (1991) also argues that involuntary minorities experience frequent discriminatory treatment with respect to being "confronted with social and political barriers, given inferior education, and derogated intellectually and culturally, and they may be excluded from true assimilation into the mainstream society" (p. 9). Obgu's caste theory is not without its critics (see, e.g., Foley, 1991, 2004, 2005; Trueba, 1991). For example, Ogbu's framework tends to assert that caste-like students' school failure is endogenously based. Once overwhelmed, such minority students

> develop a dysfunctional oppositional culture that leads them to believe that they cannot be both academically successful and ethnically different. In short, caste theory makes a powerful case that involuntary minorities are not likely to succeed in school and life.
>
> (Foley, 1991, p. 67)

Social Reproduction and Resistance

Numerous scholars have advanced this family of theories (e.g., Aronowitz & Giroux, 1993; Bowles & Gintis, 1976; De Jesús, 2005; Oakes, 1985; Pearl, 1991, 2002). This cluster is also referred to as "structural inequality" or "systemic inequalities" models. When one analyzes the poor academic achievement of many students of color in the widest cultural, economic, and political contexts, macrolevel elements pertaining to (a) vicissitudes of the national economy,

(b) political influence over school policy and practice (macropolitics), and (c) the top-down, authoritarian nature of schooling are all factors theorists deem to contribute to school failure (Pearl, 1991, 1997a, 2002). In his discussion of systemic inequities, Pearl (2002) comments on the vital role of history in understanding school failure of students of color:

> Systemic refers to established processes whereby values, traditions, hierarchies, styles, and attitudes are deeply embedded into the political, economic, and cultural structures of any society. The systems that have emerged are the consequences of historical influences modified by current political pressures. History establishes in various, often subtle or disguised forms, the means by which people are included or excluded from positions of power and influence. Unless we fully understand the consequences of a particular history we fail to appreciate how Chicano school failure [for example] is the logical consequence of a once conquered people paying a continuous price for being displaced by victors leading to systematic exclusion from positions of authority and influence (see Moreno, 1999; San Miguel & Valencia, 1998). The legacy of that history finds current expression in denial of language, particular forms of miscarriages of justice, as well as ever-recurring stereotypes that influence decisions at every juncture and at every level of an individual's life. History establishes the basis for inclusion and exclusion in various societal institutions. Most powerfully, that historical legacy of inclusion and exclusion is increasingly infused throughout education. (p. 336)

Furthermore, De Jesús (2005) remarks that according to social reproduction and resistance theories,

> The role of schools is to sort individuals and groups according to the hierarchical division of labor in society. Following in this vein, schools must shape the attitudinal and ideological dispositions and values necessary for the maintenance of asymmetrical power relations between dominant and subordinate groups. Resistance theories seek to integrate the idea of individual agency with understanding the complexity of social reproduction processes.
>
> (De Jesús, p. 345)

Deficit Thinking

Of the several theories that scholars, educators, and policymakers have advanced to explicate school failure among low-SES students of color, the deficit model, the subject of this book, has held the longest currency—spanning well over a century, with roots going back even further as evidenced by the early racist discourses from the early 1600s to the late 1800s (Menchaca, 1997). The deficit thinking model, at its core, is an endogenous theory—positing that the student who fails in school does so because of his/her internal deficits or deficiencies. Such deficits manifest, adherents allege, in limited intellectual abilities, linguistic shortcomings, lack of motivation to learn, and immoral behavior. The proposed transmitters of these deficits vary according to the intellectual and scholarly climate of the times. We shall see that proponents have postulated genetics (chapter 2), culture and class (chapter 3), and familial socialization (chapter 4) as the sources of alleged deficits expressed by the individual student who experiences school failure.

Presently, many behavioral and social scientists hold the deficit thinking model in disrepute—arguing that it ignores the role of systemic factors in creating school failure, lacks empirical verification, relies more on ideology than science, grounds itself in classism, sexism, and racism, and offers counterproductive educational prescriptions for school success. However, because deficit thinking is so protean in nature, taking different forms to conform to politically acceptable notions at the moment, and while the popularity of different revisions may change, it never ceases to influence school policy and practice. Given the continuing strong conservative ascendancy in the U.S., it is not surprising that deficit thinking is currently experiencing a resurgence (e.g., see the neohereditarian works of Lynn, 2006, 2008; Lynn & Vanhanen, 2002, 2006; and Rushton, 2000 [discussed in chapter 2 of the present book]). Furthermore, not only is deficit thinking penetrating current educational thought and practice (e.g., Ruby Payne's [2005] *A Framework for Understanding Poverty* that she utilizes in in-service teacher education programs [discussed in chapter 3 of the present book]), it is shaping national sentiment toward the "undesirables," such as immigrants (see, e.g., Brugge, 2008; Chávez, 2008; López, 2005; Mangaliman, Rodríguez, & Gonzales, 2006; Sheehy, 2006). We can see sharply contrasting perspectives on the contemporary immigrant issue in Leo Chávez' book, *The Latino Threat: Constructing Immigrants, Citizens, and the Nation* (2008), and Daniel Sheehy's book, *Fighting Immigration Anarchy: American Patriots Battle to Save the Nation* (2006).

Six Characteristics of Deficit Thinking

Blaming the Victim

In 1971, William Ryan offered the social sciences *Blaming the Victim*—a now classic book. With the striking force of a two by four board, Ryan dealt a crushing blow to the backbone of deficit thinking.[3] In a penetrating and impassioned treatise, his social construction of the phrase, "blaming the victim," masterfully got to the core of the nature of deficit thinking. Ryan's book was a reaction to deficit thinking *vis-à-vis* the "culturally disadvantaged" and subsequent policies advanced in the 1960s, a time at which the deficit thinking model hit its apex with respect to volume of literature, policy interventions, and popularity. His critique transcended deficit thinking in education and covered social programs in general. Commenting on the "terrifying sameness in the programs" (p. 7) that arose from deficit thinking, Ryan observed:

In education, we have programs of "compensatory education" to build up the skills and attitudes of the ghetto child, rather than structural changes in the schools. In race relations, we have social engineers who think up ways of "strengthening" the Negro family, rather than methods of eradicating racism. In health care, we develop new programs to provide health information (to correct the supposed ignorance of the poor) and to reach out and discover cases of untreated illness and disability (to compensate for their supposed unwillingness to seek treatment). Meanwhile, the gross inequalities of our medical care delivery systems are left completely unchanged. As we might expect, the logical outcome of analyzing social problems in terms of the deficiencies of the victims is the development of programs aimed at correcting those deficiencies. *The formula for action becomes extraordinarily simple: change the victim.*

(1971, p. 8)

Ryan's (1971) *Blaming the Victim* proved especially valuable in exposing the ideological base of deficit thinking (i.e., the more powerful blame the innocent) and in showing us how deficit thinking translates to action. First, victim-blamers identify social problems. Second, they conduct a study in order to find out how the disadvantaged and advantaged are different. Third, once they identify the differences, they define these differences as the *causes* of the social problem. Fourth, they set governmental intervention in motion to correct the differences (i.e., deficiencies). The great appeal of deficit thinking as a model of social reform in the 1960s and early 1970s lay in the framework's appearance of soundness. In reference to the above four steps, Ryan notes, "All of this happens so smoothly that it seems downright rational" (p. 8).

Building on Ryan's (1971) above notion of rationality, I believe one can advance a powerful argument as to why some scholars, educators, and lay-people are attracted to and engage in deficit thinking: *This type of cognition is a relatively simple and efficient form of attributing the "cause" of human behavior.* My reasoning here stems from what we know about the "law of parsimony"—also referred to as "Ockham's razor." The law of parsimony appears to have originated in the early study of animal behavior in psychology. In his 1932 article, Nagge tentatively expresses the law of parsimony: "Of any possible number of explanations of an animal act the simplest possible explanation should be employed" (p. 493). Over the decades, the law of parsimony has become a commonplace explanatory proposition in discussions regarding behavioral laws in histories of psychology. As noted by Simonton (1995), "*Supposedly,* the human mind is so designed that it prefers simple explanations over complex explanations. Often this preference is carried to the extreme, where reality is shortchanged" (p. 93). This second sentence in Simonton's statement can potentially lead to dangerous reductionism.[4] He notes that when

scientists apply erroneous assumptions and beliefs to groups, such an application can evoke a more encompassing law. On this, Simonton quotes
Hergenhahn (1992): "Throughout history scientific and philosophical works
have often been distorted to support political ideologies" (p. 199).

Hergenhahn's (1992) point is well taken. For example, historically scholars
used social Darwinism to explain social stratification (Valencia, 1997d). Those
groups of people whom psychologists considered wealthier, brighter, and
moral—compared to the poor, intellectually dull, and immoral—attained
their privileged positions because of their alleged fitter genetic constitutions.
Certainly, social Darwinism stands out as a classic case of deficit thinking as it
reified hereditarianism and said nothing about the inculpatory role societal
structural forces had in creating a social hierarchy.

In conclusion, the law of parsimony strongly drives deficit thinking. The
reductionist nature of this law, however, raises serious concerns about deficit
thinking as a legitimate scientific principle of attribution. Given the parsi-
monious nature of deficit thinking, it is not unexpected that advocates of the
model fail to look for external attributions of an individual student's school
failure. They hold exculpatory how schools are organized to thwart learning. In
addition, inequalities in the political economy of education and oppressive
macropolicies and practices in education are ignored in understanding school
failure. Large-scale school reform is complex and highly demanding. As such,
deficit thinkers avoid systemic approaches to school reform and focus on this
simple kind of solution: "Fix" the individual student. My analysis is consonant
with Pearl (1997b, p. 151) who asserts (in the context of 1960s deficit thinking):

> Deficit models, with their person-centered frameworks, were attractive
> to scholars and policymakers in that they were more parsimonious
> theories than ones that examined the complexity of institutionalized
> inequity. They were also safer. These deficit theories could ignore external
> forces—that is, the complex makeup of macrolevel and microlevel
> mechanisms that helped structure schools as inequitable and exclusio-
> nary institutions. By accepting the simplicity of the cultural and
> accumulated environmental deficit models, scholars and policymakers
> were excused from addressing the real issues of inequality.

Oppression

It follows logically from Ryan's (1971) analysis of "victim-blamers and victims" that deficit thinking amounts to a form of oppression—that is, the cruel
and unjust use of authority and power to keep a group of people in their place.
The history of deficit thinking in education teems with examples of how
macro- and microlevel educational policies/practices fueled by class and racial
prejudice kept economically disadvantaged students of color in their place. The
historical and contemporary bases of such oppression manifest in a range of

contexts: for example, state constitutional statutes, state educational agency policies, judicial outcomes, state legislation, local school board policies, and classroom teacher practices. Here, I briefly touch on two examples of how deficit thinking is a type of oppression: compulsory ignorance laws and school segregation.

COMPULSORY IGNORANCE LAWS

The passing of laws designed to keep enslaved Africans illiterate, hence power-less in the South, constitutes one of the most brutal forms of educational oppression (see, e.g., Erickson, 1997; Miller, 1995; Weinberg, 1977). In 1740, South Carolina passed the first "compulsory ignorance" law. This new law called for heavy fines for any person who taught Blacks to write or used them as scribes. The South Carolina law unequivocally noted:

> That all and every person and persons whatsoever who shall hereafter teach, or cause any slave or slaves to be taught to write, or shall use or employ any slave as a scribe in any manner of writing whatsoever, hereafter taught to write; every such person or persons shall, for every offense, forfeit the sum of one hundred pounds current money.
>
> (Webster, 1992, p. 187)

Later, other states in the South followed South Carolina's path of legally barring Blacks from schools or forbidding literacy instruction in any form. For example, the following states adopted such laws: Missouri (1817); Virginia (1819); Georgia (1831); Mississippi (1832) (see Johnson, 2000).

Scholars have proffered two explanations for the adoption of compulsory ignorance laws. One such reason lay in the belief that enslaved Africans were mentally deficient and thus they had severe limitations on how much they could benefit from literacy training (Miller, 1995). These notions were pre-cursors of the genetic pathology era of deficit thinking in the 1920s (Valencia, 1997d). Another, and more plausible explanation for such laws was that Southern Whites used these statutes as a major control mechanism of slavery. After all, becoming literate has the potential of raising consciousness and politicizing oppressed people. In short, knowledge takes on a liberating poten-tial. As Weinberg notes, "Whites seemed to fear not that Negroes could not learn but that they would" (p. 39). Similarly, Erickson (1997) comments: "An educated Black might realize [once literate] how horribly he was treated and revolt" (p. 206).

SCHOOL SEGREGATION

Scholars have taken great interest in the forced segregation of Mexican American and African American students, as well as their desegregation.[5] Clearly, segregationist laws and related practices directed toward the intentional separation of students of color from their White peers constituted oppression. Historical evidence dates the ideological foundations of school segregation back to the racial beliefs of the 19th century that White groups should not socially interact with peoples of colored "races" (Menchaca & Valencia, 1990). Proponents of White supremacy practices predicated these policies on the belief that colored races were biologically inferior and race mixing would contaminate the White "stock" (Menchaca, 1997; Valencia, 1997d).

Deficit thinking was highly influential in the promotion of school segregation during the rooting of separate but equal education in the late 1890s and early 1900s, and particularly in the subsequent decades of entrenchment (1920s through the 1940s; San Miguel & Valencia, 1998). School officials based the forced segregation of African American and Mexican American students, for example, on views of these children as intellectually inferior, linguistically limited in English, unmotivated, and immoral—all characteristics, officials asserted, that would hold back the progress of White classmates if racial mixing in schools were permitted. Suffice it to say, deficit thinking in its manifestation of schooling practices led to inferior schooling, hence such social thought and its subsequent policy recommendations contributed substantially to school failure for many low-SES students of color (San Miguel & Valencia, 1998). Segregation, an oppressive act, resulted in "colored" and "Mexican" schools with run-down physical plants, poorly prepared teachers, insufficient supplies, dated textbooks, and dead-end curricula for allegedly mentally retarded students (San Miguel & Valencia, 1998; Valencia, 2008, chapter 1).

It is important, however, to contextualize the early school segregation of students of color within the larger realm of historical race relations and deficit thinking. Let us take Mexican Americans as a case in point. White communities began deliberately separating Mexican American students from their White peers in public schools in the post-1848 decades following the Treaty of Guadalupe Hidalgo that ended the U.S.–Mexican War (1846–1848).[6] The signing of the Treaty and the U.S. annexation, by conquest, of the current Southwest signaled the beginning of decades of persistent, pervasive prejudice and discrimination against people of Mexican origin who reside in the U.S. (Acuña, 2007; Perea, 2003). Subsequently, Whites in the Southwest practiced the racial isolation of schoolchildren as normative—despite states having no legal statutes to segregate Mexican American students from White students (San Miguel & Valencia, 1998; Valencia, 2008, chapter 1). Whites did not, however, only segregate Mexican Americans in the schools. As a colonized people, many Mexican Americans experienced segregation from "the cradle to the grave." Whites enforced segregation in maternity wards,[7] movie theaters, restaurants, and public accommodations (e.g., swimming pools) (Acuña, 2007; Martínez, 1994). Whites imposed segregation in the Southwest so completely that many Mexican Americans even had separate cemeteries (Carroll, 2003). The treatment of Mexican Americans as nonpeers allowed Whites via deficit thinking and racist policies to maintain their system of privilege and domination.

In sum, the idea of characterizing deficit thinking as a form of oppression offers a fruitful area to develop intellectually. As *Dismantling Contemporary Deficit Thinking* unfolds, I discuss more about the linkages among deficit thinking, educability perceptions, the politics of oppression, the practice of schooling, and school failure.

Pseudoscience

Blum (1978) defines pseudoscience as a "process of false persuasion by scientific pretense" (p. 12). I assert that deficit thinking tightly fits this definition. To some extent, the appeal of the deficit thinking paradigm among scholars, laypeople, and policymakers comes from the model's wrapping—the "scientific method." We are all familiar with the core of the scientific method: that is, empirical verification. Science rests on the process that begins with sound assumptions and clear conjectures (or hypotheses), moves through the operation of collecting data with reliable and valid tools, controls for key independent variables, and concludes with objective empirical verification (or disconfirmation) of the initial conjectures.

A close examination of deficit thinkers' research uniformly shows that they frequently violate the scientific method (Valencia, 1997d). Typically, deficit thinkers base their study on unsound assumptions, use psychometrically weak instruments and/or collect data in flawed manners, do not control important independent variables, and do not consider rival hypotheses for the observed findings. Of course, the preceding scenario can, and does, characterize just plain sloppy research. How does one draw the line between (a) legitimate scientific research that contains lethal flaws that prevent its publication and (b) pseudoscience? One can argue that the difference lies in the *degree of researcher bias* (which is ubiquitous), as well as the *degree of vigor* with which the researcher pursues hypothesis verification. On these distinctions between legitimate science and pseudoscience, Blum (1978 pp. 12–13) notes:

> All scientific work is guided by assumptions, and the defense of one's assumption becomes a likely source of bias. Particularly when controversial topics are being researched, some amount of bias is inherent in the position of any investigator. The label "pseudoscience" becomes pertinent when the bias displayed by scientists reaches such extraordinary proportions that their relentless pursuit of verification leads them to commit major errors of reasoning.

In addition to the above distinction between genuine science and pseudoscience, Blum (1978) also offers advice to those who wish to discern the latter. He contends that two different kinds of occurrences must join: "First, there must be attempts at verification which are grossly inadequate. Second, the

unwarranted conclusions drawn from such attempts must be successfully dis-
seminated to and believed by a substantial audience" (p. 12). As we proceed,
these two criteria will prove useful in our analysis of the development and
maintenance of deficit thinking. For example, Valencia (1997d) draws on these
standards when discussing hereditarianism, the intelligence testing movement,
and deficit thinking from about 1900 to 1930. On a final note with regard to
pseudoscience, this notion is integral to another construct, "scientific racism,"
which I define as: *The use of pseudoscience to support an alleged scientific
paradigm of White superiority, apropos to people of color* (discussed in detail in
chapter 2).

Temporal Changes

Given the pseudoscientific, hence ideological nature of deficit thinking, it
makes sense to characterize it as a dynamic and chameleonic concept. That is,
the era and its spirit greatly influence how deficit thinking manifests itself.
Two points need to be made here. First, although deficit thinking is dynamic in
nature, typically the ideological and research climates of the time shape deficit
thinking—rather than deficit thinking shaping the climates. This is not to say
that deficit thinking has kept silent in shaping macrolevel social programs and
schooling practices. A case in point was the structuring and implementing
of Operation Head Start, a federal program of the mid-1960s built on a
"compensatory" approach (Pearl, 1991, p. 286). Another example: During the
1920s, widespread hereditarian views heavily affected deficit thinking *vis-à-
vis* racial differences in measured intelligence—via perspectives entrenched in
cross-racial research endeavors, eugenics, and the nascent psychometrics
movement (Blum, 1978; Valencia, 1997d).

Second, the protean nature of deficit thinking does not manifest in the basic,
static characteristics (endogenous; imputational; oppressive) of the model.
Rather, the perceived transmitter of the alleged deficits metamorphoses. In
the *genetic pathology variant* of deficit thinking, proponents believe that the
allegedly inferior genes of people of color lead to poor intellectual performance
(Valencia, 1997d). In the *culture of poverty variant*, adherents allege that the
purported autonomous, dysfunctional, and self-sustaining cultural systems of
the poor carry the deficits and subsequent problems, such as school failure
(Foley, 1997). In the *cultural and accumulated environmental deficits variant* of
deficit thinking, supporters claim that the alleged inferior familial and home
environmental contexts transmit the pathology (Pearl, 1997b).

Educability

As a psychology major in the late 1960s at the University of California at Santa
Barbara, I quickly learned that the social and behavioral sciences have four goals
with regard to understanding human behavior: to (a) describe, (b) explain,
(c) predict, and (d) modify behavior. In its pursuit, the deficit thinking model

also strives to attain these objectives. As we have discussed, deficit thinking typically offers a *description* of behavior in pathological or dysfunctional ways—referring to deficits, deficiencies, limitations, or shortcomings in individuals, families, and cultures. With respect to an *explanation* of behavior, deficit thinkers claim that the etiological bases of the alleged behavioral deficits lie in endogenous factors, such as limited intelligence or linguistic deficiencies. It follows, then, that deficit thinking would posit a *prediction* of the maintenance and perpetuation of deficits in the absence of intervention. In sum, the three aspects of description, explanation, and prediction of behavior are central to the way the deficit thinking model operates. It is also important to underscore that the fourth aim (*modification* or intervention) of the social and behavioral sciences regarding human behavior is integral to our understanding of the functioning of the deficit thinking framework. The point here is that deficit thinking sometimes offers a *prescription* in its approach to dealing with people from targeted populations, for example, low-SES African American students.

Understandingthe"description-explanation-prediction-modification"sequence of the deficit paradigm illustrates clearly how deficit thinkers view the educability of students of color (for a discussion of the notion of educability, see Valencia & Aburto, 1991). For an example of this point, let us examine the thoughts of Stanford University professor Lewis M. Terman (1877–1956)—hereditarian deficit thinker, eugenicist, the developer of the Stanford revision and extension of the Binet-Simon intelligence scale (which Terman named the Stanford-Binet), and the father of the intelligence testing movement in the U.S.[8] In 1916, Terman published *The Measurement of Intelligence*, a book that he intended to provide as a guide for the clinical use of the Stanford-Binet test. In his book, he discusses, in part, borderline cases of intelligence (typically between 70 and 80 IQ, according to the convention of the time). Terman describes the cases of M.P. and C.P.—Portuguese brothers with measured IQs of 77 and 78, respectively.[9] Terman's prognosis for M.P. and C.P. was disheartening, predicting that each brother would "doubtless become a fairly reliable laborer at unskilled work . . . (and) will probably never develop beyond the 11- or 12-year level (of intelligence) or be able to do satisfactory school work beyond the fifth or sixth grade" (1916, p. 90). Regarding Terman's views toward "Indians, Mexicans, and Negroes," his sentiments about these children were unequivocally racist regarding their alleged low educability. In the following quote from Terman (1916), I have underscored (in bold) each aspect of the description-explanation-prediction-modification sequence of Terman's perception of educability *vis-à-vis* Portuguese, American Indian, Mexican American, and African American children:

> What shall we say of cases like the last two [M.P. and C.P.] which test at high-grade moronity or at borderline . . .? Hardly anyone would think of them as institutional cases. Among laboring men and servant girls there

are thousands like them. They are the world's "hewers of wood and drawers of water." **And yet, as far as intelligence is concerned, the tests have told the truth. These boys are uneducable beyond the merest rudiments of training. (viz. DESCRIPTION)** No amount of school instruction will ever make them intelligent voters or capable citizens in the true sense of the word. Judged psychologically they cannot be considered normal.

It is interesting to note that M.P. and C.P. represent the level of intelligence which is very, very common among Spanish-Indian and Mexican families of the Southwest and also among Negroes. **Their dullness seems to be racial, or at least inherent in the family stocks from which they come. [viz. EXPLANATION]** The fact that one meets this type with such extraordinary frequency among Indians, Mexicans, and Negroes suggests quite forcibly that the whole question of racial differences in mental traits will have to be taken up anew and by experimental methods. **The writer predicts that when this is done there will be discovered enormously significant racial differences in general intelligence, differences which cannot be wiped out by any scheme of mental culture. [viz. PREDICTION]**

Children of this group should be segregated in special classes and be given instruction which is concrete and practical. They cannot master abstractions, but they can often be made efficient workers, able to look out for themselves. [viz. MODIFICATION] There is no possibility at present of convincing society that they should not be allowed to reproduce, although from a eugenic point of view they constitute a grave problem because of their unusually prolific breeding.

(Terman, 1916, pp. 91–92)

The above quote clearly communicates Terman's racial views about intellectual differences and the educability of children of color. It also contains references to the four social and behavioral science goals with regard to understanding human behavior, which in this case is measured intelligence. First, *description*. Terman describes the IQ of Portuguese, American Indians, Mexican Americans, and African Americans as very commonly being at the borderline level (70–80 IQ). Second, *explanation*. He suggests that the cause of such low IQ is "racial" or "inherent in the family stocks," meaning that the substantially lower intellectual performance of children of color is genetically based. Third, *prediction*. With continued scientific study, Terman predicts that huge racial differences will emerge—gaps so large that little can be done to eliminate them. Fourth, *modification* (i.e., prescription). Terman advocates the segregation of these children of color in "special classes," where instruction is to be "concrete and practical." The goal of such intervention is to produce individuals who can become "efficient (and unskilled) workers." In sum,

Terman's views of racial differences in intelligence and educability were clearly influenced by deficit thinking.

As this book proceeds, I further explore the notion of educability, particularly perceptions about the educability of economically disadvantaged students of color. This salience of educability perceptions and curricula intervention stems from the basic nature of the student–teacher (and policymaker) relationships. Available research, observations, and anecdotes all inform us that most schools are teacher-centered, top-down, and elitist—and some teachers hold perceptions of low educability of low-SES students of color and provide them with diminished encouragement to achieve (Pearl, 1991; chapter 5, present book). Deficit thinkers would have us believe that educability largely depends on individual intellectual ability and that social, political, and economic conditions within the schools and society do not appreciably relate to why variability exists in student learning and academic performance.

Heterodoxy

In Pierre Bourdieu's (1977) *Outline of a Theory of Practice* the concepts of "doxa," "orthodoxy," and "heterodoxy" are key notions in his theories of capital and symbolic power—frameworks to understand class domination. To Bourdieu, doxa consists of that part of the class society in which the social world is "beyond question" or there is a "universe of the undiscussed (undisputed)." An ensuing argument or crisis in a class society sets in motion a "universe of discourse (or argument)." According to Bourdieu, when the world of "opinion" opens, heterodoxy (i.e., unconventional opinions; dissent; nonconformity) comes into play as "the dominated classes have an interest in pushing back the limits of *doxa* and exposing the arbitrariness of the taken for granted" (1977, p. 169). On the other hand, "the dominant classes have an interest in defending the integrity of doxa or, short of this, of establishing in its place the necessarily imperfect substitute, *orthodoxy*" (p. 169).

I find Bourdieu's (1977) discussion (as described above) useful in understanding the tension between the deficit thinking and the anti-deficit thinking camps. In the evolution of deficit thinking, plenty of examples of heterodox scholars exist—White and of color alike—who have challenged deficit thinking. For instance, during the era of the genetic pathology model the reign of deficit thinking in educational thought and practice did not prevail without contestation (Valencia, 1997d).[10] Although dissenters delayed in developing their remonstrations to the orthodoxy, did not effectively organize their forces in the beginning, and at times encountered fierce resistance from deficit thinkers, they eventually mounted an effectual challenge to deficit thinking through their heterodox perspectives. One such anti-deficit thinker was Otto Klineberg, Columbia University professor, who worked in the 1920s and 1930s with vigor via his ambitious research and publication agenda to answer, or at least to offer responses, to practically all existing research that proffered the position that certain groups were racially inferior (see, e.g., Klineberg, 1935). So far-reaching were Klineberg's heterodox goals and efforts that they led historian Carl Degler to note categorically that Klineberg was to psychology as Franz Boas was to anthropology. "He [Klineberg] made it his business to do for psychology what his friend and colleague at Columbia had done for anthropology: to rid his discipline of racial explanations for human social differences" (Degler, 1991, p. 179).

Another example of heterodoxy from the genetic pathology epoch was the work of a small cadre of African American scholars in the 1920s who confronted the hereditarian assertion that Blacks were intellectually inferior to Whites (see Thomas, 1982; Valencia, 1997d). The mainstream journals were frequently controlled by editors and editorial boards who were hereditarians (for example, Lewis Terman's editorial control over the *Journal of Educational Psychology* and the *Journal of Applied Psychology*). As a result, many of these 1920s Black scholars were forced to publish their research in other outlets, such as *Crisis* and *Opportunity*, periodicals of the National Association for the Advancement of Colored People and the Urban League, respectively. These Black intellectuals' scholarly assault on 1920s mental testing falls into three categories (Thomas, 1982). First, some researchers focus on an environmental critique, for example, differences in educational opportunity between Whites and Blacks best account for racial differences in intellectual performance (e.g., Bond, 1924). Second, some of these scholars focus on methodological flaws or instrumentation problems. For example, Howard H. Long (1925) —who earned his doctorate in experimental psychology from Clark University—presents a technical criticism of IQ tests, contending that they contained numerous measurement problems, such as the inadequacy of using mental age scores for comparing IQ scores across races. Long notes that the procedure is flawed because it does not account for the correlation of mental age raw scores with chronological age. Third, some of the Black researchers conducted their own original research and generated their own data, thus providing alternative explanations to hereditarian-based conclusions drawn by White scholars. For example, Herman G. Canady (1928) in his master's thesis was one of the first scholars to investigate examiner effects on intelligence testing with White and Black children (also, see Canady, 1936).

Anti-deficit thinkers have not confined their heterodox perspectives to scholarly publications. For instance, oppressed groups of color have sometimes resorted to legal action in their struggle for equality. A case in point is the Mexican American community's long-standing legal campaign for better schools. In my 2008 book, *Chicano Students and the Courts: The Mexican American Legal Struggle for Educational Equality*, I engage the many areas that have spurred Mexican Americans to legal battle, including school segregation, school financing, special education, bilingual education, school closures, undocumented students, higher education financing, and high-stakes testing, ultimately situating these legal efforts in the broader scope of the Mexican American community's overall struggle for the right to an equal education. For example, regarding school segregation, a form of oppression guided by deficit thinking, the Mexican American community mounted a considerable campaign for over eight decades contesting inferior, separate schools. In undertaking research for the "School Segregation" chapter, I identified 35 school desegregation lawsuits that Mexican Americans brought forth, or in which they participated with African Americans (Valencia, 2008, chapter 1).

In conclusion, we can summarize the preceding discussion of six characteristics of deficit thinking in the context of schooling as follows:

1. *Victim blaming.* Deficit thinking is a person-centered explanation of school failure among individuals as linked to group membership (typically, the combination of racial minority status and economic disadvantagement). The endogenous nature of the deficit thinking framework roots students' poor schooling performance in their alleged cognitive and motivational deficits, and absolves institutional structures and inequitable schooling arrangements that exclude students from optimal learning. Finally, the model is largely based on imputation and little documentation.

2. *Oppression.* In light of the "victim-blamers/victims" nature of deficit thinking and the lop-sided power arrangements between deficit thinkers and economically disadvantaged students of color, the model can oppress its victims. As such, the deficit thinking paradigm holds little hope for addressing the possibilities of school success for such students.

3. *Pseudoscience.* The deficit thinking model is a form of pseudoscience in which researchers approach their work with deeply embedded negative biases toward people of color, pursue such work in methodologically flawed ways, and communicate their findings in proselytizing manners.

4. *Temporal changes.* Depending on the historical period, low-grade genes, inferior culture and class, or inadequate familial socialization transmit the alleged deficits.

5. *Educability.* Not only does the deficit thinking model contain descriptive, explanatory, and predictive elements, it is also—at times—a prescriptive model based on educability perceptions of low-SES students of color.

6. *Heterodoxy.* Historically, the deficit thinking model has rested on orthodoxy—reflecting the dominant, conventional scholarly and ideological climates of the time. Through an evolving discourse, heterodoxy has come to play a major role in the scholarly and ideological spheres in which deficit thinking has been situated.

2
Neohereditarianism
Pseudoscientific Explanations for Racial Differences in Intelligence

Of the three major alleged transmitters of deficit thinking (genetics; culture and class; familial socialization), the first—genetic inheritance—injures the target of the deficit thinker in the greatest degree. This harm stems from the common belief among scientific racists that genetics has a powerfully permanent influence in shaping behavior, particularly in intelligence. Let us examine hereditarian thought, the doctrine that genetics primarily accounts for individual differences in the behavior of human beings, as well as differences between groups (Valencia, 1997d; Valencia & Suzuki, 2001).[1]

The Resurgence of Hereditarianism: An Introduction to Neohereditarianism

Why do these resurgences of hereditarianism occur? In his revised and expanded edition of *The Mismeasure of Man* (1996), the late paleontologist Stephen Jay Gould explains that such resurgences are not mysterious nor predictably cyclical. Rather, Gould (1996) argues, hereditarian reoccurrences are sociopolitically driven. Note his insights for this assertion:

> No mystery attends the reason for these recurrences. They are not manifestations of some underlying cyclicity, obeying a natural law that might be captured in a mathematical formula as convenient as IQ; nor do these episodes represent any hot item of new data or some previously unconsidered novel twist in argument, for the theory of unitary, rankable, innate, and effectively unchangeable intelligence never alters very much in each sequential formulation. Each surge to popularity works with the same fallacious logic and flawed information.
>
> The reasons for recurrence are sociopolitical, and not far to seek: resurgences of biological determinism correlate with episodes of political retrenchment, particularly with campaigns for reduced government spending on social programs, or at times of fear among ruling elites, when disadvantaged groups sow serious social unrest or even threaten to usurp power. What argument against social change could be more chillingly effective than the claim that established orders, with some groups on top and others at the bottom, exist as an accurate reflection of the innate and unchangeable intellectual capacities of people so ranked?
>
> (Gould, 1996, pp. 27–28)

As our discussion of neohereditarianism unfolds, I will say more about the sociopolitical nature of these resurgences. In the remainder of this section, I focus on the primary funding source of this misguided research—the Pioneer Fund.

The Pioneer Fund

During my career as a scholar, now spanning over three decades, I have often sought funding for research projects (particularly for hiring research assistants). I am sure many readers share this concern. For scientific racists, however, they have had a fairly accessible and steady source for funding their research and writing—the Pioneer Fund (hereafter referred to as "Pioneer"). Here, I briefly discuss Pioneer and its prominent role in the funding of scientific racism.[2] In doing so, I touch upon the following aspects: (a) founding of Pioneer; (b) Harry L. Laughlin and Pioneer; (c) opposition to *Brown v. Board of Education of Topeka* (1954): the role of Pioneer; (d) organizations provided financial support from Pioneer. For this discussion, one of the major sources I rely on is William Tucker's book (2002), *The Funding of Scientific Racism: Wickliffe Draper and the Pioneer Fund*.

FOUNDING OF PIONEER

On February 27, 1937, the Board of Trustees of Pioneer filed the Certificate of Incorporation, with full incorporation on March 11, 1937.[3] Pioneer's charter contained two "charitable" objectives: Part A sought to provide financial funding to meritorious children (or their parents), and part B was intended to provide research grants for the study of heredity, eugenics, and human nature. Only part B, however, was funded (Lynn, 2001). An elaboration of parts A and B is as follows:

> A. To provide or aid in providing for the education of children or parents deemed to have such qualities and traits of character as to make such parents of unusual value as citizens, and, in the case of children or such parents whose means are inadequate therefor, to provide financial aid for the support, training, and start in life of such children. The children selected for such aid shall be children of parents who are citizens of the United States, and in selecting such children, unless the directors deem it inadvisable, consideration shall be especially given to children who are deemed to be descended predominantly from *White persons who settled in the original thirteen states* prior to the adoption of the Constitution of the United States and/or from related stocks, or to classes of children the majority of whom are deemed to be so descended.
> B. To conduct or aid in conducting study and research into the problems of heredity and eugenics in the human race generally and such study and such research in respect to animals and plants as may throw

light upon heredity in man, and to conduct or aid in conducting research and study into the *problems of race betterment* with special reference to the people of the United States, and for the advance of knowledge and the dissemination of information with respect to any studies so made or in general with respect to heredity and eugenics.[4]

Wickliffe Preston Draper (hereafter referred to as Draper; 1891–1972), founder of Pioneer, was born in 1891 in Milford, Massachusetts into an upper-class, wealthy New England family. Wickliffe's grandfather, George Draper, made his fortune via the Draper Corporation in Massachusetts. Elder Draper built up the corporation to such an extent that it became the nation's foremost manufacturer of textile machinery (Lynn, 2001). George Draper Jr., Draper's father, died in 1923 and left an estate of $10.7 million (about $129 million AFI in 2007).[5] Eventually, Draper acquired the bulk of the estate (Tucker, 2002).

Draper attended Harvard University and graduated in 1913, *cum laude* (Lynn, 2001). Beginning in the 1920s, Draper developed a desire to learn about human intelligence and the role genetics played in individual, as well as group differences. Eugenics also became an interest of his. As Draper's interests in these areas developed, he met some of the top scientists of the time. Of particular importance to Draper was Charles Benedict Davenport, a leading geneticist and eugenicist (Lynn, 2001). Tucker (2002, p. 34) has this to say about Davenport, considered the preeminent figure in the area of eugenics during the genetic pathology era of deficit thinking:

> Davenport was obsessed with the biological threat of Blacks and immigrants. One of his earliest reports on eugenics, in 1910, recommended study of the "mongrelization ... proceeding on a vast scale in this country." A year later he warned that the United States was being threatened by "blood-chaos": the "aryo-germanic race"—the "carriers of culture and civilization," whose "unparalleled successes" and "dominance in world affairs" had resulted from the qualities "bred into its protoplasm"—was now "in danger of being mixed with the blood" of immigrants "from southern and southeastern Europe and from Asia minor." In a widely cited paper in 1917, Davenport provided the scientific underpinning for this ominous prediction, explaining that genetic disharmonies were being produced by the "racial intermingling" of dissimilar groups.

Eventually, Draper funded Davenport's research. As a case in point, Draper donated $10,000 to support Davenport's study on the dangers of race mixing in Jamaica (Tucker, 2002). To Davenport, a staunch anti-miscegenationist, the underlying problem of biological amalgamation lay in the notion of "disharmony," or alleged poor fits due to disparate genetic contributions from dissimilar racial or extreme groups. As Davenport notes with his co-author

(Morris Steggerda) in *Race Crossing in Jamaica* (1929): "A hybridized people are a badly put-together people" (quoted in Klineberg, 1935, p. 121). In the 1920s, Draper started to commit his money to the mission of the eugenics movement and purity of the White race. Tucker (2002) notes:

> And although his contributions were but one of many sources of support at the time—and a minor one, at that—by the time of his death in 1972, Draper's money had become the most important and perhaps the world's only funding source for scientists who still believed that White racial purity was essential for social progress. (p. 23)[6]

HARRY H. LAUGHLIN AND PIONEER

Laughlin (1880–1943) served as one of the original founding five directors of Pioneer.[7] He also served as the first president of the organization (1937–1941), advocated programs that sought the involuntary sterilization of habitual criminals and the mentally retarded and mentally ill, and advocated quite vocally for restrictive immigration laws.[8] In these missions, Laughlin proved quite successful. Regarding immigration, Congress appointed him as "Expert Eugenics Agent," and based in large part on his writings and testimony, Congress passed the highly exclusionary Immigration Act of 1924, intentionally drafted to stop the stream of Jews and Italians, in part, whose counts as U.S. immigrants substantially increased from 1900 to 1920 (Lombardo, 2002; Valencia, 1997d). Laughlin also spearheaded a second aspect of the eugenics campaign, involuntary sterilization laws. Through his leadership, the legislatures of more than 30 states passed such statutes (Tucker, 2002).

Many authors have written of Laughlin's connection with Nazi Germany. For example, Tucker (2002, p. 46) notes:

> As editor of the *Eugenical News*, Laughlin also fawned over the Third Reich, filling the journal with praise for a government with the good sense to translate eugenic science into state policy. In emulation of the German term *Rassenhygiene* [racial hygiene], which was used more frequently in the Nazi movement than *Eugenik* [eugenics], he added the phrase Race Hygiene to the masthead of the *News* even before Hitler's seizure of power. When, shortly after the Nazi takeover, Germany enacted the Law for the Prevention of Genetically Defective Progeny—its own sterilization measure, patterned after Laughlin's model—the *News* was exultant. An unsigned editorial—unmistakably recognizable as Laughlin's work, however, from both the substance and the stilted prose—noted with obvious pride that "the text of the German statute reads almost like the 'American model sterilization law' " and extolled the Nazi regime for leading "the great nations of the world in the recognition of the biological foundations of national character. It is probable that the sterilization statutes of the several American states and the national sterilization

statute of Germany will, in legal history, constitute a milestone which marks the control by the most advanced nations of the world of a major aspect of controlling human reproduction, comparable in importance only with the states' legal control of marriage." As the Third Reich moved further toward becoming the eugenic state, Laughlin's journal followed the advancements with undisguised admiration, devoting an entire issue in 1934 to accounts of progress in Germany.

J. Philippe Rushton (2002), current President of Pioneer and Pioneer grantee, vigorously states that Laughlin was not preoccupied with German eugenics, and that Lombardo (2002)—a critic of Laughlin's fascination with Nazism—is "guilty of confirmation bias, and that he, not Laughlin, is captivated and preoccupied with Nazi politics" (p. 226). For a lively exchange regarding Pioneer and its activities, see Rushton (2002) and, on the other hand, Lombardo (2002, 2003) and Tucker (2002).

OPPOSITION TO BROWN V. BOARD OF EDUCATION OF TOPEKA (1954):
THE ROLE OF PIONEER

Following Laughlin's death in 1941, Frederick H. Osborn (1890–1980), one of the original founding directors of Pioneer[9] and recognized as a leader in eugenics during the mid-20th century, served as Pioneer president from 1941 to 1958 (Lynn, 2001). During Osborn's tenure as president, Draper's interest shifted from "science" to "policy." Citing correspondence from Malcolm Donald (Draper's attorney and close friend) to Osborn, Tucker (2002, p. 56) notes Donald's words: Draper was "not . . . concerned with research in human genetics since he felt that enough was known on the subject and that the important thing was to have something done." Draper's new mission of practicality focused its eye, in part, on the landmark U.S. Supreme Court decision, *Brown v. Board of Education of Topeka* (1954), the High Court ruling that found separate schools were inherently unequal under the Fourteenth Amendment, and thus ordered the school integration of Black and White students.[10] Draper viewed *Brown* as a major threat to his core principles (racial separation and subordination of Blacks; White racial purity) (Tucker, 2002). His objective sought not to use science in the advancement of knowledge, but rather to utilize it as an instrument to promote racial separation. Several months after Chief Justice Earl Warren delivered the historic opinion in *Brown* (May 17, 1954), Draper informed Osborn that he demanded on having research findings that would "promote . . . ethnic homogeneity" and that he would not aid investigators whose . . . "viewpoints were markedly alien" to his own (Tucker, 2002, p. 132).

In the decade that followed *Brown*, White Southerners "tried every mechanism, legal and illegal, to resist desegregation" (Jackson, 2005, p. 118). Three examples of these efforts are: (a) the 1959 founding of the Pioneer-backed International Association for the Advancement of Ethnology and Eugenics

(IAAEE; Jackson, 2004; Tucker, 2002; Winston, 1998). I discuss this organization in a later section, "Organizations Provided Financial Support from the Pioneer Fund"); (b) the legal challenge to *Brown* via *Stell v. Savannah-Chatham County Board of Education* (1963), in which several Pioneer grantees provided testimony;[11] (c) Draper's donation of $215,000 ($1,423,121 AFI in 2007) for the campaign against the civil rights bills of the mid-1960s (Tucker, 2002). Of the three preceding events, I limit my discussion to the *Stell v. Savannah-Chatham County Board of Education* lawsuit.

Not only did opponents endlessly and vigorously contest the initial *Brown* (1954) decision, the High Court's ruling in *"Brown II"* (1955)[12]—which required segregated states to comply fully and with all deliberate speed to the 1954 decision—also met with strong resistance from the South (Clotfelter, 2004; Klarman, 2004; Kluger, 2004; Ogletree, 2004). An example of such an impediment occurred in the Savannah-Chatham County Public School System in Georgia. Over 8 years had passed since *Brown*, yet the Savannah public schools in 1962 remained entirely segregated. Tucker (2002, p. 112) notes that the school board had established a "pupil placement policy" palpably

> tailored to preserve segregation by assigning students to schools on the basis of a series of guidelines that made no mention of race, but nevertheless did not place a single Black student in a "White" school—nor, of course, the reverse.[13]

To confront the obstinate White community, Ralph Stell—and a class of other African American minors—brought an action that sought to enjoin the defendants (members of the school board) from managing a biracial school system (i.e., a dual system). For relief, plaintiffs asked for an injunction to compel the school board to devise a desegregation plan that would allow the enrollment of Black students in White schools.[14] At the time of *Stell*, the Savannah-Chatham County Public School System had an enrollment of 60% White and 40% Black[15]—ideal percentages that had the potential to lead to a comprehensive desegregation plan.

Carleton Putnam—airline pioneer, writer, and segregationist—served as one of the key architects of the opposition in *Stell* (although he played a low-key role). His task was to put together a blue-ribbon panel of scientists to provide the facts about race, and thus expose the faulty logic of *Brown* (Jackson, 2006). Putnam authored the racist book, *Race and Reason: A Yankee View* (1961),[16] and Draper supported him in a number of projects (Tucker, 2002).

The Pioneer–*Stell* connection began when members of the White community in Savannah filed a motion to intervene (i.e., enter the lawsuit to assist the defendants).[17] Based on their petition to join *Stell*, the intervenors characterized themselves as: "Whites, sharing a common biological origin, cultural heritage, and consciousness of kind," who objected to their children being "forcibly compelled to associate with plaintiffs and others of their ethnic group in the common schools" of the school system (Newby, 1967, p. 197). Intervenors (including their expert witnesses [whom I discuss shortly]) carefully selected *Stell* as their test case to overturn *Brown* because observers considered the presiding judge—Frank M. Scarlett (U.S. District Court, Southern District of Georgia, Savannah Division)—to be a staunch ally of segregationists (Tucker, 1994). Thus, it was no surprise that Judge Scarlett granted the request for intervention. Civil rights attorneys knew well that Judge Scarlett was an obstructionist determined to thwart the *Brown* decree. His tenacious attempts to block Black plaintiffs' desegregative struggle in Brunswick, Augusta, and Savannah, Georgia proved effective in hindering integration in the Southern District of Georgia long after many school districts in the Fifth Circuit started to comply with court-ordered desegregation plans (Read, 1977).

The intervenors in *Stell* recruited a number of experts, most of whom were Pioneer grantees and members of the IAAEE (funded by Draper). Key individuals providing trial testimony included Drs. R. Travis Osborne, Henry E. Garrett, Wesley Critz George, and Ernest van den Haag.[18] R. Carter Pittman, articulate supporter of segregation and noted spokesperson for the racist Citizens' Council, served as attorney for the intervenors. Newby (1967) comments that the Citizens' Council of America, headquartered in Jackson, Mississippi, took on the substantial part of disseminating literature on scientific racism, in which the various authors used "science" to defend racial segregation.

Pittman's legal strategy focused on the argument that the U.S. Supreme Court in *Brown* erred in its conclusion that the segregation of Black students adversely influenced their learning. Intervenors claimed that the Supreme Court's findings did not rest on case law, but rather questionable *scientific evidence* as provided in the prominent footnote 11 of *Brown* (Tucker, 2002). The well-known footnote 11 lists scholarly citations concluding that school segregation leads to injurious psychological effects (particularly diminished self-esteem) and inferior education.[19] Several major questions arose regarding judicial interpretations in *Stell*. Historian I.A. Newby, in *Challenge to the Court* (1967, p. 188), writes:

> Did not the use of social science in the Brown decision introduce an undesirable, even dangerous, relativism into the law and violate the principle of *stare decisis*?[20] Did not the decision introduce instability and uncertainty and threaten the principle of the rule of law as opposed to the rule of man? . . . Finally, and here scientific racists came in, might not the expert opinion which the Court accepted in the *Brown* decision be disputed, perhaps even refuted, by experts equally competent to those who testified in the lower courts and/or were cited in footnote eleven?

In sum, the intervenors in *Stell* sought to argue that the *Brown* ruling did not maintain that the separate but equal principle was "bad law," but rather that the doctrine rested on "bad sociology" (Newby, p. 189). The task for experts Garrett et al.: Build a strong defense for the pedagogical and psychological justification of school segregation of Black and White students.[21] In very brief form, I next discuss this testimony, attestations that teem with deficit thinking.[22]

R. Travis Osborne, Professor of Psychology and Director of the Student Guidance Center at the University of Georgia, testified that based on academic achievement and intelligence test data gathered in Savannah-Chatham County, "major differences exist in the learning ability patterns of White and Negro pupils" and thus such test results

> were of major importance in educational planning as they indicate the necessity for changing course content, subject selection and rate of progress planning separately for each of the two groups if the schools are to endeavor to adapt to the different learning potentials of each.[23]

In short, intervenors argued that they could make a pegagogical rationale for segregation in light of these vast racial "learning abilities patterns" and the ensuing extraordinary curricular modifications that schools would need to implement.

Henry E. Garrett, Visiting Professor at the University of Virginia and Emeritus Professor of Psychology at Columbia University followed Osborne on the witness stand. Garrett testified that the observed "differences in educability between Negro and White children were *inherent* [italics added]," and that no scientific likelihood existed that the rate of learning differences between White and Black students "were either caused by or could be substantially altered by the students' environment." Furthermore, Garrett asserted that school failure among Blacks (if educated with Whites) would be so frustrating that such failure "will be compensated . . . by anti-social class behavior."[24]

Wesley Critz George, Emeritus Professor of Histology (study of the microscopic structure of tissue) and Embryology in the School of Medicine at the University of North Carolina testified next. George received a number of bank checks from Draper subsequent to authoring pamphlets and booklets that encouraged the defiance of the *Brown* ruling (Tucker, 2003). For example, George wrote "The Race Problem From the Standpoint of One Who is Concerned About the Evils of Miscegenation" (1955), in which he comments: "Intermingling of the races and miscegenation would be furthering the deterioration of our race and our civilization" (p. 5). In his well-known and widely circulated *The Biology of the Race Problem* (1962)—which Governor John Patterson of Alabama commissioned for $3,000 (Newby, 1967)—George opens by seriously questioning the *Brown* decision remarking that it relied on inaccurate "science" and the opinion of "authorities." His booklet, designed to provide a considerable amount of "established fact and pertinent evidence" that the U.S. Supreme Court neglected, discusses the alleged physiological and intellectual bases for Black inferiority (George, 1962, pp. 1, 13–34). George's main purpose in writing *The Biology of the Race Problem* "was to prove the necessity for public school segregation" (Newby, 1967, p. 107). In the *Stell* trial, George testified that the differences in the intellectual abilities between White and Black students "were innate . . . and related in both a quantitative and qualitative degree to physical characteristics which are anthropologically accepted."[25]

Ernest van den Haag, Professor of Social Philosophy at New York University and another Pioneer grantee, testified last. He claimed that groups who self-identify (i.e., by race) close their ranks when coming into contact with different groups. That is, "Prejudices, whether ethnic, religious or racial, increase rather than decrease in proportion to the degree of non-voluntary contact between separately identifiable groups." Based on studies of group intermixing in classrooms, he testified that "an increase in cross-group contacts increases pre-existing racial hostility rather than ameliorates it."[26]

Prior to the testimony of the intervenors' experts, the National Association for the Advancement of Colored People–Legal Defense Fund (NAACP–LDF) attorneys objected to having this evidence presented, but Judge Scarlett overruled their objection. Plaintiffs' counsel did not cross-examine intervenors' experts nor did they present their own experts. Attorneys for plaintiffs argued:

> The law is settled by the Supreme Court in the *Brown* case that segregation itself injures negro children in the school system. That is what the Supreme Court's decision is all about, so we do not have to prove that.[27]

Not surprisingly, Judge Scarlett denied the plaintiffs' motion for an injunction. In his opinion, he relies heavily on the intervenors' experts' testimony, citing them frequently. Ignoring systemic forces in explaining school failure of Black students, deficit thinking guided his findings. In his opinion, he writes that the differences in test scores of White and Black students in Savannah-Chatham County "are not the result of the educational system or of the social or economic differences in status or in environment of the students" (but are) "attributable in large part to *hereditary factors* [italics added], predictably resulting from a difference in the physiological and psychological characteristics of the two races."[28] In flagrant disregard for the *Brown* ruling, Judge Scarlett comments: "Plaintiffs' assumption of injury to Negro students by the continuance of segregated school is not supported by any evidence in this case."[29] As such, he further notes: "The court (his court) held that the decision in *Brown v. Board of Education of Topeka* was not binding on it."[30] Not unexpectedly, plaintiffs' counsel appealed to the Fifth Circuit Court of Appeals.[31] In a stinging rebuke, the Fifth Circuit writes that "The district court for the Southern District of Georgia is bound by the [*Brown*] decision of the United States Supreme Court, as are we." Furthermore, the appellate court notes that Judge Scarlett's ruling "was a clear abuse of its discretion for the trial court to deny appellants' motion for a preliminary injunction requiring the defendant School Board to make a prompt and reasonable start toward desegregating the Savannah-Chatham County Schools."[32] Also, the Fifth Circuit ruled that the defendants need "to make arrangements for admission of children to such schools on a racially non-discriminatory basis with all deliberate speed [as required by *Brown II*]."[33] Finally, the appellate court required that the defendants submit a desegregation plan to the Fifth Circuit no later than July 1, 1963.[34] Appellees appealed to the Supreme Court, but the Court denied the writ of certiorari.[35]

In conclusion, the *Stell* case represents

> the high-water mark of scientific racism, and its outcomes left the movement in a state of suspension and indecision. Racists had expected the case to go to the Supreme Court and become a *cause célèbre* in their controversy with integrationists.
>
> (Newby, 1967, p. 213)

Notwithstanding the scientific racists' defeat in *Stell*, their vigorous campaign against school integration continued via various publications (I discuss this later).

ORGANIZATIONS PROVIDED FINANCIAL SUPPORT FROM THE PIONEER FUND

In this final segment on Pioneer, I briefly focus on a number of organizations that received funding from Pioneer. Most of the organizations served as publishing outlets for Pioneer grantees or Pioneer-oriented activities.[36] As shown in Figure 2.1, there are six major groups. In the order of discussion, I move in a clockwise direction, denoting the chronology of the organizations' establishment.

1. *The International Association for the Advancement of Ethnology and Eugenics (IAAEE).*[37] Draper funded the IAAEE with a substantial amount of money. Henry E. Garrett and others founded the organization in Washington, D.C. in 1959 (Jackson, 2005; Tucker, 2002). Members of the Executive Committee included, among others, Ernest van den Haag and Wesley Critz George, scientific racists who testified in *Stell* (Winston, 1998). Concisely, a major purpose of the IAAEE sought "objectively to investigate racial differences and to publicize their findings" (Jackson, 2005, p. 17). Monographs, a book series, and articles based on original research formed the basis of this publicity.

Mankind Quarterly (MQ), the IAAEE's initial and most prominent publication to serve the publicizing function of the organization, surfaced in 1960.[38] From its inception, *MQ*—an international journal—has devoted considerable space to the topic of race. On the journal's 2008 website, it notes, in part: "*The Mankind Quarterly* is not and never has been afraid to publish articles in controversial areas, including behavioral group differences and the importance

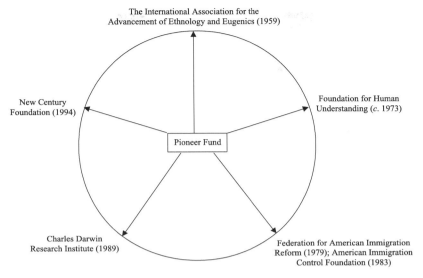

The International Association for the
Advancement of Ethnology and Eugenics (1959)

New Century
Foundation (1994)

Foundation for Human
Understanding (c. 1973)

Pioneer Fund

Charles Darwin
Research Institute (1989)

Federation for American Immigration
Reform (1979); American Immigration
Control Foundation (1983)

Figure 2.1 Organizations Provided Financial Support from the Pioneer Fund.

Source: Tucker (2002, pp. 70, 156, 182, 188, 199).

of mental ability for individual outcomes and group differences."[39] To be sure, many *MQ* articles have generated considerable controversy and criticism. Tucker (1994) notes that the journal has produced a regular "stream of scientific racism" (p. 176). Articles on race, *MQ*'s major emphasis, include subjects related to intellectual abilities of Africans, intelligence test differences of U.S. Blacks and Whites, implied support for apartheid, and the adverse effects of school integration (Winston, 1998). Winston does comment, however, that not all *MQ* articles have centered on scientific racism. "Some [articles] were discussions of ancient civilizations, prehistory, or the physical characteristics, such as eye color, of ethnic groups" (p. 193). Winston further comments that these latter subjects gave the impression of *MQ* as a regular academic journal, but on assiduous reading many of the articles' themes "hearken back to the journal's central mission [promotion of White superiority]" (p. 193). It is noteworthy to add that immediately after *MQ*'s establishment, controversy broke loose over the journal's narrow mission. Jackson (2005) comments: "*Mankind Quarterly* created a stir within anthropology not for the startling new studies it published about race but rather because evidence of what many suspected was its dedication to anything but an open discussion on race" (p. 149).

2. *Foundation for Human Understanding (FHU).* Circa 1973, a small number of Pioneer grantees (e.g., Henry E. Garrett, Ernest van den Haag, and R. Travis Osborne) established FHU, which Pioneer funded as another attempt to "win the war" against school segregation and to promote White superiority (Tucker,

2002, pp. 156–157). From 1971 to 1996, FHU received $348,700 from Pioneer.[40] In undertaking its mission, FHU's primary activity was the promotion of books and articles it approved. An example included the book of Arthur R. Jensen (a major Pioneer grantee), *Straight Talk About Mental Tests* (1981), on which FHU spent $27,000 ($60,850 AFI in 2007) "for thousands of copies [of Jensen's book] to be distributed gratis to college presidents and admission officers around the country." Tucker (2002), paraphrasing Jensen's (1981) message to the targeted universities, comments: "The decline in the number of students with high SAT scores was attributable to a declining birthrate among the 'ethnic groups' that had furnished most of the top in the past" (p. 157).

FHU also published and distributed books "that no press would accept" (Tucker, 2002, p. 158). Two examples include *Twins: Black and White* by R. Travis Osborne (1980) and *The Testing of Negro Intelligence*, Volume 2 by R. Travis Osborne and Frank C.J. McGurk (1982a), two Pioneer grantees (Lynn, 2001). One of the "most appalling" FHU publications is *America's Bimodal Crisis: Black Intelligence in White Society* by Stanley Burnham (1993),[41] a volume that offers "a succession of racist canards as self-evident truths" (Tucker, 2002, p. 158). Burnham's book is the quintessence of blaming the victim, one of the six major characteristics of deficit thinking (see chapter 1, present book). Commenting on victimology, Burnham (1993, pp. 3, 69) asserts:

> If Blacks fail in schools, or abuse welfare, or procreate randomly, or engage in too much petty theft and violent crime, or cost too much government money, it is the fault of somebody else, not Blacks themselves. . . . They [Blacks] cry exploitation, but their problem lies elsewhere—ultimately with the genetic deficiencies they cannot remedy.

In Burnham's final chapter, "What is to be Done?", he asserts that given the bimodal distribution of intelligence of Blacks and Whites which has produced a bimodal society, then bimodal reform is necessary. For example:

> Black students whose intelligence and academic performance persistently fall below acceptable standards should be steered as quickly and effectively as possible into job situations in which performance demands are less stringent . . . —such as in farm labor, dish washing, garbage collecting, and the like.
>
> (Burnham, 1993, p. 116)

3. *Federation for American Immigration Reform (FAIR) and American Immigration Control Foundation (AICF)*. Pioneer also has an interest in opposing immigration (particularly "illegal alien" Latinos) (Diamond, 1999; Tucker, 2002). Over the years, FAIR received $1,289,000 from Pioneer, and AICF $183,000.[42] Diamond (1999) notes that both FAIR and AICF, through their incendiary propaganda, have orchestrated successful campaigns—particularly the 1994

Proposition 187 in California. The initiative sought, in part, "to bar state and local governments ... from providing non-emergency health care and social services and public education to undocumented immigrants" (Johnson, 1996, p. 2). Regarding Proposition 1987, Diamond (1999, p. 180) writes:

> Both national organizations [FAIR and AICF] have contributed logistical and moral support to several dozen grass-roots groups, mostly in California. The existence of dozens of small anti-immigrant groups no doubt made a difference in the signature gathering campaign to place California's Proposition 187 on the ballot in 1994. Reportedly, a corps of 8,000 volunteers collected more than a half million signatures in all 58 of the state's counties.

Voters passed Proposition 187, in a racialized manner, by a margin of 59–41% on November 8, 1994, but the U.S. District Court for the Central District of California ruled that the initiative violated California and federal law (see Valencia, 2008, pp. 247–250).

4. *Charles Darwin Research Institute (CDRI)*. J. Philippe Rushton, President of Pioneer since 2002, founded CDRI in 1989. From its website, CDRI states it "is a scientific and educational foundation established to honor and extend the scientific revolution inaugurated by one of the greatest figures [Charles Darwin] in the history of human thought." As well, CDRI seeks "to guarantee academic freedom for research on race differences."[43] The website of the Southern Poverty Law Center (SPLC), which describes Rushton as "one of the most notorious race scientists in the world," notes that tax records show CDRI received $473,835 from Pioneer.[44]

Inspection of the CDRI website indicates that the organization is a singular showcase for Rushton's (2000) racist book, *Race, Evolution, and Behavior: A Life History Perspective* (published by CDRI, i.e., indirectly by Pioneer). CDRI is undertaking a very ambitious promotional campaign, of international magnitude, to sell Rushton's book (358 pps.), discussed later. The website provides access to printable versions (ranging from 50 to 102 pages) in English, Dutch, Romanian, Spanish, Portuguese, German, and Chinese.[45]

5. *New Century Foundation (NCF)*. The NCF, founded in 1994, also obtained funding from Pioneer—to the tune of $27,000 between 1994 and 1999 (Tucker, 2002). According to the NCF's website, the organization's purpose is "to study immigration and race relations as to better understand the consequences of America's increasing diversity." NCF holds occasional conferences, and sponsors books and publications. The main publication is the monthly *American Renaissance (AR)*, edited by Jared Taylor, who also serves as NCF president.[46]

The above description of NCF sounds innocuous, but a close reading of *AR*, its books, and publications tells otherwise: It is a White supremacy organization. In one of the early issues of *AR*, Richard McCulloch (1995), in his "Separation for Preservation" article, writes that the *AR* has given plenty of documentation to demonstrate "that a multiracial society is detrimental to the interests of European-Americans." McCulloch continues: "Separation may not be necessary to solve the problems of crime, delinquency, economic inefficiency, cultural and educational decline, etc., but it is necessary for [White] racial preservation." Such talk about separation and preservation appears as a common theme of *AR*. This is clearly illustrated in a 2003 NCF edited book by George McDaniel, *A Race Against Time: Racial Heresies for the 21st Century*, a compilation of *AR* articles on how the growth of people of color in the United States threatens White society. In the book's foreword, Jared Taylor comments:

> The authors of this book and the movement we represent are entirely in earnest about the survival of our people and our culture. Unless Whites shake off the teachings of racial orthodoxy they will cease to be a distinct people with a culture of their own. History, morality, biology, and generations of common sense justify our desire that our children should walk in the ways of their own people, that they should be the heirs to the culture and civilization of Europe, that their lives be shaped by their own history rather than by the demands of people unlike themselves. More and more Whites are awakening to the crisis they face. They will eventually shake off their lethargy and secure for themselves that to which all men have a right: survival as a people.
>
> (McDaniel, 2003, p. xiii)

Racist doctrine, a long-standing subject of Pioneer-sponsored groups, is also seen in the pages of *AR*. For example, in a recent article ("Diversity in the Army: A Thin Veneer Covers Serious Trouble") Duncan Hengest (2008) comments:

> Non-Whites in the armed forces cause three problems. The first is unit and soldier indiscipline [sic]. In the past, entire Black regiments have behaved badly, and individual Blacks often follow the same pattern. Second, Blacks and Whites sometimes think and behave differently. Bridging the gap is costly and never entirely successful, and racial divisions sap unit morale. Third, there is the added trouble of other non-White troops. An increasing number of racial and religious minorities can give rise to unique kinds of trouble.

Overall, the NCF appears to have been quite successful in carrying forth the racist tradition of Pioneer-funded groups.

When Pioneer founder Wickliffe Draper died in 1972, attorney Harry F. Weyher took over the reins, serving as president until his death in 2002. The Pioneer board then appointed J. Philippe Rushton as the new president.

Tucker (2002) comments that the reconstituted board intends to "keep Harry F. Weyher's great legacy alive" (p. 214).

In the final analysis, although some scholars find the Pioneer-funded research personally disturbing and think the conclusions to be highly suspect, a small number of authorities believe that the Pioneer-funded researchers' work is sensible, fair-minded, and directed toward human betterment (e.g., Michael E. Levin; Richard Lynn; J. Philippe Rushton). To understand the Pioneer's mission, readers are referred to Richard Lynn's (2001) hagiography, *The Science of Human Diversity: A History of the Pioneer Fund*. Regarding the future, Pioneer is soliciting money to fund investigations it deems important.[47]

Three Temporal Waves of Neohereditarianism

Based on my observations and analysis, I discern three resurgences of hereditarian thought. Stephen J. Gould (1996, pp. 29–30) and I have, independently, delineated several periods of hereditarian thought. Gould begins with early hereditarianism (c. 1920s). He follows by discussing two periods of neohereditarianism: First, Gould (1996) cites the debate generated by Arthur Jensen's controversial 1969 monograph published in the *Harvard Educational Review*. Second, Richard Herrnstein and Charles Murray published their contentious *The Bell Curve* in 1994. My framework, however, differs from Gould's (1996) in that I develop three periods of neohereditarianism, with a number of additional players as well as a contemporary era (post 2000). My periodization does not intend to be exhaustive with regard to the list of key individuals. I attempt to identify the major authors and their works. Table 2.1 presents the three waves, with the major accompanying players and their works. In the interest of space, I only discuss select authors from the three waves. Of the 16 different authors listed in Table 2.1, 11 (69%) are Pioneer grantees (indicated by a superscript "a").

Neohereditarianism: Wave I

Foley (1997) and Valencia (1997d) discuss a number of factors and events that helped contribute to the downfall of the genetic pathology era of deficit thinking, which hit its zenith in the 1920s. Around the time of the monumental 1954 *Brown* decision, however, the first wave of neohereditarianism surfaced. This resurgence of hereditarianism largely emerged as a reaction to the U.S. Supreme Court's mandate of school desegregation.[48] Table 2.1 lists the key players of wave I and their works. Due to space limitations, I focus on Shuey (1958, 1966), Garrett (1961), and Jensen (1969).

AUDREY M. SHUEY

Shuey, professor and chair of the Psychology Department at Randolph-Macon Women's College (Lynchburg, Virginia) wrote *The Testing of Negro Intelligence* in 1958 (351 pps.). Her volume is an ambitious undertaking of the literature

Table 2.1 Three Temporal Waves of Neohereditarianism

Year	Author(s)	Publication
	Wave I (1958–1982)	
1958, 1966	Audrey Shuey[a]	*The Testing of Negro Intelligence*
1961	Henry E. Garrett[a]	"The Equalitarian Dogma"
1969	Arthur R. Jensen[a]	"How Much Can We Boost IQ and Scholastic Achievement"
1971	Hans J. Eysenck[a]	*Race, Intelligence and Education*
1971	Richard J. Herrnstein	"I.Q."
1972	Arthur R. Jensen	*Genetics and Education*
1973	Richard J. Herrnstein	*I.Q. in the Meritocracy*
1973	Arthur R. Jensen	*Educability and Group Differences*
1982	R. Travis Osborne[a] & Frank McGurk[a]	*The Testing of Negro Intelligence*
	Wave II (1987–1997)	
1987	Lloyd M. Dunn	*Bilingual Hispanic Children on the U.S. Mainland*
1991	Roger Pearson[a]	*Race, Intelligence and Bias in Academe*
1994	Richard J. Herrnstein & Charles Murray	*The Bell Curve*
1995	John Philippe Rushton[a]	*Race, Evolution, and Behavior*
1997	Michael Levin[a]	*Why Race Matters*
	Wave III (2000–2008)	
2000	John Philippe Rushton	*Race, Evolution, and Behavior*
2002	Richard Lynn[a] & Tatu Vanhanen	*IQ and the Wealth of Nations*
2004	Vincent Sarich & Frank Miele[a]	*Race*
2006	Richard Lynn	*Race Differences in Intelligence*
2006	Richard Lynn & Tatu Vanhanen	*IQ and Global Inequality*
2007	Michael H. Hart	*Understanding Human History*
2008	Richard Lynn	*The Global Bell Curve*

Note: Complete citations are provided in the references. [a]Denotes Pioneer grantee.

(1913–1958). She reviews 240 empirical studies in which examiners administered 60 different measures of intelligence involving 80,000 Black elementary, high school, and college students.[49] Of Shuey's (1958) numerous conclusions, the ones most germane to this discussion are the following:[50]

1. A striking consistency in intelligence test scores appears. Combining all studies, Blacks, as a group, have a mean IQ of 1 standard deviation (15 IQ points) below the mean for Whites.

2. With regard to selective migration, Shuey finds that Black children born

in the North have an average of about 3 to 6 IQ points higher than Black children residing in the very same municipalities, but born in the South. She notes: "Assuming an IQ difference of about 9 [IQ] points between northern and southern Negro children, then from about half to two-thirds of this difference may reasonably be attributed to environmental factors and the remainder to selective migration" (p. 314).

3. Shuey raises the all-too-familiar racial hybridity hypothesis (Valencia, 1997d), commenting "[Negro] Racial hybrids have a tendency to score higher on psychometric tests, on the whole, than groups described as unmixed" (p. 313).

4. In general, when researchers control for SES, "the colored averaged [in IQ] consistently below the Whites" (pp. 317–318).

Regarding her major explanation for the mean differences in intellectual performance between Blacks and Whites, Shuey (1958) demonstrates silence throughout her lengthy review. Her conclusion does appear, however, in the *final* sentence on the *final* page. Atavistically, Shuey posits a genetic hypothesis reminiscent of 1920s hereditarian thought: "The remarkable consistency in test results. . . . all point to the presence of *native* [italics added] differences between Negroes and Whites as determined by intelligence tests" (p. 318).

Shuey, a Pioneer grantee,[51] received funding for her book from the "Human Genetics Fund" (or "Foundation"), to which Draper privately provided the money, because she proved unsuccessful in finding an academic or commercial outlet to publish her volume (Garrett,1961; Lynn, 2001; Tucker, 2002). Jackson (2005) notes that via this funding the publisher "distributed [the book] free of charge throughout the South and that the Citizens' Councils had been active distributors" (p. 116). Newby (1967) states that Shuey's book "was widely applauded by segregationists and racists of various persuasions" (p. 78). Indeed, scientific racists accepted and proselytized *The Testing of Negro Intelligence* as the definitive work on Black–White differences in measured intelligence. For example, in the *Stell* (1963) desegregation case (previously discussed), Garrett—who testified that intellectual differences between Black and White students can be innately explained—cites Shuey (1958) as his source.[52] In light of the attention garnered by her first edition, Shuey authored a second edition of *The Testing of Negro Intelligence* (1966), with the help of a grant from Pioneer (Lynn, 2001), which her benefactors used to create Social Science Press, the book's publisher (Tucker, 2002). Echoing her conclusions in her 1958 edition, Shuey's genetic explanation of mean Black–White IQ differences conveyed an even stronger conviction: "[The test results] all taken together, *inevitably point to the presence of native differences between Negroes and Whites as determined by intelligence tests*" [italics added] (p. 521). Other scholars would not forget Shuey's contribution to the belief in White intellectual superiority. After her death in 1977, R. Travis Osborne and Frank C.J.

McGurk—Pioneer grantees—published an edited book (1982a), *The Testing of Negro Intelligence* (Vol. 2). Pioneer-funded FHU published the volume, and Osborne and McGurk dedicated it to Shuey's memory. The 1982 book covers new material on Black–White studies of intellectual performance, spanning 1966 to 1979. In their conclusion, the editors parrot Shuey's (1958, 1966) judgment that Black–White mean differences on measures of intelligence "inevitably point to the presence of native differences" (Osborne & McGurk, 1982b, p. 297). As late as 2008, Pioneer's website declares: [*The Testing of Negro Intelligence*] is the "standard sourcebook on the topic [of Black–White IQ differences]."

Suffice it to say, Shuey's hereditarian explanation of racial differences in intelligence that she presents in both editions did not go unchallenged. A sampling of these critiques follows:

1. Shuey (1958) fails to distinguish the comments and conclusions of the authors she reviews from her own inferences. Bond (1958) cites examples of authors who conclude that environmental factors largely account for the observed lower IQ scores of Blacks. Yet, Shuey (1958) apparently lumps together the results of a large number of such studies and concludes that heredity largely accounts for Black–White mean differences in intelligence.

2. Bond (1958) takes Shuey (1958) to task for not fully discussing her reporting that White Southerners invariably score lower on IQ tests than do White Northerners.

3. Shuey (1958) cites a number of studies in which she claims Blacks still score significantly lower even when researchers "equated" environmental factors. Pettigrew (1964) finds fault with Shuey's analyses, however, critiquing her failure to read carefully the caveats of the authors (e.g., the assumption of socioeconomic status equality of Blacks and Whites is not entirely valid).

4. Hicks and Pellegrini (1966) offer a novel and potent rebuke of Shuey's (1958) hereditarian conclusion in that it wrongly deals with the *meaningfulness* of racial differences regarding *policy*. That is, can scientists empirically substantiate any policy implications stemming from race studies in intelligence? For example, Garrett (1962) argues that Blacks are so constitutionally inferior that miscegenation and school integration should be prohibited. Hicks and Pellegrini (1966)—arguing that researchers could make almost any study show significant differences if they use enough subjects regardless of how nonsensical the variables might be—criticize Garrett (1962) for misconstruing the meaning of "statistical significance" and erroneously equating it with "practical significance." Hicks and Pellegrini reexamine 40 studies by 26 investigators that Shuey reviews in her 1958 book and compute an estimated ω^2 (omega-square) from the t value in each case.[53] The estimated ω^2 values range from .000 to .383, with a median value of .061 (i.e., 6% explained variance). Of

the 40 studies, 24 have estimated ω^2 values less than .100, 11 of the values fall between .100 and .199, 3 between .200 and .299, and 2 between .300 and .383. One study had an astronomical t of 149.05, but researchers used 93,955 Whites and 23,596 Blacks as participants; Hicks and Pellegrini (1966) estimate the ω^2 to be .159.

Hicks and Pellegrini (1966), in sum, argue that Shuey's (1958) conclusion of innate intellectual inferiority of Blacks and any resulting policy recommendation (e.g., Garrett's [1962] call for the school segregation of Black children) have no established objective basis. Criticizing both Shuey and Garrett, Hicks and Pellegrini (1966) comment:

> The results of this [Shuey's] study reflect directly on the conflicting interpretations of racial differences in IQ. The median [estimated] ω^2, .061, is thought to best represent the strength of association between skin color and intelligence. Six percent represents only a small reduction in uncertainty. When Garrett [1962, p. 2] claims that the differences in Negro and White IQ "are real and highly useful in guidance and prediction," he has greatly exaggerated the strength of the relationship between skin color and IQ. It is concluded that studies of racial intelligence have failed to establish the existence of meaningful ethnic differences in intelligence. Therefore any interpretations of racial IQ data that stipulates differential treatment of Negroes and Whites is unwarranted. (p. 45)

HENRY E. GARRETT

Garrett, whom I introduced earlier, carries a principal role in this discussion of the first wave of neohereditarianism.[54] He received his Ph.D. in psychology from Columbia University in 1923, subsequently joined the faculty there and served as the Acting Executive Officer (head) of the Department of Psychology (1941–1955), and in 1956 the university designated him professor emeritus. It appears that during Garrett's career his colleagues held him in high esteem. They elected him president of the following prestigious professional organizations: Psychometric Society (1943), Eastern Psychological Association (1944), and American Psychological Association (1946). In addition, his peers selected Garrett as a fellow of the American Association for the Advancement of Science and member of the National Research Council (Winston, 1998).

Early in his career, Garrett held hereditarian views. In the mid-1940s, however, his "public position shifted" on racial differences in intelligence (Winston, 1998, p. 182). This change appears to be prompted by anthropologist Ashley Montagu, who wrote an article in the *American Journal of Psychology* (1945). In his analysis of the First World War Army Alpha and Beta intelligence test median scores, Montagu (1945) reports "that the Negroes from some northern states do better ... than the Whites from so many other southern states" (p. 187). He asserts that superior socioeconomic conditions in the North, not native intelligence, best explain the observed racial differences in intelligence. Garrett (1945) quickly replied to Montagu in the same year, same journal—accusing Montagu of statistical mistakes, misinterpretation, dogmatism, and researcher bias. Garrett concludes that the Black–White Army test scores differences "cannot be explained in socio-economic terms" (1945, p. 495). At this point in time, "Garrett took up the rhetorical position that he and others would use effectively for the next 25 years in the general public arena" (Winston, 1998, p. 183): Namely, environmental explanations of Black–White differences in intelligence center on ideology, while genetic explanations hinge on science.

The ideology versus science debate on racial differences in intelligence captured center stage in 1961 when, in the inaugural issue of the Pioneer-supported *Mankind Quarterly*, Garrett wrote an article entitled "The Equalitarian Dogma," a phrase that he coined.[55] Garrett asserts that contemporary social scientists do not frequently accept the historically sound judgment by most Whites that "the Negro [is] natively less gifted [intelligent] as a race than the White" (p. 253). Instead, he states, most social scientists of the day believe that all races are essentially equal in intelligence. To Garrett, this is the *equalitarian dogma*, which he remarks has become a major proposition not to be challenged in academia—particularly in anthropology, psychology, and genetics departments.

Garrett (1961) claims that five principal sources explain the change from a belief in innate racial differences to the dogma of equalitarianism.

1. *"The Rise of 'Modern Anthropology'."* Garrett credits cultural anthropologist Franz Boas, his colleague at Columbia University, whom he refers to as the "father of equalitarianism," as the most influential opponent of the argument of innate racial differences in intelligence.[56] Historians of the nature–nurture controversy and race relations agree that German-born Boas is most responsible for the development and advancement of the concept of culture (Cravens, 1978; Degler, 1991). From about 1900 to 1920, Boasian environmentalism would indelibly make its mark on the landscape of the nature–nurture debate, particularly with his 1911 book, *The Mind of Primitive Man*, which "declared war on the idea that differences in culture were derived from differences in innate capacity" (Degler, 1991, p. 62). To be sure, Boas's views on culture and race were indeed radical—considering the entrenchment of hereditarian thought during the genetic pathology era of deficit thinking. Boas's thesis underscores that the observed social differences among races (an undeniable fact) are products of "different histories not different biological experiences" (Degler, 1991, p. 62). The influence of Boas in laying the foundation for cultural relativism and the eventual sovereignty of culture as an explanation of

human behavior proved so profound it led one historian, Carl N. Degler, to comment:

> Indeed, his [Boas's] introduction of history of culture as the cause of differences among people might be said to have been the sword that cut asunder evolution's Gordian knot in which nurture was tightly tied to nature. It also constructed a single human nature in place of one divided by biology into superior and inferior peoples.
>
> (Degler, 1991, pp. 62–63)

Garrett maintains that Boas and his followers who assertively champion equalitarianism do so via "subjective and unconvincing" evidence (p. 255). The most valid and measurable data to determine racial differences in intelligence, Garrett argues, lay in intelligence tests—and the preeminent source of his assertion is Shuey's 1958 book, *The Testing of Negro Intelligence*. After summarizing Shuey's most relevant findings, he comments: "It seems clear that the evidence from psychometrics does not support the equalitarian dogma" (p. 255).

2. *"Hitler and the Nazis."* Garrett's reasoning here is that the brutalities and racial superiority beliefs of the Nazis created an advantageous atmosphere for advocates of equality to support the equalitarian dogma. He states that the equalitarian argument in which "acceptance of the *fact* of racial differences" (p. 256) triggers racial superiority beliefs, prejudice, discrimination, and oppression is a fallacious assertion. Although this equalitarian argument does have some scientific credence, Garrett dismisses it by resorting to stereotype. He comments: "Recognition of the talents of many Negroes for sports and for various forms of entertainment has if anything improved the feelings of the White majority toward Negroes generally" (p. 256).

3. *"The Rise of African Nationalism."* Here, Garrett remarks that the fight for freedom and self-rule by different groups in Africa has prompted the solicitude of many Whites and has unquestionably strengthened "the emotional appeal in the idea that all men are born equally endowed" (p. 256). But, Garrett asserts, such sentiments can be misleading because African civilizations are not worthy of being compared to, for example, European civilizations.

4. *"The Supreme Court Decision of 1954."* It is not surprising that Garrett includes this factor to explain the shift from a belief in native racial differences in intelligence to the equalitarian dogma. As I discussed earlier, scientific racists mounted a vigorous campaign to reverse the *Brown* ruling. Supporters of equalitarianism, as Garrett aptly notes, hailed the 1954 decree.

5. *"The Influence of the Communists."* Garrett comments that the politicizing activities of the communists assisted in the expansion and acceptance of equalitarian dogma. As an example, he refers to the school desegregation cases

that aided in fomenting "dissension and bitterness on which the Communist thrives" (p. 257). Garrett (1961) closes his "Equalitarian Dogma" article in *Mankind Quarterly* (p. 257) as such:

> The weight of the evidence favours the proposition that racial differences in mental ability (and perhaps in personality and character) are innate and genetic. The evidence is not all in, and further inquiry is sorely needed. Surely there are no good reasons why restrictions should be placed on further scientific research and discussion. At best, the equalitarian dogma represents a sincere if misguided effort to help the Negro by ignoring or even suppressing evidences of his mental and social immaturity. At worst, *equalitarianism is the scientific hoax of the century* [italics added].

By no means has discussion of the equalitarian dogma faded in history. Its resurrection is seen in the writings, for example, of contemporary scientific racists Roger Pearson (1991)—Pioneer grantee and *Mankind Quarterly* editor—and J. Philippe Rushton (1994), Pioneer grantee and president. Furthermore, in his hagiography of Pioneer, Richard Lynn (2001, p. 69) notes:

> This book will adopt Garrett's term, "equalitarian," for the dogma or belief that all significant human differences, between individuals or groups, are purely the result of environmental factors and that genetic factors are absent or trivial. It is useful to have an antithesis to the term, "hereditarian," which represents the position of most Pioneer grantees on the nature-nurture issue.

Prior to and after *Brown v. Board of Education of Topeka* (1954), the scientific racism of neohereditarianism, wave I, gained considerable momentum. Garrett emerged as a dominant figure in the movement committed to the prevention of race mixing and the preservation of apartheid and school segregation.[57] Likely bolstered by his very close ties with Pioneer and the funding the organization provided Garrett, he surfaced as the leader of the scientific crusade against racial integration, and later a board member of the Pioneer Fund (Tucker, 2002), and the "oracle and field marshal for scientific racists of all sorts, whether academic social scientists or outspoken White supremacists" (Newby, 1967, p. 92).

After the landmark *Brown* ruling of 1954, and the futile attempts to reverse the High Court's decision (see earlier discussion of *Stell*), Garrett dispensed with any semblance of scientific objectivity and became an indefatigable polemicist, advocating a "scientific" justification for segregation (Tucker, 1994, 2002). Compared to his more temperate racial pronouncements in respectable scholarly journals (e.g., Garrett, 1962), Garrett voiced his most egregious racial animus in a series of self-serving booklets. For example, in *Breeding Down* (*c.* mid-1960s; cited in Chorover, 1979) Garrett (n.d.) offers justification for race segregation on the grounds that Blacks are mentally inferior:

> You can no more mix the two races and maintain the standards of White civilization than you can add 80 (the average IQ of Negroes) and 100 (the average IQ of Whites), divide by two and get 100. What you would get would be a race of 90's, and it is that 10 per cent differential that spells the difference between a spire and a mud hut; 10 per cent—or less—is the margin of civilization's "profit"; it is the difference between a cultured society and savagery. Therefore, it follows, if miscegenation would be bad for White people, it would be bad for Negroes as well. For, if leadership is destroyed, all is destroyed.
>
> (quoted in Chorover, 1979, p. 47)

Garrett's mission in trying to convince others about the evils of racial integration continued unabatedly. In the year of his death (1973), Howard Allen Press, an "ultra-right-wing publisher" (Winston, 1998, p. 188), released Garrett's (1973) booklet, *IQ and Racial Differences* in which once again he spewed his racist diatribe. Examples of his onslaught against school integration:

- "In recent years it has become fashionable to depict in glowing terms the achievement of the Negro over the past 5,000 years, although the truth is that the history of the Black African is largely a blank" (pp. 1–2).
- "Egalitarianism makes a bow to heredity, but argues that almost all of the undeniable differences among mankind arise from environmental pressures, many of which are under man's control. . . . The author [Garrett] of this study holds to the thesis that egalitarianism is dead wrong. Black and White children do not have the same potential. They do not learn at the same rate" (pp. 10–11).
- "The American Negro is aided [intellectually] by his racial admixture with the American White" (p. 11).
- "The case for genetic differences in [Negro–White] intelligence is a solid one" (p. 47).
- "Since environmental theory has wrought havoc, why not try a 'new' set of premises based on genetic theory? For example . . ., institute separate and equally well-equipped schools for Negroes and Whites, wherever feasible" (p. 51).
- "It is clear there cannot be complete desegregation of our classrooms on the one hand and first-rate education on the other. Under such conditions there would only be second-rate education for the children of both races" (p. 53).

Two years later, in 1975, in the midst of the volatile school busing debate regarding school desegregation in Boston, an advertisement appeared in the *Boston Globe* announcing the publication of Garrett's (1973) *IQ and Racial Differences*.

In all, opponents of school integration doled out, gratis, 500,000 copies of Garrett's racist booklets to U.S. teachers in the 1960s (Chorover, 1979).

To sum, two points regarding Garrett are noteworthy. First, there is the subject of ethics. In the foreword of Shuey's (1966) *The Testing of Negro Intelligence,* he writes: "The honest psychologist, like any true scientist, should have no preconceived racial bias" (p. viii). Apparently, Garrett felt he was above this principle. Keep in mind that at the same time he made this statement he was voicing, in his booklets, repugnant and bigoted opinions about Blacks. Second, on the environmental hypothesis of racial differences in intelligence, he argues in the foreword of Shuey's book: "The American Negro is generally below the White in social and economic status, and his work opportunities are more limited. Many of these inequalities have been exaggerated" (p. viii). Notwithstanding all the empirical evidence that Black–White differences in intelligence are greatly accounted for by structural inequality, as well as environmental and SES factors, he shrugs off this body of data (Valencia & Suzuki, 2001, chapters 3 and 4).

ARTHUR R. JENSEN

Jensen—former educational psychologist at the University of California, Berkeley and professor emeritus since 1994—is one of the most notable Pioneer grantees, having received more than $1,000,000 in funds.[58] According to Richard Lynn (2001), author of the history of Pioneer, in the 1960s Jensen agreed with the predominant perspective that environmental factors mainly or entirely determined intelligence. His views changed, however, after receiving a Guggenheim Fellowship in 1966–1967 to devote his sabbatical at the Stanford University Center for Advanced Study in the Behavioral Sciences. His goal: to write on the negative effects of "cultural disadvantages on the intelligence and educational attainment" of American ethnic minority children (Lynn, 2001, p. 216). As Jensen immersed himself in the literature, he realized that textbooks on intelligence had omitted or even misinterpreted "the genetic aspect of mental ability" (Lynn, 2001, p. 216). As such, Jensen's subsequent publications (1969, 1972, 1973; see Table 2.1, present chapter) proved highly instrumental in galvanizing genetic pathology deficit thinking during wave I of neohereditarianism.

Upon invitation by the editorial board of the *Harvard Educational Review* (HER), Jensen wrote an article, "How Much Can We Boost IQ and Scholastic Achievement?"[59] The title of the lengthy article is highly significant. The wording—a double-barreled query—cleverly captures the core of Jensen's thesis. He asks two questions regarding Black and poor children: (a) How much can their IQ be raised? (b) How much can their school achievement be raised? To the first question his conclusion is: very little. The second: somewhat (but in a prescribed manner).

Jensen's (1969) opening line of his 123-page article got right to the point:

"Compensatory education has been tried and it apparently has failed" (p. 2). He concludes that supporters of compensatory education for "disadvantaged" children tried such programs, but they failed to increase children's IQs for any significant period of time. Given that the plasticity of human intelligence (Bloom, 1964; Hunt, 1961; Piaget, 1963) formed the theoretical basis of compensatory education programs (e.g., Operation Head Start), Jensen (1969) questions whether the efforts of these programs to raise children's intelligence are being misdirected. A reasonable and rival interpretation, Jensen asserts, is perhaps that these children lack the cognitive capacity for higher-level learning. To support this contention, he draws from research on his "Level I–Level II theory of mental abilities" (which essentially is a theory of educability). Interestingly, nearly 30 years later, A.R. Jensen (1998) clarifies matters that his Level I–Level II theory "*is not really a theory* but rather a set of generalizations about the nature of the W–B [White–Black] differences on cognitive tests" (p. 404).

In any event, Jensen (1969) claims that Level I involves lower-level skills (e.g., digit span memory; serial rote-learning; paired-associate learning). Level II, by contrast, involves higher-order skills (e.g., concept learning; problem solving). Jensen hypothesizes that, "Level I ability is distributed about the same [i.e., normally] in all social class groups, while Level II ability is distributed differently in lower- and middle-SES groups [i.e., positively skewed in low-SES children; negatively skewed in middle-SES children]" (p. 115). Jensen goes on to conclude:

> Heritability studies of Level II tests cause me to believe that Level II processes are not just the result of interaction between Level I learning ability and experientially acquired strategies and learning sets. That learning is necessary for Level II no one doubts, but certain neural structures must also be available for Level II abilities to develop, and these are conceived of as being different from the neural structures underlying Level I. *The genetic factors involved in each of these types of ability are presumed to have become differentially distributed in the population as a function of social class* [italics added], since Level II has been most important for scholastic performance under the traditional methods of instruction ... There can be little doubt that certain educational occupational attainments depend more upon g[60] than upon any other single ability. *But schools must also be able to find ways of utilizing other strengths in children whose major strength is not of the cognitive variety* [italics added]. One of the great and relatively untapped reservoirs of mental ability in the disadvantaged, it appears from our research, is the basic ability to learn. We can do more to marshal this strength for educational purposes.
>
> (Jensen, 1969, pp. 116–117)

In sum, Jensen (1969) hypothesizes that compensatory education failed to boost, to any appreciable degree, the IQs of "disadvantaged" children in such programs because these youngsters have limitations in Level II ability, which Jensen states that cognitive tests with high loadings of *g* measure. Jensen (1969) then moves into an area that would prove incendiary in the eyes of many. He discusses evidence that "social class and racial variations in intelligence cannot be accounted for [almost entirely] by differences in environment but must be attributed partially to *genetic influence*" [italics added] (p. 2). This is a reasonable hypothesis to raise, Jensen claims. He comes to this conclusion via the following two-step route in reasoning:

Based on his synthesis of the worldwide literature on various kinship correlations of measured intelligence (i.e., for White populations), Jensen (1969) concludes that .81 is "the best single overall estimate of the heritability of measured intelligence that we can make" (p. 51). It appears that Jensen's understanding of the magnitude of heritability of intelligence has changed from years past. "The broad heritability of IQ is about .40 to .50 when measured in children, [is] about .60 to .70 in adolescents and young adults, and approaches .80 in later maturity" (A.R. Jensen, 1998, p. 169). In the final section of this chapter regarding scientific research about the genetic hypothesis of racial differences in intelligence, I discuss the concept of heritability.

Although Jensen (1969) acknowledges that (a) he bases his heritability estimate on White European and North American populations, (b) no adequate investigations of heritability estimates exist on the Black population in the U.S., and (c) heritability estimates do not necessarily apply to intellectual difference between populations, he nonetheless concludes,

> So all we are left with are various lines of evidence, no one of which is definitive alone, but which, viewed all together, *make it a not unreasonable hypothesis that genetic factors are strongly implicated in the average Negro-White intelligence difference* [italics added]. The preponderance of the evidence is, in my opinion, less consistent with a strictly environmental hypothesis than with a genetic hypothesis, which, of course, does not exclude the influence of environment or its interaction with genetic factors.
>
> (*Ibid.*, p. 82)

Scholars responded swiftly, and in great numbers, to Jensen's (1969) article. Citation counts show that within a few years after *HER* published his treatise, 117 articles and chapters appeared in academic outlets.[61] Furthermore, the article caught the attention of telecasters, newspapers, and major national print sources such as *U.S. News and World Report, Time,* and *Newsweek* (Snyderman & Rothman, 1988; Tucker, 1994). Kelves (1985) comments that "No single publication did more to precipitate the revival [i.e., the issue of race and intelligence]" (p. 269) than Jensen's *HER* article. Pearson (1991), a Pioneer grantee and staunch supporter of Jensen, hails him as "the foremost researcher responsible for the revival of 'hereditarian' thought in recent decades" (p. 141). Tucker

(1994) describes Jensen's (1969) publication as "the most explosive article in the history of American psychology, triggering one of the most bitter scientific controversies since Darwin" (p. 199).

In light of the voluminous literature Jensen's (1969) article stimulated—some positive, most negative—and because others have extensively covered this debate, I touch on only five criticisms I think are the most important.[62]

1. Jensen's (1969) conclusion that preschool compensatory education proved ineffective in increasing the intellectual performance (as measured by IQ) of "disadvantaged" children stems, in part, from the massive Westinghouse-Ohio National Evaluation of Head Start study (Cicirelli, Evans, & Schiller, 1969). This investigation, based on a national sample of 102 Head Start Centers and nearly 4,000 children, concludes that Head Start failed to produce any significant and lasting cognitive and effective gains in the children. Smith and Bissell (1970), in a major critique of the Westinghouse-Ohio study, contend that serious methodological problems exist (e.g., the use of random rather than stratified sampling; an unrepresentative final sample in that more than half of the target centers refused to participate; Head Start and non-Head Start children ["controls"] not being equated adequately). Also, Tucker (1994, p. 201) notes that the "failure" of Head Start may have been related to a "helter-skelter" of poorly organized and structured programs.

2. Several scholars raise criticisms regarding Jensen's (1969) contention that the heritability estimate of intelligence is about .81 for White populations (i.e., Europeans and U.S. Whites). For example: (a) the sample sizes in kinship/heritability of intelligence studies of twins and siblings reared together are limited (Crow, 1969); (b) a number of assumptions of monozygotic twins reared apart are not met (Taylor, 1980); (c) Jensen chose the higher heritability estimate, although researchers found a range of estimates in human populations (Lewontin, 1973); (d) the original work on the heritability of intelligence by noted English psychologist Sir Cyril Burt (whom Jensen relies on considerably, for deriving his estimate of heritability) is suspected of being fraudulent (Hearnshaw, 1979; Kamin, 1974; Wade, 1976).[63]

3. For his conclusion that study after study shows U.S. Blacks, as a group, perform on the average about one standard deviation lower than the mean of U.S. Whites on IQ tests, Jensen (1969) relies heavily on Shuey's (1966) review—a work with which a number of scholars found problems (see earlier discussion, this chapter).

4. Scholars criticize Jensen (1969) for making an unwarranted leap from within-group to between-group variance regarding the estimated .81 heritability of intelligence. That is, one *cannot* apply the heritability estimated for one particular population to another population.[64]

5. Jensen's (1969) implicit schooling recommendation—that educational attempts to boost low-SES children's IQ are misdirected, and therefore schools

should focus on teaching specific skills (i.e., Level I learning) that are commensurate with the abilities of such children—prompted criticisms by several scholars. Researchers questioned Jensen's claim that his Level I–Level II theory is a hierarchical model of learning (i.e., Level I precedes Level II). Jensen views his two levels as being genetically and independently determined (factorially distinct). Phillips and Kelley (1975) point out, however, that Jensen makes an assumption that confuses his claim and contradicts his assertion that Level I–Level II abilities are independent (also, see Taylor & Skanes, 1976). The issues Phillips and Kelley raised more than three decades ago appear to have merit regarding the validity of Jensen's "theory." As I note earlier, A.R. Jensen (1998) recanted, saying that the Level I–Level II theory actually is *not* a theory.

What impact did Jensen's (1969) controversial article have on social thought and educational practice? Regarding the former, his *HER* article had tremendous influence in three ways during wave I of neohereditarianism. First, his article reinforced the conclusion of Shuey (1958, 1966) who proffers that innate factors account for Black–White mean differences in measured intelligence. Second, Jensen (1969) helped to strengthen the challenges of the equalitarian dogma articulated by Garrett (1961). Third, Jensen's *HER* article helped stimulate the work of other neohereditarianists in wave I (e.g., Eysenck, 1971; Herrnstein, 1971, 1973; Osborne & McGurk, 1982a [see Table 2.1, present chapter], all who cite and support Jensen's [1969] conclusion regarding racial differences in intelligence).[65] With respect to the influence of Jensen (1969) on educational practice, there is some evidence that his article reinforced deficit thinking beliefs that poor children of color best learn via the teaching of concrete skills. For example, Jensen's Level I–Level II theory of learning appears to have influenced Carl Bereiter (1969), who, at the time, developed curriculum for young Black children. Bereiter comments: "We were not trying to teach academic skills directly in ways that did not demand of the children abilities they demonstrably did not possess" (p. 315) (see, Nyberg, 1976, for a critique).

In sum, Jensen's (1969) account of the alleged existence of genetically driven Black–White racial differences in intelligence offers little that is new. Although he had the benefits of modern day statistical tools and an advanced knowledge base of human genetics, the core of Jensen's analysis follows the tradition of the 1920s genetic pathology model of deficit thinking (Valencia, 1997d). Close inspection of his 1969 treatise indicates a near alignment with several tenets of 50 years earlier: (a) Intelligence is innately acquired; (b) IQ tests measure innate intelligence; (c) Black–White differences in measured intelligence are largely explained by genetic differences, and environmental factors such as SES, culture, structural equality are not important, for the most part, to consider; (d) Schooling for Blacks should consist of concrete, practical instruction. At chapter's end, I provide a discussion of how Jensen's and other hereditarian scholars' conclusions that racial differences are largely genetically based rest on pseudoscientific theorizing.

Neohereditarianism: Wave II

Lloyd M. Dunn's 1987 research monograph—*Bilingual Hispanic Children on the U.S. Mainland: A Review of Research on Their Cognitive, Linguistic, and Scholastic Development*—shocked many scholars, Latinos in particular (Valencia & Suzuki, 2001). Dunn (1987) is the first research treatise of notable length (88 pps.) ever published that proffers a genetic interpretation, in part, regarding Latino–White mean differences in measured intelligence.[66] In the monograph, published by American Guidance Service, a leading producer of tests and educational materials, Dunn (1987, p. 63) claims:

> While many people are willing to blame the low scores of Puerto Ricans and Mexican-Americans on their poor environmental conditions, *few are prepared to face the probability that inherited genetic material is a contributing factor.* Yet, in making a scholarly, comprehensive examination of this issue, this factor must be included.[67]

With the exception of Dunn (1987), the other publications of neohereditarianism, wave II listed in Table 2.1 have dates of the 1990s decade. The singular publication of this period that stands out, by far, is Herrnstein and Murray's *The Bell Curve*—which received enormous attention. What Jensen's (1969) article did for wave I of neohereditarianism, Herrnstein and Murray's book did for wave II—serving as a focal point of hereditarian resurgence in the study of racial differences in intelligence. In the interest of space and time, I limit this discussion of neohereditarianism, wave II to *The Bell Curve*.

RICHARD J. HERRNSTEIN AND CHARLES MURRAY

Their book, *The Bell Curve: Intelligence and Class Structure in American Life* (1994), is a tome of massive proportions (845 pps.), and is certainly influenced by Herrnstein's earlier work on intelligence and meritocracy (Herrnstein, 1971, 1973; see Table 2.1, neohereditarianism, wave I).[68] In *The Bell Curve* the late Herrnstein (Harvard University psychology professor, 1958–1994) and Murray (current scholar at the American Enterprise Institute, a conservative research group in Washington, D.C.) seek to shed new light on the complex relations among social class, race, heredity, and intelligence. While this objective may be scientifically worthwhile, at the time of *The Bell Curve*'s publication Herrnstein and Murray had no record of having authored any peer-reviewed scientific publications on the genetic basis of intelligence and its relation to race or poverty (Dorfman, 1995).

The Bell Curve ranks as one of the most sustained treatises on genetic pathology deficit thinking ever published in regard to the poor and people of color. Herrnstein and Murray claim that cognitive differentiation among

Americans (within- and between-racial/ethnic groups) has resulted in a bifurcated society at the extreme levels of the IQ continuum—that is, the emergence of a *cognitive elite* (top 5%, IQ of 120 or higher) and the *very dull* (bottom 5%, IQ of 75 or lower).[69] In some cases, Herrnstein and Murray include the *dull* (IQs from 75 to 89) as part of the *cognitive underclass*. The authors contend that such "cognitive partitioning" is strongly linked to "socially desirable behaviors" (i.e., high schooling attainment; prestigious occupational status; high income level) as well as "socially undesirable behaviors" (i.e., poverty; high school dropouts; unemployment; divorce; illegitimate births; welfare dependency; malparenting; crime; poor civility and citizenship) (see chapters 5–12 of Herrnstein & Murray, 1994).

In their cognitive partitioning thesis, Herrnstein and Murray (1994) contend: (a) Having a high IQ greatly improves one's life chances of social mobility and possessing desirable behaviors; (b) Having a low IQ places one at substantial risk for possessing undesirable behaviors. The authors derive their thesis and larger model of social stratification according to the following nine-step sequence of reasoning:

1. High IQ is an invaluable raw material for social and economic success in American society.

2. "Intelligence itself, not just its correlation with socioeconomic status, is responsible for these group differences" (Herrnstein & Murray, 1994, p. 117). That is, different levels of cognitive ability are linked with different patterns of social behavior, and intelligence is endowed unequally across social classes. The authors' first point, regarding the relation between intelligence and SES, is the bedrock of their thesis of cognitive partitioning. Here, Herrnstein and Murray challenge the conventional view of directionality between the two variables. Note the following:

    Convention:[70]   SES → Intelligence
    Herrnstein & Murray: Intelligence → SES

3. Herrnstein and Murray (1994) confidently claim that "IQ is substantially heritable" (p. 105). Within the White population, the authors note that the heritability estimate for intelligence is between .40 and .80,[71] and for purposes of their discussion, they opt for a heritability index of .60.

Continuing from directly above, Herrnstein and Murray (1994) introduce one of the most explosive issues in *The Bell Curve*—possible explanations for racial differences in measured intelligence.[72] The authors state that they are "resolutely agnostic" (p. 311) on the relative contributions of nature and nurture to "the mix" (p. 311). Although Herrnstein and Murray say they are skeptical on the relative proportions of genetic and environmental influences on racial/ethnic differences in intelligence, they are not agnostic, however, that such influences exist, as indicated by this assertion: "It seems *highly likely* [italics added] that both genes and environment have something to do with racial differences [in intelligence]" (p. 311). But, a closer analysis of Herrnstein and Murray's discussion of racial differences shows that the sources they cite are weighted toward a genetic explanation. Herrnstein and Murray draw heavily from the writings of Pioneer grantees, for example, Arthur R. Jensen, Richard Lynn, J. Philippe Rushton, and Frank C.J. McGurk.[73]

4. The cognitive elite, through concentrated social pools and self-selection (i.e., assortative mating), has emerged. Members of this class (which are disproportionately White) have become the controllers of power, privilege, and status, "restructuring the rules of society so that it becomes harder and harder for them to lose" (p. 509).

5. Concomitant with the increasing isolation of the cognitive elite and its growing influence over the control of America, is the growth and perpetuation of the cognitive underclass (disproportionately Latinos and Blacks) and its accompanying intractable social problems. Furthermore, Herrnstein and Murray (1994) claim there is an alleged dysgenic effect presently occurring in which the intellectually disadvantaged (disproportionately Latinos and Blacks, according to the authors) are having the highest fertility rates, "which could lead to further divergence between Whites and other groups in future generations" (p. 341).

6. Given that (a) the cognitive underclass is allegedly deficient in intellectual endowments and abilities and (b) attempts to raise the IQ of members of this class have proved disappointing, a national policy agenda needs to be set in motion.

7. Such national policy considerations should include, for example: evaluation of the immigrant situation ("legal" and "illegal") in that "immigration does indeed make a difference to the future of the national distribution of intelligence" (Herrnstein & Murray, 1994, p. 358); this is particularly seen in the cases of "Latino and Black immigrants [who] are, at least in the short run, *putting downward pressure on the distribution of intelligence*" [italics added] (pp. 360–361).

8. Regarding policy directed toward educational reform, Herrnstein and Murray (1994) tangentially mention the use of "national achievement tests, national curricula, school choice, vouchers, tuition tax credits, apprenticeship programs, restoration of the neighborhood school, minimum competency tests, [and] ability grouping" (p. 435). One reform suggestion they discuss in some detail is a need for more attention and funding for the gifted, whom they claim were "out" when economically disadvantaged became "in." To meet the needs of the neglected gifted, Herrnstein and Murray advocate that the federal government "*reallocate some portion of existing elementary and secondary school federal aid from programs for the disadvantaged to programs for the gifted*" (pp. 441–442).

9. Finally, Herrnstein and Murray (1994), in *The Bell Curve*'s penultimate chapter, offer a speculation of the future impact of cognitive stratification on

American life and the workings of the government. Their prediction of the future—which can be best described as resembling a horrendous caste system—is frightening and has a calamitous tone for those people who will occupy the bottom rungs of the cognitive ability continuum. The authors comment: "Like other apocalyptic visions, this one is pessimistic, perhaps too much so. On the other hand, there is much to be pessimistic about" (p. 509). Herrnstein and Murray predict that the coming of the custodial state will be influenced, over the next two decades, by a growing acceptance of the belief that the underclass are in dire conditions "through no fault of their own but because *of inherent shortcomings* [italics added] about which little can be done" (p. 523). As such, more open discussion will occur among politicians and intellectuals that members of the underclass cannot, for example, fend for themselves (e.g., from violence, child abuse, and drug addiction) or be trusted to spend cash appropriately (thus, the custodial state will rely more on services than on cash for the underclass).

Quite similar to the reactions to Jensen's (1969) article of neohereditarianism wave I, an immense outpourings of critical writings and debate followed the publication of *The Bell Curve*. My literature search identified five books about *The Bell Curve*[74] and nearly 70 published book reviews and commentaries, as of 1999. Based on the literature I have reviewed, the responses to *The Bell Curve* are, for the most part, negative, a point even acknowledged by Charles Murray, co-author of the book. After the book's release in October 1994, Murray comments in May 1995: "The initial reaction was encouraging. . . . Then came the avalanche. . . . Most of the comment has been virulently hostile" (Murray, 1995, p. 23). Indeed some of the responses have an *ad hominem* and invective demeanor, but a good number of the reactions are thoughtful, scientifically based, and well informed. Given the enormous reaction to *The Bell Curve*, it is well beyond the scope of this chapter to provide a comprehensive and integrative analysis of these responses. I offer a very brief encapsulation of this body of criticism.[75] For ease of discussion, I organize the critiques around central themes.

1. *On what is new in The Bell Curve.* Many critics assert that there is little new in *The Bell Curve* regarding argumentation germane to race, class, and intelligence, and that the book rests on an old, disreputable, and debunked paradigm of genetic explanations of inequality.[76] Duster (1995), for example, comments,

> It should now be clear that the extraordinary success of this book is not a function of the presentation of new information, nor of the restructuring of a new line of argumentation by reassembling old data in a coherent and convincing manner. (p. 160)

2. *On statistical data presented in The Bell Curve.* Critics remark that the

observed associations (correlations) between the main predictor variables (measured intelligence and SES) and the various social behaviors are weak in strength.[77] Gould (1996) comments: "Herrnstein and Murray's correlations are very weak—often in the 0.2 to 0.4 range" (p. 376).[78] Critics also state that Herrnstein and Murray approach the use of correlational analysis in an uncritical manner, that is, drawing conclusions of causality from correlations (Carspecken, 1996; Kamin, 1995; Sowell, 1995).

3. *On the construct of intelligence embraced in The Bell Curve.* Drawing from the classicist tradition, Herrnstein and Murray embrace and defend the construct of *g* as the central, dominant perspective of what intelligence is. Some critics contend that in doing so, Herrnstein and Murray shun alternative perspectives of the intelligence construct (Kinchloe & Steinberg, 1996; Reed, 1994). Another related criticism leveled against *The Bell Curve* has to do with the basic measure of "intelligence" used by Herrnstein and Murray in their analyses—that is, the Armed Forces Qualifying Test (AFQT). Fischer et al. (1996), based on their own empirical analyses, provide an informed and insightful discussion that the AFQT (a) is more a measure of school tasks (high-school level mathematics and reading) than of general intelligence (e.g., *g*), (b) strongly correlates with years of schooling of the test taker, (c) is a better predictor of "past schooling than . . . [of] future schooling. That is, the AFQT measures what test takers have already learned, not their ability for future learning" (p. 64), and (d) is not administered under standardized conditions.

4. *On the issue of raising cognitive ability in The Bell Curve.* Based on their review of the literature, Herrnstein and Murray (1994) conclude, "No one yet knows how to raise low IQs substantially on a national level" (p. 416). A major criticism of Herrnstein and Murray is that they ignore many studies that document the advantages of educational intervention (Kinchloe & Steinberg, 1996; also, see Duster, 1995; Finn, 1995).

5. *On the political nature of The Bell Curve.* Of the different criticisms directed at *The Bell Curve*, critics appears to most frequently note that Herrnstein and Murray (1994), behind the smoke screen of science, use their book to tacitly outline and push their agendas on affirmative action bans, immigration restriction, and welfare reform.[79] For example, Kinchloe and Steinberg (1996) assert that *The Bell Curve* is "the theoretical torch bearer for the right-wing insurgency of the 1990s" (p. 4).

6. *On the nature–nurture debate in The Bell Curve.* Surprisingly, few critics of *The Bell Curve* draw from the literature in behavioral genetics that finds no support for a genetic hypothesis in explaining racial/ethnic mean differences in intelligence. One scholar who discusses this research from behavioral genetics is Nisbett (1998), who raises, for example, the extremely important point that "Estimates of heritability *within* a given population need not say anything about the degree to which differences *between* populations are genetically determined" (p. 87). In the final section of this chapter, I discuss research

findings from the behavioral genetics field that the genetic hypothesis is not scientifically supportable.

7. *On the absence of rival interpretations in The Bell Curve.* In my view, this is the most powerful criticism of Herrnstein and Murray (1994). As I discuss in chapter 1 of this volume, theories in the behavioral and social sciences describe, explain, and predict human behavior, and they often offer recommendations for behavioral change. If one's nomological net is not flexible enough to cast for competing interpretations, then dogma is likely to take form for what should be open discourse. Explicitly or implicitly stated in the many criticisms of *The Bell Curve* is the failure on the part of Herrnstein and Murray to entertain competing interpretations for their conclusions that individuals of low and high IQ end up situated in the "cognitive underclass" and "cognitive elite," respectively. In sum, what might be a rival and perhaps sounder way to explain America's system of inequality? To address this, Fischer et al. (1996)—six sociology professors at the University of California at Berkeley—reanalyzed the very same National Longitudinal Survey of Youth (NLSY) survey data Herrnstein and Murray (1994) use to come to the conclusion that inherited differences in intelligence between social classes largely explain inequality. Fischer et al. published their results and conclusion in *Inequality by Design: Cracking the Bell Curve Myth*. Through the use of a macro-level structural model involving caste status, social circumstances, social policies, unequal distribution of wealth, and challenges to deficit thinking, Fischer et al. offer a compelling study whose findings rebut the deterministic model presented in *The Bell Curve*. The authors proffer an explanation of societal inequality that is antithetical to the one generated by Herrnstein and Murray. Fischer et al. assert: "A racial or ethnic group's position in society determines its measured intelligence rather than vice versa" (p. 173). Or stated even more directly, "*Groups score unequally on tests because they are unequal in society*" [italics added] (p. 172). As I discuss in chapter 1 of the present book, the structural inequality paradigm is a powerful counterstory to the deficit thinking model.

In conclusion, *The Bell Curve* offers little new in understanding contemporary social stratification in the U.S. and is based on an old, refuted model. Valencia (1997d) identifies a number of historical ideological and "scientific" streams that helped to shape 1920s hereditarianism and are pertinent to this particular criticism leveled against *The Bell Curve*. The major forces are: (a) Galton's belief that one's social status is genetically predetermined, as are socially desirable and undesirable behaviors; (b) Terman's (and other scholars') view that intelligence is largely innately based and it predicts, fairly accurately, one's eventual social, economic, and occupational status; (c) McDougall's perspective of a society that can and should be divided between the "haves" and "have-nots," where the former are more deserving to reap societal benefits, should control the latter, and need to reproduce at greater levels than the latter.

A close examination of *The Bell Curve* reveals that Herrnstein and Murray (1994) incorporate, in whole or part, these pseudoscientific, historically refuted ideas into their work. Interestingly, the fundamental question that Herrnstein and Murray posed in 1994 is remarkably similar to what McDougall (1921) raised 73 years earlier in *Is America Safe for Democracy?*: "Does the social stratification of society correspond to, is it correlated with, a stratification of intellectual capacity?" (McDougall, p. 62). In sum, if one is to dismiss 1920s hereditarianism as bad science and policy, then *The Bell Curve* must be rejected on the same basis.

Neohereditarianism: Wave III

The wave III publications listed in Table 2.1 have two features that set them apart from the works shown in waves I and II. First, all of them have publication dates in the 2000s decade. Second, with the exception of Sarich and Miele (2004), these books focus on international comparisons of racial differences in intelligence. For example, Richard Lynn's (2008) book, *The Global Bell Curve: Race, IQ, and Inequality*, forecasts its content—an international treatise *à la* Herrnstein and Murray's (1994) *The Bell Curve*. Once again, due to space and time restrictions, I limit my discussion—in this instance to Rushton (2000) and Lynn and Vanhanen (2002).

JOHN PHILIPPE RUSHTON

This individual, a.k.a. J. Philippe Rushton, is one of the most controversial neohereditarian scholars listed on Table 2.1, present chapter. Rushton is a professor of psychology at the University of Western Ontario (London, Ontario), a grantee and current President of Pioneer, and founder of the Pioneer-funded Charles Darwin Research Institute (CDRI).

Rushton is best known for his contentious *Race, Evolution, and Behavior: A Life History Perspective* (2000), published by the CDRI.[80] The book's inside cover shows endorsement blurbs by a coterie of supporters, including a number of Pioneer grantees. These latter peers offer accolades, for example: "This brilliant book is the most impressive theory-based study . . . of the psychological and behavioral differences between the major groups" (Arthur R. Jensen). "In my view this theory has the simplicity and explanatory power that indicate truth" (Michael Levin). "Should, if there is any justice, [Rushton should] receive a Nobel Prize" (Richard Lynn).

Before I discuss critics' responses to the book, two comments are in order. First, in 1989 at the annual meeting of the American Association for the Advancement of Science (AAAS) in San Francisco, Rushton presented his genetically based theory of racial differences in a number of physical and behavioral characteristics, including intelligence (Horowitz,1995; Lynn, 2001; Pearson, 1991). He asserted that based on evolutionary history, a racial ranking exists in which "Mongoloids," "Caucasoids," and "Negroids" are in the top end of the continuum, intermediate position, and bottom end of the continuum, respectively. Subsequent to Rushton's AAAS paper, (a) Newspaper stories ensued in which reporters referred to him as a racist; (b) The Attorney General of the Province of Ontario instructed the provincial and local police to investigate whether Rushton violated federal hate crime codes; (c) Eighteen University of Western Ontario students submitted an official complaint with the Ontario Human Rights commission, claiming Rushton had contravened the Human Rights Code that guarantees equality of treatment to all subjects of Ontario; for remedy, the students asked that his job be terminated. The outcome:

> Rushton was given a negative annual performance rating, deprived of pay increases, investigated as to the ethics of his research work, convicted of minor breaches of protocol, and forced to deliver his lectures by videotape. He spent a year-and-a-half fighting the administration through a series of internal grievance procedures, eventually winning on the important issue of academic freedom.
>
> (Lynn, 2001, p. 377)

Gray (1991), in a comprehensive overview of the Rushton case at the University of Western Ontario, notes that the Psychology Department's Personnel, Promotion and Tenure Committee appealed the favorable ruling on Rushton. Yet, the Faculty Senate Grievance Committee denied the appeal. As such, Rushton's victory on grounds of academic freedom was upheld.

A second incident occurred in November and December of 1999 regarding Rushton's (2000) *Race, Evolution, and Behavior* (Alland, 2002; Lombardo, 2002; Tucker, 2002). About 30,000 anthropologists, sociologists, and psychologists (including myself) received, unsolicited, a "special abridged edition" (108 pps.) of Rushton's book, clearly as a marketing strategy to introduce the 2000 unabridged version. The abridged version (Rushton, 1999), sent in a small plain brown envelope and marked "compliments of J. Philippe Rushton," contains absolutely no references or footnotes. The booklet's back cover succinctly captures Rushton's evolutionary history theory of racial differences, based on an *r*- and *K*-selection continuum. His model is as follows: (a) At least three biological races ("subspecies") of humans exist (Asians; Whites; Blacks); (b) These three racial groups possess distinguishable profiles (e.g., in regard to brain size; intelligence; criminal behavior; sexual behavior); (c) On average, these profiles fall on a continuum from high (Asian), intermediate (White), to low (Black); (d) "This worldwide pattern implies *evolutionary and genetic*, rather than purely social, political, economic, or cultural, causes."[81]

Although the abridged version of *Race, Evolution, and Behavior* contains a copyright from Transaction Press, Pioneer provided the money to print 100,000 copies and distribute the highly condensed edition of the book. Transaction Press, which published the first (1995) and second (1997) editions of *Race, Evolution, and Behavior*, had not agreed to have its name (as copyright holder) on the abridged version—but only to assist in circulating a flyer for the booklet. In the end, Rushton agreed to Transaction's demand for destruction of the remaining 60,000 copies. For those tens of thousands of scholars who received the abridged version of *Race, Evolution, and Behavior*, numerous "were outraged at what they considered 'racial pornography,'" one recipient calling the paperback a 'wholly vile piece of work' and returning it to the publisher forthwith" (Tucker, 2002, p. 198). Here is an example of a racist statement Rushton (1999) presents in the abridged version: Racial differences exist "in brain size, IQ, crime rates, growth rate, sexual activity, even the number of multiple births and hormone levels." He continues by noting that such differences are so numerous that it is "unlikely that the causes are only due to culture. . . . *Genes seem to be involved*" [italics added] (p. 59).

Rushton's first edition of *Race, Evolution, and Behavior* (1995) prompted many responses, overwhelmingly negative.[82] The major criticisms are:

1. *Race*. Rushton (1995) asserts, wrongly, that race is a biological concept. There are no objectively measurable races, a point that scholars have discussed for decades (Graves, 2002).[83]

2. *Human variation*. Rushton (1995) fails to understand that there is far more variation within populations than variation between populations (Alland, 2002; Wahlsten, 1995). This basic principle bolsters the assertion that there are no distinct biological races.

3. *Interaction*. Rushton (1995) seems not to comprehend that environmental and genetic contributions to human behavior are inseparable (Barash, 1995; Brace, 1996), in that they interact via one's norm of reaction (Valencia & Suzuki, 2001, chapter 6).

4. *Methodology*. Rushton (1995) asserts that the keystone of his methodology is the "principle of aggregation," which is the "average across a number of measures" (p. 20). Wahlsten (1995), however, questions this methodology (also, see Barash, 1995). Wahlsten (1995) notes that utilizing aggregation ignores the role of environmental differences, and thus makes all of Rushton's data unreliable for hypothesis testing in regard to genetic influence of racial differences.

5. *Alternative hypotheses*. In light of Rushton's (1995) near exclusive emphasis on genetics to explain racial differences, he fails to consider alternative hypotheses (Barash, 1995; Brace, 1996; Graves, 2002; Wahlsten, 1995). For example, Rushton (1995) asserts that South African Blacks have very low IQs, and suggests this has a genetic base. Wahlsten (1995), however, remarks that such low measured intelligence says nothing about genes because this

diminished performance is strongly related to inferior schooling. He comments: "Rushton himself was raised in South Africa before moving to England, and he seems blind to the injustices of apartheid and how these injustices have had a particularly severe impact in the primary schooling of the Black Africans" (p. 131).

6. *Brain size and intelligence.* A significant argument Rushton (1995) maintains in his evolutionary life history theory is that brain size is positively correlated with intelligence. Given that Blacks have the smallest brain size, according to Rushton, then they fall at the low end of his *r-K*-selection continuum. In *Race, Evolution, and Behavior* (1995), Rushton presents Table 2.2 (pp. 38–39) in which he summarizes the results of 32 studies that find positive *r*s, (average of 0.30) between brain size and intelligence.[84] Graves (2002), however, has carefully examined these investigations and concludes they are useless in drawing the conclusion Rushton does. That is, only 3 (9.4%) of the 32 investigations control for height and weight. This control is essential because in humans, body size and brain size are positively correlated. Of the three studies considered legitimate, the *r*s ranged from .28 to .35, which are low correlations. To Graves' (2002) critique, I would add that the measures of "intelligence" had no uniformity, hence concerns of reliability and validity arise.[85]

To sum, experts in life history theory conclude that Rushton's (1995) work is pseudoscientific and racist. For example, Douglas Wahlsten (1995), a psychologist who specializes in brain structure and behavior, and genetic experimentation, notes:

> Rushton is an earnest believer in genetically determined race differences, and he vows to cling tenaciously to his world view unless his opponents can provide conclusive proof to the contrary. In my opinion, this is the kind of approach to be expected from religious zealots, not professional scientists. (pp. 130–131)

David Barash (1995), a psychologist specializing in evolutionary factors influencing human behavior, says this of *Race, Evolution, and Behavior*: "Bad science and virulent racial prejudice drips like pus from every page of this despicable book" (p. 1133).

RICHARD LYNN

Lynn, Emeritus Professor of Psychology of the University of Ulster (Coleraine, Northern Ireland), has long-standing connections with Pioneer. From 1971 to 1996, the Ulster Institute for Social Research (which he directed) received $609,000 from Pioneer.[86] As of 2008, Lynn is listed as an Associate Editor of Pioneer-supported *Mankind Quarterly* (see previous discussion, present chapter). Finally, since 2002 he has been serving on the Pioneer Board.

Lynn is the author of a number of books that convey a common theme—

global racial differences in intelligence explain how low-performing groups (in intelligence) create problems for themselves. In sum, his treatises are filled with a genetic pathology model of deficit thinking, gone internationally. It is telling to mention the publishers of Lynn's books. Praeger published Lynn's *Dysgenics: Genetic Deterioration in Modern Populations* (1996)[87] and *IQ and the Wealth of Nations* (2002; with Tatu Vanhanen). One may ask why Praeger, a major publisher of academic and general interest books and reference titles, many of which receive annual awards, would publish Lynn's (1996, 2002) deficit thinking books. It appears that Lynn had a connection at Praeger. Both of his books (1996, 2002) are published in the Human Evolution, Behavior, and Intelligence Series; the Series Editor is Seymour Itzkoff, a Pioneer grantee.[88] Washington Summit Publishers produced three of Lynn's books: *IQ and Global Inequality* (2006; with Tatu Vanhanen);[89] *Race Differences in Intelligence: An Evolutionary Analysis* (2006),[90] and *The Global Bell Curve: Race, IQ, and Inequality Worldwide* (2008).[91] The Southern Poverty Law Center (SPLC) classifies Washington Summit Publishers, run by Louis R. Andrews, as a White Nationalist Hate Group.[92] The SPLC notes that Andrews "has become increasingly important in academic racist circles in recent years." Furthermore, Washington Summit Publishers reprints a range of classical and modern racist tracts, along with books on eugenics, the discredited "science" of breeding better humans. Washington Summit also sells the works of Kevin MacDonald, which Andrews says show why "anti-Semitism is a naturally expected and powerful phenomenon."[93]

Now consider Richard Lynn and Tatu Vanhanen's[94] *IQ and the Wealth of Nations* (2002). I do so because of this book's close connection with Herrnstein and Murray's *The Bell Curve: Intelligence and Class Structure in American Life* (1994). Lynn and Vanhanen (2002) in *IQ and the Wealth of Nations* attempt to address the question they pose in chapter 1, which is entitled, "Why are Some Countries So Rich and Others So Poor?" In this chapter, the authors discuss eight theories that scholars proffer to explain why nations differ in wealth (e.g., culture; geography; poor nations' dependency on capitalistic countries; climate). Lynn and Vanhanen (2002) focus on another factor that researchers have not conceived previously, the intellectual level of the world's nations.

Two major variables form the basis of Lynn and Vanhanen's (2002) theoretical framework: (a) intelligence and (b) wealth. Intelligence is operationalized as a country's "national IQ," and wealth is operationalized as per capita income, measured by five types of Gross Domestic Product (GDP) and Gross National Product (GNP) ranging from the period of 1820 to 1998. The authors' bivariate model is: national IQ → national wealth, where IQ is the independent variable and wealth is the dependent variable. Lynn and Vanhanen (2002) claim, with conviction, that this connection between national intelligence and national wealth is a "causal relationship" (p. 183).

In regard to the intelligence variable, Lynn and Vanhanen (2002) calculate national IQ data for 185 nations (presented in Table 6.5, pp. 73–80 of their book)—which the authors assume are representative for each country. For the 185 nations, Lynn and Vanhanen (2002) have direct IQ data on less than a majority ($n = 81$, 44%) of the total countries.[95] The IQ data for the 81 nations come from a motley of investigations using a number of different intelligence tests[96] and a wide range of sample sizes (22–43,825 participants), ages of examinees (2–70 years), and years of published studies (1929–2000). In regard to the calculation of national IQs for the 81 nations, Lynn and Vanhanen (2002)—in a number of instances—rely on just one investigation.[97] For example, in the authors' reporting of the national IQ of Indonesia, they calculate a mean IQ of 89, drawing from the study of Thomas and Sjah (1961) who administered the Draw-a-Man Test, a performance test of intelligence (Goodenough, 1926). Another example of reliance on a singular study by Lynn and Vanhanen (2002) to calculate national IQ pertains to Uganda. Based on the investigation by Heyneman and Jamison (1980), who administered the Raven's Coloured Progressive Matrices to 2,019 11-year-olds, Lynn and Vanhanen compute the country's IQ to be 73.

As I note above, Lynn and Vanhanen (2002) report direct national estimates for only 81 of the total 185 countries that form the authors' data set in regard to intelligence, the independent variable in the analysis. Then, how do the authors calculate national IQs for the remaining 104 countries? *They do it through "estimation"!* Lynn and Vanhanen (2002, pp. 71–72) explain their procedure:

It is assumed that where the national IQs are unknown, they will be closely similar to those in neighboring countries. We have consequently taken the most appropriate neighboring countries and used their IQs to assign IQs to those countries with unknown IQs. Where there are two or more appropriate neighboring countries, the IQs of these countries are averaged to obtain an estimated IQ for the country whose IQ is unknown. For example, to estimate an IQ for Afghanistan, we average the IQs of neighboring India (81) and Iran (84), which gives an IQ of 83. Averages with decimal points have been rounded toward 100.[98]

Chapters 7 and 8 form the empirical nucleus of *IQ and the Wealth of Nations*, in which Lynn and Vanhanen (2002) provide the results of their correlational analysis between national intelligence and national wealth. The authors report (pp. 157–158):

The correlation between national IQs and per capita income increases from .625 (the average of the Pearson and Spearman correlations) in 1820, to .629 (the average of six Pearson correlations), and to .675 (the average of six Spearman correlations) in 1997 and 1998. . . . Our conclusion is that differences in national intelligence provide the most powerful and fundamental explanation for the gap between rich and poor countries.

In their concluding chapter, Lynn and Vanhanen (2002) entertain possible types of intervention (e.g., improved nutrition; increased education) that wealthy nations could invest in to help raise the intelligence of poor nations. Although the authors note that such likely remedies should be recognized by wealthy countries, "Intelligence differences between nations will be impossible to eradicate because they have a *genetic basis* [italics added] and have evolved over the course of tens of thousands of years" (p. 195).

In light of the assumption Lynn and Vanhanen (2002) make about the heritability of intelligence, their inappropriate methodology to calculate/estimate national IQs, and the authors' grim conclusions in regard to the future, *IQ and the Wealth of Nations* has captured the interest of a number of scholars. In preparation for discussion of this book, I identified 13 book reviews—10 negative and 3 positive.[99] I focus, in brief, on the major criticisms:

1. *Misinterpretation of correlation.* One of the first points a student enrolled in an introductory statistics course learns is that an observed correlation does *not* imply causation.[100] Belief that a correlation suggests causation is the mistaken belief that temporal succession suggests a causal relation (*post hoc, ergo propter hoc*—Latin for "after this, therefore because of this"). Some scholars criticize Lynn and Vanhanen (2002) for their claim that the correlation between intelligence (independent variable) and wealth (dependent variable) is a causal relation (Berhanu, 2007; Godina, 2005). As I discuss earlier, critics of *The Bell Curve* also raise this concern—that is, Herrnstein and Murray (1994) err in concluding causality from correlations.

2. *Questionable assumptions about the IQ tests and scores.* One of the most frequent criticisms leveled against Lynn and Vanhanen's (2002) analysis concerns their independent variable—intelligence, particularly as to questions about the cross-cultural utility of the various IQ tests.[101] Here, I zero in on two questionable assumptions: (a) representativeness of IQ scores and (b) cross-cultural equivalence of the IQ tests.

As a prefatory comment to their calculation of national IQs, Lynn and Vanhanen (2002) note that "most intelligence tests have been constructed in Britain and the United States" (p. 59). This means that British and U.S. intelligence test developers, in the norming of their instruments, assume that the standardization sample utilized, and the resultant distribution of scores, is representative of a targeted population (e.g., the country as a whole; a particular group, such as hearing impaired children). The norming process often involves sample stratification (i.e., typically age, gender, ethnicity, and SES) and uses a reasonable sample size. Lynn and Vanhanen (2002) erroneously assume that their method of "calculating" the "national IQ" of 81 nations and "estimating" it using "comparison countries" for the other 104 nations is valid. As I note earlier, in the calculation of national IQs for the 81 countries, Lynn and Vanhanen (2002) rely on singular studies in many instances ($n = 43$). For example, they calculate the national IQ of the Philippines, a multiethnic nation, to be 86—based on an investigation by Flores and Evans (1972) who administered the British-normed Raven's Standard Progressive Matrices to 203 children, aged 12–13 years. For Lynn and Vanhanen (2002) to generalize an IQ of 86 to an ethnically diverse nation of 81,159,644 people[102] (2000 census) based on only one measure of intelligence is psychometrically indefensible.

A second dubious assumption Lynn and Vanhanen (2002) make is that the IQ tests they rely on to calculate/estimate national IQs are cross-culturally equivalent (i.e., culture free). The authors fail to address the issue that the administration of British- and U.S.-normed intelligence tests to individuals in other countries (e.g., Ethiopia; Nigeria; Romania) may be culturally loaded or culturally biased (Valencia & Suzuki, 2001, chapter 5). For example, in a number of cases (Guatemala; Indonesia; Lebanon) researchers administered the Draw-a-Man test (Goodenough, 1926) to children. Lynn and Vanhanen's (2002) assumption that the Draw-a-Man test is culture free is patently unfounded. Klineberg (1935, pp. 158–59) comments:

> The Goodenough test of "drawing a man" is based upon the concept of a fully clothed man as seen in our society [U.S.A.]. When Porteus gave this test to the Australians, he found that they would almost invariably draw the man naked and so lose points given for correct drawing of the clothes. This test also assumes that a man is the figure most frequently drawn by children; the writer [Klineberg] found that among the Dakotas (Sioux) the horse was much more popular.

Also, Anastasi (1988) notes: "Such [cross-cultural, cross-ethnic] investigations have indicated performance on this test [Goodenough's Draw-a-Man] is more dependent on differences in cultural background than was originally assumed" (p. 306). It also appears that Goodenough (writing with Harris in 1950) a quarter century after she developed her test was of the opinion that "the search for a culture-free test [such as the Draw-a-Man], whether of intelligence, artistic ability, personal-social characteristics, or any other measurable trait is illusory" (Goodenough & Harris, 1950, p. 399).

3. *Failure to consider competing hypotheses.* As I discuss in chapter 1 of the present book, deficit thinkers fail to consider rival interpretations for observed findings. A major challenge to Lynn and Vanhanen's (2002) assertion that "intelligence has a high heritability" (p. 25) is that schooling attainment is positively correlated with measured intelligence (i.e., schooling attainment → intelligence) (see Ceci, 1991; Richards & Sacker, 2003). As evidence of this

relation, I used a subsample of Lynn and Vanhanen's (2002) data set. I conducted a correlational analysis between educational attainment (data from Barro & Lee, 2000), and national IQs from Lynn and Vanhanen (2002). Barro and Lee (2000) have educational attainment data (years of schooling completed, year 1999) for 104 of the 185 nations for which Lynn and Vanhanen (2002) provide calculated/estimated national IQ data. The results of my bivariate correlational analysis are presented in Figure 2.2. The results show a robust r of 0.80 between schooling and IQ. Assuming the educational attainment is the independent variable and national IQ is the dependent variable, this r of 0.80 suggests a strong rival interpretation for Lynn and Vanhanen's (2002) claim that national intelligence is highly heritable.

Scientific Research Investigations: Indirect and Direct Evidence Against a Genetic Hypothesis of Racial Differences in Intelligence

The cornerstone of the field of biometric genetic analysis of intellectual abilities research is the construct of "heritability" (typically symbolized as h^2).[103] Scholars typically define heritability as: "the proportion of phenotypic differences among individuals in a particular population. Broad-sense heritability involves all additive and nonadditive sources of genetic variance, whereas narrow-sense heritability is limited to additive genetic variance" (Plomin, DeFries, McClearn, & Rutter, 1997, p. 313).[104] My discussion here pertains to

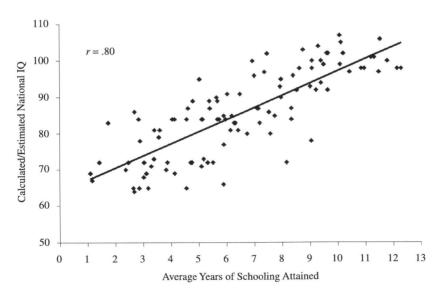

Figure 2.2 Scatterplot of Correlation between Average Years of Schooling Attained and Calculated/Estimated National IQ.

Source: Average years of schooling attained data are from Barro and Lee (2000); calculated/estimated national IQ data are from Lynn and Vanhanen (2002).

broad-sense heritability, which is the percentage of phenotypic differences due to all sources that are genetic.

It is important to comment on two major misconceptions about heritability that appear in the nature–nurture discourse. First, in the most general sense, heritability "refers to the contribution of genetic differences to observed differences among individuals for a particular trait in a particular population at a particular time . . ., not to the phenotype of a single individual" (Plomin et al., 1997, pp. 82–83). For example, the heritability of intelligence (a particular trait) might be .50 for White, middle-SES, American adults 25–50 years old (a particular population) estimated between 1980 and 1985 (a particular time period). As such, heritability estimates are protean, depending on how environmental or genetic factors might differ in diverse populations or at different times. Numerous scholars have underscored the point that heritability is a characteristic of a population, *not* an individual.[105] Unfortunately, this major point that heritability is a population, not an individual, trait is not always understood.

A second misconception involves generalizability. Given that heritability refers to a characteristic of a particular population (a *within*-group notion), *it is not generalizable from one group to another.*[106] Stated more directly, knowing within-population heritability for intelligence only for a White population in the United States, for example, does not allow one to draw conclusions about between-population differences in measured intelligence (e.g., Whites compared to African Americans; Whites compared to Mexican Americans). Put more simply, "The fact is . . . that the high heritability of a trait [i.e., intelligence] within a given group has no necessary implications for the source of a difference between groups" (Neisser et al., 1996, p. 95). This is a principle that is frequently discussed in the behavioral genetics literature, but often ignored or misunderstood by scholars. Violation of this major principle has led to unwarranted conclusions about genetic bases of racial differences in intelligence (e.g., as seen in Herrnstein & Murray, 1994; Jensen, 1969).

Of the present-day procedures used to estimate the heritability of measured intelligence, "the one with the greatest conceptual appeal" (Taylor, 1980, p. 75) uses correlations between the IQs of identical (monozygotic [MZ]) twins who have been separated—it is assumed—at birth and reared in separate and unrelated environmental settings. Notwithstanding the attraction that this research design carries, some scholars heavily criticize studies on separated MZ twins on methodological grounds,[107] as well as strongly defend them (Bouchard, 1997). One critic asserts: "In the final analysis, what we are left with is a mass of faulty methods and data, which do not permit one to conclude in favor of a significant genetic effect on IQ score" (Taylor, 1980, p. 216).

Taylor (1980) proffers one of the most sustained critiques of the research on investigations of MZ twins reared apart (MZA) twins in *The IQ Game*, a book devoted to a methodological inquiry into the heredity–environment debate.

In his chapter, "The Myth of the Separated Identical Twins," Taylor (1980) describes three requirements that MZA twin studies must meet in order to conclude that twins' measured intelligence (i.e., IQ) is very likely related to their genes. These stringent conditions are: (a) The twins were separated at birth; (b) The twins were raised in completely different and unrelated families after separation (but before any intelligence testing was done); (c) All MZA twin pairs were separated over a wide range of different environmental settings after separation. Taylor (1980) points out that a fourth condition actually exists: Prenatal (intrauterine) environmental effects on each twin pair are equal and negligible in magnitude.

To investigate whether these three requirements were met, Taylor (1980) examines three well-known MZA twin studies forming the bedrock of research concluding that intelligence is highly genetic in basis.[108] Based on his reanalysis of data from the three studies, Taylor (1980) finds "four ways in which inadvertent similarity between the presumably separated identical twins came about" (p. 77). These four sources of environmental similarity are (a) late separation, (b) reunion prior to testing, (c) relatedness of adoptive families, and (d) similarity in social environment after separation. Although not all MZA twin pairs experienced these sources of environmental similarity, a large number of twins did. For example, Taylor (1980) reports that although all 68 twin pairs across the three investigations were separated in some way, and for at least some period, about 44 pairs (65%) were united for some period prior to being tested for IQ. According to Taylor (1980), the overall picture that arises from his reanalysis of the three studies leads him to conclude that the inadvertent environmental similarity experienced by many of the MZA twin pairs resulted in artificially inflated IQ correlations, thus producing questionable estimates of heritability. In short, the authors of these three core studies fail to analyze the four sources of environmental similarity. Taylor (1980) concludes, "There is no hard and convincing evidence that the heritability of IQ is anywhere near substantial" (p. 206).[109]

In this section, I turn to a brief coverage of those empirical studies that seek to examine the hypothesis that genetics largely accounts for the persistent gap in measured intelligence between African Americans and Whites. To address the scientific grounds, there are two forms of evidence: indirect and direct (Brody, 1992; Flynn, 1999). Indirect types of evidence derive, for example, from (a) studies of heritability estimates of intelligence; (b) investigations in which researchers attempt to control for environmental variables (e.g., SES); (c) analyses of racial differences in brain size. Direct evidence, by contrast, stems from studies of (a) transracial adoptions and (b) racial admixture.

I first examine the indirect evidence, confining the discussion to heritability of intelligence. As I note earlier, some critics raise methodological and statistical issues concerning how researchers derive heritability estimates of intelligence. Notwithstanding these concerns, a strong consensus exists that intelligence in the White population is a significantly heritable trait, and data exist to support this assertion.[110] It may surprise the reader, however, that very little data are available regarding heritability of intelligence in African American samples, and these data are inconclusive.

In *Race Differences in Intelligence*, one of the most comprehensive reviews of the nature–nurture controversy pertaining to African American/White differences in measured intelligence, Loehlin, Lindzey, and Spuhler (1975) identify just a handful of pertinent studies pertaining to heritability of intelligence in the African American population.[111] Loehlin et al. (1975) address several problems with these studies, including: (a) Sample sizes are used that are too small to allow accurate estimations of heritability; (b) Strikingly different conclusions are drawn (e.g., heritability estimates are lower for Blacks compared to Whites [Nichols, 1970; Vandenberg, 1970]; heritability estimates for Blacks and Whites are comparable in magnitude [Osborne & Miele, 1969]); (c) Researchers use different measures of intelligence at different grade levels (Scarr-Salapatek, 1971).

An extremely important, but often overlooked, issue regarding the nature–nurture debate and racial differences in intelligence is the following: Let us suppose the heritability estimates for the African American and White populations are equal and high in magnitude. If this were the case, could we hypothesize that genetics largely explains the one standard deviation difference in measured intelligence? Brody (1992) assuredly notes: "It is easy to answer this question in one word—no" (p. 299). As Brody and others (e.g., Lewontin, 1975; Mackenzie, 1984) discuss, scholars base this resounding "no" on the logic derived from an understanding of the sources of between- and within-group differences. In explicating this logic, scholars frequently cite the brilliant, classic example (from plant genetics) by Lewontin (1970), who points out that Jensen (1969) fundamentally erred in his hypothesis about between-group heritability in that he confused heritability of a trait *within* a population with heritability of the difference *between* two populations. That is, it is possible to have a situation in which genetic factors explain practically all the variance within two different populations, yet environmental factors could explain an average difference between the two. Given that Lewontin's (1970) famous example (illustrated here in Figure 2.3) is quite long, here is an abbreviated version

Flynn (1999, p. 13) offers:

> He [Lewontin] imagined a sack of seed corn with plenty of genetic variation. The corn is randomly divided into two batches, each of which will therefore be equal for overall genetic quality. Batch A is grown in a uniform and optimal environment, so within that group all height differences at maturity are due to genetic variation; Batch B is grown in a uniform environment that lacks enough nitrates, so within that group all

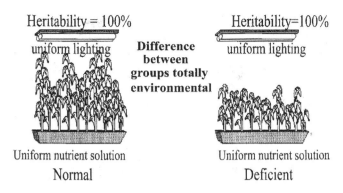

Heritability = 100%

uniform lighting

Difference between groups totally environmental

Heritability=100%

uniform lighting

Uniform nutrient solution

Normal

Uniform nutrient solution

Deficient

Figure 2.3 Heritability can be High within Each of Two Groups even though the Difference between Groups is Entirely Environmental.

Source: From "How Heritability Misleads About Race," by N. Block, 2002, *Race and Intelligence: Separating Science from Myth* (J.M. Fish, ed., p. 289). Copyright 2002 Taylor & Francis. Reprinted, with slight adaptation, by permission of Taylor & Francis via Copyright Clearance Center.

height differences are also genetic. However, the difference in average height between the two groups will, of course, be due entirely to the unequal quality of their two environments.

Now consider a short discussion of investigations of direct evidence tests of the genetic hypothesis of racial differences in intelligence. I focus on transracial adoptions and racial admixture. Based on a review by Brody (1992), two studies have measured the intelligence of African American children raised in predominantly White environmental settings (Moore, 1986; Scarr & Weinberg, 1976).[112] The design of transracial adoption studies lends itself to an interesting challenge. Scarr and Weinberg (1976) note that under the genetic hypothesis, Black adopted children probably will likely fall in IQ performance "below that of other children reared in White upper middle-class homes. On the other hand, if Black children have a range of reaction similar to other adoptees, their IQ scores should have a similar distribution" (p. 727). In their study, Scarr and Weinberg (1976) report that the Black and interracial children (adopted by highly educated, above average in occupation, White parents in Minnesota) had a mean IQ lower than the natural children of the adopted parents, but about 20 points above the mean IQ for Black children raised by their natural parents in the north central region. Scarr and Weinberg (1976) interpret the data to suggest that "the high IQ scores of the socially classified Black adoptees indicate malleability for IQ under rearing conditions that are relevant to the tests and the schools" (p. 726). In addition, Scarr and Weinberg (1976) conclude that the social environment plays a paramount role in shaping the mean IQ of the participating Black children "and that both social and genetic variables contribute to individual variation among them" (p. 739). In a 10-year follow-up of the children, Weinberg, Scarr, and Waldman (1992) find no significant differences in IQ scores (from Time 1 to Time 2) between the transracial adoptees and the natural children of the adopting parents.

Moore (1986) undertook a study of traditionally adopted Black children (i.e., Black child adopted by middle-class Black parents) and transracially adopted Black children (i.e., Black children adopted by middle-class White parents). In all, the mean Wechsler Intelligence Scale for Children (WISC) IQ of both groups (tested between 7 and 10 years of age) was significantly higher that the mean IQ typically observed (in general) in Black children, thus providing support for the environmental interpretation proffered by Scarr and Weinberg (1976). Moore did find, however, that the mean IQ of the transracially adopted group ($M = 117.1$) was significantly higher than the mean IQ of the traditionally adopted group ($M = 103.6$). Based on an analysis of styles of responding to test demands demonstrated by the two groups, Moore concludes that the transracial group scored higher on the WISC because of being raised "in environments that are [more] culturally relevant to the tests" (p. 321).

Another research design to examine the genetic versus environmental hypothesis of racial differences in measured intelligence involves racial admixture, which researchers can assess in three ways: genealogical records, biochemical assays and protein markers, and visible indicators of race such as skin color (Mackenzie, 1984). Given that the African American population is racially heterogeneous (estimated 20% to 30% European [White] ancestry; Reed, 1969), racial admixture studies can serve as potentially powerful tools for examining environmental and genetic conjectures about sources of racial differences in measured intelligence (Mackenzie, 1984; Scarr, Pakstis, Katz, and Barker, 1977).

A genetic hypothesis suggests that the amount of White ancestry in African Americans positively correlates with measured intelligence. Loehlin et al. (1975) provide an earlier review of the racial admixture literature. Based on their analysis of available publications, Loehlin et al. note that higher IQ correlated with lighter skin color among Blacks. The authors did qualify matters, however, stating that "these correlations have tended to be quite low, and thus compatible with either the genetic or environmental explanations" (p. 132). Loehlin et al. conclude, "Recent studies of U.S. interracial matings and ability–blood group correlations suffer from methodological limitations and small samples, but on the whole fail to offer positive support to hereditarian positions concerning between-group differences" (p. 132). The investigation by Scarr et al. (1977) stands as one of the most comprehensive and ambitious racial admixture studies undertaken. More than 400 Black and White children (ages 7–10 years) attending schools in Philadelphia served as participants. Based on analyses of skin color reflectance, blood group markers, and ancestral phenotype frequencies, Scarr et al. (1977) conclude that the relation between degree of African ancestry "and intellectual skills failed to provide evidence for genetic differences in intelligence" (p. 84). Other scholars who have reviewed the racial admixture literature have rendered similar or unequivocal conclusions (see, e.g., Brody, 1992; Mackenzie, 1984; Nisbett, 1998).

Conclusion

What can be concluded about the genetic pathology model of deficit thinking? Based on the indirect and direct evidence just discussed, *we cannot confirm the hypothesis of genetic differences between African American and White populations in phenotypic differences in intelligence.* So, as the new decade begins, what will likely transpire in regard to research on the hypothesis that genetics significantly accounts for racial differences in intelligence? Can we expect a neohereditarianism, wave IV on the horizon? Why has so much research on racial differences in intelligence led to little scientific value? Tucker (1994) notes that although having the imprimatur of science, such research invariably has been linked (in actual and suggested ways) to oppressive deeds. And, indeed, the U.S. has enacted many such repressive policies, starting with slavery and unfolding through the decades as witnessed by forced sterilization, anti-miscegenation laws, forced school segregation, immigration restrictions, curtailment of social welfare programs, opposition to school integration, calls for birth control to curb alleged dysgenic effects, and pressures to abandon compensatory education programs. In sum, we need to be vigilant about scientific racists who espouse a genetic pathology model regarding racial differences in intelligence and be prepared to offer vigorous and informed anti-deficit thinking responses.

3

Ruby Payne's Mindsets of Poverty, Middle Class, and Wealth

A Resurrection of the Culture of Poverty Concept

Earlier, we noted a number of deficit thinking characteristics. Deficit thinking, we saw, is a fluid notion, in which the zeitgeist of the times influences its form.

Consider the career of Dr. Ruby K. Payne, who proclaims herself as "The leading U.S. expert on the *mindsets* [italics added] of poverty, middle class, and wealth" (front cover, Payne, 2005). Payne, who received her Ph.D. in Educational Leadership and Policy Studies from Loyola University (Chicago, Illinois), earlier worked as a high school teacher, principal, and central office administrator.[1] Since 1996, she has provided training to hundreds of thousands of educators and other professionals—in 38 states, as well as areas in Canada, Ireland, England, and Australia—as to how poverty impacts "learning, work habits, [and] decision-making." As of 2006, Payne employed 25 trainers and 50 consultants who work nationwide.

In her workshops (which number over 200 per year, and in which she charges $295 per person), Payne "teaches rules and mindsets of economic classes" so as "to positively impact the education and lives of individuals of poverty throughout the world." The founder and CEO of aha! Process, Inc., a multimillion dollar corporation, she has self-published several dozen books and videos. Her 1996 seminal work—*A Framework for Understanding Poverty* (revised four times)—has sold over 1,000,000 copies, and is available in Spanish (*Un Marco para Entender la Pobreza*). Her book is a particular focus in the current chapter because of the numerous instances in which Payne voices deficit thinking. For example, in the "hidden rules among [social] classes" she notes that for people living in poverty, education is "valued and revered as abstract *but not as reality*" (Payne, 2005, p. 42).

Historical Attitudes Toward the Poor

Throughout human history, unequal social and economic orders have persisted. Attitudes of the "haves" toward the "have-nots" can be characterized as suspicious and dehumanizing in which the economically advantaged blame "those at the bottom for their own lowly position" (Goode, 2002, p. 279).[2] The U.S. has been, and continues to be, part of the "them"–"us" discourse. For example, John E. Tropman (1998) in his book, *Does America Hate the Poor?*, comments: "Suspicion of the status poor, the 'underclass,' the 'needy,' the 'homeless,' emerges in virtually every discussion of them. This suspicion, concern, or hate often seems heavily involved with negative moral judgment. Americans often morally disparage the poor" (p. 3).

For the greatest part of the 19th century in the U.S., the citizenry viewed poverty as a "natural" condition and inevitable for a large number of people. The poor, conceptualized as a shapeless, undistinguished group, "were considered necessary to the [social] system and to the elite donor of alms" (Eames & Goode, 1973, p. 254). The *haut monde* received spiritual blessings by giving some of their wealth to the virtuous poor. With the advent of technological and economic developments and a new social order, however, attitudes toward the poor shifted to negativity. The elite no longer rationalized the condition of poverty, but rather viewed the poor as the most detested social stratum and as a problem that needed to be fixed (Eames & Goode, 1973).

In discussions about poverty (academic and popular publications), many writers focus on two aspects—causes and solutions. In regard to the former, two contrasting arguments exist.[3] One is that the poor create their own problems due to insular and deviant cultures, individual shortcomings, and familial dysfunction. The other explanation is based on victimization, in which the poor are economically exploited, class discriminated, and socially ostracized by forces beyond their control (i.e., the larger economic, social, and political systems). In the next section, I focus on the culture of poverty notion, a deficit thinking idea asserting that the poor are the makers of their own material disadvantagement and deprivation.

The Culture of Poverty

Oscar Lewis's Notion of the Culture of Poverty

Oscar Lewis (1914–1970), cultural anthropologist, earned his Ph.D. in anthropology in 1940 from Columbia University, and went on to serve as a faculty member at Brooklyn College, Washington University (St. Louis, Missouri), and the University of Illinois at Urbana-Champaign.[4] He devoted much of his scholarly career to undertaking ethnographic research on families of the urban poor in Mexico, Cuba, and Puerto Rico (San Juan as well as Puerto Ricans living in New York). Among his most notable books are: *Five Families: Mexican Case Studies in the Culture of Poverty* (1959), *The Children of Sánchez: Autobiography of a Mexican Family* (1961), *La Vida: A Puerto Rican Family in the Culture of Poverty—San Juan and New York* (1966a), and *A Study of Slum Culture: Backgrounds for La Vida* (1968).

Lewis coined the term "culture of poverty" in *Five Families* in 1959, which, he notes in Lewis (1961), refers to "those people who are at the very bottom of the socio-economic scale, the poorest workers, the poorest peasants, plantation laborers, and that large heterogeneous mass of small artisans and tradesmen usually referred to as the lumpen proletariat" (p. xxv).[5] Although Lewis discusses his culture of poverty notion in his other books, the term became popularized via his *Scientific American* article (1966b), "The Culture of Poverty." Lewis (1966b) asserts that based on his research, 70 "traits" typify the culture of poverty, and the main ones may be framed in four dimensions of the poverty system: (a) the connection between the culture of poverty and the larger society; (b) the makeup of the slum community; (c) the makeup of the family; (d) the values, attitudes, and character configuration of the individual. A number of culture of poverty traits are quite descriptive and factual of people living in poverty—for example: "lower life expectancy," "lower wages," and "low level of education and literacy." Other traits (i.e., those dealing with values, character structure, and social/psychological characteristics), however, elicit a strong negative impression of poor people—for example: "wife beating," "personal unworthiness," "frequent use of violence in training children," "high tolerance for psychological pathology of all sorts" (Leeds, 1971, pp. 239–241). Although Lewis derives the culture of poverty concept from his research in Mexico (the primary site), Cuba, and Puerto Rico (San Juan and New York City), he asserts that the notion has universal implications. Lewis (1961) claims: "It seems to be that the culture of poverty has some universal characteristics which transcend regional, rural-urban, and even national differences" (p. xxv).

To sum, the insular, autonomous, fatalistic, and dysfunctional nature of Lewis's culture of poverty notion evokes a powerful deficit thinking image of the poor—a depiction of poor people with self-imposed, intractable, transgenerational problems. Note the following:

> The culture of poverty, however, is not only an adaptation to a set of objective conditions of the larger society. *Once it comes into existence it tends to perpetuate itself from generation to generation because of its effect on the children* [italics added]. By the time slum children are age six or seven they have usually absorbed the basic values and attitudes of their subculture and are not psychologically geared to take full advantage of changing conditions or increased opportunities which may occur in their lifetime.
>
> (Lewis, 1966a, p. xiv)

Appropriation of the Culture of Poverty Concept

Lewis formulates his culture of poverty model "in such a categorical, objectivist manner that it was easy [for others] to appropriate [it] as a literal, absolute truth claim" (Foley, 1997, p. 116). As the culture of poverty idea penetrated the vocabulary of 1960s scholars, Lewis's notion became redefined as cultural deprivation and cultural disadvantagement (Katz, 1989). The 1960s gushed with scholarly literature on the "culturally deprived" or "culturally disadvantaged" family, home, and child.[6] The targeted populations of 1960s deficit thinking are all too familiar: "The disadvantaged refer to Whites, Negroes, Puerto Ricans, Mexicans, and all others of the poverty group who basically share *a common design for living*" [italics added] (Marans & Lourie, 1967, p. 20). As well, scholars frequently identify the carrier of the deficit as inadequate parents who "seem to perpetuate their own conditions in their children through their child-rearing patterns . . . [and who] produce a disproportionate incidence of academic failures and of lower socioeconomic memberships among their full-grown offspring" (Marans & Lourie, p. 21).[7] With an eye closer to the home problem, it was not uncommon for deficit thinkers four decades past to comment: "Very frequently the unique environment of a given *subculture* [italics added] may not provide the prerequisite learnings or general acculturation essential to school success or to optimal life development" (Edwards, 1967, p. 64).

In addition to those scholars of the 1960s who focus on cultural and accumulated environmental deficit models (which are largely psychological in nature), a number of other scholars of the times—directly or indirectly influenced by Lewis's culture of poverty concept—write from a sociological perspective in which they center on the putative dysfunctional "way of life" of the poor. In brief form, I cover a sampling of these scholars' works, ranging from 1962 to 1982.

MICHAEL HARRINGTON

Harrington's 1962 book, *The Other America: Poverty in the United State*s, is one of the most important works of the poverty discourse. In his book, he exposes the appalling degree of poverty in the U.S., claiming that between 40,000,000 to 50,000,000 people reside in poverty, frequently going hungry and having inadequate education, medical care, and housing. *The Other America*, some scholars and journalists assert, helped to spur President John F. Kennedy (and soon after President Lyndon B. Johnson) to mount the War on Poverty in 1964.[8]

Notwithstanding the importance of Harrington's (1962) book in bringing overdue attention to the plight of the poor, he conceived his characterization of them as such: "Poverty in the United States is a culture, an institution, a way of life" (p. 17). Even Oscar Lewis notes that Harrington "used [the culture of poverty phrase] extensively in *The Other America*. . . . However, he used it in a somewhat broader and less technical sense than I had intended" (Lewis, 1966a, p. xlii).

DANIEL P. MOYNIHAN

Moynihan received his Ph.D. in sociology from Tufts University (Medford, Massachusetts) and served as Assistant Secretary of Labor for Policy Planning and Research (1963–1965) under the Kennedy and Johnson administrations. Moynihan is well known for his highly controversial 1965 government report, *The Negro Family: A Case for National Action*, popularly referred to as the "Moynihan Report."[9] Katz (1989) states: "Nowhere did he [Moynihan] mention Oscar Lewis. . . . Nonetheless informed readers could not miss the striking parallels between Lewis's culture of poverty and Moynihan's culture of poverty" (p. 24). In his chapter titled "The Tangle of Poverty" (which he borrows from Clark, 1965), Moynihan (1965, p. 30) refers to the Negro "subculture" and focuses on the matriarchal, dysfunctional family:

> Obviously not every instance of social pathology afflicting the Negro community can be traced to the weakness of family structure. . . . Nonetheless, at the *center of the tangle of pathology is the weakness of the family structure*. Once or twice removed, it will be found to be *the principal source* of most of the aberrant, inadequate, or antisocial behavior that did not establish but now serves to *perpetuate the cycle of poverty* and deprivation.

In light of its deficit thinking orientation, the Moynihan Report infuriated a number of Black leaders and many of their White advocates (Katz, 1989).

THOMAS GLADWIN

Gladwin, an anthropologist, authored *Poverty U.S.A.* (1967), which for the most part is an evaluation of President Johnson's War on Poverty program, which Gladwin finds quite positive. His book conveys a sense of ambivalence about the poor. Valentine (1968) comments that a large portion of *Poverty U.S.A. "is an intellectual wrestling match with the idea of poverty culture and its policy implications, particularly in the recent 'war on poverty' "* (p. 91). On one hand, Gladwin notes that the poor face negative stereotypes and discrimination, and that money and power need to be reallocated to those living in poverty. Yet, on the other hand, Gladwin appears to embrace the culture of poverty notion. He writes (pp. 26–27):

> The whole conception of the War on Poverty rests upon a definition of poverty as *a way of life*. The intellectual climate in which it was nurtured was created by studies of the culture of poverty, notably those of Oscar Lewis in Mexico City. . . . This lifestyle is acquired by children and stays with them throughout their lives . . . [These studies] provided the basis for programs at the national level designed very explicitly to correct the social, occupational, and psychological deficits of people born and raised to a life of poverty.

In regard to reforming the lives of the poor, Gladwin (p. 112) notes that the onus is on them:

> Among the strategic implications of the idea of a culture of poverty one stands out most clearly: if poverty is both the cause and result of a way of life in which self-defeating behaviors are learned by each

rising generation, then any attack on poverty should try to modify these behaviors. Put more positively this cultural conception of poverty means that if its cycle is to be broken poor people must among other things be taught new and more effective ways of functioning.

Banfield earned his Ph.D. in political science from the University of Chicago. Of his many books, *The Unheavenly City: The Nature and Future of Our Urban Crisis* (1970) is the most well known. In *The Unheavenly City*, Banfield mentions Oscar Lewis's culture of poverty notion in only two instances (pp. 125–126, 288–289). Banfield agrees that such a culture exists, but he asserts that "poverty is in its effect rather than its cause" (p. 125). He explains (pp. 125–126):

> Extreme present-orientedness, not a lack of income or wealth, is the cause of poverty in the sense of "the culture of poverty." Most of those caught up in this culture are unable or unwilling to plan for the future, to sacrifice immediate gratifications in favor of future ones, or to accept the disciplines that are required in order to get and to spend. Their inabilities are probably culturally given in most cases—"multiproblem" families being normal representatives of a class culture that is itself abnormal.

In light of the above quote, it appears that Banfield (1970) is intellectually closer to Lewis's culture of poverty idea than he thinks. My point is further confirmed by Banfield's "class culture" framework in which he attributes distinct characteristics to the "upper," "middle," "working," and "lower" classes (pp. 46–66). The lower class, which Banfield characterizes as possessing a litany of negative features (e.g., impulsivity; improvidence; not interested in work; violence; hypersexuality; self-contempt) that he asserts are class bound and transgenerational. In sum, to Banfield, poverty is "individualistic, a state of soul rather than a condition of society" (Harrington, 1984, p. 181).

Auletta, a journalist, is the author of the 1982 book, *The Underclass*.[10] Although his book's release date is a decade plus after the last book I discuss here (Banfield's [1970] *Unheavenly City*), *The Underclass* is important to include in this analysis because it fits tightly into the culture of poverty discourse initiated by Oscar Lewis. Although the culture of poverty and underclass expressions share very similar theoretical cores, the latter term overtook the former term in "public language" usage. Morris (1989) undertook a frequency review of poverty-related listings in the *Social Sciences Citation Index* from 1966–1987, and he reports that between 1966–1980 scholars used "culture" or "cultural" subheadings of "poverty" 46 times, and 6 times between 1981–1987.

By contrast, scholars made use of the "underclass" term 11 times between 1966–1980, and 41 times between 1981–1987.

It appears that Gunnar Myrdal, Swedish economist, is one of the first scholars to use the term, "underclass." In his 1970 book, *The Challenge of World Poverty: A World Anti-Poverty in Outline*, he writes of the increase of urban and rural poor people in the Third World, an "underclass" isolated from society whose members lack "the education and the skills and other personality traits they need in order to become effectively in demand in the modern economy" (p. 406). Myrdal notes that a close likeness exists between the rapidly growing underclass in developing nations and the U.S. underclass. In both, he asserts there is a trend to reduce the demand for the employment of the underclass, "making them, in fact, more and more superfluous" (p. 406). Notwithstanding that Myrdal's use of the underclass notion principally focuses on economic troubles of the Third World, the underclass concept garnered considerable attention describing U.S. urban poverty patterns (Sernau, 1997). The underclass notion made its first mass media debut in the U.S. in a *Time* magazine cover story on August 29, 1977.[11] Author of the article, George Russell, writes: "Behind its crumbling walls . . . of the pock-marked streets and gutted tenements . . . lives a large group of people who are more intractable, more socially alien and more hostile than almost any had imagined. They are the unreachables: the American underclass" (1977, p. 14). Russell focuses, in part, on the supposed deviant values and behavioral pathology of the underclass. He comments: "Their bleak environment nurtures values that are often at odds with those of the majority—even the majority of the poor" (p. 14).

In Auletta's (1982) *The Underclass*, he states that the underclass—the poorest of the poor—comprise about 9 million of the total 25 to 29 million people officially classified as poor. Auletta claims that broadly speaking, the underclass can be categorized into four discrete groups: (a) the *passive poor* (i.e., typically long-standing welfare recipients); (b) the *hostile* (i.e., terroristic street criminals, often drug addicts); (c) the *hustlers* (i.e., those who gain their money in the underground economy, but seldom carry out violent crimes); (d) the *traumatized* (i.e., drifters, homeless, drunks, and individuals released from mental institutions). As these descriptions in the four categories denote, Auletta focuses on deviant, pathological behavior of those individuals in the underclass, rather than examining systemic or structural factors in the larger society that lead to such grave economic and living conditions for the very poor.[12]

Critique of the Culture of Poverty Concept

Given the deficit thinking orientation of the culture of poverty concept, a number of scholars provide critiques of the notion.[13] Based on my sense of this discourse, the criticism falls into four areas.

CONCEPTUAL PROBLEMS

Several scholars raise a core concern: What is meant by the concept of the "culture of poverty" (Katz, 1989; Leeds, 1971; Valentine, 1968)? Leeds notes that a major contradiction exists in Oscar Lewis's conception of the culture of poverty. On one hand, Lewis (1966b) asserts that the culture of poverty is transgenerational, transmitted via a social system—specifically along family lines. Furthermore, this transmitting channel is not intrinsic to cultural traits. On the other hand, Lewis describes the culture of poverty in terms of traits (e.g., 1959, 1961). Leeds comments that the two conceptions are antithetical because in the transmission model the culture of poverty is conceptualized as a distinct system, and in the trait model the culture of poverty is treated as having removable and independent components, which as traits, should be able to be transmitted to any person, of any age, and at whichever time. Leeds concludes: Lewis's "model of 'traits' of a 'culture of poverty' is confused because he asserts their autonomy from some system and their independ-ence of each other, both of which are contradicted by Lewis' treatment of transmission and by the data themselves" (p. 231).

Katz (1989) remarks that the literature on the culture of poverty does not incorporate a fixed set of characteristics. Moreover, the long inventory of traits typically presented contain an *ad hoc* quality. The traits do not separate aspects of material deprivation from personality and behavior. In sum, Katz states that the traits "do not, by and large, identify the core characteristics that give shape and coherence to the whole" (p. 41) (also, see Leeds, 1971).

QUESTIONABLE GENERALIZABILITY AND REPRESENTATIVENESS

An inherent problem of case studies, the methodological approach Oscar Lewis used, is very limited generalizability, or as described in research methods—restricted external validity, a term referring to the degree that results can be generalized to other populations, situations, and conditions (Wiersma & Jurs, 2005). As I mention earlier, although Lewis undertook most of his ethnographic research in Mexico, he maintains that the culture of poverty contains some universal attributes (Lewis, 1961). In light of Lewis's insufficient evidential base, his universality claim in regard to the culture of poverty is tenuous.

A closely related issue to questionable generalizability is: How representative are Lewis's informants? A case in point is the Rios family, interviewed and stud-ied in some detail in *La Vida* (1966a). Lewis states: "The Rios family, their friends and neighbors, reflect many of the characteristics of the subculture of poverty, *characteristics which are widespread in Puerto Rico* [italics added] but which are by no means exclusively Puerto Rican" (p. xxv). Valentine (1968) notes that Lewis (1966a) fails to present concrete evidence of behaviors and beliefs attributed to the Rios family, and he does not link such characteristics to the "way of life" of the poor in Puerto Rico. Valentine continues by stating that

Rios family members are not representative of Puerto Ricans residing in the culture of poverty, but Lewis selected them for study "because they manifested deviant extremes" (p. 53).

FAILURE TO CONSIDER ALTERNATIVE HYPOTHESES

As I discuss and iterate in previous chapters, deficit thinkers frequently fail to consider rival interpretations for the alleged deviant behaviors they identify. The culture of poverty discourse is not immune to this major shortcoming. For example, in the culture of poverty literature a major assumption is the primacy of socialization. That is, familial socialization is the putative mechanism that perpetuates the culture of poverty. Katz (1989) asserts that a "situational explanation is equally plausible" (p. 41), meaning that each succeeding generation may reproduce corresponding subcultural arrangements as it adapts to comparable constraints. More specifically, Lewis (1966a) claims that culture of poverty families are disorganized and unstable. An alternative hypothesis, however, may be that although poor families may be unconventional in their structure and behaviors, such family units are organized in ways that are adaptive to exogenously imposed factors. In poor families, the socialization of young children tends to be collectively done by a wider network of kin and peers beyond the nuclear family, and such an arrangement may foster a healthy maturity and the adaptation of numerous affective relationships and likely serve as origins of emotional security.[14]

FAILURE TO CONSIDER THE RESILIENCY AND STRENGTHS OF THE POOR

Scholars who embrace the veracity of the culture of poverty notion often engage in negative stereotyping, asserting that the poorest of the poor are, for example, fatalistic, violent, intentionally insular, have pathological personalities, and are members of dysfunctional families. By contrast, some scholars reject such stereotyping, and counter these myths by providing evidence from urban ethnographies that speak to a vastly different portrait of the poor—one that characterizes many poor people (Black, Latino, and White) as resilient, tenacious, and active in their struggle for empowerment.[15]

Ethnographic research shows that the poor show highly structured work activities among all family members (Edin & Lein, 1997; Valentine, 1968; cited in Goode, 2002), engage in production such as makeshift housing and cooked food (Uzzell, 1975; cited in Goode, 2002), participate in activism for welfare rights and civil rights (Piven & Cloward, 1971, 1979; cited in Goode, 2002), and practice positive familial role-modeling and collective child rearing (Stack, 1974; Willie, 1976; cited in Foley, 1997).

Ruby Payne's Conceptual Structure for Understanding Poverty

In this section, I turn to the core of this chapter—the deficit thinking of Ruby Payne (2005) as expressed in her views of families living in "generational poverty," which she defines as "being in poverty for two generations or longer" (p. 3). She contrasts "generational poverty" with "situational poverty," which she notes as being in poverty "a shorter time and is caused by circumstance (i.e., death, illness, divorce, etc.)" (p. 3). Payne presents her conceptual structure for comprehending poverty in her self-published, best-selling 2005 book, *A Framework for Understanding Poverty* (hereafter referred to as *Framework*).[16] In 2005, the poverty guideline amounted to $19,350 for a family of four in the U.S. (48 contiguous states and Washington, D.C.).[17]

Framework includes nine chapters, covering topics such as class-bound language and hidden rules, features of generational poverty, discipline, and relationships.[18] For her sources in writing *Framework*, Payne relies on two bases. First, as she states on her aha! Process website, *Framework*

> borrows heavily from a 30-year, qualitative, ongoing case study, which uses several methodologies. The research methodology that was and is used relies heavily on an anthropological approach. In addition, the narratives/stories of a neighborhood are used extensively. The neighborhood that was and is observed is mostly White; some of the individuals are part Native American, and there are a few Hispanics. The number of people observed is between 50 and 70. Because of the greater likelihood of early death in poverty and the amount of mobility, the number fluctuates. The author is most interested in noting that the study has "ecological validity."[19]

As the reader can see, the description of the above "anthropological approach" is quite vague regarding, for example, details on location, respondents, instrumentation, and ethnographer(s).

Second, Payne (2005) draws from a number of scholarly works. These include, for example, *Consequences of Growing Up Poor* (Duncan & Brooks-Gunn, 1997); *Class: A Guide Through the American Status System* (Fussell, 1983); *The Other America: Poverty in the United States* (Harrington, 1962); *The Five Clocks: A Linguistic Excursion Into the Five Styles of English Usage* (Joos, 1967); *What Money Can't Buy: Family Income and Children's Life Chances* (Mayer, 1997); *Four Horsemen: Pollution, Poverty, Family, Violence* (Penchef, 1971); *Always Running: La Vida Loca: Gang Days in L.A.* (Rodríguez, 1993); *The Hidden Injuries of Class* (Sennett & Cobb, 1972). Payne further notes that among a number of other authors, she "pulls heavily from the research" of Oscar Lewis, particularly his concept of the culture of poverty. For example, in her "Research Notes" section of *Framework*, Payne (2005, p. 147) provides a lengthy quote from Lewis (1971) that describes a litany of culture of poverty traits (e.g., wife beating; machismo; violent behavior; alcoholism; precocious sex; present time orientation; fatalism). As well, Payne (2005, p. 140) quotes Lewis in regard to his assertion that the culture of poverty contains some universal characteristics. Although Payne cites some references in the text of

Framework, the bulk of her citations are listed in a section toward the end of the book, titled "Research Notes." She mentions that these notes "have been selected to correlate with the content of this book" (p. 119). Notwithstanding a few exceptions, Payne (2005) uses quotes from her references provided in the Research Notes, with no direct correspondence to the actual assertions and points she proffers in the text of each chapter. For the careful reader, this format makes for guesswork as to how Payne substantiates her claims. I daresay that such a referencing style would not pass muster in peer-reviewed publications.

In this section, I confine my discussion of *Framework* to three aspects of Payne's conceptual structure for understanding poverty.

Class-Bound Hidden Rules

In her chapter, "Definitions and Resources," Payne (2005) provides a working definition of poverty: "the extent to which an individual does without resources" (p. 8). She asserts, based on a motley of quotations from a number of sources provided in her Research Notes (pp. 129–135), that there are eight types of resources: (a) "financial;" (b) "emotional;" (c) "mental;" (d) "spiritual;" (e) "physical;" (f) "support systems;" (g) "relationships/role models;" (h) "knowledge of hidden rules." Payne (2005) contextualizes her discussion of these resources by using seven scenarios with an accompanying "background" and "current situation." These seven scenarios, which focus on poor families (White = 3; Black = 2; Latino = 2), are filled with people possessing dysfunctional attributes and behaviors (e.g., alcoholism; sexual precociousness; illegitimate children; drug addiction; drug dealers; gang members).

Here, I center on Payne's (2005) "hidden rules," one of the major premises in *Framework*. Payne states that hidden rules, which she asserts are class bound, originate as follows and serve as survival mechanisms:

> Economic realities create "hidden rules," unspoken cueing mechanisms that reflect agreed-upon *tacit* understandings, which the group uses to negotiate reality. These "hidden rules" come out of cause-and-effect situations. Hidden rules reflect the behaviors and *mindsets* [italics added] that are needed to survive in that economic reality.[20]

Note that Payne (2005) claims that hidden rules manifest the behaviors and mindsets utilized to survive in discernible economic spheres (i.e., among the poor, middle class, and wealthy). The notion of a mindset—"a habitual or characteristic mental attitude that determines how you will interpret and respond to situations"[21]—is of particular interest here. Take notice that Payne's usage of "mindset" is very closely related to the concept of an *attitude*, which is typically defined as "an individual's tendency or predisposition to evaluate an object or the symbol of that object in a certain way" (Katz & Stotland, 1959, p. 428) (also, see Albarraci, Johnson, & Zanna, 2005; Crano & Prislin, 2008). Scientifically speaking, the notions of mindset and attitude lay in the scholarly domain of psychology (the study of *individual differences and behavior*), and not, as Payne more than suggests, in the purview of sociology (the study of *group differences and behavior*). For Payne to assert—in the absence of empirical, valid data—that members of a given "economic reality" (i.e., class) have ways of life governed by collective mindsets, or attitudes, is a scientifically indefensible, futile exercise in grand theorizing. As a number of scholars discuss, a communal mindset among the poor simply does not exist (e.g., Abell & Lyon, 1979; Gans, 1995; Katz, 1989; Leeds, 1971; Ng & Rury, 2006). Among the poor a wide range of attitudes, beliefs, and abilities exist as to how to cope.

In her chapter, "Hidden Rules Among Classes," Payne (2005) introduces matters by presenting three "quizzes" for the reader, titled "Could You Survive in Poverty?," "Could You Survive in Middle Class?," and "Could You Survive in Wealth?" Examples of an item from each "quiz" are as follows:

> "I know which grocery stores' garbage bins can be accessed for thrown-away food." (poverty)

> "I know which stores are most likely to carry the clothing brands my family wears." (middle class)

> "I have several favorite restaurants in different countries of the world." (wealth)

Payne comments that the point of this exercise

> is that if you fall mostly in the middle class, the assumption is that everyone knows these things. However, if you did not know many of the items for the other classes, the exercise points out how many of the hidden rules are taken for granted by a particular class, which assumes they are a given for everyone.
>
> (2005, p. 41)

Payne (2005) then proceeds to ask: "What, then, are the hidden rules?" (p. 41). She responds by providing a 3×5 matrix, consisting of 15 categories (e.g., "possessions;" "food;" "education;" "destiny") in which these hidden rules, she claims, describe the behavior of three classes (i.e., poverty; middle class; wealth). It is here that Payne, in her centerpiece of *Framework*, engages in stereotyping of epic proportions.[22] An example is the category of "education." Payne asserts that the hidden rule among people of poverty is: Education is "valued and revered as abstract but not as *reality*." By contrast, the hidden rules for middle-class and wealthy people are that education is "crucial for climbing [the] success ladder and making money" and is "[a] necessary tradition for making and maintaining connections," respectively (pp. 42–43). The assertion that low-SES people, particularly of color, do not value, or devalue, education is a long-standing myth. A case in point involves Mexican Americans (Valencia & Black, 2002).[23] The myth persists that these parents are indifferent toward and devalue education. Valencia and Black, for example, in their article " 'Mexican Americans Don't Value Education!'—On the Basis of the Myth, Mythmaking, and Debunking," note that the fallacy has appeared in sources as variable as (a) early master's theses (e.g., Gould, 1932; Lyon, 1933; Taylor, 1927); (b) published scholarly literature (e.g., Frost & Hawkes, 1966; Hellmuth, 1967; Marans & Lourie, 1967; Sowell, 1981); (c) newspaper articles and columns (e.g., Martin, 1997; Roser & Tanamachi, 1997; Snider, 1990). Valencia and Black debunk the myth by showing that Mexican Americans do indeed value education as a *reality, not an abstraction.* The authors' evidentiary bases are (a) the Mexican American people's enduring struggle for equal educational opportunity (e.g., via litigation; see Valencia [2008]); (b) the scholarly literature documenting Mexican American parental participation in education (e.g., see Moreno & Valencia, 2002); (c) a case study of transgenerational Mexican American parental involvement in education (Black, 1996).

Language

In *Framework*, Payne (2005) devotes a chapter to "The Role of Language and Story," in which she also stereotypes and makes claims *sans* scientific support. Drawing from the book by Martin Joos (1967)—*The Five Clocks: A Linguistic Excursion into the Five Styles of English Usage*—Payne states that "*Every language in the world* [italics added] has five registers" (p. 27)—that is: (a) "frozen;" (b) "formal;" (c) "consultative;" (d) "casual;" (e) "intimate." These universal registers, noted by Joos, are pure speculation. Although Joos is a noted linguist, in *The Five Clocks* he provides no empirical evidence for the existence of five language registers. In his book, he only provides *one* scholarly source (Fries, 1952), and this involves a transcript of a telephone conversation (in the "consultative" register). My point that Joos has no empirical base to support his contention that there are five registers is corroborated by the analysis of Bomer, Dworin, May, and Semingson (2008). This whole discussion of language is an example of how Payne (2005) in *Framework* often draws from dubious sources, or misrepresents them.

In regard to Payne's claim that usage of the five registers is class bound, she remarks:

> How then does this register impact students from poverty? First of all, the work of Dr. Maria Montaño-Harmon (1991) found that the majority (of the students in her research) of minority students and poor students do not have access to formal register at home. As a matter of fact, these students cannot use formal register.
>
> (2005, p. 28)

Payne continues (p. 28):

> This use of formal register is further complicated by the fact that these

students [living in poverty] do not have the vocabulary or the knowledge of sentence structure and syntax to use formal register. When student conversations in the casual register are observed, much of the meaning comes not from word choices, but from the non-verbal assists. To be asked to communicate in writing without the non-verbal assists is an overwhelming and formidable task, which most of them try to avoid. It has very little meaning for them.

The above statement by Payne that minority and poor students lack access to formal register (which is the register frequently used in classrooms), or are unable to use formal register, has no basis in fact. My close reading of Montaño-Harmon's article indicates that Payne has no basis in her assertion. Montaño-Harmon draws no such conclusion about register usage among poor and minority students. Her research investigates differences between the discourse features in texts written in Spanish by Mexican *secundaria* [secondary] students in Mexico and those written in English by White high school students in the U.S. Her original research design also included "Mexican American/ Chicano students" and "Spanish-dominant ESL students" writing in English, but Montaño-Harmon excluded these two groups from the analysis. Montaño-Harmon found significant differences in the discourse features of the texts written by Chicano students, which she attributed to "a clash between a non-standard dialect of English, Chicano English . . ., and the standard-academic English required for the formal transference of information in expository written form to a general audience" (p. 419). She makes no such claims about Chicano students' access to, or their ability to use the formal register. Once again, my point that Payne fails to base her claims on scientific evidence is supported by independent analysis. Bomer et al. (2008) also find that the Montaño-Harmon study has nothing to do with Payne's assertion that poor students lack a formal register.

Another example of a stereotype and nonscientific-based assertions in regard to language among the poor involves Payne's claim that children in poverty rely heavily on non-verbal cues because "these students do not have the vocabulary or the knowledge of sentence structure and syntax to use formal register" (2005, p. 28). And, she asserts, this lack of language facility can lead to trouble. Payne notes (p. 41):

Being able physically to fight or have someone who is willing to fight for you is important to survival in poverty. Yet, in middle class, being able to use words as tools to negotiate conflict is crucial. Many times the fists are used in poverty because the words are neither available nor respected.

This stereotype also appears in a book published by Payne's organization, aha! Process, Inc. Jodi R. Pfarr (2009), in her *Tactical Communication: Law Enforcement Tools for Successful Encounters with People from Poverty, Middle Class, and*

Wealth (designed for police officers), appears to champion Payne's views about class differences. Pfarr informs the readers that poor people are primarily non-verbal and this leads to a propensity for violence. Note the following:

> Being able to see, feel, and hear nonverbal signals that are sent to you will help you survive in poverty; in fact, this ability is absolutely mandatory. Teachers have reported students in school hitting other students without recognizable provocation. When asked to explain the behavior, the aggressors' most common responses were along the lines of, "Because s/he was looking at me." Absolutely! In poverty, if someone gives you a dangerous look, it may be in your best interest to attack preemptively before you yourself are attacked. Because nonverbal cues communicate information, they are being interpreted quickly and are relied upon as heavily as verbal communication. Law enforcement personnel must be conscious of what their nonverbals are communicating. I can't stress this enough: In a neighborhood in poverty, *nonverbal communication is as important as verbal communication.*
>
> (Pfarr, 2009, p. 46)

Payne's (2005) and Pfarr's (2009) contentions that poor children have a proclivity for violence because they rely strongly on nonverbal cues to communicate do not hold up in light of available research. For example, in empirical investigations of the hypothesis that low-SES, inner-city Black children are prone to aggression when confronted with a potentially violent situation (i.e., a scenario of a smaller child who picks a fight with a larger child), the Black participants overwhelmingly gave responses that the larger child should show restraint (e.g., tell him or her you don't want to fight because of possible harm to the smaller child).[24]

Discipline

In *Framework*, Payne (2005) has a chapter on the subject of "Discipline," in which she proceeds to partake in stereotyping and continues to be very selective in drawing from literature to make her *ad hoc* observations about the poor. Payne declares (p. 77):

> *In poverty, discipline is about penance and forgiveness, not necessarily change.* Because love is unconditional and because the time frame is the present, the notion that discipline should be instructive and change behavior is not part of the culture in generational poverty. . . . The culture of poverty does not provide for success in middle class because middle class to a large extent requires the self-governance of behavior. To be successful in work and in school requires self-control concerning behavior. What, then, do schools need to do to teach appropriate behavior?

To address the query in the above quotation, Payne (2005) displays a chart consisting of two columns—one labeled "Behavior Related to Poverty," and a corresponding column titled "Intervention" (pp. 79–80). Thirteen different behavior-intervention links comprise the chart. Here are several examples: First, Payne asserts that poor children are very disorganized (e.g., fail to plan; do not prioritize). The intervention: The teacher should utilize a color-coded procedure to instill organizational skills. Second, Payne claims that poor children demonstrate a lack of respect for the teacher, and are not cognizant of a single adult who merits respect. The intervention: The teacher needs to instruct students in the right voice tone and acceptable choice of words. Third, Payne contends that poor children steal or cheat, and this is indicative of poor role models. The intervention: The teacher should underscore that such behavior is illegal and not a choice at school.

Payne's (2005) above assertions about alleged dysfunctional behavior among poor children carry far-reaching implications for classroom intervention. As such, it is important to examine the sources of Payne's claims. As I note earlier, Payne provides the vast amount of her sources for text discussion and contentions in each chapter in the Research Notes section near book's end (typically presented as quoted material from the sources listed in her References, pp. 187–193). For the "Discipline" chapter in *Framework*, Payne cites three sources in the Research Notes (Mayer, 1997; McLanahan, 1997; Rodríguez, 1993).

McLanahan's (1997) chapter, "Parent Absence or Poverty: Which Matters More?," is a straightforward literature review that covers, in part, the effects on children who grow up in a nonintact family (which tends to be collinear with living in poverty). McLanahan concludes that such children have more "behavioral" and "psychological" problems as they grow up. McLanahan's discussion of the nature of these problems are quite vague, nowhere coming close to the specificity of the discipline problems Payne alleges exist among poor children.

Payne (2005), in her "Discipline" chapter, also draws from an autobiography by award-winning poet Luis J. Rodríguez. *Always Running: La Vida Loca: Gang Days in L.A.* (1993) is a skillfully written and nerve-racking narrative of his life as he grew up in Watts and Las Lomas *barrio* (located east of Los Angeles). Rodríguez, a Mexican American, discusses how he and his family endured the shame of poverty and racial discrimination when they arrived from Mexico. He also writes about his drug usage, gang membership, and encounters with police brutality. As Rodríguez matures, he finds the futility of "always running" and turns to political action to reform himself and others. At book's end, he comments:

> I've talked to enough gang members and low-level dope dealers to know they would quit today if they had a productive, livable-wage job. You'll

find people who don't care about who they hurt, but nobody I know wants to sell death to their children, their neighbors, and friends. If there was a viable alternative, they would stop. If we all had a choice, I'm convinced nobody would choose *la vida loca*, the "insane nation"—to "gang bang." But it's going to take collective action and a plan.

(Rodríguez, 1993, p. 251)

Payne is quite selective in her Research Notes in drawing from Rodríguez's work. She fails to build on his transformation from gang member to political activist. Instead, she lifts two quotes from *Always Running* in an *ad hoc* manner that helps support her claims about supposed dysfunctional behavior among the poor. Payne (p. 153) comments: "He [Rodríguez] said his father 'didn't get angry or hit me. That he left to my mother' " (Rodríguez, p. 47). Payne continues: "An example of punishment was given. He [Rodríguez] said his 'mother carved into my flesh with a leather belt' " (Rodríguez, p. 74).

A third source that Payne (2005) cites for the "Discipline" chapter in *Framework* is Susan E. Mayer's (1997) book, *What Money Can't Buy: Family Income and Children's Life Chances*, a volume that deals with little of the discipline problems Payne discusses in her "Discipline" chapter. Mayer does briefly note, however, that poor parents—compared to more economically advantaged parents—are more probable to engage in "power-assertive" disciplinary tactics "such as physical punishment, rather than reasoning, more likely to value obedience, and less likely to be supportive of their children" (p. 115). According to psychologists, states Mayer, the stress of poverty helps to facilitate these attributes. Nonetheless, Payne (pp. 152–153) zeroes in on Mayer's thesis that improved parental behavior trumps the importance of money for the poor by providing this quote:

A school counselor said, " 'Giving the family money can improve the standard of living, but it won't give the children the tools they need for success.' Her colleague added, 'I think it is the parenting values—the parenting style—matters more than the money.' "

(Mayer, 1997, p. 113)

Besharov and López (1997), in a review of Mayer's (1997) *What Money Can't Buy*, comment that her findings are not that convincing—particularly in that she takes her analysis and conclusions "both too far and not far enough" (p. 114). For example, Besharov and López remark that Mayer overgeneralizes, painting with a brush that leaves a portrait that all poor families are alike. Another criticism Besharov and López raise is that Mayer's design is static, in which she employs a one-point-in-time cross-sectional analysis. Thus, the reviewers comment: "She cannot predict the long-term consequences of giving [poor] parents more money" (p. 115).

Improving Academic Achievement

In the beginning of Payne's (2005) chapter in *Framework*, "Improving Academic Achievement," she comments: "One of the overriding purposes of this book is to improve the achievement of students from poverty" (p. 87). In itself, this a laudable objective, given that, *as a group*, low-SES students (particularly of color) experience school failure (e.g., reading below average) disproportionately more so than their economically advantaged peers (see Preface, present book). Yet, Payne approaches her goal of improving academic achievement of poor children in a scientifically unjustifiable and deficit thinking manner. Here, I discuss and counter several of her assertions.

THE RELATION BETWEEN SES AND ACADEMIC ACHIEVEMENT

Early in discussion, Payne (2005) states: "Numerous studies have documented the correlation between low socioeconomic status and low achievement" (p. 87). While researchers indeed have found correlations between SES and measures of academic achievement (and intelligence) to be positive, the magnitudes vary dramatically depending on the unit of analysis. Karl R. White (1982), employing meta-analytic techniques, conducted one of the most comprehensive reviews of the literature on the relation between SES and measures of academic achievement and intelligence.[25] In his review, White found a number of methodological problems. One of these issues centers on the "unit of analysis" used in computing the correlation coefficient. White found that in the 101 studies he reviewed, researchers varied in their unit of analysis. White coded these units as "aggregated," "confounded," or "student." He describes them as follows:

> When an aggregated unit (such as school or district) was used, both the SES measure and the achievement measure were averages for the aggregated unit, and the correlation was computed between the average scores. When the unit of analysis was confounded, SES was measured at an aggregated level, and achievement was measured at the student level or vice versa. For instance, all students in the same school might be given the same SES rating but could have individual achievement scores. The student was identified as the unit of analysis when both SES and achievement were measured separately for each student.
>
> (White, 1982, p. 465)

In his review, White (1982) finds that the magnitude of the correlation between SES and academic achievement/intelligence is significantly related to a number of variables (e.g., year of study; grade level of participant; number of participants in the study; number of items in the SES measure). He reports that the most dramatic difference in correlation magnitude is related to the unit of analysis. That is, when correlations are computed from aggregated data the resultant magnitudes are considerably higher than correlations computed using individual students as the unit of analysis. White notes that it is well known among statisticians that using aggregated units of analysis results in spuriously high correlations (Knapp, 1977; Robinson, 1950). To illustrate, White presents data of mean correlations between SES for measures of academic achievement and intelligence. Table 3.1 presents these data.

It is exceedingly clear from the data in Table 3.1 that using the aggregated unit of analysis results in substantially higher correlations than does using the student unit of analysis, the more valid unit (Robinson, 1950). Of the various measures (Verbal, Math, Composite Achievement, and IQ), when the more accurate unit of analysis (i.e., student) is used, the r values range from a low of .20 (Math) to a high of .33 (IQ); these are low magnitudes.

On a final point of interest, White (1982) collapsed his data across all coding variables and for all studies and finds the mean correlation coefficient between SES and "achievement" (which includes IQ measures)[26] to be .35. The median, which is the best estimate of central tendency in a skewed distribution, is only .25. When White analyzed the data with student as the unit of analysis, the mean and median are .25 and .22, respectively. By sharp contrast, when White analyzed the data using aggregated units of analysis, the mean and median jump to .68 and .73, respectively.

In sum, White's (1982) comprehensive review of the literature provides strong evidence against the prevailing "belief that socioeconomic status . . . and various measures of academic achievement are strongly correlated" (p. 461) (also, see Boocock, 1972; Charters, 1963). This is a point that Payne in *Framework* is not aware of, but should be. In theorizing about factors associated with students' academic achievement and intellectual performance, researchers would be prudent in their empirical investigations to utilize data in which the individual student is the unit of analysis.

Table 3.1 Mean Correlations between SES and Measures of Achievement and Intelligence

Category	Verbal		Math		Composite Achievement[a]		IQ	
	M	N or n^b	M	N or n	M	N or n	M	N or n
All Correlations	.31	225	.25	143	.37	66	.40	102
Aggregated	.68	35	.70	14	.64	15	.73	18
Confounded	.29	16	n.a.	n.a.	n.a.	n.a.	.34	10
Student	.23	174	.20	128	.27	46	.33	74

Source: Valencia and Suzuki (2001, p. 79, Table 3.8).

Note: SES = socioeconomic status; n.a. = nonavailable data. [a]Composite Achievement measure refers to data in which total achievement was assessed. [b]N or n refers to number of correlations.

THE ALLEGED COGNITIVE IMPAIRMENTS OF POOR CHILDREN

Payne (2005), *sans* any supportive evidence, claims: "Increasingly, students, mostly from poverty, are coming to school without the concepts, but more importantly, *without the cognitive strategies*" [italics added] (p. 89). By "concepts," she means: "*Concepts* store information and allow for retrieval" (p. 89) and by "cognitive strategies," she refers to "fundamental ways of processing information" (p. 89). Furthermore, again without empirical evidence, Payne (2005, pp. 92–93) asserts that "these students" (i.e., children living in poverty) have seven cognitive impairments (e.g., "impaired verbal tools;" "impaired spatial orientation;" "lack of precision and accuracy in data-gathering;" "inability to hold two objects or two sources inside the head while comparing and contrasting").

Although low-SES children, *on the average*, tend to score lower than their economically advantaged peers on measures of intelligence (especially verbally loaded and culturally loaded tests), this point needs to be taken with great caution.[27] It is important to clear up a common misconception demonstrated by laypeople and scholars alike when referring to "racial/ethnic group differences" (as well as SES group differences) in measured intelligence. This phrase of "group differences" is misleading and tends to perpetuate stereotypes. What the group differences actually refer to are *average* intellectual differences in performance of the *individuals* who are linked to racial/ethnic group membership (e.g., Whites; African Americans; Mexican Americans) and SES groups (e.g., working class; middle class). Thus, an important question to ask is: How large are the average differences between groups relative to the range of variation that occurs within groups? Although "different observers vary considerably in the emphasis they place on average differences between groups compared with variation within groups" (Loehlin, Lindzey, & Spuhler, 1975, p. 15), the major finding is that "the majority of the variation in . . . levels of [intellectual] ability lies within U.S. racial/ethnic and socioeconomic groups, not between them" (p. 235). That is, for measured intelligence, average differences in performance *between* groups tend to be quite modest relative to the range of differences *within* groups. In any event, the indiscriminate use of the term *group differences* in referring to patterns in intelligence scores among racial/ethnic and SES populations ignores the reality of overlap of individual scores between groups and perpetuates the myth that nearly everybody of one racial/ethnic group (e.g., Whites) performs higher than practically everybody of another group (e.g., African Americans).[28]

Research findings exist, including my own studies, that present antithetical evidence to Payne's (2005) above contention that poor children come to school without cognitive strategies, as well as with cognitive impairments. For example, during the early part of my career I collected a considerable amount of intelligence test data on English-speaking and Spanish-speaking

Mexican American children primarily attending preschools, either in Head Start programs or preschools serving children from working-class backgrounds (Valencia, 1988). I determined that the SES of a strong majority of my participant children, based on the Hollingshead Two-Factor Index of Social Position (Hollingshead & Redlich, 1958), fell at the very low end of the scale. For my measure of intelligence, I administered the McCarthy Scales of Children's Abilities (MSCA; McCarthy, 1972), a very well standardized, individually administered test.[29] The MSCA is comprised of 18 subtests which are grouped into six scales: Verbal (V), Perceptual-Performance (PP), Quantitative (Q), General Cognitive Index (GCI), Memory, and Motor. A number of GCI subtests measure various conceptual abilities—such as: early language development; verbal concept formation; numerical reasoning; concentration; spatial relations; directionality; logical classification; divergent thinking; nonverbal reasoning (Kaufman & Kaufman, 1977; Valencia, 1990), the kinds of cognitive skills that Payne asserts poor children do not possess when they come to school. The GCI is an estimate of the child's global intellectual functioning. The GCI is formed by combining performance on the V, PP, and Q scales, which do not overlap in content. A mean of 100 is set for the GCI, and the standard deviation is 16. For the other five scales, the mean and standard deviation are 50 and 10, respectively.

In Valencia (1988), I present my research findings—as well as those of other scholars—of 700 young Mexican American children's performance on the MSCA. For the Mexican American English-speaking children ($n = 307$), aggregated across a number of different studies, they had a weighted mean of 99.9 on the MSCA GCI, and when rounded it was identical to the MSCA standardization mean of 100, which the test developer derived from a predominantly (84%) White, middle-class norm group. For the Spanish-speaking Mexican American children ($n = 302$), they had a weighted mean GCI of 92.7, about one-half a standard deviation below the MSCA standardization mean.

In sum, based on this relatively large sample size of considerably low-SES Mexican American children (predominantly preschoolers), Payne's (2005) blanket generalization that poor children come to school without cognitive strategies and with cognitive impairments is patently false and smacks of deficit thinking.

PAYNE'S PROPOSED INSTRUCTIONAL INTERVENTION

Immediately after Payne (2005) claims in her "Instruction and Improving Achievement" chapter that students, primarily from poverty, are entering school in increasing numbers without the necessary "concepts" and "cognitive strategies" to learn (p. 89), she notes with glaring resignation: "We simply can't assign them all to special education" (p. 89). My sense of Payne's remark is that she is saying poor children come to school in such great numbers with cognitive deficits that special education programs are unable to accommodate them all. Once again, in making her statements and drawing conclusions, Payne ignores the available scholarly evidence. First, she exaggerates the number of students in special education classes or programs. It is important to obtain reliable data in regard to the actual placements of students into educational settings, for example, children with mild or educable mental retardation (fairly interchangeable terms)—Payne's likely target population, noted above.[30] For example, in evaluating the *Larry P.* decision of the early 1970s (*Larry P. v. Riles*, 1972), Prasse and Reschly (1986) report that Black students constituted 10% of the K–12 student population in California.[31] However, they represented 25% of the students placed in classes for the mildly mentally retarded. Therefore, many assumed that 25% of Black students were in classes for the mildly retarded. In actuality, the percentage of Black students placed in special classes for the mildly retarded constituted 1%. Thus, "overrepresentation statistics need to be carefully analyzed to avoid exaggeration and distortion" (Reschly, 1988, p. 320). A second problem with Payne's statement about poor children and mild mental retardation (disproportionately students of color, especially Black and Latino; see Valencia, 2008, chapter 3; Valencia & Suzuki, 2001, chapter 7) is she fails to discuss that many of these children's placements in special education are largely due to issues other than cognitive impairments —mainly inappropriate and biased assessments, leading to false positives.[32]

After stating that more and more poor children arrive to school with cognitive impairments, Payne (2005) asks: "What are these cognitive strategies [these children lack], and how do we build learning structures inside the heads of these [poor] students?" (p. 89). For her suggested intervention, she draws heavily from the work of Reuven Feuerstein and associates. Feuerstein, born in 1921 in Butosani, Romania, studied, in part, under Jean Piaget (noted child developmentalist) at the University of Geneva. In 1970, Feuerstein earned his doctorate in Developmental Psychology from the Sorbonne in Paris, France. He is internationally known for his work with children with learning problems (e.g., children with Down Syndrome; autism).[33]

Feuerstein is also well known for his research on facilitating the learning of children with mental retardation, as seen, for example, in these books: *The Dynamic Assessment of Retarded Performers: The Learning Potential Assessment Device, Theory, Instruments, and Techniques* (Feuerstein, Rand, & Hoffman, 1979) and *Don't Accept Me as I Am: Helping Retarded People to Excel* (Feuerstein, Rand, & Rynders, 1988).[34] Feuerstein's work has been greatly influenced by Russian developmental psychologist Lev Vygotsky, who frames his learning theory around a social context in which learning is facilitated by a mediator (Vygotsky, 1978). Feuerstein believes very much in cognitive modifiability. In regard to modification of cognitive abilities in individuals with mental retardation, Feuerstein's model has three essential steps. Detterman, Gabriel, and Ruthsatz (2000, p. 152) succinctly capture these phases:

The first step is the evaluation of the individual through the learning potential assessment device (LPAD). This device is meant to measure an individual's capacity to learn. The LPAD is a dynamic approach to discover a child's readiness or ability to learn and is different from traditional IQ tests, which are considered a static form of assessment. Once the assessment is done the individual enters the second stage of the program, Instrumental Enrichment (IE), which entails learning to learn. The program provides the child with strategies to enhance performance in academic and real-world situations. The final phase of the program is the adjustment of the environment to produce supportive formats for people with mental retardation.[35]

Utilizing diverse cultural groups, scholars have tested and applied Feuerstein's cognitive interventions in over 45 countries (Burgess, 2008). Feuerstein and associates' model has demonstrated, experimentally, promising results. For example, Rand, Tannenbaum, and Feuerstein (1988; cited in Detterman et al., 2000; also, see Feuerstein et al., 1988, pp. 237–238) studied the effect of IE on a sample of 600 12- to 15-year-old "culturally deprived" Israeli children with mental retardation (IQs between 60 and 90); 300 children formed the experimental group, and 300 children comprised the control group, who received instruction in mathematics, reading, and writing. After a period of 1 year, the experimental group, compared to the control group, showed higher scores on the Primary Mental Abilities Test (for more on this test, see Thurstone, 1941; Thurstone & Thurstone, 1962). This statistically significant difference persisted throughout the assessment period, and continued until 2 years after intervention terminated.

In addition to the interest generated by encouraging findings for individuals with mental retardation, Feuerstein and associates' model of cognitive assessment and learning facilitation has also attracted attention among researchers who study other populations and issues. These are: children in regular classrooms (i.e., non-special education; Tzuriel & Klein, 1987; Lidz, 1991); Mexican American English learners (Peña, 1996; Peña, Iglesias, & Lidz, 2001); multicultural assessment (Armour-Thomas & Gopaul-McNicol, 1998; Lidz, 2001); gifted students (Lidz & Macrine, 2001). Such interest by other researchers in regard to the Feuerstein and associates' model lay in the paradigm shift from static to dynamic assessment (Lidz, 1987, 1991). Dynamic assessment, which utilizes a test–teach–retest approach, provides a much richer source of information about how the student learns, and what types of interventions might most benefit him or her. Such individualized approaches are a great advantage over standardized assessment in that the assessment and intervention processes are tailored to individual students' strengths and needs.[36]

In sum, Payne's (2005) statement about the relation between SES and academic achievement, her claim that poor children come to school with cognitive deficits (i.e., without concepts or strategies), as well as her proposed Feuerstein et al. method of intervention to "build learning structures inside the heads" (p. 89) of poor children, all have very questionable scientific merit. First, she overstates the strength of the association between SES and school achievement. Second, she fails to acknowledge the research findings that many poor children, including youngsters of color, come to school with various strengths in their cognitive abilities. Third, her suggested Feuerstein et al. approach to intervention is misleading. For Payne to juxtapose her assertion that poor children have cognitive impairments *with* the proposed intervention model of Feuerstein and associates leads one to believe that most poor children have mental retardation. This is blatant deficit thinking on Payne's part.

Critique of Ruby Payne's Conceptual Structure for Understanding Poverty

In the previous section, I introduce Payne's (2005) *Framework*, and I also offer criticisms of a number of her assertions in various chapters. This present section is designed to present a more systematic and quantitative critique of *Framework*. In my literature search for germane material in which scholars proffer critiques of Payne's (2005) *Framework* and related works, I identified 13 publications—focusing on various issues.[37] A number of these critiques are consonant with the concerns I raise in the previous section; some are new. One thread, however, ties together the 13 publications: The authors deem that Payne engages in considerable deficit thinking. Another interesting point: The dates of publication range from 2005 to 2008, and one "in press" article, with a mode of 2006 ($n = 5$). Given that Payne published her first edition of *Framework* in 1996, why did scholarly critiques only begin to appear about a decade later? The answer is quite simple. The work of Payne and the work of scholars lay in vastly different spheres.[38] Payne is a self-promoting, self-publishing individual whose work is utterly free of peer review. By sharp contrast, the work of scholars is subject to rigorous review by peers. As such, these two realms seldom interact. When they do, the substantive and methodological adroitness of trained scholars comes to bear when they come across the declarations of deficit thinkers. A case in point is Nana Osei-Kofi, Assistant Professor of Educational Leadership and Policy Studies at Iowa State University. In her 2005 article, "Pathologizing the Poor: Understanding Ruby Payne's Work," she reflects:

> I was first exposed to Payne's work through my role as a consultant to a number of school districts. These districts were seeking to develop K-16 partnerships for the purpose of increasing access to higher education for underserved students. Soon after my introduction to these school districts, I started to hear about the incredible work Payne was doing to help teachers and administrators understand issues of class and poverty. My interest was immediately peaked. This praise was curious to me in

light of the wide-spread resistance within the education community to critically engage issues of oppression and domination. As I began to learn more about Payne's work and had an opportunity to attend one of her seminars, my cautious interest turned to great concern. Payne's ideas about "understanding" poverty do great violence to any ideas of education as a positive force in creating a socially and economically just society.

(Osei-Kofi, 2005, p. 368)

What follows is an overview of the 13 critiques of Payne's work. They largely center on her *Framework* (2005). Rather than summarizing each critique, I thought it would be more efficient and informative to provide a content analysis of the 13 critical reviews of Payne's work. A content analysis is a research methodology designed to systematically examine the content of communication. In my approach, I sought to capture relatively common subjects that appear across the 13 critiques.[39] Table 3.2 presents these themes with the accompanying publications.

The five subjects are not mutually exclusive. For example, the Culture of Poverty theme involves false perceptions and misrepresentations of reality —that is the Stereotyping theme. Nonetheless, I believe each of the five themes is dissimilar enough to stand alone as informative markers for this analysis. Next, I briefly discuss each theme.

Culture of Poverty

As the subtitle of the present chapter expresses, Payne's (2005) *Framework,*

Table 3.2 Content Analysis of 13 Critiques of Payne's *Framework*

Publication	Theme				
	Culture of Poverty	Stereotyping	Nonscientific Research Base	Deficit Thinking	No Consideration of Alternative Explanations
Bohn (2006)	X	X	X	X	X
Bohn (2007)		X		X	
Bomer et al. (2008)	X	X	X	X	X
Dudley-Marling (2007)	X		X	X	
Dworin & Bomer (2008)	X	X	X	X	X
Gorski (2005)	X	X	X	X	X
Gorski (2006a)		X	X	X	X
Gorski (2006b)		X		X	X
Gorski (2008)	X	X	X	X	X
Kunjufu (2006)	X			X	X
Ng & Rury (2006)	X	X	X	X	X
Osei-Kofi (2005)	X	X	X	X	X
Smiley & Helfenbein (in press)	X	X		X	

in my view and those of others, is a "Resurrection of the Culture of Poverty Concept." As Table 3.2 shows, 10 (77%) of the 13 critiques note that Payne frames her discussion of the poor in the context of the culture of poverty notion. For example, Bomer et al. (2008) comment that Payne quotes from the work of Oscar Lewis who, as I discuss earlier, paints the poor as being homogenous, dysfunctional, and self-perpetuating entities. Osei-Kofi (2005), another critic, remarks that in her *Framework* Payne incorporates Lewis's culture of poverty concept, as well as the concepts of those who appropriate Lewis's research (e.g., Edward Banfield), and the final result is "a stringing together of worn-out conservative platitudes to rationalize poverty as a choice of the individual" (Osei-Kofi, p. 368).

Stereotyping

Table 3.2 indicates that of the 13 critiques forming the corpus of the content analysis, 11 (85%) find that Payne in her *Framework* engages in considerable stereotyping. Bohn (2006), for example, states: "On my first read-through of the [hidden] 'rules' I didn't know whether to laugh at the sheer stupidity of some of them or to rage at the offensive stereotyping of people in poverty and the thinly veiled bigotry reflected in others" (p. 2). Bomer et al. (2008) take Payne to task for her racialization of poverty by depicting poor persons as people of color, "rather than acknowledging the fact that most poor people in the U.S. are White" (p. 2506). In support of this fact, Bomer et al. (2008) cite Roberts (2004). Although Payne (2005) in *Framework* notes that "while the number of Caucasian children in poverty is the largest group, the percentage of children in most minority groups is higher" (p. 6), she nonetheless racializes poverty in her scenarios and case studies in *Framework*, as Bomer et al. (2008) discuss. The authors continue: "Payne is perpetuating negative stereotypes by equating poverty with people of color. Although there is a correlation between race and class, this does not justify her use of racialized 'case studies' " (p. 2506).

Nonscientific Research Base

Table 3.2 shows that of the 13 critiques, 9 (69%) point out that in her *Framework* Payne lacks scientific rigor in using the research literature to support her many claims about the poor. That is, in a number of different instances she (a) fails to use credible sources to substantiate her assertions, (b) has no source at all to support her claims, (c) misrepresents the research findings of others, and (d) is highly selective in drawing from the existing research base. For example, Dworin and Bomer (2008, pp. 110–11) express great concerns about Payne's alleged research base for *Framework*:

> Payne describes herself as having gathered information over years, later saying "I had been gathering data for 24 years" (p. 1). Her "data" seem to

be the impressions she collected about her former husband, his family, and people who lived in the neighborhood where her former husband grew up, and her thoughts when she was a principal of an affluent elementary school. No researcher would consider anything in this book data—there is not one particle of data, not one empirical fact, not one datum in the book—but the use of the term invokes the discourse of science, apparently enough to enlist many readers' trust for authority.

The critique by Bomer et al. (2008) is of particular interest in regard to Payne's (2005) lack of scientific competence in *Framework*. In their well-designed and executed investigation, Bomer et al. (2008) extracted 607 "truth claims" Payne asserts in *Framework*. In turn, Bomer and associates—after coding and grouping all the data—identified 102 codes. The authors collapsed the codes into 15 categories, which are further collapsed into 4 superordinate categories: "social structure," "daily life," "language," and "characteristics." In the superordinate category of "social structure," they found five categories— "poverty;" "culture of poverty;" "race, ethnicity, and gender;" "hidden rules;" and "class." Regarding "class," Payne (2005) makes a truth claim, *sans* research documentation, that three SES groupings exist—the "poor," "middle class," and the "wealthy" (pp. 42–43). By sharp contrast, Bomer and associates cite evidence that multiple classes, as well as substrata within, describe U.S. class structure. For example, sociologist Dennis Gilbert (2003; cited in Bomer et al., 2008) offers a class analysis of the U.S. in which he estimates that 12% of the population belong to the "underclass," 13% comprise the working poor, 30% are working class, 30% make up the middle class, 14% comprise the upper-middle class, and 1% are deemed the capitalist class. In sum, Bomer et al. (2008) demonstrate that Payne's numerous truth claims are contradicted by empirical research findings on poverty in sociology, anthropology, and other disciplines.

Deficit Thinking

Table 3.2 shows that 100% of the 13 critiques find Payne's *Framework* to be guided by a stream of deficit thinking. This unanimity is not surprising, given that the linchpin of Payne's theorizing about the etiology of poverty rests on an endogenous model—that is, blame the poor for their condition. Some examples of how the authors of the 13 critiques zero in on Payne's deficit think-ing are illustrative. Dudley-Marling (2007) remarks: From "A deficit-oriented perspective. . . . Ruby Payne . . . pathologizes poor families while situating high levels of school failure among poor and minority children in their heads, homes, and communities" (p. 8). Gorski (2008) comments: "The root of her framework—that people in poverty must learn the culture of the middle class in order to gain full access to educational opportunities—is steeped in deficit thinking" (p. 138). Kunjufu (2006), in reference to Payne's theorizing, states:

"The deficit thinking model is prescribed and based on the idea that there is something wrong with our [African American] children, and we need a workshop to describe what is wrong with it" (p. xv).

No Consideration of Alternative Explanations

In chapter 1, present book, I discuss six characteristics of deficit thinking—one being pseudoscience. In addition to basing their research on flawed assumptions, using psychometrically weak instruments, and not controlling for key variables, pseudoscientists also do not consider rival explanations for their observed findings. Table 3.2 shows that 10 (77%) of the 13 critiques mention that Payne, in her *Framework*, fails to entertain exogenous factors as to why poor people are in their "world." For example, critics Bomer et al. (2008) note that Payne constantly pathologizes the poor, but "She never considers the alternative, that social, economic and political structures—not their [the poor's] own behavior and attitudes—have provided barriers to success in schools for poor children" (p. 2507). In a similar vein, Ng and Rury (2006) comment: "Payne overlooks the predominant social and economic causes of poverty highlighted in social science literature such as deindustrialization, discrimination, unequal educational resources, and socioeconomic segregation" (p. 6).

Conclusion

In this concluding section on the work and influence on Ruby Payne, I focus on three topics.

Payne's Popularity in Educational Training Sectors

Anita P. Bohn, a critic of Payne's work, writes: "Ruby Payne's reign as avatar of social class consciousness in America continues, or so a recent article in the *New York Times Magazine* would have one believe" (Bohn, 2007, p. 1). Bohn is referring to an article, "The Class-Consciousness Raiser," written by journalist Paul Tough.[40] In all, Tough, in his 2007 article, is quite nice to Payne. Bohn (2007) notes: "Tough's uncritical five-page infomercial for Payne's consulting company spotlights her already lucrative business in a publicity spread for which most companies would kill" (p. 1). Bohn (2007) also states that Tough "dismisses Payne's critics as 'a few angry assistant professors' who hound her 'like gnats at a backyard barbeque' " (p. 1). In his article, Tough records a workday for Payne who presents her standard workshop, using her ubiquitous *Framework*, for 1,400 individuals employed by the Glynn County (Georgia) School System. Due to her great demand, the Board of Education was forced to book Payne's presentation 2 years in advance. At the morning break, Tough notes that Payne met her admirers and signed books. Tough also writes: "A few of the teachers hugged Payne. One woman kissed her hand. Another burst into tears." Tough further mentions a Charlotte Lawson, who worked as an "instructional coach" in one of the district's elementary schools. Lawson, a veteran of Payne's intensive four-day certification course, authorizes her to provide training, on the basis of *Framework*, to other teachers. Tough notes that Lawson had never personally met Payne. Lawson gushed, exclaiming, "I'm so excited. This is like a dream."

Ruby Payne's popularity is also evidenced by the sheer number of school districts that turn to Payne's workshops and her *Framework*, in districts' desperate needs for ideas to improve the schooling of low-SES students. On December 29, 2008, I conducted a Google search using "School Improvement Plan" + "Ruby Payne," and received 1,500 hits.[41] Even further evidence of Payne's reach on teaching her views about the poor is seen in teacher education courses. Nana Osei-Kofi (2005), another critic of Payne, based on a Google search generated more than 5,000 web documents using these search terms: "Ruby Payne, Syllabus, and Education." From these search results, Osei-Kofi reviewed close to 60 syllabi for teacher education courses offered at numerous institutions (e.g., University of Michigan; Indiana State University; The Ohio State University). Osei-Kofi states that exposure to Payne's work in higher education could possibly be used to encourage critical analysis. She concludes, however, that her review of the syllabi

> provide little to no evidence to support such a claim. Instead, alarmingly, Payne's work is used in education and social work programs today simply as a pragmatic tool to "help" students "recognize" and learn to "address" issues with poor students/clients in their work and internships/field experiences.
>
> (Osei-Kofi, 2005, p. 368)

Why do Educators Espouse Payne's Framework?

A number of the authors who provide critiques of Payne's work (Table 3.2, this chapter) ask a very important question, as the one posed by Jennifer C. Ng and John L. Rury: "What explains the popularity of her book [Payne's *Framework*] and the apparent success of her workshops?" (2006, p. 7). Ng and Rury point out that Payne's attraction and influence are somewhat puzzling, given that Payne's "viewpoint is heavily tilted toward a certain perspective and the research base for her work is so questionable" (p. 7). It appears that Payne's appeal to educators (incumbent and preservice) lay in their negative conceptions about the poor, which are reflective of the long-standing, prejudicial societal perceptions of the poor. Ng and Rury (2006, p. 7) incisively capture this point, which some other critics of Payne would agree:

> If they [educators] are predisposed to believing that the poor are lazy and impulsive as well as unreliable and temperamental, they are more likely to agree with Payne's analysis than to question it. In short, Payne may be popular simply because she echoes commonplace assumptions

about why some individuals appear to succeed in American society while others do not.

In regard to the argument that educators find comfort and pedagogical value in Payne's work because of preconceptions about the poor, Joel E. Dworin and Randy Bomer (2008) provide a valuable investigation of Payne's work by utilizing a critical discourse analysis (CDA) of *Framework*. Drawing from Gee (2004), Dworin and Bomer describe CDA as such:

> CDA analyzes passages of language, not only to describe the structures in the language and to interpret the meanings of those structures, but also to connect the structures and meanings to larger sociopolitical patterns of privilege and power, oppression and silencing.
> (Dworin & Bomer, 2008, p. 106)

Dworin and Bomer (2008) find that Payne's (2005) success in capturing her audience via *Framework* is very much related to a number of text features in the book, to wit: (a) "scientism and authority" (e.g., Payne as an "expert" on mindsets of classes); (b) "indirection" (e.g., obliquely stating her rather strong claims); (c) "spaciousness, cohesion, and gaps" (therefore leaving the reader and writer to assume what the text says); (d) "pronoun reference—whom is this about?" (conflating class with race, thus distancing the White middle-class reader from poor students of color). In sum, Dworin and Bomer note: "The success of Payne's program is, at least in part, attributable to the ways it taps into discourses already present in the U.S., including but not limited to the middle class, of which many educators are a subset" (p. 105).

Another insightful investigation of how and why Payne and her *Framework* appeal to educators is by Azure D. Smiley and Robert J. Helfenbein (in press), university teacher educators. Smiley and Helfenbein seek to examine the influence of *Framework* on the "pedagogical and professional identity development" (p. 2) of two preservice special education teachers, "Vicki" and "Linda"—who both identify as White, with middle-class backgrounds. The authors' methodology includes the participants' exposure to *Framework* via the curriculum, as well as interviews, field observations, and a focus group. Smiley and Helfenbein report that based on their initial interviews, they asked the participants to indicate which courses or curricular aspects seemed most significant in assisting them to prepare for the pending practicum. Although both participants had read, for example, the work of noted multicultural education expert, James A. Banks, they "immediately referred to Ruby Payne's book" (p. 11). Vicki shares: "I think Ruby Payne's work helped a lot. I really liked that one. It just explained a lot. I could think back and say, oh that's why that was like that" (p. 11). Linda expresses a similar reaction:

> The poverty book by Ruby Payne. It's a really good book. I really like it. I

could relate it to my life and really see where I stand or my family stands. I think that's the only class [the course using Payne's book] so far that has taught me to be more understanding and deal with poverty. It taught me about diversity. It made me open my eyes and kind of understand what to expect.

(Smiley & Helfenbein, in press, p. 11)

After Smiley and Helfenbein (in press) collected and coded all data, five themes emerged from their study: "encouraged separation," "deficit mode," "messiah mentality," "urban education," and "contradiction." In regard to the deficit mode, the authors remark that both participants—whose field work was in an urban setting—"began to look for confirmations of the deficit perspectives they brought to the experience" (p. 16), and Vicki and Linda's "views appear to be deeply impacted by the variety of examples of deficit perspectives offered in Payne's book. Vicki's disgust of her students' 'little habits' are validated by Payne's text" (p. 17). Vicki also comments: "Being loved, they [her students] may go home and their parents may not care about their homework and teaching them right from wrong" (p. 24). Smiley and Helfenbein conclude by noting that preconceived notions of preservice teachers play a large role regarding their future work. The authors comment:

Students often made comments about the young people and teachers in urban settings that are not only offensive, but in direct contrast with the mission of this teacher preparation program. After comments had been made verbally or in written form, often students cite *A Framework* as the source of their newfound epiphany. Vicki and Linda seem to agree that this particular text provided a welcome and unique insight on teaching in areas of poverty—it was a favorite.

(*Ibid.*, p. 28)

The Rising Tide of Scholarly Critique of Payne's Views of the Poor

As I discuss earlier, although Payne's *Framework* first appeared in 1996, the first published critiques of her work did not surface until 2005 (i.e., Gorski, 2005; Osei-Kofi, 2005). Yet, as seen in Table 3.2 (present chapter), 11 more such publications have appeared since (i.e., by the end of 2008; plus the "in press" article)—a 550% increase. I gather that the number of publications raising serious concerns about Payne and her *Framework* will increase as more and more scholars interested in social justice, equal educational opportunity, and the schooling of students of color and low-SES backgrounds become aware of Payne's work—and similar entrepreneurs who profit from informing educators about the "culture of poverty."[42] Furthermore, it is incumbent for teacher educators, and concerned allies in education, to introduce our preservice teacher students, counselors, and administrators to Payne's theoretical underpinnings and intervention proposals *vis-à-vis* the education of low-SES students, and to encourage these future leaders to engage this introduction in a critical fashion.

Although Payne's *Framework* is heavily based on the long discredited culture of poverty notion and the oppressive nature of deficit thinking, her empire is unlikely to implode on its own. Critiques, such as the ones cited in this chapter, must continue with critical analysis, scientific scrutiny, and the discussion of workable, democratic school reform. As Professor Anita P. Bohn advises: "Ruby Payne has flown under the radar for too long. It's time for teachers and administrators to take a critical look at her immensely popular message" (2006, p. 2).

Epilogue

Shortly after I completed this chapter, Randy Bomer—my University of Texas at Austin colleague—informed me (R. Bomer, personal communication, May 18, 2009) that Ruby Payne (2009) had responded to the Bomer et al. (2008) critique of Payne's (2005) *Framework* in which Bomer and associates (2008) provide a critique of Payne's book, underscoring that it lacks scientific competence.[43] In Payne's (2009) response to the critique of her *Framework* by Bomer et al. (2008), she asserts that the authors in their refutation of her work are, for example, narrowly focused by relying on "social determinism." Also, Payne (2009) criticizes Bomer et al. (2008) for noting that she has no valid research findings to support her claims about mindsets of the poor.[44] Another criticism raised by Payne (2009) of Bomer et al. (2008) is in regard to the authors' use of the deficit thinking model in describing Payne's (2005) *Framework*. In a sweeping statement, and *sans* independent scientific support, Payne (2009, p. 2) asserts:

> The authors [Bomer et al., 2008] apply the criticism of "deficit model" to my work and define it using Valencia. . . . As Valencia (as cited in Bomer et al., 2008, p. 2523) states: "Deficit thinking is a person-centered explanation of school failure among individuals linked to group membership . . . [and] is largely based on imputation and little documentation." *The irony of this is that the "deficit model" is a theoretical model in itself that has little scientific research to support it* [italics added]. I can say that the glass is half full of water or half empty. Regardless of the language I assign to it, the level of water in the glass does not change. *So to assign the label "deficit model" is simply a theoretical construct* [italics added] (p. 2).

Given that Payne (2009) summarily dismisses the heuristic value of the deficit thinking model that I and my contributors have extensively studied (Valencia, 1997a), I felt obligated to challenge her claim. In my response, I focus on (a) the theoretical nature of the deficit thinking model and (b) the applicability of the model in understanding the linkages among deficit thinking, educability perceptions of poor students and students of color, the politics of oppression, the practice of schooling, and school failure (Valencia, 2009).

In regard to theory, I point out that although Payne's (2009) assertion that the deficit thinking model "has little scientific research to support it" (p. 2) has some veracity, she fails to understand that deficit thinking is grounded in a *confluence of science and ideology,* which leads to a variant called "pseudo-science" in which numerous researchers strongly believe that their findings and conclusions are valid (see chapter 1, present book).

Regarding the applicability of the deficit thinking model, I comment on Payne's fallacious claim that "The label 'deficit model' is simply a theoretical construct" (p. 2). On the contrary—as I underscore in chapter 1 (present volume)—the model demonstrates great utility in understanding the connection between theory and practice.[45] I also write in my response to Payne (2009) that fortunately there are numerous scholars who also discuss the prescriptive dimension of the deficit thinking paradigm, but they do so from a proactive, constructive perspective with the goal of dismantling deficit thinking (see chapter 5, present book). For example, there is the topic of pre-service teacher education, in which college students exhibit deficit thinking toward poor students and students of color. As a case in point, in my response (Valencia, 2009) I briefly discuss the work of teacher educator Sherry Marx (2006) who has proved successful in identifying deficit thinking among her preservice teacher education students—and more importantly—in developing workable interventions to help students recognize and dismantle their deficit thinking (see chapter 5, present volume). In sum, for Ruby Payne (2009) to maintain that the deficit thinking model has no scholarly utility is a baseless claim (Valencia, 2009). And so the scholarly struggle against deficit thinking continues.

4

At-Risk Students or At-Risk Schools?

My goal in this chapter is to provide a comprehensive coverage of the social construction of the "at-risk" term,[1] a deficit thinking notion. I do so by organizing this discussion around four sections.

Historical Origins of the At-Risk Notion

Laosa (1984) notes that in every epoch over the past four centuries, specific populations of children have been determined to be "at-risk" for having problems. These groups comprised children, for example, who had severe diseases, physical handicaps, mental retardation, and emotional disturbances. Such groups also included children deemed delinquent, antisocial, indigent, neglected, illegitimate, abused, and destitute.[2] As Laosa comments, such children identified at risk (then and now) "thus become a major focus of social concern and public responsibility" (p. 1). A good historical example of this concern for children at risk is what transpired during the U.S. colonial period with the Puritans. A major societal task involved the insurance of children's salvation, typically via the acts of "baptism or conversion" (Wollons, 1993, p. x). Indeed, adults considered children's salvation to be a high priority. Wollons comments:

> Puritans considered children to be depraved from birth, and the child at risk was one who might not ultimately find a home with God. While risks to children's health were high, control over a child's health was minimal, making salvation an even greater imperative. Insuring salvation was the responsibility of the parents; fathers, as a matter of law and custom, had absolute authority over the child and were responsible for instilling discipline, obedience, and self-denial in the child, all essential to a child's ultimate salvation.
>
> (p. x)

Another useful framework for understanding the historical contexts or forerunners of the modern at-risk construct is offered by Swadener (1990) who identifies the etiological frames for the term in a number of disciplines. These include: special education, child welfare, sociology, social work, medicine and public health, early childhood education, developmental psychology, demography, and economics. In her article, Swadener (1990) focuses on three of these disciplines. Next, I provide a synopsis of each of these three disciplines' contributions in shaping the construct of at risk.

Medical and Public Health

As Swadener (1990) notes, it appears that this model—sometimes referred to as the "epidemiological model"—is the most conspicuous and straightforward (also, see Richardson, Casanova, Placier, & Guilfoyle, 1989). This framework involves themes, for example, as: kindergarten screenings; epidemiology of disorders during childhood; health and nutrition programs for the poor; medical intervention for hyperactivity; immunizations against specific contagious diseases. Swadener (1990) remarks that the anchoring of the at-risk notion in a medical model focuses on "prevention, early intervention, and developmental screenings" (p. 22). A medical example she provides regarding the intervention for academically at-risk students is Operation Head Start, an early childhood education program established for low-SES children (particularly of color) in the 1960s War on Poverty. Deficit thinking helped drive these initial early education programs, also viewed as the compensatory education strategy. Pearl (1991, p. 285) notes:

> The dominant theoretical explanation for disproportionate school failure of the poor and the minority was "accumulated environmental deficit"—that is, students entered school with a build-up of handicaps incurred in early formative years that would be irreversible unless significant action was taken when children were very young. . . . If, however, intervention begins early enough the child can recover from the lack of intellectual stimulation at home and the dearth of language. . . . The compensation for the deficits that are hypothesized to have occurred before a child enters school results in the leveling of the playing field giving everyone an equal chance at a desirable future.

Swadener (1990) comments that Head Start and similar early intervention strategies sought to prevent "later school failure (anticipated 'disease') through an early 'shot in the arm,' academically and socially speaking" (p. 22).

Child Psychology and Early Education

This theme is somewhat related to the medical and public health model in that young children at risk remain a focus. Yet, the child psychology and early education model tends to focus on *intervention*, whereas the medical model places greater emphasis on *prevention*. Swadener (1990) comments that the former discipline's historical etiological bases of at risk are, for example: the 1860s German-style kindergartens,[3] compulsory schooling, and compensatory education. Swadener (1990) remarks that a number of scholars who have written on early childhood education and these historical developments frequently focus on the powerful role of the incipient reformers ("social ameliorists") in regard to the establishment of infant schools, early public schools, and kindergartens for low-SES and immigrant children. These social ameliorists centered on "child saving" and, as such, formed the basis of the "at-risk" construction.

Child Welfare and Social Policy

It is this category of historical contributions of the construction of the at-risk notion that has the closest connection to the deficit thinking theme of the present book. Swadener (1990) mentions that it is in this discipline, which is shaped by sociopolitical forces (e.g., social work; economics; political science; demography), that "the *deficit model*, [italics added] child-saving slogans, recurrent references or insinuations of cultural deprivation, and labeling and analysis of a growing number of family and community risk variables have been most thoroughly articulated, analyzed, and promoted" (pp. 24–25). Some of the historical roots of the at-risk notion Swadener lists are: forced school segregation of Black and Mexican American students (Klarman, 2004; Kluger, 2004; Ogletree, 2004; Valencia, 2008, chapter 1); language suppression of Mexican American students (Valencia, 2008, chapter 4); culture of poverty influences on the War on Poverty (chapter 3, present book); the "culturally deprived" and dysfunctional families of the 1960s (Pearl, 1997b); emphasis on child abuse and neglect; welfare reform; focus on teenage pregnancy and drug abuse. Swadener (1990) also notes that an anti-deficit thinking paradigm became a part of the at-risk discourse of the child welfare and social policy discussions. The "institutional deficiency model" articulated via the work of heterodox scholars provided forums challenging the deficit thinking nature of the at-risk construct. Such scholars have called for comprehensive, systemic schooling transformations.[4]

The 1980s Excellence Movement: Framers and Critics

Although the "excellence movement" for U.S. school reform can be traced to the 1980s, one has to go back a decade to understand that some reform continuity flowed from the 1970s to the 1980s. Falling standardized test scores characterized a number of students' (particularly low-SES pupils of color) academic performance throughout the 1970s (Airasian, 1988; Pipho, 1986). Beginning in the late 1970s, reformers advanced a wide range of improvements as responses to the perceived need to improve educational quality in the country. The strategies that surfaced as the winners can be characterized best as "new forms of standardized testing and accountability programs" (Airasian, p. 305). Given that a growing number of assessment programs at the state level, coupled with additional state laws that focused on minimal student and teacher competency, led to no perceptible upward trend in achievement patterns in the 1970s, the seed of the modern epoch of the excellence movement began to germinate—eventually maturing in the early 1980s (Pipho).

Ground zero for the 1980s excellence movement can be traced to August 26, 1981, when Terrell E. Bell, Secretary of Education (1981–1984) during the middle period of President Ronald W. Reagan's administration, created the National Commission on Excellence in Education. David P. Gardner, University of Utah President and University of California President-Elect, served as Chair of the 18-member Commission. Six particular charges comprised the Commission's charter, calling for:

- Assessing the quality of teaching and learning in our Nation's public and private schools, colleges, and universities;
- comparing American schools and colleges with those of other advanced nations;
- studying the relationship between college admissions requirements and student achievement in high school;
- identifying educational programs which result in notable student success in college;
- assessing the degree to which major social and education changes in the last quarter century have affected student achievement; and
- defining problems which must be faced and overcome if we are successfully to pursue the course of excellence in education.
  (National Commission on Excellence in Education, 1983, pp. 1–2)

The Commission's charter instructed it to pay specific attention to teenagers in high school.

On April 26, 1983, the Commission released its brief, but powerful report, *A Nation at Risk: The Imperative for Educational Reform* (National Commission on Excellence in Education, 1983). The authors of the report intended it to serve "as much as an open letter to the American people as it is a report to the Secretary of Education" (p. 6). Briefly into its text, the widely circulated report uses a war metaphor in a scathing attack on contemporary U.S. education:

Our Nation is at risk. Our once unchallenged preeminence in commerce, industry, science, and technological innovation is being overtaken by competitors throughout the world. . . . We report to the American people that while we can take justifiable pride in what our schools and colleges have historically accomplished and contributed to the United States and the well-being of its people, the educational foundations of our society are presently being eroded by a rising tide of mediocrity that threatens our very future as a Nation and a people. What was unimaginable a generation ago has begun to occur—others are matching and surpassing our educational attainments. *If an unfriendly foreign power had attempted to impose on America the mediocre educational performance that exists today, we might well have viewed it as an act of war* [italics added]. As it stands, we have allowed this to happen to ourselves. We have even

squandered the gains in student achievement made in the wake of the Sputnik challenge. Moreover, we have dismantled essential support systems which helped make those gains possible. We have, in effect, been committing an act of unthinking, unilateral educational disarmament.
(National Commission on Excellence in Education, 1983, p. 5)

In doing its work, the Commission relied, for the most part, on information from five sources: (a) 40 commissioned papers from experts with diverse educational expertise (pp. 44–48); (b) testimony, for example, by students, teachers, parents, administrators, scholars, and public officials given at a number of meetings with the full Commission present—that is, panel discussions, public hearings, and a symposium; (c) current analyses of problems in education; (d) letters from concerned administrators, teachers, and citizens; (e) scrutiny of noteworthy educational programs and promising educational approaches.

In *A Nation at Risk*, the commissioners' conception of "risk" has a strong global economic theme, underscoring that risk is not only due to Japanese technology in making more efficient automobiles than U.S. manufacturers, and not only because the South Koreans have built the most proficient steel mill, and not only due to the development of superior German machine tools. In addition, these technological developments signal a redistribution of educated capability throughout the world. The report explains: "Knowledge, learning, information, and skilled intelligence are the new raw materials of international commerce and are today spreading throughout the world as vigorously as miracle drugs, synthetic fertilizers, as blue jeans did earlier" (p. 7). As such, the commissioners note that if the U.S. is to maintain and improve its slight competitive edge in global markets, the nation must make a commitment to investing in and reforming its educational system for the type of learning that is a requirement for success in the "information age" the country is entering (p. 7). The report states that the time has come for producing extremely skilled workers in recently developed fields, such as computer knowledge, laser technology, robotics, and radical technological transformations in many occupations (e.g., medical science; food processing; health care; energy production).

In order to attain the above technological advances, *A Nation at Risk* calls for "excellence" in the educational system, which the report defines to mean several interrelated aspects. First, at the *individual learner* level, one must perform at the upper boundary of personal limits—not only in school, but in the workplace. Second, at the *school or college* level, goals must be set at high expectations for success. Third, at the *society* level, policies must be adopted to help prepare its citizens for skill development that will be utilized to respond to the challenges of a world that is rapidly changing. In addition to the goal of excellence, the report does devote some discussion to the "twin goal" of "equity" (i.e., equitable educational treatment of all, regardless of race or class). Such discourse, however, amounts to lip service. The major goal of *A Nation at Risk* is to develop a "Learning Society" in which minimum standards are no longer tolerable, and schools and colleges must strive to become of exceedingly great merit to reverse the current decline in technological supremacy. This failure by the Commission to discuss equity issues in greater detail will be covered later.

In light of the commissioners' conclusion that educational performance was on the decline due to "disturbing inadequacies in the way the educational process itself is often conducted" (National Commission on Excellence in Education, 1983, p. 18), the report proposed five recommendations for reform. A common theme that runs through the proposals is an emphasis on quantity—more is better. In brief, the recommendations call for changes in:

Content

A Nation at Risk comments that high school curricula have been transformed to a "homogenized, diluted, and diffused" program of study that no longer maintains a principal purpose. The report asserts that students in large numbers have drifted "from vocational and college preparatory programs to 'general track' courses" (National Commission on Excellence in Education, 1983, p. 18). As such, the report recommends that high school requirements for graduation include the "Five New Basics" (i.e., specified number of years in English, mathematics, science, social studies, and computer science; p. 24).

Standards and Expectations

The report notes, for example, that homework has decreased, the time in class spent on various classes (i.e., chemistry; biology) is less than that in other industrialized countries, "minimum competency" examinations have become the "maximum" in expectations, and publishers have "written down" textbooks to continually lower reading levels (pp. 20–21). To counter these concerns, *A Nation at Risk* recommends that the educational pipeline adopt more demanding and measurable standards and increased standards for student academic performance and conduct. Furthermore, institutions of higher education need to raise their admission requirements.

Time

Somewhat related to the above concern involving declines in time spent on learning, the report points out that U.S. schools, in comparison to schools in other industrialized countries (e.g., England), provide considerably less time on school work, homework, and development of study skills. To correct these deficiencies, the report recommends that substantially more time be allocated to learning the New Basics. Thus, this means that more effective utilization is needed for the school day, and a longer school day or school year should be implemented.

Teaching

A Nation at Risk claims that teachers in U.S. schools are drawn from the bottom ranks of graduating students (both in high school and college), teachers are underpaid, and they are poorly prepared in substantive courses (at the expense of "methods" courses), and severe shortages exist in fields such as science and mathematics. In light of these problems, the report recommends a number of proposals—such as: higher standards for admission to teacher preparation programs; the development of career ladders; involvement of master teachers in designing teacher education programs and in supervising beginning teachers in the classroom, and the implementation of merit-based salary increases.

Leadership and Fiscal Support

The report recommends that local principals and superintendents play critical roles in garnering community support for the Commission's proposals. Furthermore, the primary responsibility for school financing and governance should lie in the hands of school board members and local and state officials. Also, the federal government's task is to take on the primary responsibility to pin down the national interest in education and provide the ultimate leadership to address the concerns raised in *A Nation at Risk*.

In sum, *A Nation at Risk* constitutes the beginning of the modern era of the excellence movement, with its strong message for reform along the lines of schooling increases (e.g., more: course requirements; homework; time for learning; qualified teachers), and higher standards. The 1983 release of *A Nation at Risk* triggered a rash of concurring national reports on school reform by, for example, the Carnegie Forum on Education and the Economy, the Committee for Economic Development, the Twentieth Century Fund, and the National Governors' Association. By year's end in 1984, 30 national reports had been produced (Cross, 1984). Lytle (1990, p. 199) comments that:

> All of these reports began with the premise that the continuing health of our economy and the preservation of the American way of life were contingent on more effective schooling and a development of our human resources. All used Japan and Western Europe as contrasts to illustrate the shortcomings of American education.

Very soon after the framers released the national reports on school reform, a number of states (e.g., Arkansas; California; Georgia; Texas) joined the excellence movement with comprehensive legislative mandates, with barely any facet of schooling untouched (Pipho, 1986). Furthermore, over 300 task forces in a number of states had been organized in order to study public education concerns (Cross, 1984). These state reform pursuits had at least two principal themes: more rigorous standards for student academic performance and greater recognition and increased standards for teachers. By 1986, 45 states and the District of Columbia had implemented higher standards for students (e.g., for high school graduation), and 35 states had required testing for the initial certification of teachers (Pipho). These numerous reports of the 1980s excellence movement did not go uncontested. Advocacy groups for poor students and students of color, in particular, quickly followed with a number of reports criticizing the "mainstream" reports. I turn next to these critiques.

Barriers to Excellence: Our Children at Risk (National Coalition of Advocates for Students, 1985) surfaced as the earliest of the advocacy documents.[5] Co-chairs Harold Howe II (Commissioner of Education in the 1960s in Lyndon B. Johnson's administration) and Marion Wright Edelman (President of the Children's Defense Fund) presided over public hearings for 15 days in 10 cities during 1983–1984. In its first page of text, *Barriers to Excellence* challenges the positioning of the at-risk notion—locating it from a modifier identifying a nation that has lost its technological dominance and superiority, to a modifier of failing schools.

> Our study began with a different perspective from other recent efforts to understand and improve public education in the United States. Our approach was to determine the changes needed in the schools by examining the problems of young people whose learning is hampered by schools that do not serve them adequately; by expectations on the part of educators that they will not or cannot succeed; by denial of access to special needs programs; by fiscal policies that limit educational services; and by inattention to the difficulties young people face in moving from school to work. *Students in schools where these conditions exist are clearly "at risk" in our social and economic system* [italics added].
>
> (National Coalition of Advocates for Students, 1985, p. iv)

The language of *Barriers to Excellence* is unswervingly direct in its criticism of the educational system, asserting that discrimination and differential treatment *vis-à-vis* students abound in public schools—along the lines of class, race, culture, gender, and special education. The report also discusses various barriers to excellence, for example: inflexibility of school structure, abuses of ability grouping and tracking, misuses of testing, narrowness of curriculum and teaching practices, lack of democratic governance, and lack of early childhood education programs.

In regard to recommendations for school reform, *Barriers to Excellence* strongly disagrees with the more the better theme of *A Nation at Risk* (National Commission on Excellence in Education, 1983). The former report asserts that the latter document's reform proposals fail to address adequately the basic pedagogical and curriculum problems of the nation's schools. *Barriers to Excellence* remarks that *A Nation at Risk*'s reform suggestions are misdirected:

> For the most part, they are quantitative solutions that focus on the numbers of minutes of instructional time allowed and the numbers of

credits for graduation required. But, in fact, the problems are qualitative. They have to do with the content being taught, as well as the process of teaching and learning that is going on during that "instructional time" or "credit hour." *Until the qualitative issues become central to the debate such reforms will be misdirected* [italics added].

(National Coalition of Advocates for Students, 1985, p. 52)

As such, *Barriers to Excellence* focuses on systemic reform recommendations, including, for example, such aspects as follows among the report's 14 goals: ample federal, state, and local funding of programs for low-SES children in order to minimize class discrimination; eliminating racially identifiable classes, programs, and schools; minimizing discrimination against language minorities (i.e., need to implement bilingual education programs and foster the value and importance of bilingualism); ending of rigid curriculum differentiation; implementing early childhood education programs.

A number of scholars have also critiqued the excellence movement of the 1980s. For example, Apple (1986) states that reports such as *A Nation at Risk* "are as much political as they are educational documents" (p. 175), with the intent of reconstructing a consensus over a partly broken educational system during the 1970s. This call, notes Apple, involved the using of language couched in the "common good" that seeks to provide something for everybody, but with particular emphasis on mobilizing the powerful to attain specified goals (as seen in *A Nation at Risk*). Apple remarks that the language of the excellence reports necessitates an analysis not particularly for their veracity, but in their "rhetorical use" (p. 175). In a similar vein, Stedman and Smith (1983) characterize the excellence reports as political documents in which polemics take the place of reason and empirical substantiation. The authors assert that "Rather than carefully marshalling facts to prove their case, they [the reports] present a litany of charges without examining the veracity of their evidence or its uses" (p. 176).[6] Other critics of the excellence movement—Gitlin, Margonis, and Brunjes (1993)—comment that the blatantly top-down nature of the excellence reports focuses on raising standards so that those students who are already achieving success might perform even better. Another critique of *A Nation at Risk* and concurring reports is offered by Reyes and Valencia (1993).[7] The authors assert that these reports make a number of questionable assumptions. For example, schools are marketplaces. That is, schools are conceptualized as markets where competition and choice would somehow take care of the problems experienced in schools. Another assumption is that schools are homogenous. The excellence movement assumes that all schools are alike, driven by the same structures and technology, and have few or no ties to the local communities that support them. Of course, this assumption flies in the face of the U.S. school reality. Schools are similar at the macrolevel but different within. These differences are determined by the community's ability to provide the structural and technological means for their operation. Some schools have inadequate facilities, lower quality of laboratories, fewer incentives to motivate teachers to perform at higher levels, and fewer human resources to enhance the quality of curriculum and instruction than other schools.

One of the most interesting treatises on the excellence movement—and one that is particularly germane to the focus of the present book (i.e., deficit thinking)—is proffered by Frank Margonis in his article "The Cooptation of 'At-Risk': Paradoxes of Policy Criticism" (1992). Margonis explains that the term at-risk was first used by critics of the excellence movement.[8] These critics sought to move educators and policymakers away from "the belief that educational success and failure hinge primarily on individual effort" (Margonis, 1992, p. 343), a view popularized by excellence reforms. Critics contended that school failure was largely systemically based. Margonis further argues that the term was co-opted by the proponents of the excellence movement that it was first used to challenge. He claims that the co-optation of the at-risk notion has done the reverse of what critics of the excellence movement intended. That is, critics sought to use the term at-risk to demonstrate the short sightedness of the movement, arguing that standardization in curricula (tracking) and testing—coupled with large workloads of teachers—created insensitive and impersonal school environments and thus placed students in jeopardy for school failure. Nevertheless, excellence proponents won the semantic war over the terminology. As Margonis notes, "The educational goals embodied in the ideas of excellence became the standard, and students who could not reach these goals came to be at risk" (p. 344). Margonis further notes that the co-optation of the at-risk notion constitutes deficit thinking. He states:

> The transformation of the concept *at risk* into a deficit notion has been accomplished as policymakers have conveniently neglected the account of institutional injustice that previously accompanied the term. *What was an alternative to deficit thought—a way of blaming institutions rather than victims—has become a new and potentially more resilient version of deficit thinking* [italics added]. The redefinition of at risk has occurred as the concept was appropriated by national reformers who have subordinated its meaning to an administrative agenda. Concerned with preparing a work force and preventing the enlargement of welfare rolls, national leaders have aggressively adopted the concept *at risk* as a means of identifying failure before it occurs and shaping students likely to fail into productive and dependable citizens.
>
> (Margonis, 1992, p. 344)

Early At-Risk Discourse

In this and the following section ("Contemporary At-Risk Discourse"), I attempt to capture a scholarly sense of discussions about the at-risk discourse.

My intent is not to provide a comprehensive review of this corpus of publications. The literature base on at-risk students is immense, thus I seek to get a sense of how scholars, from 1983 to 2008, communicate their perspectives about the at-risk notion. My focus is to obtain an understanding of how scholars view academic risk—predominantly from a student-centered *or* a systemic perspective.

In early 2009, I undertook a search of the Education Resource Information Center (ERIC) database, the most extensive digital library of educational literature in the world.[9] I delimited the search to "at-risk students" and "academic achievement" keywords in order to focus on academic performance of at-risk students, and to avoid literature that centered on, for example, social competence of students (Luthar, 1991), newborns and older children at risk for later special education placement (Goldberg, McLaughlin, Grossi, Tytun, & Blum, 1992; Campbell, Goldstein, Schaefer, & Ramey, 1991), and risk factors for drug use among students (Vega, Zimmerman, Warheit, Apospori, & Gil, 1993). Furthermore, I delimited the search to school-age children and youths by using not "higher education or two year college students or college freshmen or college" keywords. The search results are presented in Figure 4.1.

From 1983 to 2008, the search produced 1,255 hits. The number of citations that appear during the first several years after the 1983 release of *A Nation at Risk* (National Commission on Excellence in Education, 1983) is scant. Figure 4.1 also shows that the number of at-risk student citations peaks between 1990 and 1993 ($n = 341$; 27% of total 1,255). From 1994 to 2008, the number of citations reaches a relative plateau, with a yearly average of close to 50. In regard to the "early" and "contemporary" periods of at-risk student citations, I arbitrarily make the break at the year 1999 for the trend analysis.

In the following discussion of the "Early At-Risk Discourse" period, I first focus on representative literature that views the at-risk notion from a

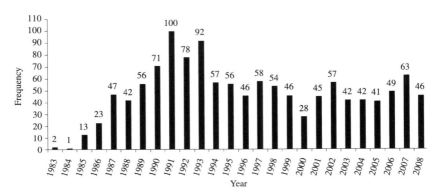

Figure 4.1 Number of At-Risk Student Citations (1983–2008).

Source: ERIC database.

student-centered perspective. Then, I briefly cover examples of scholarly work of this period that offers a systemic point of view of school failure. In the 1989 edited book, *Effective Programs for Students at Risk*, Robert E. Slavin and contributors offer a number of discussions about programs the authors state, based on empirical evidence, are effective in improving academic achievement for students deemed at risk for school failure. These programs include, for example, effective preschool (Karweit, 1989a), kindergarten (Karweit, 1989b), and pullout programs (Madden & Slavin, 1989) for students at risk. At risk, by the way, is defined in one possible manner by Slavin (1989) as: "Students who are at risk are those who, on the basis of several risk factors, are unlikely to graduate from high school" (p. 5). Slavin (1989) also notes that included among these student risk factors are grade retention, low achievement, poor attendance, low SES, and attendance at schools with a substantial number of poor pupils. During the early at-risk discourse period, researchers frequently identified at-risk students via an inventory of factors believed to predispose some students for school failure. For example, Frymier and Gansneder (1989) report the results of the collaborative Phi Delta Kappa (PDK) Study of Students at Risk.[10] The major assumption grounding the investigation was that students are at risk if they have the probability to fail—"either in school or life" (p. 142). In the PDK study, researchers collected data from participating students, teachers, and counselors, in which questions regarding 45 risk factors (suggested by previous studies) framed the interviews. Frymier and Gansneder report that of 22,018 students attending 276 schools, between 25% and 35% had a serious at-risk status—that is, "over the line" on 6 of the 45 factors, for example, having experienced grade retention, course failure, school suspension, and having a language other than English as the primary spoken home language (other non-academic factors include drug abuse, sexual abuse, and pregnancy).

In sum, although the use of an inventory of indicators to identify at-risk students may have some utility in flagging pupils who have a probability of serious schooling problems, such a procedure is misdirected because it masks the presence of systemic bases of academic failure such as schools with inferior resources and unqualified teachers. Furthermore, given that at-risk students are concentrated among pupils of color, from poverty households, single-parent families, and immigrant populations, the at-risk inventory approach has the strong tendency to stereotype. As Levin (1992) notes, we must be cognizant that at-risk factors "are only *indicators* of at-risk populations rather than definitions." He continues by remarking that many students from these groups are not at risk for school failure, "and we must take care not to stereotype children from these populations in a mindless way that precludes their educational success" (p. 285).

Baker and Sansone (1990) conducted a dropout prevention program at an urban high school ($N = 1,632$ students; 75% White, 25% Black). The authors, with the assistance of school staff, identified 70 at-risk students via a number of typical indicators: cutting classes, failing grades, having drug or alcohol problems, and exhibiting noncompliant behavior. Baker and Sansone developed and implemented four highly student-centered, authoritarian interventions, to wit: (a) individual accommodations (e.g., student contracts; sign-in system); (b) available school-level structures (e.g., a segregated homeroom for at-risk ninth graders; school-wide "sweeps" to investigate students' location); (c) district-level structures (e.g., transfer to alternative schools); (d) community-level structures (e.g., liaison outreach with community groups, such as juvenile court, group homes, and drug and alcohol treatment). Baker and Sansone's draconian interventions did not prove very successful, as 45% of the students prematurely left school (10 students dropped out at 17 years of age; records of 21 students could not be found).

Another example of scholars from the early at-risk discourse period who utilize inventories of at-risk indicators, as well as advocating student-centered interventions, is seen in Louis J. Kruger's 1990 edited book, *Promoting Success with At-Risk Students: Emerging Perspectives and Practical Approaches* (Kruger, 1990a). In this volume, the contributors center on fixing at-risk students by proposing student-focused interventions, for example: behavioral self-management (Mace & Shea, 1990), contingency contracts (Kruger, 1990b), applied behavior analysis (Piersel & Lee, 1990), and reduction of academic related anxiety (Huberty, 1990). Still another example of student-centered construction of academic risk during the early at-risk discourse time frame is presented in Swanson (1991). She is rather explicit in her deficit thinking, remarking that the academic achievement problems of at-risk students are rooted in the cyclical nature of the life of low-SES families (reminiscent of the culture of poverty concept). That is, low-SES parents produce children who fail in school, and who in turn, beget children who also fail. Furthermore, Swanson asserts that a large number of Hispanic English-limited students have disabilities (she does not mention which type), and for such students, English has little usefulness in their everyday lives. Swanson also delves deeply into the deficit thinking claim that low-SES parents do not value education:

> Many at-risk students today come from homes that do not have the same reverence for our institutions and desire for an education. Their parents do not have the same respect for teachers, and they don't demand excellence in the schools or from their children. They don't place work ahead of television, telephone, and hanging out. They don't communicate to their children that educational achievement will pay big dividends in their lives. They don't want to hassle their children about schoolwork and leave motivation to the schools. You bet it's tough to teach under such conditions.
>
> (Swanson, 1991, p. 74)

At this juncture, I shift to representative coverage of scholars during the early at-risk discourse period who viewed academic risk from a systemic or structural analysis. This perspective is presented by a number of contributors in Barbara Z. Presseisen's book, *At-Risk Students and Thinking: Perspectives from Research* (Presseisen, 1988a). For example, Presseisen (1988b) offers a cogent argument that students identified as at-risk certainly can improve and attain success. She maintains that the problems faced by such students are exogenous to the learner, rooted in the schools that are supposed to assist him or her to acquire knowledge and become competent. In rejecting genetic pathology and cultural deprivation models of deficit thinking, Presseisen (1988b) asserts that academic risk can be mitigated if interventions are based on research-based knowledge, and a shift by educators from a focus on the circumstances of students' daily lives to a centering of what students can achieve. Mirman, Swartz, and Barell (1988)—authors of a chapter in Presseisen (1988a)—assert that schools must provide equal educational opportunity, teachers need to share control of power with their students, and schools must be restructured to allow teachers to become change agents in collaboration with their students.

Toward the end of the early at-risk discourse period, Beth B. Swadener and Sally Lubeck's edited book appeared, *Children and Families "at Promise": Deconstructing the Discourse of Risk* (1995a).[11] At the time, the volume represented the most comprehensive analysis and critique of the at-risk notion. Swadener and Lubeck (1995b) note that the at-risk concept is based on a deficit model, frequently taking the embodiment of blaming the victim in which the systemic societal practices of exclusion and oppression are ignored. That is, the use of the "at-risk" label is very troublesome because it is a classist, racist, ableist, and sexist term—a 1990s rendering of the 1960s cultural deficit framework that locates pathologies in the individual, family, and community, rather than focusing on institutional arrangements (e.g., White privilege; political conservatism; class stratification) that generate and perpetuate inequality. As is the case of deficit thinking in general, the notion of at risk fails to acknowledge the strengths, competencies, and promise of low-SES children and parents. The contributors in Swadener and Lubeck's volume speak forcefully to this point of "at promise" regarding African American, Latino, Asian American, and American Indian children and their families.[12]

Contemporary At-Risk Discourse

Based on the data presented in Figure 4.1 (present chapter), mean calculations of the number of at-risk citations per year for the early at-risk discourse period (1983–1999) and for the contemporary at-risk time frame (2000–2008) are 50 and 46, respectively. As such, this is evidence that scholarly discourse concerning the at-risk notion had been fairly steady over the past 2½ decades. In this section, I cover representative contemporary scholarly at-risk discourse that proffers student-centered and systemically-based perspectives on the at-risk concept.

An example of a student-centered investigation of the contemporary at-risk discourse period is by Solberg, Carlstrom, Howard, and Jones (2007). The authors, in this non-intervention study, used a cluster analysis design to identify at-risk youth in a predominantly low-income high school, the majority of students being of color (67% of the participants identified as Latino/Latina). Solberg et al. used five self-report measures (e.g., high school intrinsic motivation; exposure to violence; high school self efficacy) to classify five at-risk profiles (ranging from most vulnerable [high] to not-at-risk [low]). Subsequently, the authors used several measures (i.e., health status; high school stress; academic outcomes [GPA]; retention status) to examine differences between the cluster groups. Solberg et al. report that exposure to violence constituted the distinguishing feature in three of the five at-risk profiles. As is the case of other student-centered studies of academic risk, Solberg et al. did not include any systemic factors for study (e.g., teacher quality; school funding) in their investigation.

A number of contributors in Mavis G. Sanders' edited volume, *Schooling Students Placed At Risk* (2000), offer systemic-based analyses of students put at risk for school failure. A. Wade Boykin (2000), who writes the Foreword, notes that the "at-risk" notion, which has long been used to label low-SES students of color, is undergoing a paradigm shift. He remarks that the label, a deficit conception, is gradually being viewed by advocates as students "placed at risk" for academic failure. Describing characteristics of an anti-deficit thinking perspective, Boykin notes:

> Referring to students as at risk effectively locates the problem of schooling "inside" the children or in their putative problematic home and community circumstances. In this manner, students and their families are conceived to have afflictions that must be cured if positive schooling outcomes are to accrue. In defining the problem of schooling this way, the prescription most often is to repair the child or fix the family in some way.
>
> (Boykin, 2000, p. xii)

Franklin (2000), contributor to Sanders' (2000) volume, maintains that the epidemiological inventory model to discern academic risk—which has some utility in identifying student and familial features that make academic performance arduous—still when used alone focuses on individual risk and vulnerability for school failure. On the other hand, Franklin advocates the use of an ecological framework that has the potential to recognize (a) families that foster at-promise youth (e.g., via inculcating favorable values about education; setting homework routines); (b) schools that foster at-promise youth (e.g., via teachers who are informed about the structures and systemic factors that shape urban communities and schools; a determined principal who helps set a school climate of high expectations); (c) communities that foster at-promise youth (e.g., via support systems developed by social service providers, churches, and businesses).

Another example of a publication in which some scholars proffer systemic analyses of the at-risk notion is the edited volume by Sam Stringfield and Deborah Land, *Educating At-Risk Students: One Hundred-First Yearbook of the National Society for the Study of Education* (2002). Contributing to this volume, Land and Legters (2002, p. 3) assert:

> Troubled by the classist and racist implications and potentially stigma-tizing effects of the cultural-deficit risk model implied by targeted compensatory education programs, educators and researchers welcomed the shift in focus away from individual student characteristics toward factors that characterize school systems and the political and economic contexts in which they operate.

In a similar vein, Padrón, Waxman, and Rivera (2002)—contributors to the Stringfield and Land book—comment that deficit frameworks used to examine academic risk focus on individual students and their families, instead of the circumstances that place such pupils at risk. Padrón et al., citing the work of Waxman (1992), note that certain aspects of "at-risk environments" are implicated in shaping school failure, such as: teachers' low expectations for certain students (e.g., Latinos), student alienation, and unresponsive class-room practices of teachers.

One of the most recent publications on at-risk students is *Saving Our Students, Saving Our Schools* by Robert D. Barr and William H. Parrett (2008)—which appears to be a textbook for preservice teachers. The book's subtitle is *50 Proven Strategies for Helping Underachieving Students and Improv-ing Schools*, a discussion which takes up 92% of the book's text pages. Each of the strategies—most of which are about 3–4 pages long and presented in a cookbook-like fashion—consists of a "Research" section (*sans* citations)[13] and a "Take Action" section. It is difficult to understand Barr and Parrett's perspec-tive on the at-risk notion. On one hand, the authors discuss a number of struc-tural factors implicated in how schools fail students and produce low academic achievement (factors such as: inequalities in school funding, grade retention, unsupportive teachers, and curricular tracking). Yet, at times, Barr and Parrett engage in deficit thinking. A case in point is seen in strategy #6 ("Work With The Externally Centered Student"). Here, the authors discuss how the "culture of poverty" predisposes people to be "externally centered" (see Conrath, 2001). Reminiscent of the pathology, fatalism, and hopelessness attributes ascribed to poor people (see chapter 3, present volume), Barr and Parrett (2008, p. 70) claim:

> Children of poverty grow up being externally centered and believing that external events control their lives. They see no relationship between hard

work, sacrifice, self-reliance, and success. These students often arrive at school with little or no concept of educational success and the reality that this success often depends on their efforts to conform to classroom procedures.

In regard to intervention for the "externally centered student," Barr and Parrett (in the "Take Action" for strategy #6) provide some advice for preservice teachers. For example, "learn about the culture of poverty" and "help poor students understand the hidden rules of the middle class." These two points are similar to the recommendations Ruby Payne gives (see chapter 3, present book), but Payne is not cited at all. In any event, how is a preservice teacher supposed to interpret Barr and Parrett's book—from a systemic or deficit thinking lens?

At-Risk Schools

This section speaks to a major paradigm shift about the at-risk notion *vis-à-vis* students who are experiencing academic problems. An anti-deficit perspective asserts that it is morally unacceptable and scientifically indefensible to hold students and their parents accountable for academic success, if schools are structured in such ways that thwart optimal learning. I provide ample, valid data that numerous students are not at-risk for school failure, but they are placed at risk by schools that are organized along lines that make it very difficult for many students to attain school success. The following discussion on "At-Risk Schools" covers three aspects regarding inequities in schools.

The Relation Between Teacher Quality and Student Academic Performance

A basic question is necessary to ask at the beginning of any discussion of at-risk schools: Is there a positive relation between the quality of teachers and student learning and academic performance? Substantial evidence exists to answer this query in the affirmative.[14] Research investigations inform us that a number of teacher attributes have an instrumental role in this effect. The lowest performing schools—compared to the highest performing schools—have considerably greater percentages of teachers: (a) not fully certified, (b) assigned to out-of-field classes, (c) with little experience, (d) with beginning employment status, (e) with higher turnover rates, and (f) having failed certification examinations (Fuller, Carpenter, & Fuller, 2008). A solid example that demonstrates the positive association between teacher quality and student academic achievement is seen in the recent investigation by Fuller et al., *Teacher Quality & School Improvement in Texas Secondary Schools*. Table 4.1 shows the results of one aspect of this comprehensive study of teacher quality. Fuller and associates examined the relation between six measures of high school teacher quality (e.g., teaching out-of-field; failure on certification tests) and the percentage of all students passing all Texas Assessment of Knowledge and Skills (TAKS) subtests, a state-mandated academic achievement battery.[15]

Table 4.1 High School Teacher Quality, Turnover, and Certification Tests Performance by Student TAKS Performance

Teacher Quality Measure		School Performance by Quintile[a]					Difference
		Q1	Q2	Q3	Q4	Q5	(Q5–Q1)
Teaching Out-of-Field							
	Core Courses	26.2	21.4	19.2	15.6	13.4	−12.8**
	English	23.2	17.7	16.5	12.1	11.7	−11.5**
	Mathematics	18.9	15.3	13.0	8.1	7.8	−11.1**
	Science	42.2	32.9	29.7	24.8	19.8	−22.4**
	Social Studies	22.3	21.3	18.8	18.3	14.4	−7.9**
Not Fully Certified							
	Core Courses	16.8	13.8	10.7	9.2	8.8	−8.0**
	English	14.1	12.2	8.5	7.8	8.3	−5.8**
	Mathematics	17.5	14.0	9.9	9.1	9.8	−7.8**
	Science	21.5	16.3	12.4	12.3	8.9	−12.7**
	Social Studies	14.6	12.2	10.9	7.8	7.5	−7.0**
Beginning Teachers							
	Core Courses	10.8	8.9	6.8	5.1	4.3	−6.5**
	English	10.4	8.3	6.8	4.5	4.0	−6.4*
	Mathematics	9.9	8.1	6.8	4.8	4.0	−5.9**
	Science	14.1	12.6	8.4	6.7	4.7	−9.4**
	Social Studies	9.2	6.5	5.2	4.6	4.7	−4.5**
Years of Experience							
	Zero	9.5	10.1	7.2	5.9	5.5	−4.1**
	1–5	27.8	25.4	23.2	21.8	20.9	−6.8**
	6–10	17.2	17.5	18.6	18.5	20.6	−3.3**
	11–20	22.2	25.4	26.7	28.7	28.0	−5.8**
	> 20	23.3	21.6	24.3	25.2	25.0	−1.8
Teacher Turnover							
	2006–2007	23.7	23.4	21.7	20.4	18.0	−5.7**
	Avg. One-Year	22.1	22.0	20.4	19.6	17.9	−4.2**
	Five-Year	60.5	58.2	53.9	52.6	50.3	−10.3**
Certification Tests							
	% Failed Pedagogy	24.7	17.9	14.5	13.0	11.5	−13.2**
	Q1 Pedagogy	32.3	24.7	21.0	19.1	17.0	−15.3**
	Q5 Pedagogy	13.0	16.4	17.2	18.5	20.6	−7.6**
	% Failed English	24.6	16.7	15.6	15.0	13.4	−11.2**
	% Failed Mathematics	38.0	32.5	26.7	25.4	21.8	−16.2**
	% Failed Science	38.2	36.7	29.9	29.0	24.8	−13.4**
	% Failed Social Studies	28.5	33.8	30.6	29.1	28.7	−0.2

Source: From Fuller, Carpenter, and Fuller (2008, p. 58, Table A–5A). Adapted with permission of the Association of Texas Professional Educators.

[a] School Performance is based on percent of all students passing all TAKS tests at all grades.
* $p < .01$; ** $p < .001$.

The data in Table 4.1 show that a consistent relation exists between the indices of high school teacher quality and student TAKS pass rates.[16] That is, Fuller et al. found a rather strong and steady positive association between greater aggregate teacher quality and TAKS achievement. The authors also note: "Even when selecting sets of schools with similar student demographics, the lowest performing schools had lower measures of teacher quality than high-performing schools" (p. 4).

Inequities in the Distribution of Teacher Quality Characteristics

Numerous research studies report that teacher quality characteristics are inequitably distributed across race and class in the nation's schools, meaning that low-SES students and pupils of color (which are frequently collinear) are shortchanged on teacher quality.[17] For instance, Barton (2003)—drawing from a study by the National Center for Education Statistics (Mayer, Mullins, & Moore, 2000)—reports that among correlates of student academic achievement (e.g., teacher preparation; rigor of curriculum; teacher experience and attendance [teacher presence or absence]), gaps exist between students of color and White students, as well as between students from low-income and high-income families. In another investigation, Craig D. Jerald (2002) of the Education Trust reports out-of-field teaching (based on a national survey of middle school and high school teachers).[18] A major finding shows that in middle schools, teachers lacking at least a college minor taught core academic classes more frequently in high-poverty schools (53%) than low-poverty schools (38%), and in high-minority schools (49%) than low-minority schools (40%).[19] Similar patterns exist for high schools, but not as grave. Jerald's report is quite comprehensive as data across race and case show consistent findings for the vast majority of the 50 states, although the percentages of out-of-field teaching vary widely. In yet another study, Darling-Hammond (2004a) reports that in California there is a strong relation between teacher underqualification (i.e., teachers who do not have a preliminary or clear credential in their field of teaching) and achievement performance of low-SES students on the state's Academic Performance Index (API).[20] Students who score in the lowest decile of the API, compared to those scoring in the highest decile, are six times more probable to be taught by unqualified teachers. Darling-Hammond states: "The presence of underqualified teachers is strongly related to student socioeconomic status and to student achievement" (p. 1939).

Inequities in the Distribution of Economic Resources for Schooling

In addition to being shortchanged on teacher quality, considerable evidence exists that many low-SES pupils and students of color also face inequities in basic economic resources in their schools.[21] For example, in a report by Carey (2004), he notes that there is a national per-pupil funding gap of $1,099 between school districts with the fewest students of color ($7,605 per-pupil funding) and the most students of color ($6,506 per-pupil funding) in 48 states in which data are available (2001–2002 school year). In another report, Barton (2003) discusses national differences in technology-assisted instruction across schools with low and high enrollments of students of color. Based on teacher survey data from 1999, 84% of students in schools with a low percentage of students of color (less than 6%)—compared to 77% of students in schools with a high percentage of students of color (50% or more)—have computers available in classrooms. Furthermore, Barton (2003) reports that 61% of students in schools with low enrollments of students of color—compared to 35% of students in schools with high enrollments of students of color—are given assigned research (by the teachers) using the Internet.

A related economic resource issue has to do with teacher salary. The Education Trust (2008), using Texas as a case in point, reports average teacher salary gaps among the highest- and lowest-enrollments of schools with students of color (across the 25 largest districts in Texas). These data (for the 2005–2006 school year) are shown in Table 4.2 opposite.[22] Although there are a very small number of exceptions to the pattern, elementary, middle, and high school teachers in districts with the lowest enrollments of students of color, compared to their teacher peers in districts with the highest enrollments of students of color, earn larger salaries. For example, in the Austin Independent School District, Table 4.2 shows salary gaps of $3,010, $2,862, and $2,413 for teachers in the elementary, middle, and high schools—respectively. Such teacher salary gaps are no trivial issue. These discrepancies are likely related, in part, to the high teacher turnover rate in U.S. public schools—which is associated with the achievement gap among low-SES and high-SES schools. Furthermore, there is a collateral effect of the high turnover rate. It is estimated that the national cost of teacher turnover is 7.3 billion dollars per year due to the expenditures related to the recruiting, hiring, and training of replacement teachers (National Commission on Teaching and America's Future, 2007).

One of the most demonstrative sources of evidence pertaining to inequities in the distribution of economic resources for schooling originates from the *Williams v. State of California* (2000) lawsuit.[23] Attorneys for *Williams* filed the case on May 17, 2000—46 years to date that Chief Justice Earl Warren penned the historic opinion of the U.S. Supreme Court in *Brown v. Board of Education of Topeka* (1954). The *Williams* complaint is based on two foundational principles (Oakes, 2004). First, the State has the responsibility to make certain that each public school student (elementary through high school) has the essential resources of education (e.g., qualified teachers; ample supply of instructional materials, such as textbooks; decent, satisfactory school buildings). Second, based on the California Constitution, education is a fundamental right that has to be made available to all students on equal conditions. The *Williams* complaint involved both issues of inequities in the distribution of teacher quality

Table 4.2 Average Teacher Salary Gaps Among the Highest and Lowest Enrollments in Schools with Students of Color in the 25 Largest Districts in Texas (2005–2006 School Year)

District Name	Elementary School	Middle School	High School
1. Houston ISD	−$1,074	$425	$1,080
2. Dallas ISD	−$424	$1,522	−$1,088
3. Cypress-Fairbanks ISD	−$2,066	−$1,535	−$2,367
4. Austin ISD	−$3,010	−$2,862	−$2,413
5. Fort Worth ISD	−$1,666	−$2,492	−$1,413
6. Northside ISD	−$521	−$3,014	−$972
7. Fort Bend ISD	−$418	−$513	−$1,411
8. El Paso ISD	$1,077	−$1,156	−$309
9. Arlington ISD	−$3,070	−$4,750	−$3,194
10. North East ISD	−$1,338	−$5	−$398
11. Garland ISD	$482	$725	$836
12. Aldine ISD	−$1,798	−$520	$805
13. San Antonio ISD	$109	$843	$590
14. Plano ISD	−$525	−$666	−$699
15. Pasadena ISD	−$1,166	−$2,678	−$308
16. Brownsville ISD	−$1,547	−$2,780	−$621
17. Katy ISD	−$2,036	−$328	−$24
18. Alief ISD	$431	−$1,107	−$1,296
19. Lewisville ISD	$107	−$696	$2,002
20. Ysleta ISD	−$597	$1,967	−$796
21. Conroe ISD	$234	$1,019	−$719
22. Klein ISD	−$1,616	−$2,358	−$2,208
23. Corpus Christi ISD	$1,510	−$1,086	−$686
24. Round Rock ISD	−$2,493	−$1,076	−$5,048
25. Socorro ISD	−$1,113	−$695	−$2,731

Source: Adapted from The Education Trust (2008, p. 12, Table 2).

Note: ISD = Independent School District. Negative numbers indicate that the average teacher salary in schools with the highest enrollments of students of color was less than the average teacher salary in schools with the lowest enrollments of students of color.

characteristics *and* inequities in the distribution of educational resources. Here, I primarily focus on the latter.

The *Williams* case is both similar and different to lawsuits in the past that dealt with inequities in interdistrict school financing (e.g., California's *Serrano v. Priest* [1969] and Texas's *Rodriguez v. San Antonio Independent School District* [1971]).[24] Oakes (2004, p. 1891) comments:

> Rather than focusing directly on money, *Williams* seeks to make real the state's constitutional responsibility by attending to what is provided to individual students in classrooms. It seeks a system of accountability that ensures that basic tools are provided on an adequate, continuing,

and equal basis. Importantly, the case does not presume to guarantee a high-quality education to all the state's children. It merely seeks a minimum threshold for educational provisions, below which no child must be made to suffer.[25]

Plaintiffs in *Williams*, a class action lawsuit, number 106,338 elementary, middle, and high school students (the main and subclass groups of plaintiffs).[26] Practically all the plaintiffs are low-SES students of color (Black; Latino/Latina; Asian/Pacific Islander), and in 42 (91%) of the 46 affected schools, students of color constitute far greater than 50% of the student body. In 30 (65%) of the 46 schools, English learners account for more than 30% of the student enrollment (p. 7). Plaintiffs' legal claims rest largely in *Williams* on state constitutional violations of principles of equality. For example: Plaintiffs cite the Equal Protection Clauses of the California Constitution (Constitutional Article I, §7[a]; Article IV, §16[a]) and the California Constitution principle that states access to public schooling is a right to be enjoyed by all, not a privilege procurable for purchase (Article IX, §5) (p. 11).

The *Williams* complaint begins with a statement that tens of thousands of schoolchildren and youngsters attending schools from Southern to Northern California are being deprived of fundamental educational opportunities available to their more advantaged peers. Although compulsory education is state law, far too many children and youngsters attend "*schools that shock the conscience*" [italics added] (p. 6). Shortly following this opening statement, there is page after page of accounts of the appalling substandard conditions of many of the plaintiffs' elementary, middle, and high schools (pp. 26–58). Here are a few examples of descriptions of elementary, middle, and high "schools that shock the conscience":

- *Frank D. Parent Elementary School in Inglewood* (located in the Inglewood Unified School District in Los Angeles County).

  At Parent, students cannot bring books home for homework in many classes. These students take home incomplete photocopied papers instead; the papers often lack instructions and background material. Without books or background material, students often cannot understand their homework assignments and parents often cannot help students with their homework. Seventh- and eighth-grade students do not have science textbooks to use in class or to take home. Many texts in use at the school are long out of date. For example, a literature book in use at the school was published in 1969. . . . School toilets often lack toilet paper and students have urinated or defecated on themselves because they could not access bathrooms with toilet paper. Parents have spent hundreds of dollars of their own money to purchase toilet paper for the bathrooms in efforts to rectify the lack of essential supplies for their children. (p. 55)

• *Wendell Helms Middle School in San Pablo* (located in the West Contra Costa Unified School District in Contra Costa County [in the San Francisco Bay Area]).

Helms does not have enough textbooks for all the students in the school. One algebra class has no books at all—not even books for students to use in class. The students must use class time to copy problems into their notebooks from the blackboard. And students must rely on notes they took in class for instruction on how to do their math problems because they have no books anywhere to which they can refer for clarification. In science and history classes for which the school does have books, there are not enough books for students to take home for homework, so students may use books only during class time in school. Several students at Helms compare the school to the schools they used to attend when they lived in Mexico, and the students are surprised that in the United States students do not have books to take home and safe places to learn, as the students had when they lived in Mexico. . . . Ceiling tiles at Helms are cracked and falling off, and the school roof leaks in the rain. Students worry that they will be hit with falling tiles when they enter the library and other areas of the school. Students sometimes cannot use the gym on rainy days because the leaks cause dangerous puddles on the gym floor. . . . Toilets often do not work in the school bathrooms. The bathrooms regularly are strewn with used condoms, cigarette butts, and empty liquor bottles. Most of the stalls in the boys' bathrooms are missing doors. The bathrooms only rarely have soap, toilet paper, or paper towels. (p. 30)

• *Susan Miller Dorsey Senior High in Los Angeles* (located in the southern part of Los Angeles Unified School District).

Students in some classes at Dorsey have to stand or sit on counters for entire semesters because the school does not have enough seats for all the students in their classes. . . . Students routinely see rats in their classes. Teachers set rat traps in some classes, and janitors take dead rats away from the traps as frequently as every other day when the teachers set these traps. . . . Some classes at Dorsey do not have permanent teachers when the school year begins. These students take instruction from a series of substitute teachers for weeks until the school hires a permanent teacher or a long-term substitute teacher to teach the class. The students cannot learn with the series of substitutes because the lack of continuity prevents the substitute teachers from creating lesson plans and teaching material that develops on past lessons. . . . The school does not have enough books for all the students. Students in some math classes do not have any books at all. These students must copy down problems and notes from the board, often without accompanying written instructions and examples. Students in some English classes do not have full class sets of books, so students read different books at different times. Students in these classes cannot engage in class discussions and lessons about the books they read because the students read different books. . . . The school does not have enough open and unlocked bathrooms for all the students. Those bathrooms that are open for student use are filthy and lack toilet paper, soap, and paper towels. Many of the stalls lack doors. . . . The windows in some classrooms do not shut and the classrooms do not have heat, so in the winter the classrooms become extremely cold. Students must wear coats, hats, and gloves in class to keep warm because the temperature falls so low during class time. The students find it difficult to learn because of the extreme chill. . . . Approximately half the classrooms at Dorsey do not have air conditioning and temperatures in these classrooms become extremely hot during the spring and early summer. Students sweat in class and are unable to concentrate on their lessons because of the heat. . . . Glass in two or three of the windows in the school gym have been broken and not repaired for at least two full years. (pp. 46–47)

In *Williams*, the State engaged (via the leadership of Governor Gray Davis) in a vigorous and costly defense—spending $15 million on expensive private lawyers and numerous expert witnesses.[27] Some of the State's experts (e.g., Susan E. Phillips; Christine H. Rossell) have a history of serving for the defendants in civil rights lawsuits.[28] Shortly after assuming office on November 17, 2003, Governor Arnold Schwarzenegger recognized that the *Williams* plaintiffs were correct in their claims of inequities, and requested that State Attorney General Bill Lockyer enter a settlement negotiation. On June 30, 2004, Governor Schwarzenegger provided an interview for the *Capital Morning Report*. He expressed the state's current position on *Williams*:

It's terrible. It should never have happened. Every child is guaranteed to get equal education, equal quality teachers, equal textbooks, homework materials, all of this stuff ought to be equal, but it hasn't been. And this is why the State was sued. And it was crazy for the State to then go out and hire an outside firm and to fight the lawsuit. Fight what? To say this is not true what the ACLU is saying, that they actually got equal education? All anyone has to do is to just go to those schools, and I've gone to those schools because of my after-school programs. I've seen how inner city schools are falling behind because they're not getting the equal teaching and the equal books, equal learning material. So, of course, we are settling that lawsuit. We are very close in settling that, and it is part of the budget negotiation, because we've got to give every child in this state equal opportunities, equal education, equal learning materials, equal books, everything equal.

(Oakes, 2004, p. 1897)

In 2004, the plaintiffs and defendants settled *Williams*. The State allocated the following amounts of money: (a) $138 million in new funds for "standards-aligned instructional materials" for schools in the first and second deciles of achievement, as determined by the state's Academic Performance Index (API); (b) another $50 million for "implementation costs and other oversight-related activities" for schools in deciles one through three based on the API; (c) another $800 million for "critical repair of facilities in future years" for schools in deciles one through three as determined by the API. Legislation adopted in August 2004 (SB6 and 550, and AB 1550, 2727, and 3001) implemented the settlement. About 2.3 million California children and youngsters are likely to benefit from the *Williams* settlement funding.[29] Suffice it to say, the near $1 billion settlement embodied a major victory for the *Williams* plaintiffs. Yet, the settlement signals only the initial step toward a revitalization of California's public schools; still remaining, for example, is the very challenging issue of the recruitment/retention of highly qualified teachers for the many schools populated by low-income students of color. As well, there is the serious need to establish structural changes in order to measure and report the provision of "opportunities for teaching and learning" to allow longitudinal cross-school comparisons (Oakes, 2004, p. 1897).

Conclusion

Discourse on the at-risk notion has gone unabated from the mid–1980s to the current time. As presented in this chapter, this discussion has focused on two quite different perspectives. One position is that via indicator inventories, at-risk students—and by extension, their families—can be identified. As such, this deficit thinking perspective asserts that students, due to their putative cognitive, motivational, and familial deficiencies are at risk for school failure. By sharp contrast, another position is that the academic problems faced by many students—particularly low-SES students of color—stem from an exogenous nature. That is, systemic inequities in society are central to understand why numerous students are predisposed to experience serious academic problems. I have presented ample empirical evidence and argumentation why the structural framework has far greater veracity as an explanatory model for comprehending the school failure of many students. In short, students are not at risk for academic problems due to their alleged deficits. Rather, schools are organized and run in such oppressive ways (e.g., inequities in the distribution of teacher quality characteristics and inequities in the distribution of economic resources for schooling) that many students are placed at risk for school failure.

5

Deconstructing Deficit Thinking
Practical Solutions for Teacher Educators, Educational Leaders, and Educational Ethnographers

In light of the pervasiveness of deficit thinking in schools, it is important to discuss how some individuals have attempted to eliminate the pathologization of poor students and students of color. In this chapter, I provide examples of a number of proactive, anti-deficit thinking suggestions that many readers can utilize to help promote a more equitable and democratic schooling for all students. In particular, I draw from the literature that speaks to deconstructing deficit thinking in five areas.

Preservice Teacher Education

A major reality of contemporary teacher education programs in our nation's universities and colleges is the racialization of the students in preservice teacher education tracks. Overwhelmingly, the vast majority of these students are White.[1] Many of these young women and men, upon completion of their training and with teaching credential in hand, often select to seek employment in urban school districts—districts with an ever-increasing percentage of students of color.[2] The focus here is to examine a number of studies in which researchers (mostly teacher trainers) report on how the effects of White racism by preservice teachers, as manifested via deficit thinking, influence their attitudes and behavior toward culturally and linguistically different children of color. In some of these investigations I cover, the authors (teacher educators) discuss their intervention attempts to deconstruct the deficit thinking expressed by their preservice teacher education students. The category of preservice teacher education is a logical point to begin this discussion because it is here, at ground zero in educational training, that deficit thinking among White preservice teachers first manifests, and more importantly, can be challenged by informed teacher educators.

A major authority in the area of preservice teacher education and deficit thinking is Sherry Marx, professor in the Department of Secondary Education at Utah State University. Marx—a White, female, teacher educator—has authored a number of publications that explore and challenge Whiteness and White racism among White preservice teachers.[3] Included in this work is her book, *Revealing the Invisible: Confronting Passive Racism in Teacher Education* (2006). In her studies, Marx draws from the theoretical perspectives of critical White studies and critical race theory (Marx, 2003, 2004a, 2004b). A small group of White, English-speaking students in her teacher education classes (Second Language Acquisition) who primarily tutor low-SES Mexican-origin English learners in elementary school participated in her research. For her methodology, Marx (2006) incorporates field notes taken during observations of the tutors, in-depth interviews (audiotaped and transcribed) of the tutors, and analysis of the tutors' reflective journals.

Marx (2006) notes that deficit thinking, particularly toward children of color and English language learners (ELLs), is quite prevalent in colleges of education where students in teacher education courses learn, via stereotypes, that children of color and ELLs have low educability and are difficult to teach. In her research with preservice teachers, Marx (2006) comments that the women express deficit thinking in four main ways—that is, perceived deficits in (a) culture; (b) language; (c) families; (d) self-esteem and intelligence. For example, in perceived deficits toward language, Marx (2006) relates the account of one of her students, Ashley (a pseudonym). In regard to her attitude toward Tex-Mex (a language blend of Spanish and English),[4] Ashley remarks:

> Augh! Tex-Mex is *low*. . . . It's like you take a genuine Hispanic and a White person and you mix them together and you have an offspring kid. The kid's both, you know. That kid's kind of a mix. So Tex-Mex is just kind of a, you know, it's a *mix*! It's not really a genuine thing! Either speak English or speak Spanish! Just don't speak both.
>
> (Marx, 2006, p. 55)

Marx (2006) reports that her students also reveal fears of people of color, thus making attempts to create distance between themselves and individuals of color. Furthermore, Marx (2006) comments that the students' deficit thinking lead to expressions of White superiority.

> As the young women articulated the deficits in the cultures, families, characteristics, and languages of the children they tutored, as well as the other people of color and learners of English they described, they silently praised their own White culture, families, characteristics, and English fluency. As they did this, it became clear that the perceived deficiency of color went hand-in-hand with the perceived superiority of Whiteness.
>
> (Marx, 2006, p. 67)

In light of the frequent deficit thinking, low expectations, and stereotypes demonstrated by the preservice teachers toward students (and people) of color, Marx (2006) developed an intervention program that sought to confront and change her students' racism via seven discrete steps, as follows: (a) acknowledging one's own racism; (b) bringing attention to contradictions; (c) catching a glimpse of the shaky evidential base students relied on to attest to their lack of racism; (d) challenging easy answers that might alleviate any racist beliefs that may affect the students' teaching; (e) drawing attention to the larger context of White racist effects on children of color; (f) recognizing and admitting their own racism and taking responsibility for their part in perpetuating it; (g) moving past the guilt associated with White racism.[5] Finally, Marx (2006) comments that future research on White racism in preservice teacher education needs to focus on the possibility of moving from individually centered attempts at antiracist mediations to full classroom interventions. Though such group-based engagements may challenge students' beliefs and statements, Marx (2006) asserts: "Specifically introducing the notions of White talk (McIntyre, 1997) and deficit thinking (Valencia, 1997[a]) would likely make these quagmires easier to name and avoid" (p. 169).

In addition to Sherry Marx, other teacher educators have reported successful interventions in having their preservice teacher education students recognize and dismantle their deficit thinking. For example, Patricia A. Young—an African American, female professor of Education at the University of Maryland, Baltimore County—teaches a multicultural course, "Cultural Pluralism in Elementary Schools." Her preservice teachers are predominantly White (87%). Young (2007) sought to use the theoretical and practical foundations of multiculturalism, critical pedagogy, culturally responsive pedagogy, race, and ethnicity to inform and transform her students to understand how the "dominant culture denounces the cultural ways of being, doing, and seeing expressed by minority groups" (pp. 111–112). In addition to her main class text (Bennett's [1999] *Comprehensive Multicultural Education: Theory and Practice*), Young incorporated a class reader including contributions from Valencia (1997a) and other readings.[6] Young's students also had a number of required assignments (e.g., weekly journals; case study of an ELL or a student who speaks a different dialect; final research paper). Young's primary methodology included the administration of an open-ended question—"What does it mean to think outside the box?," which she administered in a precourse–postcourse design (pp. 116–117, 121). Young chose critical discourse analysis (CDA) as a method of analyzing the participants' responses.[7] She reports that the postcourse responses demonstrated a thematic structured "awakening" perspective in which participants used "I" in a self-reflective manner (e.g., "I have come to realize") rather than an egocentric fashion (pp. 121–122). Furthermore, some participants responded in a "transformative" perspective, which Young defines as: "Transformative educators critically understand, interpret, and postulate the different worlds of others and themselves, and incorporate an intellectuality that transcends 'into, through, and beyond'; their practice is always culturally responsive and critically conscious" (p. 124). In sum, Young underscores that teacher educators need to teach preservice teachers to "think racially" so as to develop a critical consciousness that they can use in their eventual teaching to transform the lives of low-SES children and children of color (p. 126).

We see another example of how teacher education researchers have helped their preservice teachers identify and eliminate their deficit thinking in the study by Julie Horton and Linda Pacifici (2003), teacher educators in the Department of Curriculum and Instruction at Appalachian State University. Horton and Pacifici co-taught an undergraduate course, "Literacy, Technology, and Instruction" geared for preservice teachers (all White). At the beginning of the course, the researchers administered a survey to the students—an instrument designed to gather information about "students' ideas surrounding 'good' teachers and students" (p. 3), concepts that could disclose the students' understandings of multiculturalism. The open-ended questions consisted of:

1. What does it mean to be a good teacher? Please describe.
2. What pictures do you have in your mind of a "good" student? Please describe.
3. *Are you familiar with the concept of deficit thinking? If so, what does that mean to you* [italics added]*?*
4. In your own words, define or explain the concept of "diversity."
5. How does diversity relate to teaching and learning?

(Horton & Pacifici, 2003, p. 3)

Subsequent to administering the survey, Horton and Pacifici introduced the students to the deficit thinking construct by having them read a chapter from Valencia (1997a)—that is, Valencia and Solórzano (1997). The students also read Victoria Purcell-Gates' book, *Other People's Words: The Cycle of Low Poverty* (1995).[8] At the end of the five-week unit of instruction, students submitted a reflection paper in which they related deficit thinking to the Purcell-Gates book.

Based on their analyses of the reflection papers, Horton and Pacifici (2003) report that the preservice teachers demonstrated they could "identify acts of deficit thinking and this led them to attribute negative outcomes to stereotyping and negative perceptions" (p. 9). Furthermore, Horton and Pacifici note that the preservice teachers showed an understanding of "internalized deficit thinking" (p. 10). For example, one preservice teacher wrote in her reflection paper that Jenny and Donny (main characters in *Other People's Words* by Purcell-Gates [1995]) believed in the negative perceptions of themselves:

> After being told time and time again that Urban Appalachian culture was the factor that restrained Donny and her from reading and writing, Jenny seemed to have engaged in deficit thinking herself . . . Jenny illustrated deficit thinking herself because she believed her hillbilly or countrified language hindered her from becoming a successful reader, while she felt Donny's inability to read and write was due to his laziness.
>
> (Horton & Pacifici, 2003, p. 10)

Such intervention studies with regard to preservice teachers' deficit thinking are not limited to White teacher education students. John A. Sutterby, Reneé

Rubin, and Michelle H. Abrego—professors of education at the University of Texas at Brownsville (a Hispanic-serving university)—undertook an investigation involving preservice teachers (85% Latinas). In Sutterby, Rubin, and Abrego (2007),[9] the teacher education students—as a part of their course work—participated in an afterschool reading tutoring program with prekindergarten through first-grade pupils attending an elementary school (100% Latino; 99% low SES; 55% ELLs) located within a mile of the Texas–Mexico border. A component of the tutoring program required that the preservice teachers communicate with the children's parents before and after the tutoring period.

Sutterby et al. (2007) collected data on the preservice teachers, including open-ended questions (pre- and postsurveys), weekly journal reflections, and end-of-course reflections. The researchers also collected data from the parents by the use of focus groups, conducted mainly in Spanish. Sutterby et al. report that the preservice teachers viewed the parents as possessing a number of strengths in supporting their children, including *esfuerzo* (effort) in desiring to help in any way they could to assist their children succeed. The parents also demonstrated *orgullo* (pride) in the accomplishments of their children and held high expectations for their youngsters. Sutterby et al. (2007, pp. 88, 91) conclude:

> The findings support previous research that preservice teachers who have experiences with family involvement during teacher preparation will feel more comfortable interacting with families and value family involvement more than those who lack this preparation. . . . Viewing diversity from a strength perspective allows for preservice teachers to move away from the deficit thinking toward families that exist in many of today's schools.

I close this discussion of preservice teacher education and deficit thinking by shifting slightly to a focus not on White students in teacher education programs, but on the predominant deliverers of such training—White professors. Wendy W. Brandon—a White, middle-class, female teacher educator at Rollins College (Winter Park, Florida)—has written an insightful and valuable article, "Toward a White Teachers' Guide to Playing Fair: Exploring the Cultural Politics of Multicultural Teaching" (2003). In her article, Brandon tackles the critical issue of "being a White professor teaching White [preservice] teachers how to successfully teach diverse children" (p. 37). One of Brandon's main conceptual tools in addressing her concern is the use of "metonymy," which is defined as "a figure of speech in which one word or phrase is substituted for another with which it is very closely associated."[10] In her discussion of metonymy and multicultural education, Brandon draws from, in part, Gale and Densmore (2000) and Bourdieu (1997).

In brief, Brandon (2003) asserts that the cultural and social capital of White professors can become metonymical when they get "positioned in relationships to the 'Other' " (p. 40). That is, sometimes White professors can become metonymical when they become representations of the entire field of multicultural education. As such, the bias of the field of multicultural education goes "unmarked when the whole takes on the character of the part (White teacher education)" (p. 40). In turn, White teacher educators in predominantly White institutions become the "legitimate" transmitters of multicultural knowledge, particularly in how to teach the "Other" and in "doing for" the "Other" who is deemed weaker, disadvantaged, and deficient (p. 40). To rectify this problem of imbedded deficit thinking in their teacher education programs, Brandon argues that teacher educators of multicultural education must adopt a "recognitive view of social justice for guiding White educators in the practice of fair play in diverse classrooms" (p. 31).

Parental Engagement in Education

An abundant corpus of literature documents the positive relation between the degree of parents' participation in education (e.g., monitoring homework) and their children's educational achievement, particularly improving students' academic performance, lowering dropout rates, and promoting positive attitudes toward the learning process.[11] Although researchers have found this correlation between parental educational particpation and student achievement to exist across ethnicity and SES, one aspect of deficit thinking that fails to die is the major myth that low-SES parents of color typically do not value the importance of education, fail to inculcate such a value in their children, and seldom participate—through parental engagement activities—in the education of their offspring.[12] In this discussion, I cover, in brief, this pathologizing. Also, I discuss some promising research findings that scholars recommend to enhance the active participation of low-SES parents in their children's education.

As I note above, some scholars pathologize low-SES parents, particularly parents of color, claiming as evidence these parents' alleged lack of participation in their children's education.[13] As a case in point, I note the article by Valencia and Black (2002), " 'Mexican Americans Don't Value Education!'— On the Basis of the Myth, Mythmaking, and Debunking."[14] Valencia and Black assert that the basis for the myth that Mexican Americans do not value education stems from the general model of deficit thinking, and from the specific variant of putative familial deficits. The argument goes as follows: Given that Mexican Americans do not (allegedly) hold education high in their value hierarchy, this leads to inadequate familial socialization for academic competence, which in turn, contributes to the school failure of Mexican American children and youths. Furthermore, the myth of Mexican Americans' indifference to the value of education can be more fully understood when viewed as part of a historical tradition of deficit thinking in which Mexican Americans are described under the "Mexican American cultural model (stereotype)" in which their value orientations are presented as the root cause of their social problems (Hernández, 1970; for critiques of the stereotype model, see Menchaca, 2000; Romano-V, 1968). In a broader sense, the Mexican American stereotype model is grounded in the long-standing myth that behavior is equated with values (Valencia & Solórzano, 1997). As Allen (1970, pp. 372–373) notes:

> Behavior cannot be equated with values. In other words, simply because a person behaves in a certain way does not mean he desires to do so because of his beliefs or values. Another problem is that the concept is tautological: values inferred from behavior are used to explain behavior. To be useful for explaining behavior, values should be measured independently of the behavior to be explained, or no advantage can be claimed for the gratuitous labeling of the behavior.

We see a good example of how some scholars wrongly equate behavior with values in the work of economist Thomas Sowell who wrote in his chapter on "The Mexicans" (*Ethnic America: A History*, 1981): "*The goals and values of Mexican Americans have never centered on education*" (p. 266). How does Sowell, who has written a history of racial and ethnic groups in the United States, support this sweeping generalization? What specific evidence does he marshal to defend such a blatant assertion? Sowell does so by noting comparative high school completion rates across race and ethnicity: "As of 1960, only 13 percent of Hispanics in the Southwest completed high school, compared to only 17 percent for Blacks in the same region, 28 percent among non-Hispanic Whites, and 39 percent among Japanese Americans" (p. 266). It appears that Sowell is making this argument: *Because Mexican Americans have the lowest high school completion rate of the groups he compares,*[15] *then this means that Mexican Americans do not value education.* Clearly, Sowell frames his interpretation of the ethnic high school completion gap in a deficit thinking manner. Explicit in his argument is that Mexican Americans are the makers of their own educational shortcomings. Furthermore, he fails to discuss the far different interpretations of the achievement gap proffered by the authors who presented the original data Sowell describes above (Grebler, Moore, & Guzmán, 1970, p. 143, Table 7–1). Grebler et al. attribute the achievement gap, in part, to intra-group (i.e., Anglo and Mexican American) variations in "rural-urban background, to immigrant status, and to poverty and other aspects of the home environment" (p. 170). They also present a structural inequality hypothesis to explain the gap:

> *The extreme disparities in different locales suggest also a hypothesis concerning a strategic determinant in a larger society: the extent to which local social systems and, through these, the school systems have held the Mexican American population in a subordinate position.*
>
> (Grebler et al., 1970, p. 170)

Sowell's (1981) claim that Mexican Americans' goals and values have never focused on education stands out as one of the most egregious and unfounded statements ever made about Mexican Americans and their schooling. His assertion is not only wrong,[16] but he presents it in a book on the history of ethnic groups in the United States—a type of source that should be committed to the highest level of interpretive scholarship, not mythmaking.

As I note earlier, other scholars have also discussed the pathologization of parents of color and low-SES parents regarding their educational involvement. Cooper (2003) asserts that the basis of such deficit thinking is rooted in the "power of teacher ideology" (p. 103). That is, teachers who adhere to the view that society is meritocratic are inclined to believe that the schools are also.[17] Cooper notes that such teachers are not apt to see schools as agencies of social reproduction that restrict the ability of students from families who possess few socioeconomic assets to acquire the necessary skills, knowledge, and cultural capital to move upward to the levels of their more privileged peers. In light of this meritocratic perspective, Cooper remarks, teachers can lapse into deficit thinking and display bias toward students and their parents. To eliminate such bias, Cooper comments that teachers must examine their ideological persuasions in order to create and maintain democratic and equitable classrooms. Specifically, teachers—in addition to demonstrating subject matter competency and sound pedagogy—need to hold three basic beliefs about their teacher roles *vis-à-vis* students and their parents: (a) "teaching is a political rather than a neutral act . . . (b) teachers must work to achieve 'political and ideological' clarity . . . and (c) teachers must resist forces that promote educational and social inequality within schools" (p. 104).

At this juncture of the present coverage of parental engagement in education, I shift to a discussion of how some scholars have proffered suggestions in regard to enhancing the educational participation of low-SES parents, particularly those of color. Lott (2003), in her literature review article, notes that given the frequent stereotype of low-SES parents being disinterested and apathetic about the education of their children, suggestions for change are in order. Lott discusses five strategies,[18] but for the sake of brevity, I only cover three.

Replacing Stereotypes with Recognition of Strengths

Lott (2003) comments that schools must accept two basic principles. First, schools should consider families and their children as positive resources and that they constitute the foundation for educational improvement. Second, school officials need to encourage parents and provide them the opportunity to participate thoroughly in the educational process. Certainly, these two fundamental principles are at odds with deficit thinking *vis-à-vis* parents. Yet, the propositions can be extremely useful if educators embrace them.

Helping Parents Deal with Obstacles to School Participation

Lott (2003) discusses a number of obstacles that thwart low-SES parents' educational involvement, such as: parents believe that schools are external to their field of influence; parents worry about teachers' reprisals if they advocate for their children; many low-SES parents' economic plight (e.g., child care problems; job insecurity) create obstacles to school participation. Lott suggests that schools can minimize the preceding barriers (and others) if they are proactive: for example, making parents feel welcome, providing child care and transportation, using translators, and scheduling parent–teacher conferences in the evening times.

Expanding Parental Roles in the Schools

Lott (2003) notes that schools provide low-SES parents few opportunities to participate in their children's schooling, and often limit these opportunities to quite minimal roles (e.g., signing permission slips for field trips; serving as volunteer classroom aides, but only in ways narrowly prescribed by teachers). In comparison to the participatory roles exhibited by middle-class parents in classrooms (e.g., serving as sources of particular expertise; providing information about possible careers), schools seldom seek out low-SES parents for such roles. Although Lott does not discuss the specific strategy of "funds of knowledge," research has shown, empirically, this suggestion to be a way of building upon the strengths of low-SES Mexican-origin parents. González et al. (2005, pp. 91–92) note:

> Funds of knowledge refers to those historically developed and accumulated strategies (skills, abilities, ideas, and practices) or bodies of knowledge that are essential to a household's functioning and well-being. . . . A key finding from our research is that funds of knowledge are abundant and diverse; they may include information about, for example, farming and animal husbandry, associated with households' rural origins, or knowledge about construction, and building, related to urban occupations, or knowledge about many other matters, such as trade, business, and finance on both sides of the U.S.–Mexico border.

López, Scribner, and Mahitivanichcha (2001) conducted a 5-month study of four migrant-impacted school districts in Texas and Illinois in which 15 schools proved successful in involving migrant parents in their children's education. López et al. identified a number of strategies used by the schools, for example: (a) reliance on nontraditional contact methods, such as the use of radio and television to establish initial relationships with families; (b) affirmation of the parents' demonstrated valuing of education; (c) provision of educational/vocational programs for skill enhancement (e.g., English as a Second Language; U.S. citizenship classes; Graduate Equivalency Degree);

(d) offering of "parent education" discussions ("*pláticas*") designed to inform parents of valuable information in a variety of areas (e.g., how to withdraw students in the appropriate manner; knowledge of courses students can transfer to when they matriculate to another school district).

Educational Leadership

As noted by a number of scholars, institutional leadership is a very powerful factor, if not the strongest, in the promotion and realization of school success, particularly regarding low-SES students and students of color.[19] Such leadership is especially germane to school principals, but also to school district superintendents. Here, I discuss how principals, via successful leadership practices, can help teachers avoid and even dismantle their deficit thinking. Such leadership, however, does not materialize from thin air. School principals need to be aware of their own biases and learn how to lead schools that are diverse along SES and racial lines. Most of the scholars in this area are strong anti-deficit advocates and well trained in the areas of educational administration and social justice.[20]

In this discussion, I confine myself to one study because of its excellent representativeness of this corpus of literature. McKenzie and Scheurich (2004) developed the construct of "equity traps" with the explicit goal of assisting departments of educational administration to train school leaders, especially principals, to be successful in promoting school success in racially diverse schools (i.e., the elimination or reduction of the persistent and pervasive academic achievement gap in the nation between White students and students of color). McKenzie and Scheurich (2004) define equity traps as "ways of thinking or assumptions that prevent educators from believing that their students of color can be successful learners" (pp. 601–602). The authors derive the equity trap notion from a qualitative research study involving comprehensive discussions with eight experienced White teachers employed in a high-enrollment, small elementary school (in a Southwestern city) with 56% African American and 40% Mexican American/other Latino students. The interviews included questions about the teachers' impressions of students of color, their personal racial identity, and the relation between the two factors.

Based on the interviews, McKenzie and Scheurich (2004) identified four equity traps ("Racial Erasure," "Avoidance and Employment of the Gaze," "A Deficit View," and "Paralogical Beliefs and Behaviors"), and then discussed strategies to address them. For brevity's sake, I confine my discussion to the latter two equity traps.

Equity Trap: A Deficit View

Drawing directly from Valencia (1997a), McKenzie and Scheurich (2004) report that the teachers in the investigation attributed their students' lack of success to endogenous deficits (e.g., poor motivation; inadequate cultures). The authors note that one teacher remarked:

> [I blame the parents] 100%. Not that it's their fault. But it's the culture that they are living in . . . our kids come to us at pre-K, 2 or 3 years below grade level already . . . we are playing catch up from preschool on.
>
> (McKenzie & Scheurich, 2004, p. 608)

Another teacher commented:

> I think that's where the schools are having a hard time is because the parents are not . . . motivating their children to do well. So, the school is hardly going to undo that lack of motivation. And I think that's a sad thing.
>
> (*Ibid.*, p. 608)

Overall, however, McKenzie and Scheurich (2004) state that the prevailing view expressed by the teachers in their study regarding the students' alleged poor motivation and achievement had to do with the belief that parents do not value education. In sum, the teachers consistently identified the students as possessing "built in" or "endogenous" deficits that teachers could not expect to surmount (p. 609).

McKenzie and Scheurich (2004) provide several strategies that principals can utilize to assist teachers to obviate deficit thinking as an equity trap. The rationale underlying these strategies is to provide opportunities for teachers so they can transform their deficit orientation to an assets-based perspective regarding communities of color, and the families and students residing there. The first strategy McKenzie and Scheurich (2004) have found successful in allowing teachers to know their students and families better is the idea of "neighborhood walks," which involve door-to-door welcomes by teachers and the distribution of important school information. These activities helped establish teacher–parent rapport, which in turn led to increased parental participation in school functions and a greater willingness of parents to inquire about their children's schoolwork.

A second strategy that McKenzie and Scheurich (2004) suggest principals use to help teachers eliminate deficit thinking as an equity trap is to have teachers and students, working together, conduct "oral histories" from individuals in the local community. In the process of gathering the oral histories, students can take notes, or videotape or audiotape the respondents. Subsequently, students assemble the information and construct, for example, public displays, homemade books, and scripts for speaking parts in stories. In sum, the oral history strategy effectively brings together teachers, community members, and students so as to build a union "in which everyone learns about each other and in which solidarity and [a sense of] community are being built" (p. 611).

The third strategy that McKenzie and Scheurich (2004) proffer in order for principals to assist teachers deconstruct deficit thinking as an equity trap is the establishment of "three-way conferencing," that includes the student, his/her family member, and the teacher. McKenzie and Scheurich (2004) note that three-way conferencing not only improves understanding between all concerned, but it assists the child and his significant other in becoming more involved "in making instructional decisions that support the student both at home and at school" (p. 612). Finally, the authors report that the parents informed them the three-way conferencing proved superior compared to the conventional parent–teacher conference.[21]

Equity Trap: Paralogical Beliefs and Behaviors

McKenzie and Scheurich (2004) comment that this equity trap has to do with the nature of a "paralogism," which the authors state "exists when a conclusion is drawn from premises that logically do not warrant that conclusion" (p. 624)—in short, fallacious reasoning involving self-deception. As a case in point, McKenzie and Scheurich (2004) state (based on their original research study) that the teachers described their own behaviors as treating the students in ill-mannered ways (e.g., screaming at them; losing control). The teachers concluded that such disrespectful behaviors came about from the students' bad behavior toward them. That is, the teachers rationalized their personal beliefs and behaviors by drawing the fallacious conclusion that their own discourteous treatment of the students "was caused by the behaviors of the students [which constituted an] erroneous premise" (p. 624).

McKenzie and Scheurich (2004) provide three suggestions to confront the equity trap of paralogical beliefs and behaviors. First, the authors propose that school principals have teachers pay a visit to schools and classrooms where teachers have demonstrated success with students of color.[22] Such a trip can assist the visiting teachers call into question their deficit thinking attitudes and illogical behavior toward their students. Second, McKenzie and Scheurich (2004) suggest that school principals have teachers engage in role modeling. This strategy involves a master teacher or instructional coach visiting the classroom to observe the teacher in order to identify the teacher's specific domains of challenge. Then, the master teacher or coach models the appropriate ways to teach the students. After, the teacher instructs for several days, followed by the master teacher or coach observing again. The cycle continues until the teacher finally exhibits the suitable beliefs and behaviors toward the students. Third, McKenzie and Scheurich (2004) propose that principals develop a critical mass of equity advocates among the teaching staff. The rationale for this strategy stems from the reality that principals need support. Principals often realize that they cannot, alone, implement systemic change at the local school level. McKenzie and Scheurich (2004, p. 627) assert:

They [principals] need advocates. They need at least some teachers who truly believe in equity and who are willing to stand up for, argue for, and speak out for equity. Thus, we believe that if you can get a group of educators, however small this group is initially, to openly advocate for equity, the erroneous and illogical blaming of students for teachers' destructive behaviors can be ended.

In conclusion, McKenzie and Scheurich (2004) offer sound advice how principals can develop and implement strategies that have the potential to lead to school success for students of color. The authors' suggestions for identifying and eliminating the equity traps of deficit thinking and several other traps are certainly worth considering.

Social Justice

This is another area that I expect has particular interest for the readership of the present book. The topic of social justice is gaining considerable momentum among scholars, especially critical theorists. This is likely related to the ever-increasing presence of marginalized student groups (e.g., based on race, class, gender, language status, and sexual orientation) and the failure of many status quo public schools to engage in programs and activities that will lead to equity and justice for all students that experience constant marginalization. In this discussion, I cover the following three aspects of social justice.

Conceptions of Social Justice

Beginning around the late 1990s, the notions of leading and teaching for social justice have gained prominence in the field of education. We can see such attention, for example, in a number of books, such as: *Teaching for Social Justice: A Democracy and Education Reader* (Ayers, Hunt, & Quinn, 1998); *Learning to Teach for Social Justice* (Darling-Hammond, French, & García-López, 2002); *Leading for Social Justice: Transforming Schools for All Learners* (Frattura & Capper, 2007); *Radicalizing Educational Leadership: Dimensions of Social Justice* (Bogotch, Beachum, Blount, Brooks, & English, 2008).

As Theoharis (2007a) underscores, the social justice leadership literature is "rife with definitions" (p. 222). In light of this state of affairs, it is beneficial to examine some of these denotations to see how common conceptual ground exists.[23] Gewirtz's (1998) definition centers on the disruption and subversion of arrangements that contribute to marginalization and processes of exclusion *vis-à-vis* the subaltern. The conception of social justice by Goldfarb and Grinberg (2002) focuses on transforming those institutional and organizational structures by vigorously engaging in the reclamation, appropriation, and advancement of rights concerned with equality. The conception of social justice by Bogotch (2002) differs somewhat in that he focuses on the social construction nature of the concept: "There are no fixed or predictable meanings of social justice prior to actually engaging in educational leadership practices" (p. 153; quoted in Theoharis, 2007a, p. 223). George Theoharis, a leading scholar of social justice leadership,[24] draws from these various authors and grounds his definition in the day-to-day realities of school leadership. He states:

> I define social justice leadership to mean that these principals make issues of race, class, gender, disability, sexual orientation, and other historically and currently marginalizing conditions in the United States central to their advocacy, leadership, practice, and vision. This definition centers on addressing and eliminating marginalization in schools. Thus, inclusive schooling practices for students with disabilities, English language learners (ELLs), and other students traditionally segregated in schools are also necessitated by this definition.
>
> (Theoharis, 2007a, p. 222)

Theoharis (2007a) notes that a good question to ask is: How does leadership for social justice differ from educational leadership (the latter topic covered earlier in this chapter)? First, the social justice area focuses not only on the characteristics of the educational leader (typically the school principal), but also very much on how to bring about institutional change. Second, the social justice area, although emphasizing race and class concerns, is more inclusive, covering other marginalized groups (i.e., gender; disability; language; sexual orientation). Third, scholars make a number of relatively sharp distinctions between a "good leader" and a "social justice leader" (p. 252, Table 3). Theoharis comments, for example, that a good leader "works long and hard to make a great school," while a social justice leader "becomes intertwined with the life, community, and soul of the school" (p. 252).

Countervailing Pressures against Leadership for Social Justice

Theoharis (2007b) provides a comprehensive analysis of obstacles to the attainment of social justice. In his article, he notes that some scholars use "barriers" or "resistance" to social justice, but he prefers "countervailing pressures," which "refer to all of the situations, incidences, issues, and people that apply pressure against leaders who are trying to enact a social-justice agenda" (Theoharis, 2007b, p. 5). Based on his review of pertinent social justice literature, Theoharis (2007b) identifies and synthesizes six countervailing pressures. Due to some overlap, I confine this discussion to four of the countervailing pressures. They are:

- *Deficit thinking as status quo.* The pervasiveness of deficit thinking across schools (Valencia, 1997a)—characterized as the ubiquitous blame the victim mentality, where educators view differences as defects, and value certain groups of students over others—represents a notable countervailing pressure against advancing a social justice agenda.

• *Marginalization of types of difference.* The point here is that many educators, policymakers, and community members maintain varied degrees of understanding and acceptance of differences (e.g., class; language). Particular cases in mind are the failure of teachers to discuss issues of race and sexual orientation, which lead to muted conversations. As such, these attitudes and policies exacerbate the marginalization of specific student groups.

• *Predilection for technical leadership.* Citing a study by Brown (2004), Theoharis (2007b) mentions that "90% of educational leaders, administrators, and professors reaffirm the value of technical leadership over that of moral and courageous leadership" (p. 12). In light of the safer, less controversial nature of technical leadership in schools, it becomes a more highly valued approach for school leaders. Because of this preference, social justice issues seldom surface in school leadership professional training. Thus, the value of technical leadership takes on a self-fulfilling countervailing pressure through the processes of hiring leadership personnel and allocating educational resources—all at the expense of a social justice agenda.

• *Specific national and local policies.* As a major case in point, Theoharis (2007b) discusses how the standards-based school reform movement—via high-stakes testing—represents a good example of policy as a countervailing pressure to social justice leadership (see chapter 6, present book). The results of such assessments tend to lead to disparate impact on marginalized students (especially along lines of race, class, and language), create a curriculum of hegemony (e.g., sharp control of what knowledge is important), and help form negative stereotypes of low-performing schools that hinder the hiring of highly qualified teachers.

Strategies for the Enactment of Leadership for Social Justice

In his qualitative study (using purposeful sampling) involving seven principals of elementary, middle, and high schools, Theoharis (2007a) interviewed individuals deeply committed to social justice leadership. He identifies four strategies in which the participants enacted leadership for social justice. They are:

• *Increasing student academic achievement.* Given the persistent and pervasive achievement gap between marginalized and non-marginalized public school students (particularly along lines of race and class), it is not surprising that the principals devoted considerable time to raising their students' achievement.[25] Although the principals showed awareness of the criticism of the standards-based school reform system of assessment, they nonetheless believed that they had a duty and moral obligation to attempt to increase their students' achievement. Incorporating a strategy that involved high expectations, feedback results from statewide *and* local test data, and testing as many as students as possible, the principals reported substantial increases in test scores (Theoharis, 2007a). For example, in regard to reading test scores, Latino students in the schools—as a whole—demonstrated significant gains in achievement.[26]

• *Improving the structure of schools.* This strategy for enacting social justice by the participant principals involved a powerful combination of actions to change their school structures (Theoharis, 2007a). For example, these practices involved (a) detracking of math programs; (b) full inclusion of special education students; (c) greater access of advanced courses for students; (d) informal portfolio assessments; (e) challenging teachers' deficit thinking.

• *Recentering and strengthening staff capacity.* The principals in Theoharis's (2007a) study refused to accept the assumption that their teachers had undergone adequate social justice training. As such, the participant principals implemented staff development programs designed to promote open and frank discussions, for example, around race, ELLs, current injustices, and historical inequalities. Furthermore, principals demonstrated commitments to empowering their staff and allowing them greater professional freedom.

• *Strengthening school culture and community.* This final strategy the principals enacted to promote social justice involved efforts to create a pleasant and welcoming school atmosphere for the community as a whole, and in particular for marginalized and disenfranchised families. One principal described his work with staff and community members as follows:

> [Working together, we] physically transformed the inside and outside of the school . . . so that every hallway and entranceway was bursting with beautiful children's art . . . and creating a beautiful, vibrant playground that dramatically changed the nature and time of recess. . . . Students and community were involved in developing and maintaining the environment; they felt connected, they took responsibility for the school.
>
> (Theoharis, 2007a, p. 237)

Via these efforts, Theoharis (2007a) reports that not only did marginalized families' school involvement increase, but the negative stereotypes exhibited by White, middle-class parents began to change, and the school staff gained insights that there are ways to comprehend, find, and value participation of marginalized parents other than the conventional parent–teacher methods (e.g., parent–teacher conferences at the school).

Ethnography of Schools

This discussion differs from others (e.g., preservice teacher education; educational leadership) in that the unit of analysis is broader. Here, the research typically focuses on the whole classroom, school, or the community—rather than on the teacher or the principal. Furthermore, the construct of culture has a major role in the study of the schooling process. A particularly germane question is: "What is the relationship between anthropology, culture, and research on teaching and learning?" (Foster, Lewis, & Onafowora, 2003, p. 262). In this coverage, I center on three aspects of how ethnography of schools assists in better understanding deficit thinking orientations.

The Investigative Application of Anthropology of Education in Challenging Deficit Theory

A number of educational anthropologists and human developmentalists note that psychological paradigms have dominated the study of education for decades. As Foster et al. (2003) state, these approaches have been problematic because they often view low-SES students and students of color with a deficit thinking lens, ranging along a continuum of putative genetic, cultural, and familial deficits (Foster, 2000; Foster et al., 2003). In light of the entrenchment of psychological approaches, it is not unexpected that anthropologically driven investigations of teaching and learning processes have faced obstacles in gaining a secure footing in the field of education. Foster et al. comment:

> Although such studies have been the centerpiece of some educational journals since the 1970s—the *Anthropology of Education Quarterly*, for instance—it was not until 1987, when the *American Educational Research Journal* introduced the topic of anthropological and ethnographic research on education, classrooms, and teaching and learning that anthropology and its essential concept—culture—began to appear more regularly.
>
> (Foster et al., 2003, p. 262)

In a collective response to the psychologically based deficit thinking perspectives,[27] anthropologically informed investigators have developed a paradigm shift—focusing on "studies of cultural congruence, conflict, and discontinuity" (Foster, 2000, p. 162). A case in point are asset-based microethnographic studies of communication patterns of African American children and other children of color in which their language is found to be rule-governed, systematically organized, and complete (Foster et al., 2003)

Another way in which scholars have applied the anthropology of education to challenging deficit thinking is discourse on the role of power relations between the oppressor and the oppressed. González (2004) discusses how deficit conceptions of the "Other" create an implicit binary. That is, researchers almost always view the valence of the dominant culture as positive. By sharp contrast, the culture of the poor, whom scholars perceive as pathological, lies at the bottom end of the continuum (González, 2004, 2005). González (2004) notes that this simplistic (and erroneous) conception of the highly complex nature of culture often leads to a "small leap of reification and reductionism" (p. 20). Furthermore, González (2004) maintains that it is this cultural metamorphosis and reductionism initiated by the powerful that has prompted the heterodoxic challenge to deficit thinking—as evidenced by the critical discourse of many scholars' writings seen in the present book.

As does González (2004), Gutiérrez (2002) also speaks to the unfortunate history of culture being utilized reductively and categorically. She comments that although there have been notable anti-deficit challenges to reductive views of culture, conventional educational research has not attended to the fluid and multidimensional nature of culture. Rather, such research "has isolated it as an independent variable, or has regarded it from a deficit perspective" (p. 318). As I discuss in chapter 3 of the present book (which covers in part the "culture of poverty" notion), Gutiérrez states that researchers—in their quest for cultural reductionist explanations of the incessant problems of the poor— fail to examine the roles of sociopolitical, economic, and historical factors in perpetuating the many issues faced by the poor. Gutiérrez continues by underscoring the detrimental

> consequences of conflating culture with social categories, i.e., race/ ethnicity and its proxies, language and ability. Some of our more recent studies show how defining culture as a social category results in overly deterministic, weak, and uncomplicated understandings of both individuals and the groups or practices of which they are a part. This work shows how equating culture with race, ethnicity, linguistic character, and national origin, for example, minimizes the tremendous diversity within groups who may share particular linguistic and sociocultural histories.
>
> (Gutiérrez, 2002, p. 318)

Gutiérrez asserts that such reductionism, in terms of educational policies and practices, provides scant practical information and is short on specificity. In a related article, Gutiérrez and Rogoff (2003) offer a number of suggestions how the field of anthropology of education can challenge the discourse of culture as a social category (e.g., avoid overgeneralizations based on single observations; treat participants' community dimensions as a constellation of factors, and avoid the tendency to control for independent variables).

The New Educational Ethnographer of Color

Educational anthropologist Douglas Foley (2001) recalls that when he joined the field at the close of the 1960s, White middle-class men dominated educational anthropology and sociology. He comments that one of the most invigorating developments concerning research in education is the arrival of the "ethnic educational ethnographer" (p. 17).[28] Foley (2001)—noting that educational ethnographers of color possess clear cultural, linguistic, and political advantages—states that the emergence of these scholars signaled "the end of anthropology as a colonial/neocolonial enterprise and acknowledges that 'insiders' studying their own culture elevates the quality of ethnographic fieldwork" (p. 17). Foley (2001) first discusses the work of White scholars *vis-à-vis* deficit thinking; Foley, Levinson, and Hurtig (2000) then cover how scholars of color build on these critiques.

In regard to deficit thinking, Foley (2001) discusses three principal critiques proffered by White educational ethnographers (also, see Foley et al., 2000). I only discuss two of the critiques.[29] First, there is the stream that flows from theorists who focus on Marxist and cultural reproduction thought (e.g., Bourdieu & Passeron, 1977; Bowles & Gintis, 1976). Initially, these early theorists confined their analysis to the ways that schools maintained structures (e.g., tracking) to reproduce class inequality. Later, "post-Marxist" perspectives entered the discourse and emphasized that race and gender, not only class, underpinned the presence of deficit thinking in education.[30] Foley (2001) refers to these post-Marxist views as "cultural production" and/or "practice" perspectives, generally emphasizing various struggles of cultural identity groups against gender, class, race, and ethnic dominance in education.[31]

Foley (2001) notes that White educational ethnographers developed a second major critique of deficit thinking in the late 1960s, stemming from the groundbreaking work of American sociolinguists Dell Hymes and John Gumperz (e.g., Hymes & Gumperz, 1964). For example, in later years Shirley Heath (1983) and Susan Phillips (1983)—educational ethnographers with sociolinguistic orientations—endeavored to refute the culture concept of deficit thinking by identifying the functional nature of the home language of children of color. Via microethnographic studies, such scholars found that students of color—although having a sound linguistic system—faced disadvantages due to linguistic and cultural insensitivities in school. Foley (2001, p. 21) comments:

> Here again, we see these scholars shifting the blame from the victim to the schooling institution, which is characterized as preferential toward the language and culture of middle-class youth. But like the Marxists, sociolinguists rarely explored how race and gender factors articulated with class factors.

Foley et al. (2000) next discuss how the educational ethnographers of color—with counterhegemonic voices—build on the earlier critiques of deficit thinking by White progressive educational ethnographers, to wit:

• *Shift of blame.* Many ethnographers of color quite effectively have discredited deficit thinking as an explanation of school failure among low-SES students and students of color. Furthermore, these scholars—through their ethnographic investigations—have shifted the blame of school failure from endogenous bases (e.g., the alleged "deficit" student) to schools that are uncaring, reproduce unfavorable racial and gender stereotypes, implement biased teaching and curricular practices, and engage in preferential treatment of White students, the middle class, and males (Foley et al., 2000).

• *Student agency, resiliency, and success.* Many of the new ethnographers of color have not just confined their research to how schools reproduce barriers and inequalities. These scholars have also engaged in a paradigm shift in which reputed deficit students have demonstrated keen intelligence, positive attitudes, strong motivation, and sound communicative skills—all necessary to succeed in school and life (Foley et al., 2000).

• *Liberating curriculum.* A number of the new ethnographers of color have brought forth another paradigm shift by documenting pedagogical and curricular practices that are intended to raise the consciousness of marginalized people of color and women. This transformation has come about by the work of multicultural and gender scholars who have developed training programs for educators. Such programs are designed so educators can infuse a curriculum that is sensitive to culture and gender (Foley et al., 2000).

• *Research methodology.* The new ethnographers of color have also made solid contributions by advancing the state of research methodology. Such advancements are in the form of collaborative research methods, decolonization, multiple epistemologies, narratives, and providing voice to subaltern groups. Foley et al. (2000) conclude: "Ultimately, outsider and insider ethnographers need each other. The more diverse our accounts of a given phenomenon, the better" (p. 81).

Critical Ethnography and Community Transformation: A Case Study

The ethnographic account of Guajardo and Guajardo (2002) and Guajardo, Guajardo, and del Carmen Casaperalta (2008) is a powerful story of a community's transformation. The site of activity is the Llano Grande Center for Research & Development (hereafter referred to as the Center) at Edcouch-Elsa High School (hereafter referred to as E-E H.S.) located in Elsa, Texas, 15 miles north of the Texas–Mexico border (Guajardo & Guajardo, 2002). Brothers Miguel Guajardo and Francisco Guajardo are Mexican immigrants, attended E-E H.S., graduated from The University of Texas at Austin, returned to teach at E-E H.S., and eventually earned their Ph.Ds. The Guajardos are founding members of the Center (Guajardo et al., 2008).

The Center, a non-profit organization, emphasizes school- and community-based emancipatory activities. The Center rejects deficit thinking as a paradigm to approach education. Rather, the organization's structure and activities stem from an "assets-based approach." Guajardo and Guajardo (2002, pp. 286–287) explain:

While the Llano Grande Center is acutely conscious of the needs of our youth, our schools, and our community, the needs approach is not what defines the core of our philosophy. To the contrary, the Center has deliberately departed from the traditional deficit-driven model to education and community development by creating an aggressive assets-based approach (Kretzmann & McKnight, 1996). The conventional approach suggests that because the majority of people in our community do not speak, read, or write English, they are deficient. On the other hand, our students and staff believe that we have extraordinary assets in our community because many of our residents are very proficient in Spanish. Because we have used this approach, we are in the process of developing various microenterprises.

In its endeavors, the Center focuses on community-based research, programming for youth development, and school reform initiatives that emphasize the creation of positive cultural, social, and institutional change (Guajardo & Guajardo, 2002). The Center prides itself on activist research, employing critical ethnographies (many student led) that involve conducting local oral histories (videotaped, audiotaped, and published in the *Llano Grande Journal*). Also, the Center has secured funds to support the work of community projects (run by youth and adults). Such projects include a radio station, community centers for neighboring towns, and an extensive database. Many E-E H.S. students have matriculated to Ivy League universities, and the college matriculation rate, in general, has significantly increased.[32] As well, organizations in many areas around the country replicate and practice the Center's framework (M.A. Guajardo, personal communication, July 30, 2009). In regard to their mission and accomplishments, it is worth noting these words of Guajardo and Guajardo:

> We have many assets in our community, and we must create the vehicles and space for them to share their stories of success and challenges. For as we begin to tell our stories, we begin to document our community change, and community change begins with people sharing their stories, with people sharing their vulnerabilities publicly. But we have learned much from our short experience and we are aware we will continue to face many of the same challenges we have faced historically, including the racism and patron democracy that has prevented our community from healing. However, we are a little older and a little wiser as we include more of our community in the process. This inclusion will continue to convey the stories of our elders and the spirit and innocence of our youth. Thus, as we collectively struggle with very painful issues, we will then begin to heal cognitively, economically, and spiritually. Further the inclusion of young people in the process will also help us

prepare for our future, and we know that our future is now! (pp. 300–301)

Conclusion

The coverage presented in this chapter demonstrates the numerous ways in which the various authors in their respective areas of research identify and discuss how the deficit thinking construct provides scholarly utility in understanding the ubiquitous pathologization of low-SES students and students of color. More importantly, however, this discussion points out that many scholars go much further that just documenting and describing such pathologization. As discussed, a number of scholars provide many suggestions as to how anti-deficit thinking interventions and strategies can improve the educational lot for *all* students.

6
Conclusion
(A) The Bankruptcy of the Standards-Based School Reform Movement; (B) Toward the Construction of Meaningful School Reform: Democratic Education

RICHARD R. VALENCIA AND ARTHUR PEARL

The Bankruptcy of the Standards-Based School Reform Movement

The general notion of accountability in education is that public schools should be held accountable to the public, the logic being that the public provides the lion's share of funding schools through property taxes.[1] Milliken (1970) describes this idea as a collective sense "that people are increasingly demanding to know how their children are learning, what they are learning, and why they are being taught whatever they are being taught" (p. 17). Although test scores have been important elements in holding public schools accountable since the 1920s, the modern roots of the current public accountability movement go back to the early 1980s.[2] What has arisen is the standards-based school reform movement in which state-mandated, high-stakes achievement tests are heavily used to hold local school districts, schools, administrators, teachers, and students accountable for meeting specific standards of academic performance. It is the latter component, high-stakes testing, that is the driving mechanism of the standards-based school reform movement, in which the latter is embedded in the larger accountability scheme. Figure 6.1 (opposite) represents the conceptualization of these three elements.

The standards-based school reform movement has now swept across the terrain of K–12 public education in the U.S.[3] As of 2005, 19 states had exit-level tests that all students must pass to graduate from high school, and 7 other states will phase in exit exams by 2012 (Center on Education Policy, 2005).[4] About 72% of all U.S. students enrolled in high school in 2012 will be required to pass exit-level exams in order to graduate, a sharp increase from the 50% of students affected by such exams in 2005. High school exit-level exams will have an even greater effect on students of color. An estimated 82% of minority group students and 87% of ELLs will be required to pass exit exams by 2012 (Center on Education Policy). In addition to the growing use of mandated exit-level high school tests, calls by politicians, policymakers, and others

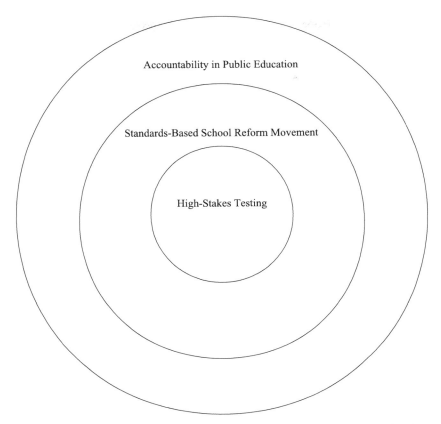

Figure 6.1 Embeddedness of High-Stakes Testing, the Standards-Based School Reform Movement, and Accountability in Public Education.

have influenced the implementation of test-based requirements in controlling grade promotion. The American Federation of Teachers (AFT) has provided comprehensive national information on states that have passed these practices for ending social promotion. When the AFT first began to monitor such policies in 1996, only three states used test data, in part, to decide a student's promotion or retention. In its most recent report (2001), the AFT notes that 16 states and the District of Columbia have institutionalized promotion policies at the elementary level.[5]

To be sure, critics have not let the standards-based school reform movement go uncontested, particularly in regard to high-stakes testing. This literature is quite massive in quantity, and will not be reviewed here.[6] What we do briefly discuss, however, are some of the main criticisms scholars raise.

Measurement-driven Instruction[7]

Madaus (1988) characterizes measurement-driven instruction as the power of testing to shape what is taught and learned and how it is learned. In more familiar terms, this notion is called "teaching to the test." On the surface, measurement-driven instruction sounds appealing, if one assumes that higher test scores truly are indicative of higher achievement. Such an inference, however, is highly questionable. Madaus notes that proponents believe that high-stakes tests can serve to improve student achievement because such tests, via measurement-driven instruction, influence teachers to focus their teaching on the skills measured by the test. The only kind of evidence that supports measurement-driven instruction, however, is that test scores rise. Yet, there is little evidence that the skills a high-stakes test purports to measure have actually improved. This misunderstanding of the effects of measurement-driven instruction arises, according to Madaus, because people fail to distinguish between the actual skills ostensibly learned and the "secondary and fallible indicator [test scores]" (p. 90). Therefore, measurement-driven instruction distorts the learning process by forcing teachers to shift the focus away from teaching their students to read well, for example, and toward teaching them only the skills needed to perform well on the test.

Failure to Use Multiple Data Sources in Assessment[8]

"In all . . . educational decisions, test scores provide just one type of information and should be supplemented by past records of achievement and other types of assessment data. *No major educational decision should ever be based on test scores alone*" (Gronlund, 1985, p. 480). This principle voiced by Gronlund is also echoed by the Board on Testing and Assessment of the National Research Council:

> An educational decision that will have a major impact on a test taker should not be made solely or automatically on the basis of a single test score. Other relevant information about the student's knowledge and skills should also be taken into account.
>
> (Heubert & Hauser, 1999, p. 3)

To this proposition advanced by Gronlund, and Heubert and Hauser, we add: When a test, whose results will have a major impact on a student's educational progress (i.e., high-stakes testing), is used with other assessment data (e.g., grade point average; taking the required courses), *that test should not have determinative weight*. We contend that these two principles—(a) no major decision should be made on test scores alone, and (b) no test should carry the determinative weight even when other assessment data are available—should be the *sine qua non* of educational assessment. Together, these two essential principles form the basis of best-case practices of using multiple data sources in high-stakes testing.

Adverse Impact on Students of Color

The adverse impact of high-stakes testing on students of color is pervasive in U.S. public schools. What is adverse impact? The following conceptualization is informative:

> Differential performance occurs when passing rates for African-American and Hispanic students (minority groups) are lower than the passing rates for White students (majority group). When the differential performance between minority and majority groups becomes too great, it is labeled *adverse impact*. An important issue in this context is determining when differential performance becomes large enough to qualify as adverse impact.
>
> (Phillips, 2000, p. 363)

Such adverse impact is seen, for example, on required high-stakes testing for high school diploma award or denial in Texas (Valencia & Bernal, 2000), and mandated high-stakes testing that is used for grade promotion or retention in Louisiana (Valencia & Villarreal, 2003). In sum, Mexican American and African American students fail these high-stakes tests at disproportionately higher rates than their White peers. In some instances, this adverse impact has prompted civil rights lawsuits.[9]

The Impact of Campbell's Law

In their book, *Collateral Damage: How High-Stakes Testing Corrupts America's Schools* (2007), Sharon L. Nichols and David C. Berliner discuss "Campbell's Law," named for renowned social psychologist, Donald Campbell. More than three decades ago, Campbell proffered the precept: "The more any quantitative social indicator is used for social decision-making, the more subject it will be to corruption pressures and the more apt it will be to distort and corrupt the social processes it was intended to monitor" (quoted in Nichols & Berliner, pp. 26–27).[10] Nichols and Berliner comment that Campbell's Law is ubiquitous. Drawing from the business sector, the authors note that for a long time economists have recognized that when stakes are high, corruption follows. For example:

> Incentives such as big bonuses for increased sales are common in business, but when stakes are attached to sales, then the business of selling could become corrupt. Cars may be sold that are lemons, houses may be sold with concealed defects, guarantees may be made that are not genuine. It is the sale that is important. In California, Sears once stopped paying salaries to its auto mechanics, instead putting them on commission for the repairs they sold to customers. It wasn't long before California authorities had to threaten to close Sears's auto shops because of all the complaints about unnecessary repairs that were being sold.

Other businesses have similar problems. Enron, Tyco, and Qwest, to name just a few examples, all needed to keep their stock prices high (their indicator of successful corporate management), and all did so by cheating. Shell needed its stock price high, so it overstated oil reserves. Pharmaceutical companies needed their share prices high, so they lied about the effectiveness of some of their drugs, and people died as a result.

(Nichols & Berliner, 2007, p. 28)

In regard to high-stakes testing in education, Nichols and Berliner (2007) comment that based on Campbell's Law, the measurement system becomes corrupted, thus making the instrument of measure less accurate. That is, you are likely to have (a) higher stakes and diminished certainty about test validity or (b) lower stakes, but increased certainty about test validity. You are not likely, however, to have both high stakes and high validity. In short, "Uncertainty about the meaning of test scores increases as the stakes attached to them become more severe. The higher the stakes, the more likely it is that the construct being measured has been changed" (Nichols & Berliner, 2007, p. 27).

Structural Misdirection

The standards-based school reform movement is structurally misdirected because it treats the symptoms of school failure (i.e., poor academic achievement indices such as low reading test scores and high dropout rates), rather than the root causes (inferior schools; see chapter 4, present book). Viewed in this manner, we consider the standards-based school reform to be riddled with deficit thinking. An undeniable fact about high-stakes testing is that it does not alter life chances any more than measuring temperature reduces fever. In the haste to eliminate the achievement gap and improve education for students of color, there has been no serious effort to distinguish standards from obstacles. School success for low-SES students of color can be fully understood only when analyzed in the broadest political, economic, and cultural contexts. Macropolicies establish the boundaries of possibilities.[11]

Toward the Construction of Meaningful School Reform: Democratic Education

The alternative to deficit thinking in every form or manifestation is "democratic education." Unfortunately, deficit thinking fits current education policy and practice and neatly meshes with admissions to higher education and the configuration of the job market. Institutions of higher education have the capacity and the resources to accommodate only slightly more than half of all those who should be considered for admission—were it not for dropouts and other forms of failure to meet admission requirements. High dropout rates, runaway tuition increases, and ever-rising admission requirements have kept down the number of potential higher education students among the African American, Latino, and American Indian populations. Deficit thinking undoubtedly influences the dropout numbers, and thus the demographic characteristics of higher education students (especially along lines of race and class). The exact extent to which there are fewer eligible applicants to institutions of higher education is at present unknowable, and only will be knowable when there are K–12 classrooms where deficit thinking has been eliminated. Then, and only then, will it be possible to determine the true impact of deficit thinking on student achievement and future job prospects.

The bifurcation of the work force also has bearing on deficit thinking. The best jobs currently go to college graduates who earn professional credentials. Poor jobs go to those with limited education. At an earlier time in the heyday of IQ tests, schools would unabashedly direct students to different stations in life (Valencia, 1997d). It is still being done via high-stakes testing, but more surreptitiously now. Over the past two decades the workforce has been divided into roughly an equal number of good and bad jobs. For all the talk of "leaving no child behind," the distribution in jobs by demographic factors (e.g., race and class) remains largely unchanged in recent years. Good jobs disproportionately go to middle-class and upper-class White males, and poor jobs disproportionately to low-SES African Americans and Latinos.

The two-tiered economy has led to the greatest ally of deficit thinking, "competitive advantage." Because of the growing gulf between the strata of the two-tiered structure of the economy, parents will go to any length to ensure that their children remain eligible for the good jobs—that is, those jobs requiring a credential. Unfortunately, some parents will also go to any length to ensure that *other parents' children do not get considered for the good jobs.*

> Public education has increasingly come to be perceived as a private good that is harnessed to the pursuit of personal advantage; and, on the whole, the consequences of this for both school and society have been profoundly negative.
>
> (Labaree, 1997, p. 42)

As the organization of work has evolved and education has become increasingly important in the determination of who gets what kind of work, deficit thinking becomes ever more important as a means to maintain and legitimate inequalities. How would a democratic education change that? A democratic education has two main objectives: (a) developing an understanding of democracy through the experiencing of democracy, and (b) developing the skills of informed and responsible citizenship by exercising citizenship. A number of features characterize democratic education. What follows is a brief discussion of seven components.

Democracy as Equal Access to an Optimum Learning Environment

This feature of democratic education emphasizes opportunity to grow within the most favorable learning environment. Macpherson (1977, p. 4) comments:

> The liberal-democratic society maximizes men's human powers, that is, their potential for using and developing their uniquely human capacities. This claim is based on a view of man's essence not as a consumer of utilities but as a doer, a creator, an enjoyer of his human attributes.

Deficit thinking arbitrarily denies students the opportunity to maximize human powers. Maximizing human powers in school, the institution designed to do just that, requires the conscious creation of an optimum learning environment and taking the necessary pains to ensure that *all* students have access to such an environment. Furthermore, for such an environment to exist, it must be precisely defined. The characteristics of an optimum learning environment include the following:

• Instilling a sense of competence in all students. Because deficit thinking instills the opposite notion, the democratic educator must believe that all students can succeed and consciously make the effort to build that feeling in his/her students. Such efforts are not easy to do. If a student victimized by the sustained application of deficit thinking begins to believe in his/her own inferiority, then he/she may cease to try. It is possible, however difficult, for democratic educators to persuade even the most defeated student to try, and when they seriously attempt such persuasion, they see dramatic positive effects (Pearl & Knight, 1999; Pearl & Pryor, 2005).

• Building a learning community where conscientious effort is made to equally encourage all students to become members.

• Creating opportunities for all students to put what they have learned to use as tutors, co-teachers or in community development projects.

• Making the classroom a secure place, one feature of which is encouraging all students to take intellectual risks, express opinions, and hazard guesses.

• Eliminating all unnecessary discomforts—excessive boredom, humiliation, and loneliness. And when some discomfort is unavoidable, make sure that it is equally distributed.

• Taking the time to make the case for the importance of the lesson and making sure all students know what it is that they are expected to do.

• Inspiring hope and meaning, according to West (1993), are the two essential attributes necessary for Black students to attain maximum powers. Currently, schools do much to crush both aspects. Bertrand Russell made a similar observation about hope, only he applied it more generally (Russell, 1927). The more teachers engage students in efforts to shape their own futures, the more the conditions of hope and meaning are met.

- Bringing the excitement of discovery and a sense of creativity that comes with the thrill of invention are not only attributes of an optimum learning environment, but are important recommendations by brain researchers (E. Jensen, 1998).

The Nature of Classroom Authority

The classroom teacher is an unelected authority. The acceptance of that authority ranges from enthusiastic acceptance to active resistance. The nature of classroom authority was the subject of what was considered groundbreaking research by Kurt Lewin and his students (White & Lippitt, 1960). Almost no significant research has been conducted on this important topic in the last half century. In the White and Lippitt studies, students appeared to benefit more from democratic authority than they did from authoritarian or a laissez-faire approach. Deficit thinking is teacher perception of the student. The extent to which the student accepts the teacher as an authority is a function of student perception of the teacher. Deficit thinking and acceptance of teacher authority are obviously related, although there is not a 100% overlap. It is safe, however, to say that both victims of deficit thinking and resisters to classroom authority are found among populations not doing well in school. If all students are to reach maximum growth, the teacher must use persuasion and negotiation to gain acceptance as the classroom authority. The elimination of the achievement gap depends on all students perceiving their teachers as legitimate authorities.

Inclusion

A distinguishing feature of a democracy is the extent to which all members of society are included as equally empowered citizens. If the Republic came into existence as a response to the abuse of authority, the sustaining efforts toward democracy came as a consequence of its marginalized members' struggles for inclusion. The elimination of the property requirement for the vote, the abolition of slavery, workers' struggle for the right to organize, the recurring efforts by various immigrants to be included, women's suffrage, and the campaign for civil rights all furthered the cause of democracy. Today, the most devastating form of exclusion occurs in schools. Schools decide who will be poor and who will escape poverty by determining admission into a credential society. And, deficit thinking plays a prominent role in making the selection.

Meaningful Curriculum

Here, we can learn from the words of President George Washington, who stated in his farewell address:

> Promote then, as an object of primary importance, institutions for the general diffusion of knowledge. In proportion as the structure of

a government gives force to public opinion, it is essential that public opinion be enlightened. As a very important source of strength and security, cherish public credit.

(Washington, 1797)

As George Washington understood, and the next three presidents affirmed, a democracy depends on an enlightened citizenry. In the early days of the Republic, minimal literacy would suffice. Today, in a rapidly changing and extremely complicated world, much more is required of democratic citizens. Unfortunately, even the best educated people often are not able to comprehend, let alone have the capability of solving such monumental problems as global warming, war, poverty, and injustice. Given the inferior education they receive, students victimized by deficit thinking are not only less likely to participate meaningfully in critical societal decisions; they also will be insufficiently prepared to make wise personal decisions. Moreover, those that have had the advantage of incorporation into decision-making bodies will continue to make decisions that will further disadvantage those who have been excluded. A democratic education mandates that all students be equally prepared to be responsible citizens. One necessary concentration for a student-based research curriculum would be an examination of the employment policies and the development of proposals that would increase the "good" jobs in a society. As long as half the jobs for adults in a society are bad, it will be almost impossible to prevent competitive advantage. Thus, the impetus for competitive advantage in turn will reinforce deficit thinking.

Development of Citizenship Skills

A democratic education encourages all students to think independently. Effective citizenship, however, requires collective action. Students can develop such democratic skills as the capacity to listen, to formulate a proposal, to disagree without being disagreeable, to engage in negotiation, to organize a constituency, and to plan and execute a political campaign, and by engaging in school-based citizenship activities. Through a revitalized school government, whose basic unit is the classroom, and through cooperative group projects designed to bring about change in the school or local community, students gain a nuanced understanding of how the society works and how they can be influential participants in it. Here again, deficit thinking undermines democracy. Only those students who have been encouraged to succeed, who remain in school until graduation, and who are eligible for leadership roles are given the opportunity to hone these citizenship skills. Student responses to deficit thinking are largely a growing disinterest in school. This is a logical rejoinder to a schooling that has shown little interest in a student prejudged to have limited academic potential. The more the student is given opportunity to engage in citizenship development activities, the more the student will be able to provide evidence of an educational potential in which deficit thinking has not been allowed to emerge.

Unalienable Rights

Although the Declaration of Independence decreed unalienable rights to be self-evident, there is no such understanding in school. The Bill of Rights did not apply to students or teachers for nearly the first 200 years of the Republic. It was not until 1969 that the Supreme Court extended the rights guaranteed in the Bill of Rights to students and teachers (*Tinker v. Des Moines Independent Community School District*, 1969). That particular case concerned the First Amendment (Freedom of Speech). Other rights guaranteed in our Bill of Rights include the right of privacy, and a right to a special due process system (presumption of innocence; habeas corpus; speedy trial before peers; right to counsel; protection against cruel and unusual punishment) and rights to movement.

Schools tend to undermine rights in three distinctive ways. First, many schools simply ignore student rights. Second, most schools link rights to responsibilities. This is saying, in effect, only the responsible can enjoy rights. Thus, the students that need rights the most are the ones most likely to be denied them. The Bill of Rights, however, makes no such discrimination. The limited number of rights in the first 10 Amendments are unalienable, available to all, responsible and irresponsible alike. Third, some schools ration rights.

Rights and deficit thinking have a relationship. The victims of deficit thinking are deemed too irresponsible for rights. Currently these basic and precious rights are endangered because they are very seldom practiced or discussed in school. Because of the Bill of Rights, the United States has managed to avoid losing its vestiges of democracy in periodic surges toward authoritarianism.

Equality

All democracies claim equality, but none come close to attaining it. One reason for this is the multiple and opposing definitions of equality. Equality remains unattainable because no agency or government instrumentality has the scope and power to bring it about. For a democratic education to be successful, equality can be limited to equal encouragement for all students to succeed. Equality can be further operationalized to mean making all the components of a democracy equally available to all students—for example, equal access to rights, knowledge for citizenship, being an equally celebrated member of a learning community. School will go a long way toward eliminating deficit thinking if the emphasis is on equal access to an optimum learning environment. Although the features of a democratic education have been necessarily given short shrift, it should be apparent that deficit thinking is incompatible with any principle of democracy. Furthermore, a serious effort to apply democratic principles to classrooms would help bring an end to deficit thinking.

Notes

Preface

1. The following text regarding the two anecdotes and the brief discussion of the focus and plan of the book draw from, with minor revisions, Valencia (1997b, pp. ix–xii).
2. See, for example: Bartolomé (2003); Darling-Hammond (2005); de los Santos and de los Santos (2006); Dei (1994); Fuentes (2006); Hale (1986, 2001); Irvine (1990); King, Houston, and Middleton (2001); Ladson-Billings (1994); Meece and Kurtz-Costes (2001); Menchaca (2003); Montaño and Metcalfe (2003); Ochoa (2003); Quijada and Álvarez (2006); Rumberger and Rodríguez (2002); Thompson (2004); Valencia (2002).
3. Scholars have produced considerable literature to substantiate the structural inequality thesis in schooling. Regarding Mexican American students, see, for example, Donato (1997), Moreno (1999), Pearl (1997a), San Miguel (1987), San Miguel and Valencia (1998), and Valencia (1991, 2002). With respect to African American students, see, for example, Feagin and Feagin (1999), Kozol (1991), and Lomotey (1990).

Chapter 1

1. This discussion of Drake's (1927) study draws from, with minor revisions, Valencia (2002, pp. 11–12).
2. The remaining portions of this chapter build on, with revisions, Valencia (1997c). The section on "caste theory" of school failure draws from Valencia and Suzuki (2001, p. 76).
3. Ryan did not use the term deficit thinking in his book. He did, however, refer to "defect" situated "within the victim" (1971, p. 7). In any event, it is very clear that the theory he was critiquing was the deficit thinking model. Following Ryan's (1971) book, and prior to the publication of Valencia (1997a), a number of authors discussed the notion of deficit thinking in various ways. For example, Bronfenbrenner (1979) explores the "deficit model" in child and family policy. Margonis (1992) refers to the "deficit notion" and "deficit thinking" regarding "at-risk" students. Wright (1993) uses the notion of "blaming the victim" in her discussion of poverty and homelessness.
4. According to Jessor (1958), the core of reductionism appears to include four interrelated general propositions:

   (a) The several disciplines or sciences may be considered as hierarchically ordered from, for example, physics at the base through chemistry, biology, and psychology, to the social and historical disciplines at the top. (b) The second essential aspect of reductionism is the proposition that the terms or concepts and the relations or laws of one discipline may fully and without loss of meaning be translated into or deduced from those of another discipline. (c) Such deduction or derivability proceeds only in one direction, from lower to higher levels in the hierarchical ordering, and hence the term "reductionism"; terms and laws of the higher discipline are "reduced" to those of a lower one. Thus, in our earlier example, the psychological term "cognitive structure" is considered translatable into—deducible from—terms belonging to neurophysiology. (*d*) The final aspect is the implicit or explicit proposition that the lower the level of terms employed to explain a given phenomenon, the more causal or fundamental or basic the explanation. (p. 171)

5. See, for example: Clotfelter (2004); González (1990); Klarman (2004); Kluger (2004); Ogletree (2004); Valencia (2005, 2008, chapter 1); Valencia, Menchaca, and Donato (2002); Weinberg (1977); Wollenberg (1978).
6. This historical discussion of Mexican Americans builds on Valencia (2008, p. 7).
7. *Cisneros v. Corpus Christi Independent School District*, 324 F. Supp. at 613 (S.D. Tex. 1970).
8. This section on Terman draws from, with revisions, Valencia (1997d, pp. 60–62, and 100 [note 23]).
9. Terman defined borderline cases as "those which fall near the boundary between that grade of mental deficiency [70–80 IQ] which will be generally recognized as such and the higher group usually classified as normal but dull. They are the doubtful cases, the ones we are always trying (rarely with success) to restore to normality" (1916, p. 87).
10. This section on heterodoxy builds on Valencia (1997d, pp. 83, 86, and 92–94).

Chapter 2

1. Scholars have amply covered historical hereditarianism in context of the deficit thinking paradigm (i.e., the genetic pathology model). For a discussion of historical hereditarianism in regard to key players, nature over nurture, race psychology research, educability, and heterodoxy, see Valencia (1997d). For coverage of the collapse of historical hereditarianism, see Foley (1997).
2. Overall, Pioneer has served as a major funder of scientific racism—to the tune of $15,148,568 from 1971 to 1996 (see *http://www.ferris.edu/ISAR/Institut/pioneer/ pfspread/pfp6.htm*). For expanded discussion of Pioneer, see: Kenny (2002); Lombardo (2002, 2003); Lynn (2001); Rosenthal (1995); Rushton (2002); Tucker (1994, 2001, 2002, 2003); Weyher (1998, 1999a, 1999b).
3. For a copy of the Certificate of Incorporation, see: *http://www.ferris.edu/ISAR/ Institut/pioneer/pfund.htm*. A copy is also available in Lynn (2001, Appendix, pp. 555–562).
4. See note 3, above.
5. "AFI" means "adjusted for inflation." Calculated from The Inflation Calculator at: *http://www.westegg.com/inflation/*.
6. Writing in 2002, Tucker notes that Pioneer provides more than half a million dollars per year for research (p. 7).
7. See Certificate of Incorporation (note 3, this chapter).
8. Lynn (2001, pp. 21–22). Laughlin also advocated against interracial marriage (Lombardo, 2002, p. 756). For coverage of Laughlin, see Tucker (2002, pp. 44–56), Lynn (2001, pp. 21–28), and Lombardo (2002, pp. 755–765).
9. See Certificate of Incorporation (note 3, this chapter).
10. *Brown v. Board of Education of Topeka*, 347 U.S. 483 (1954), Supp. op. 349 U.S. 294 (1955).
11. *Stell v. Savannah-Chatham County Board of Education*, 220 F. Supp. 667 (S.D. Ga. 1963). For a discussion of *Stell*, see Jackson (2004, pp. 533–536; 2005, pp. 131–137,

186–187, 192–194, and 200–201); Newby (1967; pp. 191–210); Tucker (1994, pp. 166–169; 2002, pp. 112–116).

12. *Brown v. Board of Education of Topeka*, 349 U.S. 294 (1955).
13. See Newby (1967, p. 196) for a list of the complex, and somewhat obscure "educational, psychological, and sociological" criteria that the school board designed to decide the policy of pupil placement. The school board developed the criteria as such to avoid the use of race, but nonetheless they served as proxies for it (e.g., "the scholastic aptitude and relative intelligence or mental energy of the pupil"; "the home environment of the pupil").
14. *Stell v. Savannah-Chatham County Board of Education*, 220 F. Supp. at 667 (S.D. Ga. 1963).
15. *Id.* at 683.
16. In *Race and Reason*, Putnam (1961) sought to refute the U.S. Supreme Court's ruling in *Brown* and provide "documented facts" about Blacks' alleged inferiority that the High Court should have considered (p. iii). Several signatories, including Henry E. Garrett and Wesley C. George (members of the Pioneer-backed IAAEE and *Stell* experts for the intervenors), signed the book's Introduction. They wrote: "We do not believe that there is anything to be drawn from the sciences in which we work which supports the view that all races of men, all types of men, or all ethnic groups are equal" (p. vii).

To seek attention for his segregationist views, Putnam (1961) wrote a lengthy letter on October 13, 1958 to President Dwight D. Eisenhower in which he protested the Supreme Court's decision in *Brown*. Eventually, a number of Southern newspapers reprinted Putnam's "open letter to the President." Putnam received thousands of letters. He comments:

> College students wrote me they had framed the letter and hung it on the walls of their rooms. Schools assigned it for class discussion. Editors of law journals asked to print it. Judges wrote me from chambers. Senators and Congressmen simultaneously requested permission to inset in the Congressional Record, and I was embarrassed as to the proper protocol in reply. The Birmingham *Post-Herald* alone supplied 22,000 demands for reprints . . . It looked as if many Southerners felt I had presented their viewpoint on integration. (p. 11)

In all, Putnam's book proved very successful, selling 60,000 copies within a period of six months (Tucker, 2002, p. 160). Chapter 3 occupies the majority of print space in *Race and Reason* ("Point by Point"; 68% of total text pages). Here, he has a number of questions from readers regarding his letter to President Eisenhower (and a second letter to Attorney General William P. Rogers sent on March 16, 1959—five months after Putnam's letter to the President). Putnam carefully selected letters to respond to, ones that favored his segregationist position. For example, here is one Q&A exchange:

> Are there any good reasons why Southern White children shouldn't be made to go to school with Negroes?
>   There are several, among them the fact that their parents don't want them to, but I will suggest the fundamental reason. There is no basis in sound science for the assumption, promoted by various minority groups in recent decades, that all races are biologically equal in their capacity to advance, or even to sustain, what is commonly called Western civilization. They most emphatically are not. (p. 36)

17. To *intervene* means "to obtain the court's permission to enter into a lawsuit which has already started between other parties and to file a complaint stating the basis for a claim in the existing lawsuit" (Hill & Hill, 1995, s.v. "intervene").

18. For the fullest coverage of these experts' testimony, see *Stell v. Savannah-Chatham County Board of Education*, 220 F. Supp. 667 (S.D. Ga. 1963). For other discussions of this testimony, see Newby (1967, pp. 201–210), Jackson (2005, pp. 135–147), and Tucker (1994, pp. 166–168). Garrett also testified as a key expert for defendants in another desegregation case (see Newby, 1967, pp. 54–57), *Davis v. County School Board of Prince Edward County*, 103 F. Supp. 337 (E.D. Va. 1952). In a three-judge panel's ruling, the *Davis* court unanimously subscribed to the segregationist position of the school board. The opinion notes: "Maintenance of the separated [school] system has not been social despotism . . . whatever its demerits in theory, in practice it has begotten greater opportunities for the Negro. . . . We have found no hurt or harm to either race" (*Davis v. County School Board of Prince Edward County*, 103 F. Supp. at 340 [E.D. Va. 1952]). Eventually, NAACP-LDF lawyers proved successful in getting the U.S. Supreme Court to consolidate *Davis* and four other desegregation cases to form under *Brown*.

19. In its entirety, footnote 11 reads as follows:

> K.B. Clark, Effect of Prejudice and Discrimination on Personality Development (Mid-century White House Conference on Children and Youth, 1950); Witmer and Kotinsky, *Personality in the Making* (1952), c. VI; Deutscher and Chein, The Psychological Effects of Enforced Segregation: A Survey of Social Science Opinion, 26 *J. Psychol.* 259 (1948); Chein, What are the Psychological Effects of Segregation Under Conditions of Equal Facilities?, 3 *Int. J. Opinion and Attitude Res.* 229 (1949); Brameld, Educational Costs, in *Discrimination and National Welfare* (MacIver, ed., 1949), 44–48; Frazier, *The Negro in the United States* (1949), 674–81. And see generally Myrdal, *An American Dilemma* (1944). (*Brown v. Board of Education of Topeka*, 347 U.S. at 495 [1954])

20. *Stare decisis* (New Latin, to stand by things that have been settled) is defined as "the doctrine under which courts adhere to precedent on questions of law in order to ensure certainty, consistency, and stability in the administration of justice with departure from precedent permitted for compelling reasons (as to prevent the perpetuation of injustice)" (*Merriam Webster's Dictionary of Law*, 1996, s.v. "stare decisis"; available online at: *http://dictionary.lp.findlaw.com/*). In *Stell*, it appeared that the intervenors made the argument that because the *Brown* ruling relied on *fact*, not *law*, then *Plessy* (1896) was controlling.

21. Conversely, see John Jackson's (2001) book, *Social Scientists for Social Justice: Making the Case Against Segregation*, for a comprehensive account of how social scientists associated with Brown asserted that segregation was damaging to Black students.

22. In the intervenors' brief, a list of "scientific" publications supported the alleged inferiority of Blacks, as well as arguments for school segregation. Newby (1967) remarks: "As these names [authors of the works] indicate, the brief was a distillation of the scientific racism of recent years, and the Stell case is best understood as a culmination of that racism" (pp. 201–202). Newby (1967, pp. 201–202, note 17) mentions that the list of exhibits includes:

> van den Haag, "Social Science Testimony in the Desegregation Cases—A Reply to Professor Kenneth Clark" (1960); Osborne, "Racial Differences in

Mental Growth and School Achievement: A Longitudinal Study" (1960); Osborne, "School Achievement of White and Negro Children of the Same Mental and Chronological Ages" (1961); Osborne, "Racial Difference in School Achievement" (1962); Garrett, "Klineberg's Chapter on Race and Psychology: A Review" (1960); Garrett, "The Equalitarian Dogma" (1961); Garrett, *Great Experiments in Psychology* (New York, 1951); Shuey, *The Testing of Negro Intelligence* (1958); McGurk, "Psychological Test Score Differences and the Cultural Hypothesis" (1961); McGurk, "A Scientist's Report on Race Differences" (1956); Weyl, *The Negro in American Civilization* (1960); Hall, "The Zoological Subspecies of Man" (1946); Burt, "The Inheritance of Mental Ability" (1958); Gates, *Human Genetics* (1946); Carothers, *The African Mind in Health and Disease* (1953); David C. Rife, *Heredity and Human Nature* (New York, 1959); and Carleton Coon, *The Origin of Races* (New York, 1962). In addition the exhibits included several articles which purported to prove that the average Negro brain is inferior to the average White brain. These were Raymond Pearl, "The Weight of the Negro Brain," *Science*, November 9, 1934, pp. 431–434; H.L. Gordon, "Amentia in the East African," *Eugenics Review*, XXV (January, 1934), 223–235; F.W. Vint, "The Brain of the Kenya Native," *Journal of Anatomy*, LXVIII (January, 1934), 216–223; and James H. Sequeira, "The Brain of the East African Native," *British Medical Journal*, I (March 26, 1932), 581.

23. *Stell v. Savannah-Chatham County Board of Education*, 220 F. Supp. at 669, 671 (S.D. Ga. 1963).
24. *Id.* at 672.
25. *Id.* at 673.
26. *Id.* at 674. The assertions of van den Haag did not take into account the prevailing "contact hypothesis" of the time (Allport, 1954) that having optimal conditions of contact (e.g., cooperative activities; close personal interactions) can improve intergroup relations (i.e., reduction of prejudice).
27. *Stell v. Savannah-Chatham County Board of Education*, 220 F. Supp. at 676 (S.D. Ga. 1963).
28. *Id.* at 683.
29. *Id.* at 684.
30. *Id.* at 667.
31. *Stell v. Savannah-Chatham County Board of Education*, 318 F.2d 425 (5th Cir. 1963).
32. *Id.* at 427.
33. *Id.* at 428.
34. *Id.* As part of its ruling, the Fifth Circuit ordered Judge Scarlett to instruct the school board to present a plan that would provide for the desegregation of no less than one grade by September 1963. "As a consequence, nineteen Black youths entered the twelfth grade at Savannah and Grove high schools in September 1962, *nearly 10 years* [italics added] after the United States Supreme Court in the *Brown* case outlawed segregation in public schools" (Billingsley, 1999, p. 56).

For coverage of what transpired with the desegregation plan, see *Stell* chronology in the present reference list (records from August, 1965, to November 19, 1971—that is, *Stell v. Savannah-Chatham County Board of Education*, 255 F. Supp. 83 (S.D. Ga. 1965) to *Stell v. Savannah-Chatham County Board of Education*, 334 F. Supp. 909 (S.D. Ga. 1971).

35. *Roberts v. Stell*, 379 U.S. 933 (1964). Certiorari: "a writ (order) of a higher court to

a lower court to send all the documents in a case to it so the higher court can review the lower court's decision." (Hill & Hill, 1995, s.v. "certiorari").

36. The organizations I discuss here serve as examples of key groups funded by Pioneer or directly by Wickliffe Draper. See Tucker (2002, pp. 70–71) for coverage of instances of other Pioneer-funded groups or activities.

37. For further discussion of IAAEE, see: Newby (1967); Jackson (2005); Tucker (1994, 2002); Winston (1998).

38. Tucker (2002) states:

> Strictly speaking, the *Quarterly* was not a publication of the IAAEE and thus did not receive Draper's money directly, it was clearly created to serve as the house organ of the group that was funded by the Colonel [Draper] and as a vehicle through which the members of the association, many of whom also enjoyed his financial support for their work, could express their views. (p. 90)

For further coverage of *MQ*, see: Billig (1979); Newby (1967); Jackson (2005); Tucker (1994, 2002).

39. *MQ* website available online at: *http://www.mankindquarterly.org/*.

40. This is not to suggest funding began in 1971; see the website of the Institute for the Study of Academic Racism: *http://www.ferris.edu/ISAR/Institut/pioneer/pfspread/pfp6.htm*.

41. Stanley Burnham is a pseudonym (see book review by Thomas Jackson, available online: *http://www.amren.com/ar/1993/04/index.html#article2*). FHU originally published *America's Bimodal Crisis* in 1985 and a second edition in 1993.

42. See: *http://www.ferris.edu/ISAR/Institut/pioneer/pfspread/pfp6.htm*.

43. For CDRI's website, see: *http://www.charlesdarwinresearch.org/#Disseminating%20Research%20Findings*.

44. For SPLC's website, see: *http://www.splcenter.org/intel/intelreport/article.jsp?aid = 83*.

45. See note 43, present chapter ("Visit the Race, Evolution, & Behavior Book Page" on the CDRI website. Available online at: *http://www.charlesdarwinresearch.org/reb.html*).

46. For NCF's website, see: *http://www.nc-f.org/index.html*.

47. See "The Future" page on the Pioneer Fund website. Available online at: *http://www.pioneerfund.org/Future.html*.

48. Frank C.J. McGurk's (1956) article in *U.S. News and World Report* "was apparently the first systematic effort by a social scientist to dispute the social science incorporated in the Brown decision" (Newby, 1967, p. 65). For discussion of the scientific racist opposition to *Brown*, see Jackson (2004, 2005); Newby (1967); Tucker (1994, 2002).

49. Shuey (1958, p. 4). For coverage of Shuey, see Jackson (2005), Lynn (2001), Newby (1967), Tucker (2002), and Valencia and Suzuki (2001).

50. Portions of this discussion of Shuey build on, with revisions, Valencia and Suzuki (pp. 161–163, 312).

51. See "Grantees" page on the Pioneer Fund website: *http://www.pioneerfund.org/Grantees.html*.

52. *Stell v. Savannah-Chatham County Board of Education*, 220 F. Supp. at 685 (note 2) (S.D. Ga. 1963). Garrett served as Shuey's mentor as she worked on her Ph.D. at Columbia University. It could be that by way of academic inbreeding Garrett may have influenced her research interests in Black–White intellectual performance

and her hereditarian conclusion in both the first and second edition of her book. Garrett wrote the foreword in both editions, and in *The Testing of Negro Intelligence* (1958), he states: "Dr. Shuey concludes that the regularity and consistency of the results [higher mean IQ of Whites compared to Blacks] strongly imply a racial [native] basis for these differences. I believe that the weight of the evidence supports her conclusion" (Garrett, 1958, p. viii).

53. Estimated ω^2 measures the association between the independent and dependent variables, calculated after an investigator runs a statistical test of significance. Estimated ω^2 has the element of "practical significance." That is, it estimates the proportion of variance in the dependent variable that can be accounted for by specifying the independent variable. Estimated ω^2 is more meaningful than statistical significance because researchers can use it to inform decisions about practical matters.

54. For discussion of Garrett, see Jackson (2005), Lynn (2001), Tucker (1994, 2002), and Winston (1998). Part of this coverage of Garrett draws from, with revisions, Valencia and Suzuki (2001, pp. 163–165).

55. Lynn (2001, p. 67). For further coverage of Garrett's "Equalitarian Dogma" article, see Jackson (2005), Lynn (2001), Newby (1967), Tucker (1994, 2002), and Winston (1998).

56. This coverage of Boas draws from, with revisions, Valencia (1997d, p. 44).

57. An example of Garrett's fight for school segregation is evidenced in his testimony in *Stell* and *Davis* (see note 18, present chapter).

58. Southern Poverty Law Center website. Available online at: *http://www. splcenter.org/intel/intelreport/article.jsp?aid* = 912. For further discussion of Jensen's connection with Pioneer, see Jackson (2005), Lynn (2001), and Tucker (1994, 2002). This section on Jensen draws from, with revisions, Valencia and Suzuki (2001, pp. 31, 166–169, and 313).

59. For interesting discussions of the events that led to the publication of Jensen's (1969) article and accounts of what transpired shortly after publication, see Fancher (1985), Jensen (1972), and Pearson (1991). These accounts attest to the highly politicized climate surrounding the publication of Jensen's (1969) treatise.

60. Spearman (1927), one of the developers of factor analysis, hypothesizes that intelligence consists of a general factor (g) and two specific (s) factors, verbal ability and fluency. His discovery of g, the first unrotated factor of an orthogonal factor analysis, fits well within his theory that intelligence is a general and hereditary ability. With regard to racial/ethnic differences, Spearman hypothesizes that g differs in distribution between groups and that measures of g would reveal group differences. A.R. Jensen (1998), in his book titled *The g Factor: The Science of Mental Ability*, continues to support the g factor as accounting for individual and group differences in intelligence. A.R. Jensen (1998) addresses the question of whether the g factor is the same in Black and White groups. Based on his review of 17 studies, he concludes that the same g factor exists across various measures of intelligence for both Black and White samples.

61. See references in Jensen (1972, pp. 356–364). A.R. Jensen (1998) notes that based on citation data from the Institute for Scientific Information, his 1969 *HER* article soon became a "citation classic"—a publication that has an unusually high frequency of being cited in the scientific literature. Based on a list of the 100 most frequently cited articles in the social science literature (1969–1978), Tucker (1994, p. 206 and p. 331, note 103) remarks that Jensen's (1969) article ranks number 6. Tucker (1994) does comment, however, that the other articles tend to be "seminal

works" in their fields, whereas scholars frequently cited Jensen's (1969) article because it was a subject of controversy.

62. For examples of publications in response to Jensen (1969), and writings about the debate that ensued, see: Alland (2002), Block and Dworkin (1976), Dobzhansky (1973), Eysenck (1971), Fancher (1985), Flynn (1980), Herrnstein (1973), Jackson and Weidman (2004), Jensen (1972), Kamin (1974), Modgil and Modgil (1987), Pearson (1991), Snyderman and Rothman (1988), and Tucker (1994). Also, see "References of Articles About 'How Much Can We Boost IQ and Scholastic Achievement?' by Arthur R. Jensen" (in Jensen, 1972, pp. 356–364).

63. Over the years, however, the case of fraud against Burt appears to have weakened. Fletcher (1991) and Joynston (1989) present defenses of Burt's work and reputation. Part of these authors' cases criticize Hearnshaw's (1979) biography, who writes, in part, a comprehensive exposé of Burt's alleged fraudulent publications on monozygotic twins reared apart. Fletcher (1991) and Joynston (1989) claim that Hearnshaw makes numerous errors, questionable assumptions, and false conclusions. For book reviews (pro, con, and neutral) of Fletcher and Joynston's work, see: Apple (1992a, 1992b), Beloff (1990), Blinkton (1989), Eysenck (1989), Fancher (1991), Fletcher (1990), Skrabanek (1989), and Zenderland (1990). What the "Burt affair" truly means in the final analysis is not clear. Drawing from Mackintosh's (1995) book, *Cyril Burt: Fraud or Framed?*, Plomin, DeFries, McClearn, and Rutter (1997) observe: "Although the jury is still out on some of the charges . . ., it appears that some of Burt's data are dubious" (p. 137).

64. See: Bodner and Cavalli-Sforza (1970); Cronin, Daniels, Harley, Kroch, and Webber (1975); Gage (1972a, 1972b); Golden and Bridger (1969); Wallace (1975).

65. Following his 1969 *HER* article, Jensen wrote two books (1972, 1973; see wave I of neohereditarianism in Table 2.1, current chapter) in which he reaffirms his conclusion regarding Black–White intelligence differences and educability. In *Educability and Group Differences*, Jensen (1973) states:

> In view of all the most relevant evidence which I have examined, the most tenable hypothesis, in my judgment, is that genetic, as well as environmental, differences are involved in the average disparity between American Negroes and Whites in intelligence and educability, as here defined. All the major facts would seem to be comprehended quite well by the hypothesis that something between one-half and three-fourths of the average IQ difference between American Negroes and Whites is attributable to genetic factors, and the remainder to environmental factors and their interaction with the genetic differences. (p. 363)

66. Historical and contemporary studies of genetically based explanations of group differences in intelligence predominantly target Black–White comparisons. Such studies of Mexican American children are mostly confined to the 1920s (see Valencia & Suzuki, 2001, p. 11 for eight citations of these studies).

67. For a sustained critique of Dunn (1987) and a rejoinder to his critics, see Fernández (1988). Also, see Valencia and Suzuki (2001, pp. 169–172) for a synopsis of this critique.

68. This section on *The Bell Curve* builds on, with revisions, Valencia and Solórzano (1997, p. 174, 200–201), and Valencia and Suzuki (2001, pp. 172–178, 314).

69. Herrnstein and Murray (1994), based on the normal distribution of IQ scores, break the continuum into five "cognitive classes" (p. 121). The classes, names given, IQ intervals, and percentage of cases are, respectively: Class I (very bright; 125 and above; 5%); Class II (bright; 110–124; 20%); Class III (normal; 90–109;

50%); Class IV (dull; 75–89; 20%); Class V (very dull; 74 and below; 5%). These classifications by IQ are very similar to the interval breaks testing specialists have used since the time of Lewis Terman (see Valencia, 1997d, pp. 73 and 102, note 38). Herrnstein and Murray note (p. 122), however, that they substituted more "neutral" terms ("very dull") for "less damning terms" ("retarded").

70. For scholarly examples of studies in which research investigations assert that SES is the independent variable and intelligence (as well as academic achievement) is the dependent variable, see White (1982) and Valencia and Suzuki (2001, chapter 3).

71. For their sources on the heritability index, Herrnstein and Murray (1994) cite: Bouchard and McGue (1981); Bouchard, Lykken, McGue, Segal, and Tellegen (1990); Pedersen, Plomin, Nesselroade, and McClearn (1992); Plomin and DeFries (1980).

72. Herrnstein and Murray's (1994) discussion of intelligence being substantially inherited exclusively focuses on Whites (see chapters 5–12 and note 11 of Part II, p. 125). Discussion of Black–White and Latino–White differences in cognitive ability is confined to chapter 13, yet the authors' coverage is a major flashpoint of *The Bell Curve*.

73. See: Graves (2002); Lane (1995); Reed (1994). A tally shows that Herrnstein and Murray cite Jensen and Lynn 23 times each, Rushton 11 times, and McGurk 5 times.

74. See: Dickens, Kane, and Schultze (1996); Fischer et al. (1996); Fraser (1995); Jacoby and Glauberman (1995); Kinchloe, Steinberg, and Gresson (1996). Of these five books, two (Fraser, 1995; Kinchloe et al., 1996) consist of collections of short reviews—all unfavorable to *The Bell Curve*. The book by Jacoby and Glauberman (1995) also contains brief reviews and commentaries, but of diverse views. Dickens et al. (1996) and Fischer et al. (1996), in contrast, base their books in large part on reanalysis of the National Longitudinal Survey of Youth study data Herrnstein and Murray (1994) use in *The Bell Curve*. The authors of both books draw very different conclusions about structure formation from those presented by Herrnstein and Murray.

75. For Murray's response to the critics, see Murray (1995).

76. See: Duster (1995); Fischer et al. (1996); Gardner (1995); Gould (1996); Jones (1995); Nisbett (1998); Reed (1994); Scott (1994).

77. See: Gardner (1995); Gould (1995); Hendricksen (1996).

78. As Gould (1996, p. 376) notes, a correlation of .40 yields an R^2 of only .16. R^2 is a statistic known as the coefficient of determination. It is the square of the observed correlation coefficient and is useful in explaining how much of the variance in the dependent variable (e.g., dropping out of high school) can be accounted for by the independent variable (e.g., IQ). Gould (1996) comments that the values of R^2 presented in Appendix 4 (pp. 593–623) of *The Bell Curve* are very low.

79. See: Carspecken (1996); Cary (1996); Cross (1996); Gardner (1995); Giroux and Searls (1996); Hauser (1995); Jones (1995); Kinchloe and Steinberg (1996); Lugg (1996); Worthen (1995).

80. Transaction Publishers released the first edition of *Race, Evolution, and Behavior* in 1995 (see neohereditarianism, wave II in Table 2.1, present chapter), and the second edition in 1997. The third edition (2000) contains a new Preface, and Afterword (same as provided in the 1997 edition). Sandwiched between the Preface and Afterword in the third edition is the identical text that appears in the first edition.

81. Rushton's (2000) framework of racial differences rests on r-K life history theory from evolutionary biology. From his glossary in *Race, Evolution, and Behavior*, he writes:

> r-SELECTION. Selection for the qualities needed to succeed in unstable, unpredictable environments, where ability to reproduce rapidly and opportunistically is at a premium, and where there is little value in adaptations to succeed in competition. A variety of qualities are thought to be favored by r-selection, including high fecundity and, in mammals, short life and small brains. Contrast with K-selection. It is customary to emphasize that r-selection and K-selection are the extremes of a continuum, most real cases lying somewhere between.
>
> K-SELECTION. Selection favoring the qualities needed to succeed in stable, predictable environments where there is likely to be heavy competition for limited resources between individuals well equipped to compete, at population sizes close to the maximum that the habitat can bear. A variety of qualities are thought to be favored by K-selection, including in mammals, long life, large brains, and small numbers of intensively cared-for offspring. Contrast with r-selection. K and r are symbols in the conventional algebra of population biologists. (pp. 303, 305)

82. See, for example: Ahmad (1995); Armelagos (1995); Barash (1995); Brace (1995); Graves (2002); Kamin (1995); Lewontin (1996); Lieberman (2001); Peters (1995); Relethford (1995); Wahlsten (1995).

83. See, for example: Brace (1995); Cann, Brown, and Wilson (1987); Cavalli-Sforza, Menozzi, and Piazza (1994); Diamond (1994); Graves (1993, 2001); Montagu (1974); Nei and Livshits (1989); Templeton (2002).

84. Of the 32 studies summarized in Table 2.2, Rushton (1995) has three parts: A (children and adolescents by external head measurements, $n = 13$ studies), B (adults by external head measurements, $n = 15$ studies), and C (adults by magnetic resonance imaging, $n = 4$ studies).

85. In the 32 investigations, the various researchers administered 12 different intelligence tests. Several measures had no name (e.g., "Basic"), and in a few studies the researchers used "teachers' estimates" and "grades" as proxies for measured intelligence.

86. See: *http://www.ferris.edu/ISAR/Institut/pioneer/pfspread/pfp6.htm*.

87. For book reviews of Lynn (1996), see, for example: Bouchard (1999); Jackson (1997); Lamb (1997); Mackintosh (2002); Van Court (1998); Whitney (1998); Wilmoth (1997). I should make readers aware, however, that some of the reviews lack objectivity. Jackson (1997) and Lamb (1997) published their reviews in Pioneer-supported *American Renaissance* and *Mankind Quarterly*, respectively. Bouchard (1999) and Whitney (1998) are Pioneer grantees. Van Court (1998) coauthored an article with Lynn (Lynn & Van Court, 2004). My caveat of bias also applies to some of the other reviewers I cite of Lynn's books.

88. For a biographical sketch of Itzkoff, see Lynn (2001, pp. 417–426). Itzkoff, who earned his Ph.D. in philosophy, has written a number of books on intelligence (i.e., evolution of human intelligence; racial differences in intelligence; importance of intelligence for economic viability of contemporary nations). In *The Decline of Intelligence in America* (1994), Itzkoff proposes a eugenics plan to curb the diminution of American intelligence:

Our intelligence levels are declining because more children are entering our schools from the lowest intellectual classes than from our elites. . . . It is all so simple in terms of a solution. We need to stimulate our finest to form families of the traditional sort in which children are conceived, born, raised, and educated to the highest levels for which they are capable. The helpless need to be encouraged and guided not to have children that they cannot rear and educate to functional cultural levels. (p. 204)

89. For book reviews of Lynn and Vanhanen (2006), see: Davies (2007); Nuenke (2007); Rushton (2006a).
90. For book reviews of Lynn (2006), see: Loehlin (2007); Mackintosh (2007); Meisenberg (2006); Rushton (2006b).
91. For book reviews of Lynn (2008), see: Ellis (2009); Rushton (2008).
92. See: *http://www.splcenter.org/intel/map/hate.jsp?T* = 39&m = 5#s = GA.
93. See: *http://www.splcenter.org/intel/intelreport/article.jsp?sid* = 371.
94. Vanhanen is Professor Emeritus of Political Science at the University of Tampere (Tampere, Finland). In 2002, the National Bureau of Investigation in Finland considered launching a criminal investigation of racist comments Vanhanen made against Africans. In Finland, authorities consider such remarks hate crimes (see: *http://www.hs.fi/english/article/1076153484261*).
95. For Lynn and Vanhanen's (2002) calculation of national IQs for the 81 nations, information on the various intelligence tests used, sample sizes, ages of examinees, and years of the published studies, see Appendix 1 (pp. 197–225) in *IQ and the Wealth of Nations*.
96. In the various studies, researchers used, by far, the Raven's Standard Progressive Matrices (RSPM) and the Raven's Coloured Progressive Matrices (RCPM), initially British-normed measures of nonmotor, nonverbal intelligence (Harris, Reynolds, & Koegel, 1996). Lynn and Vanhanen (2002) identified 160 different investigations in their analysis of IQ data for the 81 nations. Of the total 160 investigations, researchers used the RSPM or RCPM in 87 investigations (54%). The British standardization sets the means of the RSPM and the RCPM at 100 and the standard deviation at 15. For the mean national IQs of nations, in which the RSPM and RCPM served as the IQ estimate, Lynn and Vanhanen (2002) calculate these means using the Matrices as a yardstick (p. 197).
97. For the national IQ estimates of the 81 countries, Lynn and Vanhanen (2002) use a singular study 53% of the time (n = 43).
98. See Lynn and Vanhanen (2002, Table 6.5, pp. 73–80) for the respective 104 nations with estimated IQs and their respective "comparison countries."
99. For negative book reviews, see: Barnett and Williams (2004); Berhanu (2007); Ervik (2003); Godina (2005); Nechyba (2004); Palairet (2004); Richards (2002); Richardson (2004); Volken (2003); Whetzel and McDaniel (2006; this is not a book review per se; the authors reanalyze the data in Lynn and Vanhanen [2002] four different ways and disagree with the causal conclusions drawn in *IQ and the Wealth of Nations*). For the positive reviews, see: Dickerson (2006; this is not a book review, as such; the author reanalyzes the data in Lynn & Vanhanen [2002] using exponential correlation and suggests there is "a real and logical connection between IQ and the acquisition of national wealth" [p. 291]); Miller (2002); Rushton (2003).
100. See, for example: Gay (1994, p. 14); Spence, Underwood, Duncan, and Cotton (1968, p. 116); Tanur et al. (1989, p. 45); Worthen, Borg, and White (1993, pp. 111–112).

101. See: Berhanu (2007); Ervik (2003); Godina (2005); Palairet (2004); Richards (2002); Richardson (2004); Volken (2003); Whetzel and McDaniel (2006).
102. See: *http://www.airninja.com/worldfacts/countries/Philippines/population.htm.*
103. This section on scientific research investigations draws from, with revisions, Valencia and Suzuki (2001, pp. 154–156, 178–181, 310–311).
104. Lewontin (1975) comments that to have a proper study of heritability, investigators must meet six requirements (e.g., large sample sizes [at least several hundred families]); the various relationship pairs must be representative of the population to which the researcher applies the h^2 estimate, such as representativeness in schooling attainment or SES. Lewontin concludes: "In fact, no study of the genetics of IQ has even come close to fulfilling the six requirements, and all studies fail all tests in a significant way" (p. 394).
105. See: Bouchard (1997); Brody (1992); Brody and Brody (1976); Jensen (1969); Plomin et al. (1997); Taylor (1980); Tucker (1994).
106. See: Dorfman (1995); Lewontin (1975, 1976); Mackenzie (1984); Mercer and Brown (1973); Neisser et al. (1996); Taylor (1980, 1992).
107. See: Farber (1981); Kamin (1974); Steen (1996); Taylor (1980).
108. See: Juel-Nielsen (1965); Newman, Freeman, and Holzinger (1937); Shields (1962).
109. Bouchard (1983, 1997) challenges Taylor's (1980) reanalysis of the MZA twin data.
110. I need to note, however, that some scholars contend that calculations of heritability estimates of intelligence frequently violate critical assumptions of the statistical models used and employ statistical techniques that are insensitive to identifying heredity–environmental interactions (see Wahlsten, 1990, and those who concur with his position: Bullock, 1990; Chiszar & Gollin, 1990; Schönemann, 1994). Also, a number of scholars (including leading geneticists) assert that the heritability construct is a misguided notion (see Tucker, 1994, pp. 224–225). For example, Otto Kempthorne, an expert in biostatistics, maintains that "heritability does not even exist in the human context" (Kempthorne, 1978, p. 19). Finally, see note 104, present chapter.
111. See: Jensen (1973); Nichols (1970); Osborne and Gregor (1968); Osborne and Miele (1969); Scarr-Salapatek (1971); Vandenberg (1969, 1970).
112. I have located several other studies (Scarr & Weinberg, 1977; Scarr, Weinberg, & Waldman, 1993; Weinberg, Scarr, & Waldman, 1992).

Chapter 3

1. I culled this biographical information of Ruby Payne from her website (*http://www.ahaprocess.com/About_Us/Ruby_Payne.html*), the back cover of Payne (2005), Dworin and Bomer (2008), Gorski (2008), and Kunjufu (2006).
2. For related works in which the economically advantaged claim that the poor have moral flaws and shortcomings, see, for example: Betten (1973); Eames and Goode (1973); Gans (1995); Katz (1986, 1989, 1995); Piven and Cloward (1971); Rank (2004); Seligman (1968); Steinberg (2001); Tropman (1998).
3. See, for example: Bullock, Williams, and Limbert (2003); Eames and Goode (1973); Feagin (1975); Goode (2002); Katz (1989); Kluegel and Smith (1986); Prins and Schafft (2009); Rank (2004); Valentine (1968).
4. See: *http://www.mnsu.edu/emuseum/information/biography/klmno/lewis_oscar.html.*
5. The German term "lumpen proletariat" (or "lumpenproletariat"), coined by Karl Marx and Friedrich Engels in *The German Ideology* (1845), is approximately

translated as "slum workers" or "the mob." Lumpen proletariat refers to the outcast that comprises a part of the population residing in industrial centers. This class includes prostitutes, gangsters, beggars, swindlers, racketeers, tramps, petty criminals, and the chronically unemployed. Writers of the *Communist Manifesto* used *lumpenproletariat*, where it is translated as the "dangerous class" (see "Encyclopedia of Marxism: Glossary of Terms website," s.v. "lumpenproletariat" at: *http://www.marxists.org/glossary/terms/l/u.htm#lumpenproletariat.*

6. See, for example: Frost and Hawkes (1966); Hellmuth (1967). This brief discussion on 1960s deficit thinking builds on, with revisions, Valencia and Solórzano (1997, pp. 192, 202).

7. Although Marans and Lourie (1967) do acknowledge that "the issue of the effects of malnutrition, inadequate prenatal care and the like, on the physical constitution of the children is an extremely important one" (p. 21), such concerns carry a secondary importance. According to Marans and Lourie, the onus of the deprivation lay in the parents and the home environment.

8. Dionne, E.J., Jr. (2000, March 31). Michael Harrington's "America Can" reflects an optimism about America's social possibilities that needs to be rekindled. *Washington Post*, p. A29. Available online at: *http://www.commondreams.org/views/033100-105.htm.* Also, see: Harrington (1981, p. 212), Lewis (1966a, p. xlii), Donavan (1967); Isserman (2000).

9. For critiques of Moynihan (1965), see, for example: Katz (1989, pp. 24–29, 44–52); Valentine (1968, pp. 29–42).

10. According to a biographical note in *The Underclass* (1970), Auletta worked as a writer for *The New Yorker* and a columnist for the *New York Daily News*. He has a master's degree in political science from the Maxwell School of Citizenship and Public Affairs at Syracuse University.

11. Russell, G. (1977, August 29). The front cover of this issue is, "The American Underclass: Minority within a Minority."

12. For discussion and critique of the underclass notion, see: Katz (1989, chapter 5); Reed (1992); Valencia and Solórzano (1997, pp. 183–189).

13. See: Barnes (2001); Coward, Feagin, and Williams (1974); Gould (1999); Jargowsky (1996); Jones (1993); Jones and Luo (1999); O'Connor (2001). Also, see Valentine's 1968 book, *Culture and Poverty: Critique and Counter-Proposals*, for the most extended critique of Oscar Lewis's culture of poverty notion. For 14 reviews of Valentine (1968)—some negative ($n = 6$), most positive ($n = 8$)—see: Berndt (1969); Boissevain (1969); Bushnell (1969); Carstens (1969); Gladwin (1969); Hannerz (1969); Kochar (1969); Leacock (1969); Lewis (1969); Mangin (1969); Matza (1969); Mead (1969); Miller (1969); Moynihan (1969). See Valentine (1969) for a reply to these reviews.

14. Valentine (1968, p. 132). See Valentine (1968, pp. 129–134) for a discussion of culture of poverty hypotheses and rival hypotheses.

15. See, for example: Anchor (1978); Eames and Goode (1973); Edin and Lein (1997); Foley, Mota, Post, and Lozano (1988); Goode (2001); Leeds (1971); Naples (1991, 1998); Pardo (1998); Peattie (1968); Piven and Cloward (1971, 1979); Sharff (1987, 1998); Stack (1974); Uzzell (1975); Valentine (1978); Williams (1981); Willie (1976).

16. Payne also has authored/co-authored a number of other self-published books via her publication firm, aha! Process, Inc. Examples are: *Removing the Mask: Giftedness in Poverty* (Slocumb & Payne, 2000); *Bridges Out of Poverty: Strategies for Professionals and Communities* (Payne, DeVol, & Smith, 2006; designed for health, social, and legal services professionals); *Hidden Rules of Class at Work* (Payne &

Krabill, 2002; geared for the business sector); *Understanding Learning: The How, the Why, the What* (Payne, 2002); *Working with Students: Discipline Strategies for the Classroom* (Payne, 2006a); *Working with Parents: Building Relationships for Successful Students* (Payne, 2006b). A common theme that runs through most of Payne's publications is the subject of "hidden rules" ("the unspoken cues and habits of a group," Payne [2005, p. 37]) that are particular, she asserts, for people in poverty, the middle class, and the wealthy.

17. The 2005 U.S. Department of Health and Human Services Poverty Guidelines. Available online at: *http://aspe.hhs.gov/poverty/05poverty.shtml.*

18. The chapters in *Framework* are titled as follows: "Definitions and Resources" (chapter 1); "The Role of Language and Story" (chapter 2); "Hidden Rules Among Classes" (chapter 3); "Characteristics of Generational Poverty" (chapter 4); "Role Models and Emotional Resources" (chapter 5); "Support Systems" (chapter 6); "Discipline" (chapter 7); "Instruction and Improving Achievement" (chapter 8); "Creating Relationships" (chapter 9).

19. See: *http://www.ahaprocess.com/School_Programs/Research_&_Development/ Research_Base.html.*

20. *Id.*

21. Free Online Dictionary. See: *http://www.thefreedictionary.com/mindset.*

22. Stereotypes permeate Payne's (2005) *Framework*. It is important to note that stereotypes are false perceptions and misrepresent reality. As noted psychologist Gordon Allport (1954) states, "Whether favorable or unfavorable, *a stereotype is an exaggerated belief associated with a category. Its function is to justify (rationalize) our conduct in relation to that category*" (p. 191). A more technical definition is: "From a cognitive perspective . . . *a stereotype* can be defined as a *cognitive structure that contains the perceiver's knowledge, beliefs, and expectancies about some human group*" (Hamilton & Trolier, 1986, p. 133). For an excellent coverage of stereotype formation, see Stephan (1999).

23. This discussion of Mexican Americans valuing education draws from, with revisions, Valencia (2008, p. xiii), and Valencia and Black (2002, p. 81).

24. See: Koh, Abbatiello, and McLoughlin (1984); Miele (1979). These studies are investigations of possible cultural bias on the Wechsler Intelligence Scale for Children (WISC; Wechsler, 1949). Black and White children participated. The researchers examined a number of WISC items for likely bias. The scenario I note is from an item ("What is the thing to do if a fellow (girl) much smaller than yourself starts a fight with you?") from the Comprehension subtest of the WISC.

25. This coverage of White (1982) comes from, with revisions, Valencia and Suzuki (2001, pp. 78–80, 304).

26. Although White (1982), in this particular analysis, collapsed studies across dependent measures (achievement and intelligence), the observed *r* of .35 can be fairly generalizable to studies that examine only the relation between SES and intelligence. That is, achievement and intelligence tests share much in common. This assertion is based on the observation that achievement and intelligence tests show a typical range of correlations of .60 to .70 for elementary schoolchildren, and .50 to .60 for high school students (Jensen, 1980).

27. This discussion on average differences between racial/ethnic and SES groups draws from, with revisions, Valencia and Suzuki (2001, pp. xxii, 295).

28. To some extent, this assertion about stereotypic thinking regarding racial/ethnic group differences in intelligence is supported by empirical research. Results from a 1990 survey conducted by the National Opinion Research Center at the University

of Chicago finds that a majority of White respondents believe that Blacks and Hispanics are less intelligent than Whites (cited in Duke, 1991).

29. This description of the MSCA comes from, with revisions, Valencia (1988, pp. 82–83).

30. For discussions of this type of mental retardation, see, for example: Glick (1998); Keogh and Jones (1986); Langone (1996); MacMillan, Siperstein, and Leffert (2006); Tymchuk, Lakin, and Luckasson (2001).

31. Discussion of the *Larry P.* case comes from, with revisions, Valencia and Suzuki (2001, p. 204).

32. See Valencia (2008, chapter 3) for a comprehensive coverage of how three landmark legal cases in the early 1970s involving incorrect diagnosis and placement of Black, Mexican American, and Yaqui Indian children in classes for the educable mentally retarded led to a sea change in nondiscriminatory assessments in special education. See Harry and Klingner (2006) for a current discussion of explanations that compete with the opinion that special education placement reflects authentic learning and behavioral deficits requiring such placement.

33. This biographical sketch comes from: *http://www.icelp.org/asp/Professional_ Team.shtm*. For a comprehensive biography of Feuerstein's life and work, see Burgess (2008).

34. In regard to Feuerstein and associates' impact on special education theory and practice, see, for example: Detterman, Gabriel, and Ruthsatz (2000); Feuerstein, Rand, Hoffman, Hoffman, and Miller (1979); Feuerstein et al. (1985, 1986); Missiuna and Samuels (1988).

35. For further discussion on the nature of Feuerstein and associates' model of cognitive assessment and learning facilitation, see: Feuerstein (1990); Feuerstein, Rand, and Hoffman (1979); Feuerstein, Rand, Hoffman, Hoffman, and Miller (1979); Feuerstein, Rand, Hoffman, and Miller (1980); Feuerstein et al. (1985, 1986); Feuerstein, Rand, and Rynders (1988).

36. These last two sentences are from, with revisions, Valencia, Villarreal, and Salinas (2002, p. 293).

37. See Bohn (2006, 2007); Bomer, Dworin, May, and Semingson (2008); Dudley-Marling (2007); Dworin and Bomer (2008); Gorski (2005, 2006a, 2006b, 2008); Kunjufu (2006); Ng and Rury (2006); Osei-Kofi (2005); Smiley and Helfenbein (in press).

38. An example of this spherical disconnect is the experience of Professor Anita P. Bohn (2006), who relates:

> I first heard the name Ruby Payne from teachers and school administrators about eight years ago when interviewing a school district about professional development opportunities in multicultural education in their district. Several teachers and an administrator told me Payne had been brought to town to conduct workshops for the teachers and that the district had bought each participant a copy of her book *A Framework for Understanding Poverty*. Over the next few years I heard references like this over and over again, not only in my home state of Illinois, but from teachers and administrators around the country. (p. 1)

I daresay that those of us in the academy have had similar word-of-mouth testimonials finding out about Ruby Payne. As for me, I became aware of Payne in 2005 in one of my graduate courses when I was giving a lecture on deficit thinking. One of my students, Elizabeth, a former school principal who was pursuing her doctorate in Educational Administration, mentioned that she had attended one of Payne's workshops, and that *Framework* was the required reading. During class discussion, after the students had a chance to think about the nature of the deficit thinking notion, Elizabeth remarked that Payne's views of the poor are laced with deficit thinking. Suffice it to say, I wanted to know more about Ruby Payne.

39. Gorski (2008) also undertook a content analysis of Payne's *Framework*. His corpus of critiques contains 8 of the 13 references I use; he also analyzes a number of papers presented at professional conferences. Gorski (2008) found eight core concerns in Payne's work, which he refers to as "elements of oppression" that contribute to "classism," "racism," and "other inequities." Gorski (2008) discusses these elements: (a) "uncritical and self-serving 'scholarship,' " (b) "the elusive culture of poverty," (c) "abounding stereotyping," (d) "deficit theory," (e) "invisibility of classism," (f) "the 'it's not about race' card," (g) "peddling paternalism," and (h) "compassionate conservatism." Three of Gorski's (2008) elements (b, c, and d) are strikingly similar to three of my themes (Culture of Poverty; Stereotyping; Deficit Thinking), indicating some consonance across independent content analyses.

40. See Tough, P. (2007, June 10). The class-consciousness raiser. *New York Times Magazine*. Available online at: *http://www.nytimes.com/2007/06/10/magazine/10payne-t.html?scp* = 1&sq = %22class+consciousness+raiser%22&st = nyt.

41. I thank Anita P. Bohn (2007) for this search suggestion.

42. A case in point is Dr. Mary Montle Bacon, of the National Professional Resources, Inc., a professional development organization. Bacon has written *Working with Students from the Culture of Poverty*. On her website, the product description of her book states:

> The culture of poverty refers to a unique set of beliefs, behaviors, and ways of living that impoverished people transmit to their children from generation to generation. Because the vast majority of educators hold middle class values, which are very different from those held in the culture of poverty, they can find it difficult to understand and work with students who come from impoverished backgrounds.

See: *http://www.nprinc.com/ell/vwcp.htm*.

43. This epilogue draws from, with revisions, Valencia (2009).

44. For a response to Payne (2009), see Bomer, Dworin, May, and Semingson (2009). Bomer and associates offer a further critique of the validity of her research findings she notes in her response, and the authors rebut her claim that their position is a deterministic perspective.

45. For example, see my discussion of Terman (1916) in chapter 1, present volume, Jensen (1969) in chapter 2, present volume, and Payne (2005), present chapter.

Chapter 4

1. Some scholars consistently place the term "at-risk" in quotation marks, indicating they question the validity of the construct (e.g., Fine, 1995; Lubeck, 1995; Swadener, 1995; Swadener & Lubeck, 1995a; Tabachnick & Bloch, 1995). I also raise serious concerns about the soundness of the at-risk notion, but to avoid repetitiveness I do not place the term in quotation marks.

2. Laosa (1984, p. 1). For further discussion of the historical origins of the at-risk notion, see: Cuban (1989); Horn (1993); Schlossman and Turner (1993); Swadener (1990); Tropea (1993); Wollons (1993).

3. Swadener (1990) is referring to the kindergartens developed by German educator

Friedrich Froebel, who developed this early childhood education program to allow the child to explore his/her world through inquisitive play and discovery (see, Brosterman & Togashi, 1997). Swadener (1990) notes that the Froebelian kindergarten was "based on the assumption that early education could defer moral and other deficiencies in homes of [the] poor, immigrants, etc." (p. 28).

4. Swadener (1990) notes that some of these scholars are Michael Apple, Stanley Aronowitz, Michelle Fine, Henry Giroux, Ivan Illich, and Lois Weis. To this distinguished list, I would add the likes of Arthur Pearl, Tony Knight, Peter McLaren, Kofi Lomotey, Daniel Solórzano, Tara Yosso, and Pedro Noguera—just a sampling of heterodox scholars.

5. Other such reports, are, for example: *An Imperiled Generation: Saving Urban Schools* (Carnegie Foundation for the Advancement of Teaching, 1988); *America's Shame, America's Hope: Twelve Million Youth at Risk* (Smith & Lincoln, 1988); *Visions of a Better Way: A Black Appraisal of Public Schooling* (Joint Center for Political Studies [U.S.] & Franklin, 1989); all cited in Lytle (1990).

6. For a similar observation, see David C. Berliner and Bruce J. Biddle's *The Manufactured Crisis: Myths, Frauds, and the Attack on America's Public Schools* (1995).

7. This discussion of questionable assumptions that frame the excellence reports draws from Reyes and Valencia (1993, pp. 307, 310).

8. This discussion of Margonis (1992) draws from Ronda and Valencia (1994, p. 366).

9. I thank Dr. Bruno Villarreal for assisting with this search.

10. In all, 87 PDK chapters participated. Members took part in the study by collecting data from students, teachers, and counselors. Only students in "typical" classrooms served as participants (e.g., not students in classes for the mentally retarded or full-time students in alternative programs). Researchers collected data on 22,018 students (fourth and seventh graders; high school sophomores; others).

11. This discussion on Swadener and Lubeck (1995a) draws from, with revisions, Valencia and Solórzano (1997, pp. 196–197).

12. See: Arnold (1995); Cook and Fine (1995); Hauser and Thompson (1995); Quintero and Rummel (1995); White (1995).

13. Barr and Parrett (2008) do have a section at book's end (pp. 359–373), which they title "50 Strategies Suggested Reading." The authors note that these suggested resources are meant to "complement" the 50 strategies as teachers use them in the classroom. In any event, it is difficult to ascertain if the suggested reading for each strategy is supposed to provide empirical support for the respective "Research" points.

14. See, for example: Betts, Rueben, and Danenberg (2000); Darling-Hammond (2000, 2004a); Darling-Hammond and Post (2000); Darling-Hammond and Youngs (2002); Fuller, Carpenter, and Fuller (2008); Rice (2003); Rivin, Hanushek, and Kain (2005); Wayne and Youngs (2003); Wright, Horn, and Sanders (1997).

15. All 9th- and 10th-grade students must take TAKS subtests in reading and mathematics. In addition, tenth graders also take the TAKS English language arts subtest, while eleventh graders take the TAKS Exit-Level test, consisting of English language arts, mathematics, science, and social studies subtests (Texas Education Agency, 2006, p. 13).

16. Fuller et al. (2008) also found a similar pattern for middle schools (see p. 60, Table A–6A).

17. See, for example: Barton (2003, 2004); Carroll, Fulton, Abercrombie, and Yoon (2004); Darling-Hammond (2004a); Darling-Hammond and Post (2000);

Education Trust (2008); Fuller et al. (2008); Jerald (2002); Peske and Haycock (2006); Rivin et al. (2005).

18. Richard M. Ingersoll performed the data analysis. The data are from the U.S. Department of Education's 1999–2000 Schools and Staffing Survey, which utilized a sizeable and statistically representative sample of schoolteachers (Jerald, 2002, p. 2).

19. Jerald (2002, p. 6). High-poverty schools and low-poverty schools are operationalized as having 50% or more and 15% or less of the students, respectively, being eligible for the federally funded free- and reduced-lunch program. The same percentage cutoff points held for the definitions of high-minority and low-minority schools (*Id.* at 4).

20. The API is the keystone of California's *Public Accountability Act of 1999*. The index measures the academic achievement performance and the growth of schools via a number of academic indicators (e.g., pass rates on state-mandated tests; graduation rates; attendance rates). See: *http://www.cde.ca.gov/ta/ac/ay/documents/overview09.pdf*.

21. See, for example: Barton (2003, 2004); Carey (2004); Education Trust (2007, 2008); Grubb, Goe, and Huerta (2004); Oakes (2002, 2004); Oakes and Lipton (2004); Oakes and Saunders (2004); Rumberger and Gándara (2004).

22. Education Trust (2008, p. 12, Table 2). In this table, data are reported for the 50 largest school districts in Texas. For brevity's sake, I only report data for the 25 largest districts.

23. *Williams v. California*, Civil Action No. 312236 (Superior Court, San Francisco County, California, March 23, 2005).

24. *Serrano v. Priest*, Civil Action No. 93824 (Superior Court, Los Angeles County, California, January 8, 1969); *Rodriguez v. San Antonio Independent School District*, 337 F. Supp. 280 W.D. Tex. 1971). For a discussion of these cases, see Valencia (2008, chapter 2).

25. Considerable legal materials germane to *Williams* are available online. Go to the *Williams v. California* website, *http://www.decentschools.com*. There, one can locate, for example, selected papers filed with the Superior Court (e.g., plaintiffs' first amended complaint; various briefs) and the appellate court. Also, accessible at this website are the plaintiffs' and defendants' expert reports, as well as all experts' deposition testimonies.

In addition to the legal documents, scholars have produced numerous publications in regard to the *Williams* case. See, for example: Oakes (2002); Oakes and Lipton (2004); Powers (2004). Also, see the special double issue of *Teachers College Record* (2004, *106*, no. 10 and 11). This special issue contains 15 articles that analyze the claims of the plaintiffs in *Williams*. The articles are: Darling-Hammond (2004a); Fine, Burns, Payne, and Torre (2004); Grubb, Goe, and Huerta (2004); Koski and Weis (2004); Mintrop (2004); Noguera (2004); Oakes (2004); Oakes and Saunders (2004); Ortiz (2004); Ready, Lee, and Welner (2004); Rogers (2004); Rumberger and Gándara (2004); Russell, Higgins, and Raczek (2004); Teranishi, Allen, and Solórzano (2004); Timar (2004). For this special issue of *Teachers College Record*, the lead article by Oakes (2004) is particularly instructive. She provides background information on *Williams*, the plaintiffs' claims, the State's response via its experts, and a brief discussion of the settlement. Finally, Oakes (2004) briefly introduces each of the 14 remaining articles.

26. First Amended Complaint for Injunctive and Declaratory Relief (pp. 23–34), filed August 14, 2000, *Williams v. California*, Civil Action No. 312236 (Superior Court,

San Francisco County, California, March 23, 2005). Retrieved March 17, 2009, from: *http://www.decentschools.com/court_papers.php.*

27. Oakes (2004, p. 1896). In a deficit thinking posturing, the Davis administration filed a lawsuit on December 12, 2001 against 18 plaintiff school districts in *Williams*, claiming that the districts are to blame for the substandard conditions. See: *http://www.aclunc.org/news/press_releases/civil_rights_groups_respond_to_governor_gray_davis%27_action_to_sue_18_school_districts_in_landmark_education_lawsuit.shtml.*

28. In regard to Phillips, see, for example, Valencia (2008, pp. 294–296). Regarding Rossell, see, for example, Valencia (2008, pp. 72–73). For the deposition testimonies and expert reports of Phillips and Rossell (as well as for the other 13 defendants' experts), see: *http://www.decentschools.com/experts.php.*

29. See: *http://www.cde.ca.gov/eo/ce/wc/wmslawsuit.asp.* Also, see the following website at the California Department of Education: *http://www.cde.ca.gov/eo/ce/wc/index.asp.* Settlement information is also available at: *http://www.decentschools.com.* Furthermore, for the most recent update on *Williams*, see "*Williams v. California: A Progress Update*" (report released on May 29, 2009). Available at: *http://www.decentschools.com.*

Chapter 5

1. It is difficult to obtain data on ethnic breakdown for students enrolled in teacher education programs. One can extrapolate such proportions, however, by examining the ethnic composition of the K–12 public school teaching force. For example, in California and Texas, the states with the first and second largest public K–12 school enrollments (respectively) as of the 2007–2008 school year, a disparity analysis of teachers by ethnicity reveals the following:

Disparity Analysis of Teachers by Race/Ethnicity in California and Texas K–12 Schools: 2007–2008

| State | White Students | | White Teachers | | |
	No.	Total Enrollment (%)	No.	Total Teaching Force (%)	Disparity Percentage[a]
California[b]	1,790,513	29.4	219,499	71.7	+143.9
Texas[c]	1,619,426	34.8	217,159	67.5	+94.1

| State | Students of Color | | Teachers of Color | | |
	No.	Total Enrollment (%)	No.	Total Teaching Force (%)	Disparity Percentage[a]
California	4,293,631	70.6	86,561	28.3	−59.9
Texas	3,032,090	65.2	104,571	32.5	−50.2

Note: [a]In the percentage disparity category, a plus sign (+) indicates overrepresentation and a minus sign (−) indicates underrepresentation. [b]Data are from California Department of Education (2008a). [c]Data are from Texas Education Agency (2008a).

2. In many of the largest public school districts in the nation, data for the 2007–2008 school year show that students of color account for the majority of the K–12 enrollments. For example, of the 689,283 students in the Los Angeles Unified School District (California), students of color comprise 91.1% (n = 628,013 students) of the district's enrollment, while White students account for 8.9% (n = 61,270) of the total enrollment (California Department of Education, 2008b). In the Chicago Public Schools (Illinois), students of color constitute 91.8% (n = 362,957 students) of the district's total enrollment of 395,592 students; White students account for only 8.3% (n = 32,635) of the total enrollment (Illinois State Board of Education, 2008). Of the 343,432 students enrolled in the Miami-Dade County Public Schools (Florida), 90.7% (n = 311,538) of the district's enrollment are students of color; White students comprise only 9.3% (n = 31,894) of the district's total enrollment (Florida Department of Education, 2008). Finally, Houston Independent School District (Texas) enrolls 198,769 students, with 92.0% (n = 182,852) of the district's enrollment consisting of students of color; the remaining 8.0% (n = 15,917) of students are White (Texas Education Agency, 2008b).
3. See: Marx (2001, 2003, 2004a, 2004b, 2006) and Marx and Pennington (2003).
4. "Tex Mex" is the self-ascribed language (i.e., speech practices) spoken by numerous Mexican Americans of South Texas. Historically, however, the dominant Anglo society of the region has imposed a pejorative label on the term. Tex Mex involves inter- and intrasentential code-switching, but also "the linguistic repertoire of Tex Mex speakers includes lexical features specific to the region that are neither codified English nor Spanish morphemes such as *lonche* (lunch)" (Kells, 2006, p. 187). Furthermore, although it is a "marked status, Tex Mex operates as an important solidarity marker, helping to establish and maintain social access among speakers" (Kells, 2006, pp. 187–188). For a comprehensive discussion of the nature of Tex Mex, see Kells (2002, 2004, 2006).
5. Marx (2006, 128–134). Also, see Marx (2006, pp. 155–169) for a discussion of a number of recommendations that could be used to foster greater discussion of White racism among preservice teachers in their teacher preparation experience.
6. See: Delpit (1988); Macedo (2000); Ogbu (1990); Watkin (2000).
7. For a discussion of the nature of CDA, see my coverage of Dworin and Bomer (2008) in chapter 3, present book.
8. Purcell-Gates' (1995) book is a case study of an urban Appalachian mother, Jenny, and her son, Donny. Jenny (a pseudonym) is a "low-caste," nearly nonliterate woman. Donny (also a pseudonym) had just been promoted to second grade, but was not able to read any words more than his own name. In *Other People's Words*, Purcell-Gates describes her journey in helping Jenny and Donny gain literacy. The author is a strong anti-deficit thinking advocate. She comments:

> Efforts to explain the overall failure of low socioeconomic status minority populations to attain literacy levels commensurate with the middle class have fallen short, and closing the achievement gap has proved elusive. For years, professionals and public opinion have held on to the notion that poor and minority peoples are deficient in important ways. The list of supposed deficiencies is long and inclusive: deficient cognitive abilities, deficient language, poor motivation, devaluation of education, poor parenting skills. To a large degree these attitudes and beliefs about this segment of the population persist. "*Those people*" don't care about education, or are genetically unfit, or cannot even speak correctly, much less learn to read and write

standard English. From the level of policymaking to the individual class-room, such deficit-ridden views of children who come from poor and minority homes continue to have an impact on the education to which they are exposed. (p. 3)

For her theoretical lens, Purcell-Gates draws from a sociocultural view of learning, in which all cultural communities are seen as having cognitive strengths, and language variations are viewed as normative for the respective groups.

9. For a closely related study by these researchers, see Abrego, Rubin, and Sutterby (2006). See Munter (2004) for a related study of preservice teachers who engage in collaborative inquiry with Latino parents whose children attend school on the U.S.–Mexico border. Finally, for another investigation involving a group of preservice teachers from diverse ethnic groups, see Quartz and the TEP Research Group (2003).
10. See *http://www.thefreedictionary.com/metonymy*.
11. See, for example, Barnard (2004); Fan (2001); Fan and Chen (2001); Feuerstein (2000); Henderson and Berla (1994); Jeynes (2003, 2005); McWayne, Hampton, Fantuzzo, Cohen, and Sekino (2004); Patall, Cooper, and Robinson (2008); Scrib-ner, Young, and Pedroza (1999); Seefeldt, Denton, Galper, and Younoszai (1998); Sheldon (2003).
12. This statement on the major myth comes from, with a slight revision, Valencia and Solórzano (1997, p. 190).
13. For brief discussions of deficit thinking regarding parental engagement in education, see, for example: Allexsaht-Snider (2006); Ceja (2004); Cooper (2003); Jackson and Remillard (2005); López, Scribner, and Mahitivanichcha (2001); Lott (2003); Moreno and Valencia (2002); Valencia and Black (2002).
14. The following discussion builds on, with revisions, Valencia and Black (2002, pp. 81, 83, 88). In their article, Valencia and Black examine the myth in three ways. First, they suggest that the basis for the myth lies in the pseudoscientific notion of deficit thinking, a mind-set molded by the fusion of ideology and science that blames the victim, rather than holding oppressive and inequitable schooling arrangements culpable. Second, the authors explore the course of the myth-making itself. In doing so, they examine several sources (e.g., early master's theses; published scholarly literature, particularly from the "cultural deprivation" and "at risk" child categories). Third, Valencia and Black discuss how they debunk the myth by providing strong evidence that Mexican Americans do indeed value education—that is: (a) the Mexican American people's long-standing struggle for equal educational opportunity; (b) the scholarly literature documenting parental involvement; (c) a case study of transgenerational parental involvement.
15. Actually, it was American Indians who had the lowest high school completion rate (11.4%), not Mexican Americans (see Grebler, Moore, & Guzmán, 1970, p. 143, Table 7–1).
16. See Valencia and Black (2002, pp. 92–98) as to how the authors debunk the claim that Mexican Americans do not value education.
17. For a critique of the status quo version of meritocracy, see Valencia, Menchaca, and Valenzuela (1993, pp. 10–12).
18. In her literature review, Lott (2003) cites a number of references to support her assertions and conclusions. See Lott for these citations.
19. See, for example: McKenzie and Scheurich (2004, 2007); McKenzie, Skrla, and

Scheurich (2006); Reyes (2005); Reyes and Wagstaff (2005); Shields (2006); Skrla and Scheurich (2001); Skrla, Erlandson, Reed, and Wilson (2001); Skrla, Scheurich, Garcia, and Nolly (2004).

20. Prominent scholars, for example, are professors Kathryn B. McKenzie, James J. Scheurich, and Linda Skrla of the Educational Administration and Human Resource Department at Texas A&M University, College Station.

21. McKenzie and Scheurich (2004, p. 612). McKenzie and Scheurich cite Lam and Peake (1997) and Ricci (2000) as sources of more information on three-way conferencing.

22. For examples of schools that have shown success with the students of color, McKenzie and Scheurich (2004) cite: Koschoreck (2001); Reyes, Scribner, and Scribner (1999); Skrla and Scheurich (2001).

23. For this examination of definitions of social justice, I draw from the discussion by Theoharis (2007a, pp. 222–223).

24. See: Theoharis (2004a, 2004b, 2004c, 2007a, 2007b).

25. The proportion of students of color in the seven schools ranged from 34% to 99%, and the proportion of students in poverty ranged from 5% to 90% (see Theoharis, 2007a, p. 228, Table 1).

26. In 2000, 18% of the Latino students attained proficient or advanced status; in 2004, 100% of them did so (Theoharis, 2007a, pp. 233, Table 2).

27. Foster (2000, pp. 162–163) cites the early work of such scholars as (chronologically listed): Cazden, John, and Hymes (1972); Labov (1972); Michaels (1981); Gilmore and Glatthorn (1982); Philips (1983); Watson-Gegeo (1992).

28. Although I do not discuss it here, Foley, Levinson, and Hurtig (2000) also cover the emergence of feminist ethnographers who examine the gendered terrain of education and student culture (pp. 58–79). Furthermore, for a discussion specific to the work of Chicano(a)/Latino(a) critical ethnographers, see Villenas and Foley (2002).

29. The third critique concerns the work of educational anthropologist John Ogbu. I cover the criticism of his work in chapter 1, present book.

30. For such perspectives, Foley (2001) refers readers to Foley and Moss (2001) and Levinson and Holland (1996).

31. For an especially good example of a multiple-dominance perspective, see McCarthy (1998; cited in Foley, 2001).

32. See Guajardo et al. (2008) for a chronicle of "Carmen," who eventually earned her Ph.D.

Chapter 6

1. This paragraph builds on, with revisions, Valencia, Villarreal, and Salinas (2002, pp. 254–255).

2. See chapter 4, present book.

3. This paragraph, and the next, and accompanying notes (4–6) draws from Valencia (2008, pp. 268–269, and p. 287).

4. The 26 states are Alabama, Alaska, Arizona, California, Florida, Georgia, Idaho, Indiana, Louisiana, Maryland, Massachusetts, Minnesota, Mississippi, Nevada, New Jersey, New Mexico, New York, North Carolina, Ohio, Oklahoma, South Carolina, Tennessee, Texas, Utah, Virginia, and Washington.

5. The 16 states are Arkansas, California, Connecticut, Delaware, Florida, Georgia, Hawaii, Louisiana, Mississippi, New Mexico, North Carolina, Oklahoma, South Carolina, Texas, Virginia, and Wisconsin (see American Federation of Teachers, 2001, p. 33, Table 12). Of these 16 states, all but Arkansas, Georgia, and Hawaii

have promotion policies at the middle school level (D.C. also does not have a promotion policy at this level).

6. Interested readers are referred to the writings of the following scholars, for example, who have leveled criticisms at high-stakes testing and the standards-based school reform movement: Amrein and Berliner (2002), Darling-Hammond (2004b), Darling-Hammond and Wise (1985), Flores and Clark (1997), Gunzerhauser (2003), Haney (2002), Horn (2003), McNeil (2000), Meier (2002), Nichols, Glass, and Berliner (2005), Orfield and Kornhaber (2001), Pearl (2002), Valencia and Guadarrama (1996), Valencia, Valenzuela, Sloan, and Foley (2001), Valencia and Villarreal (2003), and Valenzuela (2005). For a comprehensive volume that offers commentaries from both sides of the equity/accountability debate, see Skrla and Scheurich (2004).

In addition to criticisms of high-stakes testing expressed in scholarly publications, as of 2006 over 70 professional organizations (e.g., American Educational Research Association; American Psychological Association) have opposed, via official statements, high-stakes testing (see *http://www.educationalequity.net/opposition.htm*).

Finally, considerable critiques have been directed toward the No Child Left Behind (NCLB) Act of 2002 (P.L. 107–110), the federal government's omnibus bill designed to eliminate the academic achievement gap between White students and students of color. The NCLB Act, one of the most ambitious school reform attempts in U.S. history to close the achievement gap, has faced considerable criticism. See, for example: Gamoran (2007); Hursch (2007); Lee (2007); Meier and Wood (2004); Rebell and Wolff (2008).

7. This section comes from, with revisions, Valencia and Villarreal (2003, pp. 616–617).

8. This section builds on, with revisions, Valencia, Villarreal, and Salinas (2002, pp. 295–296).

9. See: Valencia (2008, chapter 8); Valencia and Bernal (2000).

10. See Campbell (1975).

11. The latter part of this paragraph draws from, with revisions, Pearl (2002, pp. 335, 348).

References

Abell, T., & Lyon, L. (1979). Do the differences make a difference? An empirical evaluation of the culture of poverty in the United States. *American Anthropologist, 6,* 602–621.

Abrego, M.H., Rubin, R., & Sutterby, J.A. (2006). They call me *maestra*: Preservice teachers' interactions with parents in a reading tutoring program. *Action in Teacher Education, 28,* 3–12.

Acuña, R.F. (2007). *Occupied America: A history of Chicanos* (6th ed.). New York: Longman.

Ahmad, W. (1995, July 22). Race is a four letter word [Review of the books *The bell curve wars* and *Race, evolution, and behavior*]. *New Scientist,* 44–45.

Airasian, P.W. (1988). Symbolic validation: The case of state-mandated, high-stakes testing. *Educational Evaluation and Policy Analysis, 10,* 301–315.

Albarraci, D., Johnson, B.T., & Zanna, M.P. (Eds.). (2005). *The handbook of attitudes.* Mahwah, NJ: Lawrence Erlbaum.

Alland, A., Jr. (2002). *Race in mind: Race, IQ, and other racisms.* New York: Palgrave Mcmillan.

Allen, V.L. (1970). The psychology of poverty: Problems and prospects. In V.L. Allen (Ed.), *Psychological factors in poverty* (pp. 367–383). Chicago: Markham Press.

Allexsaht-Snider, M. (2006). Editorial: Urban parents' perspectives on children's mathematics learning and issues of equity in mathematics education. *Mathematical Thinking and Learning, 8,* 187–195.

Allport, G.W. (1954). *The nature of prejudice.* Reading, MA: Addison-Wesley.

American Federation of Teachers. (2001). *Making standards matter 2001: A fifty-state report on efforts to implement a standards-based system.* Washington, DC: Author.

Amrein, A.L., & Berliner, D.C. (2002). High-stakes testing, uncertainty, and student learning. *Education Policy Analysis Archives, 10*(18). Available at: *http://epaa.asu.edu/epaa/v10n18/.*

Anastasi, A. (1988). *Psychological testing* (6th ed.). New York: Macmillan.

Anchor, S. (1978). *Mexican Americans in a Dallas barrio.* Tucson: University of Arizona Press.

Apple, M. (1986). National reports and the construction of inequality. *British Journal of Sociology of Education, 7,* 171–190.

Apple, M.W. (1992a). [Review of the book *The Burt affair*]. *Isis, 83,* 699–700.

Apple, M.W. (1992b). [Review of the book *Science, ideology, and the media: The Cyril Burt scandal*]. *Isis, 83,* 699–700.

Armelagos, G.J. (1995). Race, reason, and rationale [Review of the books *The evolution of racism, Human biodiversity, The bell curve,* and *Race, evolution, and behavior*]. *Evolutionary Anthropology, 4,* 103–109.

Armour-Thomas, E., & Gopaul-McNicol, S. (1998). *Assessing intelligence: Applying a bicultural model.* Thousand Oaks, CA: Sage.

Arnold, M.S. (1995). Exploding the myths: African American families at promise. In B.B. Swadener & S. Lubeck (Eds.), *Children and families "at promise": Deconstructing the discourse of risk* (pp. 143–162). Albany: State University of New York Press.

Aronowitz, S., & Giroux, H.A. (1993). *Education still under siege* (2nd ed.). Westport, CT: Bergin & Garvey.

Auletta, K. (1982). *The underclass.* New York: Random House.

Ayers, W., Hunt, J.A., & Quinn, T. (Eds.). (1998). *Teaching for social justice: A democracy and education reader.* New York: New Press.

Baker, J., & Sansone, J. (1990). Interventions with students at risk for dropping out of school: A high school responds. *Journal of Educational Research, 83,* 181–186.

Banfield, E.C. (1970). *The unheavenly city: The nature and future of our urban crisis.* Boston: Little, Brown.

Barash, D.P. (1995). [Review of the book *Race, evolution, and behavior: A life history perspective*]. *Animal Behaviour, 49,* 1131–1133.

Baratz, S.S., & Baratz, J.C. (1970). Early childhood intervention: The social science base of institutional racism. *Harvard Educational Review, 40,* 29–50.

Barnard, W.M. (2004). Parent involvement in elementary school and educational attainment. *Children and Youth Services Review, 26*, 39–62.

Barnes, S.L. (2001). Debunking deficiency theories: Evaluating non-traditional attitudes and behavior among residents in poor urban neighborhoods. *Journal of Poverty, 5*, 43–66.

Barnett, S.M., & Williams, W. (2004). [Review of the book *IQ and the Wealth of Nations*]. *Contemporary Psychology, 49*, 389–396.

Barr, R.D., & Parrett, W.H. (2008). *Saving our students, saving our schools: 50 proven strategies for helping underachieving students and improving schools* (2nd ed.). Thousand Oaks, CA: Corwin Press.

Barro, R.J., & Lee, J-W. (2000, April). *International data on educational attainment: Updates and implications.* CID Working Paper No. 42, Center for International Development at Harvard University, Cambridge, MA. Retrieved July 17, 2008, from: *http://www.cid.harvard.edu/cidwp/042.htm.* Dataset available at: *http://www.cid.harvard.edu/ciddata/ciddata.html.*

Bartolomé, L.I. (2003). Democratizing Latino education: A perspective on elementary education. In V.I. Kloosterman (Ed.), *Latino students in American schools: Historical and contemporary views* (pp. 33–46). Westport, CT: Praeger.

Barton, P.E. (2003). *Parsing the achievement gap: Baselines for tracking progress.* Princeton, NJ: Educational Testing Service.

Barton, P.E. (2004). Why does the gap persist? *Educational Leadership, 62*, 8–13.

Beloff, H. (1990). [Review of the book *The Burt affair*]. *British Journal of Psychology, 81*, 395–397.

Bennett, C.I. (1999). *Comprehensive multicultural education: Theory and practice* (4th ed.). Boston: Allyn & Bacon.

Bereiter, C. (1969). The future of individual differences. *Harvard Educational Review, 39*, 310–318.

Berhanu, G. (2007). Black intellectual genocide: An essay review of *IQ and the Wealth of Nations. Education Review, 10*(6). Retrieved June 6, 2007 from: *http://edrev.asu.edu/essays/v10n6index.html.*

Berliner, D.C., & Biddle, B.J. (1995). *The manufactured crisis: Myths, frauds, and the attack on America's schools.* Reading, MA: Addison-Wesley.

Berndt, C.H. (1969). [Review of the book *Culture and poverty: Critique and counter-proposals*]. *Current Anthropology, 10*, 182.

Besharov, D.J., & López, M.H. (1997). Good parents not money [Review of the book *Consequences of growing up poor*]. *Public Interest, 129*, 112–115.

Betten, N. (1973). American attitudes toward the poor: A historical overview. *Current History, 65*, 1–5.

Betts, J.R., Rueben, K.S., & Danenberg, A. (2000). *Equal resources, equal outcomes? The distribution of school resources and student achievement in California.* San Francisco: Public Policy Institute of California.

Billig, M. (1979). *Psychology, racism, and fascism.* Birmingham, England: A.F. & R. Publications.

Billingsley, A. (1999). *Mighty like a river: The Black church and social reform.* New York: Oxford University Press.

Black, M.H. (1966). Characteristics of the culturally disadvantaged child. In J.L. Frost & G.R. Hawkes (Eds.), *The disadvantaged child: Issues and innovations* (pp. 45–50). Boston: Houghton Mifflin.

Black, M.S. (1996). *Historical factors affecting Mexican American parental involvement and educational outcomes: The Texas environment from 1910–1996.* Unpublished doctoral dissertation, Harvard University, Cambridge, MA.

Blinkton, S. (1989). [Review of the book *The Burt affair*]. *Nature, 340*, 439–440.

Block, N.J., & Dworkin, G. (Eds.). (1976). *The IQ controversy: Critical readings.* New York: Pantheon Books.

Bloom, B.S. (1964). *Stability and change in human characteristics.* New York: Wiley.

Blum, J. (1978). *Pseudoscience and mental ability: The origins and fallacies of the IQ controversy.* New York: Monthly Review Press.

Boas, F. (1911). *The mind of primitive man.* New York: Macmillan.

Bodner, F.W., & Cavalli-Sforza, L.L. (1970). Intelligence and race. *Scientific American, 223*, 19–29.

Bogotch, I. (2002). Educational leadership and social justice: Practice into theory. *Journal of School Leadership, 12*, 138–156.

Bogotch, I., Beachum, F., Blount, J., Brooks, J., & English, F. (2008). *Radicalizing educational leadership: Dimensions of social justice.* Rotterdam: Sense Publishers.

Bohn, A.P. (2006, Winter). A framework for understanding Ruby Payne. *Rethinking Schools Online*, *21*(2). Available online at: *http://www.rethinkingschools.org/archive/21_02/fram212.shtml*.

Bohn, A.P. (2007, Fall). Revisiting Ruby Payne. *Rethinking Schools Online*, *22*(1). Available online at: *http://www.rethinkingschools.org/archive//22_01/ruby221.shtml*.

Boissevain, E. (1969). [Review of the book *Culture and poverty: Critique and counter-proposals*]. *Current Anthropology*, *10*, 183–184.

Bomer, R., Dworin, J.E., May, L., & Semingson, P. (2008). Miseducating teachers about the poor: A critical analysis of Ruby Payne's claims about poverty. *Teachers College Record*, *110*, 2497–2531.

Bomer, R., Dworin, J.E., May, L., & Semingson, P. (2009, June 3). What's wrong with a deficit perspective? *Teachers College Record*. Retrieved June 9, 2009, from: *http://www.tcrecord.org/Content.asp?ContentId* = 15648.

Bond, H.M. (1924). What the army "intelligence" tests measured. *Opportunity*, *2*, 197–202.

Bond, H.M. (1958). Cat on a hot tin roof. *Journal of Negro Education*, *27*, 519–525.

Boocock, S.S. (1972). *An introduction to the sociology of learning*. Boston, MA: Houghton-Mifflin.

Bouchard, T.J., Jr. (1983). Do environmental similarities explain the similarity in intelligence of identical twins reared apart? *Intelligence*, *7*, 175–184.

Bouchard, T.J., Jr. (1997). IQ similarity in twins reared apart: Findings and responses to critics. In R.J. Sternberg & E. Grigorenko (Eds.) *Intelligence, heredity, and environment* (pp. 126–160). New York: Cambridge University Press.

Bouchard, T.J., Jr. (1999). [Review of the book *Dysgenics: Genetic deterioration in modern populations*]. *American Journal of Human Biology*, *11*, 272–274.

Bouchard, T.J., Jr., Lykken, D.T., McGue, M., Segal, N.L., & Tellegen, A. (1990). Sources of human psychological differences: The Minnesota study of twins reared apart. *Science*, *250*, 223–228.

Bouchard, T.J., Jr., & McGue, M. (1981). Familial studies of intelligence: A review. *Science*, *212*, 1055–1059.

Bourdieu, P. (1977). *Outline of a theory of practice*. New York: Cambridge University Press.

Bourdieu, P. (1997). The forms of capital. In A. Halsey, H. Lauder, P. Brown, & A.S. Wells (Eds.), *Education: Culture, economy, and society* (pp. 46–57). Oxford: Oxford University Press.

Bourdieu, P., & Passeron, J.-C. (1977). *Reproduction: In education, society and culture*. Beverly Hills, CA: Sage.

Bowles, S., & Gintis, H. (1976). *Schooling in capitalist America: Educational reform and the contradictions of economic life*. New York: Basic Books.

Brace, C.L. (1995). Region does not mean "race": Reality versus convention in forensic anthropology. *Journal of Forensic Sciences*, *40*, 29–33.

Brace, C.L. (1996). Racialism and racist agendas [Review of the book *Race, evolution, and behavior: A life history perspective*]. *American Anthropologist*, *98*, 176–177.

Brandon, W.W. (2003). Toward a White teachers' guide to playing fair: Exploring the cultural politics of multicultural teaching. *International Journal of Qualitative Studies in Education*, *16*, 31–50.

Brody, N. (1992). *Intelligence* (2nd ed.). San Diego, CA: Academic Press.

Brody, E.B., & Brody, N. (1976). *Intelligence: Nature, determinants, and consequences*. New York: Academic Press.

Bronfenbrenner, U. (1979). Beyond the deficit model in child and family policy. *Teachers College Record*, *81*, 95–104.

Brosterman, N., & Togashi, K. (1997). *Inventing kindergarten*. New York: H.N. Abrams.

Brown v. Board of Education of Topeka, 347 U.S. 483 (1954), Supp. op. 349 U.S. 294 (1955).

Brown, K.W. (2004). Leadership for social justice and equity: Weaving a transformative framework and pedagogy. *Educational Administration Quarterly*, *40*, 79–110.

Brugge, D. (2008). Pulling up the ladder: The anti-immigrant backlash. *The Public Eye*, *9*(2). Original article appeared Summer 1995 and updated with permission of author. Retrieved June 30, 2008, from: *http://www.publiceye.org/magazine/v09n2/immigran.html*.

Bullock, D. (1990). Methodological heterogeneity and the anachronistic status of ANOVA in psychology. *Behavioral and Brain Sciences*, *13*, 122–123.

Bullock, H.E., Williams, W.R., & Limbert, W.M. (2003). Predicting support for welfare policies: The impact of attributions and beliefs about inequality. *Journal of Poverty*, *7*, 35–56.

Burgess, R.V. (2008). *Changing brain structure through cross-cultural learning: The life of Reuven Feuerstein*. Lewiston, NY: Edwin Meller Press.

Burnham, S. (1993). *America's bimodal crisis: Black intelligence in White society* (2nd ed.). Athens, GA: Foundation for Human Understanding.

Burt, C. (1958). The inheritance of mental ability. *American Psychologist, 13,* 1–15.

Bushnell, J.H. (1969). [Review of the book *Culture and poverty: Critique and counter-proposals*]. *Current Anthropology, 10,* 184.

California Department of Education. (2008a). *State summary, number of staff by ethnicity: teachers: 2007–2008; Statewide enrollment by ethnicity: 2007–2008.* Data available through the California Department of Education's Dataquest database at: *http://dq.cde.ca.gov/dataquest/.*

California Department of Education. (2008b). *2007–08 district enrollment by ethnicity: Los Angeles Unified.* Data available through the California Department of Education's Dataquest database at: *http://dq.cde.ca.gov/dataquest/.*

Campbell, D.T. (1975). Assessing the impact of social change. In G.M. Lyons (Ed.), *Social research and public policies: The Dartmouth/OECD conference* (pp. 3–45). Hanover, NH: Public Affairs Center, Dartmouth College.

Campbell, F.A., Goldstein, S., Schaefer, E.S., & Ramey, C.T. (1991). Parental beliefs and values related to family risk, educational intervention, and child academic competence. *Early Childhood Research Quarterly, 6,* 167–182.

Canady, H.G. (1928). *The effects of "rapport" on the IQ: A study in race psychology.* Unpublished master's thesis, Northwestern University, Evanston, IL.

Canady, H.G. (1936). The effect of "rapport" on the IQ: A new approach to the problem of racial psychology. *Journal of Negro Education, 5,* 209–219.

Cann, R.L., Brown, W.M., & Wilson, A.C. (1987). Mitochondrial DNA and human evolution. *Nature, 325,* 31–36.

Carey, K. (2004). *The funding gap 2004: Many states still shortchange low-income and minority students.* Washington, DC: The Education Trust.

Carnegie Foundation for the Advancement of Teaching. (1988). *An imperiled generation: Saving urban schools.* Princeton, NJ: Author.

Carothers, J.C. (1953). *The African mind in health and disease: A study in ethnopsychiatry.* Geneva: World Health Organization.

Carroll, P. (2003). *Felix Longoria's wake: Bereavement, racism, and the rise of Mexican American activism.* Austin: University of Texas Press.

Carroll, T.G., Fulton, K., Abercrombie, K., & Yoon, I. (2004). *Fifty years after Brown v. Board of Education: A two-tiered education system.* Washington, DC: National Commission on Teaching and America's Future. Retrieved March 17, 2009, from: *http://www.nctaf.org/resources/research_and_reports/nctaf_research_reports/rr_04_special_report.htm.*

Carspecken, P.F. (1996). The set-up: Crocodile tears for the poor. In J.L. Kinchloe, S.R. Steinberg, & A.D. Gresson (Eds.), *Measured lies: The bell curve examined* (pp. 109–125). New York: St. Martin's Press.

Carstens, P. (1969). [Review of the book *Culture and poverty: Critique and counter-proposals*]. *Current Anthropology, 10,* 184–185.

Cary, R. (1996). IQ as commodity: The "new" economics of intelligence. In J.L. Kinchloe, S.R. Steinberg, & A.D. Gresson (Eds.), *Measured lies: The bell curve examined* (pp. 137–160). New York: St. Martin's Press.

Cavalli-Sforza, L.L., Menozzi, P., & Piazza, A. (1994). *The history and geography of human genes.* Princeton, NJ: Princeton University Press.

Cazden, C.B., John, V.P., & Hymes, D. (Eds.). (1972). *Functions of language in the classroom.* New York: Teachers College Press.

Ceci, S.J. (1991). How much does schooling influence general intelligence and its cognitive components? A reassessment of the evidence. *Developmental Psychology, 27,* 703–722.

Ceja, M. (2004). Chicana college aspirations and the role of parents: Developing educational resiliency. *Journal of Hispanic Higher Education, 3,* 338–362.

Center on Education Policy. (2005). *State high school exit exams: States try harder, but gaps exist.* Washington, DC: Author.

Charters, W.W., Jr. (1963). The social background of teaching. In N.L. Gage (Ed.), *Handbook of research on teaching* (pp. 715–813). Chicago: Rand McNally.

Chávez, L.R. (2008). *The Latino threat: Constructing immigrants, citizens, and the nation.* Stanford, CA: Stanford University Press.

Chiszar, D.A., & Gollin, E.S. (1990). Additivity, interaction, and developmental good sense. *Behavioral and Brain Sciences, 13,* 124–125.

Chorover, S.L. (1979). *From genius to genocide: The meaning of human nature and the power of behavior control.* Cambridge, MA: The Massachusetts Institute of Technology Press.

Cicirelli, V., Evans, J.W., & Schiller, J.S. (1969). *The impact of Head Start: An evaluation of the effects of Head Start on children's cognitive and affective development.* Report of a study undertaken by Westinghouse Learning Corporation and Ohio University (Contract B89–4536, Office of Economic Opportunity).

Cisneros v. Corpus Christi Independent School District, 324 F. Supp. 599 (S.D. Tex. 1970).

Clark, K.B. (1965). *Dark ghetto: Dilemmas of social power.* New York: Harper & Row.

Clotfelter, C.T. (2004). *After Brown: The rise and retreat of school desegregation.* Princeton, NJ: Princeton University Press.

Conrath, J. (2001). Changing the odds for young people: Next steps for alternative education. *Phi Delta Kappan, 82,* 585–587.

Cook, D.A., & Fine, M. (1995). "Mother-wit": Childrearing lessons from African American mothers of low income. In B.B. Swadener & S. Lubeck (Eds.), *Children and families "at promise": Deconstructing the discourse of risk* (pp. 118–142). Albany: State University of New York Press.

Coon, C.S. (1962). *The origin of races.* New York: Alfred A. Knopf.

Cooper, C.W. (2003). The detrimental impact of teacher bias: Lessons learned from the standpoint of African American mothers. *Teacher Education Quarterly, 30,* 101–116.

Coward, B.E., Feagin, J.R., & Williams, J.A., Jr. (1974). The culture of poverty debate: Some additional data. *Social Problems, 21,* 621–634.

Crano, W.D., & Prislin, R. (Eds.). (2008). *Attitudes and attitude change.* New York: Psychology Press.

Cravens, H. (1978). *The triumph of evolution: American scientists and the heredity-environment controversy, 1900–1941.* Philadelphia: University of Pennsylvania Press.

Cronin, J., Daniels, N., Hurley, A., Koch, A., & Webber, R. (1975). Race, class, and intelligence: A critical look at the IQ controversy. *International Journal of Mental Health, 3,* 46–132.

Cross, K.P. (1984). The rising tide of school reform reports. *Phi Delta Kappan, 65,* 167–172.

Cross, W.E., Jr. (1996). *The bell curve* and transracial adoption studies. In J.L. Kinchloe, S.R. Steinberg, & A.D. Gresson (Eds.), *Measured lies: The bell curve examined* (pp. 331–342). New York: St. Martin's Press.

Crow, J.F. (1969). Genetic theories and influences: Comments on the value of diversity. *Harvard Educational Review, 39,* 338–347.

Cuban, L. (1989). The "at risk" label and the problem of urban school reform. *Phi Delta Kappan, 70,* 780–784, 800–801.

Darling-Hammond, L. (2000). Teacher quality and student achievement: A review of state policy evidence. *Education Policy Analysis Archives, 8.* Retrieved March 17, 2009, from: *http://epaa.asu.edu/epaa/v8n1/.*

Darling-Hammond, L. (2004a). Inequality and the right to learn: Access to qualified teachers in California's public schools. *Teachers College Record, 106,* 1936–1966.

Darling-Hammond, L. (2004b). Standards, accountability, and school reform. *Teachers College Record, 106,* 1047–1085.

Darling-Hammond, L. (2005). New standards and old inequalities: School reform and the education of African American students. In J.E. King (Ed.), *Black education: A transformative research and action agenda for the new century* (pp. 197–223). Mahwah, NJ: Lawrence Erlbaum.

Darling-Hammond, L., French, J., & García-López, S.P. (Eds.). (2002). *Learning to teach for social justice.* New York: Teachers College Press.

Darling-Hammond, L., & Post, L. (2000). Inequality in teaching and schooling: Supporting high-quality teaching and leadership in low-income schools. In R.D. Kahlenberg (Ed.), *A notion at risk: Preserving public education as an engine for social mobility* (pp. 127–167). New York: Century Foundation Press.

Darling-Hammond, L., & Wise, A.E. (1985). Beyond standardization: State standards and school improvement. *Elementary School Journal, 85,* 315–336.

Darling-Hammond, L., & Youngs, P. (2002). Defining "highly qualified teachers:" What does "scientifically-based research" actually tell us. *Educational Researcher, 31,* 13–25.

Davenport, C.B. (1917). The effects of race intermingling. *Proceedings of the American Philosophical Society, 56,* 364–368.

Davenport, C.B., & Steggerda, M. (1929). *Race crossing in Jamaica.* Westport, CT: Negro Universities Press.

Davies, C. (2007). [Review of the book *IQ and global inequality*]. *Economic Affairs, 27*, 104–105.

Davis v. County School Board of Prince Edward County, 103 F. Supp. 337 (E.D. Va. 1952).

De Jesús, A. (2005). Theoretical perspectives on the underachievement of Latino/a students in U.S. schools: Toward a framework for culturally additive schooling. In P. Pedraza & M. Rivera (Eds.), *Latino education: An agenda for community action research* (pp. 343–371) Mahwah, NJ: Lawrence Erlbaum.

de los Santos, A.G., Jr., & de los Santos, G.E. (2006). Latinos and community colleges. In J. Castellanos, A.M. Gloria, & M.A. Kamimura (Eds.), *The Latina/o pathway to the Ph.D.: Abriendo caminos* (pp. 37–53). Sterling, VA: Stylus.

Degler, C.N. (1991). *In search of human nature: The decline and revival of Darwinism in American social thought.* New York: Oxford University Press.

Dei, G.J.S. (1994). Afrocentricity: A cornerstone of pedagogy. *Anthropology & Education Quarterly, 25*, 3–28.

Delpit, L. (1988). The silenced dialogue: Power and pedagogy in educating other people's children. *Harvard Educational Review, 58*, 483–502.

Delpit, L. (1995). *Other people's children: Cultural conflict in the classroom.* New York: The New Press.

Detterman, D.K., Gabriel, L.T., & Ruthsatz, J.M. (2000). Intelligence and mental retardation. In R.J. Sternberg (Ed.), *Handbook of intelligence* (pp. 141–158). Cambridge: Cambridge University Press.

Diamond, J. (1994). Races without color. *Discover, 15*, 82–91.

Diamond, S. (1999). Right-wing politics, and the anti-immigration cause. In S. Jonas & S.D. Thomas (Eds.), *Immigration: A civil rights issue for the Americas* (pp. 175–189). Wilmington, DE: Scholarly Resources.

Dickens, W.T., Kane, T.J., & Schultze, C.L. (1996). *Does the bell curve ring true?* Washington, DC: Brookings Institution.

Dickerson, R.E. (2006). Exponential correlation of IQ and the wealth of nations. *Intelligence, 34*, 291–295.

Dobzhansky, T. (1973). *Genetic diversity and human equality.* New York: Basic Books.

Donato, R. (1997). *The other struggle for equal schools: Mexican Americans during the civil rights era.* Albany: State University of New York Press.

Donavan, J.C. (1967). *The politics of poverty.* New York: Western.

Dorfman, D.D. (1995). Soft science with a neoconservative agenda [Review of the book *The bell curve: Intelligence and class structure in American life*]. *Contemporary Psychology, 40*, 418–421.

Drake, R.H. (1927). *A comparative study of the mentality and achievement of Mexican and White children.* Unpublished master's thesis, University of Southern California, Los Angeles.

Dudley-Marling, C. (2007). Return of the deficit. *Journal of Educational Controversy, 2*(1). Available online at: *http://www.wce.wwu.edu/Resources/CEP/eJournal/v002n001/a004.shtml.*

Duke, L. (1991, January 9). Racial stereotypes found to persist among Whites. *Austin American-Statesman*, pp. A1, A6.

Duncan, G.J., & Brooks-Gunn, J. (Eds.). (1997). *Consequences of growing up poor.* New York: Russell Sage Foundation.

Dunn, L.M. (1987). *Bilingual Hispanic children on the U.S. mainland: A review of research on their cognitive, linguistic, and scholastic development.* Circle Pines, MN: American Guidance Service.

Duster, T. (1995). [Review of the book *The bell curve: Intelligence and class structure in American life*]. *Contemporary Sociology–A Journal of Reviews, 24*, 158–161.

Dworin, J.E., & Bomer, R. (2008). What we all (supposedly) know about the poor: A critical discourse analysis of Ruby Payne's "Framework." *English Education, 40*, 101–121.

Eames, E., & Goode, J.G. (1973). *Urban poverty in a cross-cultural context.* New York: Free Press.

Edin, K., & Lein, L. (1997). *Making ends meet: How single mothers survive welfare and low-wage work.* New York: Russell Sage Foundation.

Education Trust. (2007). *Their fair share: How teacher salary gaps shortchange poor children in Texas.* Washington, DC: Author. Retrieved March 17, 2009, from: *http://www2.edtrust.org/NR/rdonlyres/B58606FA-2AE0–4BFE-A5B9-BD21554FAFB5/0/07TexasPoverty.pdf.*

Education Trust. (2008). *Their fair share: How Texas-sized gaps in teacher quality shortchange low-income and minority students.* Washington, DC: Author. Retrieved March 17, 2009, from: *http://www2.edtrust.org/NR/rdonlyres/0E68E606-0371-4C7D-BEF5–9D07CA415171/0/TXTheirFairShare.pdf.*

Edwards, T.J. (1967). Pedagogical and psycho-social adjustment problems in cultural deprivation. In J. Hellmuth (Ed.), *Disadvantaged child* (Vol. 1, pp. 161–171). New York: Brunner/Mazel.

Ellis, F. (2009). [Review of the book *The global bell curve: Race, IQ, and inequality worldwide*]. *Economic Affairs, 29,* 96–97.

Erickson, F. (1987). Transformation and school success: The politics and culture of educational achievement. *Anthropology & Education Quarterly, 18,* 335–356.

Erickson, R. (1997). The laws of ignorance designed to keep slaves (Blacks) illiterate and powerless. *Education, 118,* 206–209, 220.

Ervik, A.O. (2003). [Review of the book *IQ and the wealth of nations*]. *The Economic Journal, 113,* 406–408.

Eysenck, H.J. (1971). *Race, intelligence, and education.* London: Temple Smith.

Eysenck, H.J. (1989). Sensitive intelligence issues [Review of the book *The Burt affair*]. *The Spectator, 263,* 26–27.

Fan, X.T. (2001). Parental involvement and students' academic achievement: A growth modeling analysis. *Journal of Experimental Education, 70,* 27–61.

Fan, X.T., & Chen, M. (2001). Parental involvement and students' academic achievement: A meta-analysis. *Educational Psychology Review, 13,* 1–22.

Fancher, R.C. (1985). *The intelligence men: Makers of the IQ controversy.* New York: W.W. Norton.

Fancher, R.C. (1991). The Burt case: Another foray [Review of the book *Science, ideology, and the media: The Cyril Burt scandal*]. *Science, 253,* 1565–1566.

Farber, S.L. (1981). *Identical twins reared apart: A reanalysis.* New York: Basic Books.

Feagin, J.R. (1975). *Subordinating the poor.* New York: Prentice Hall.

Feagin, J.R., & Feagin, C.B. (1999). *Racial and ethnic relations* (6th ed.). Upper Saddle River, NJ: Prentice Hall.

Fernández, R.R. (Ed.). (1988). Achievement test: Science vs. ideology [Special issue]. *Hispanic Journal of Behavioral Sciences, 10*(3).

Feuerstein, A. (2000). School characteristics and parental involvement: Influences on participation in children's schools. *Journal of Educational Research, 94,* 29–39.

Feuerstein, R. (1990). The theory of structural cognitive modifiability. In B.Z. Presseisen (Ed.), *Learning and thinking styles: Classroom interaction* (pp. 68–134). Washington, DC: National Education Association.

Feuerstein, R., Hoffman, M.B., Rand, Y., Jensen, M.R., Tzuriel, D., & Hoffman, D.B. (1986). Learning to learn: Mediated learning experiences and instrumental enrichment. *Special Services in the Schools, 3,* 49–82.

Feuerstein, R., Rand, Y., & Hoffman, M.B. (1979). *The dynamic assessment of retarded performers: The learning potential assessment device, theory, instruments, and techniques.* Baltimore: University Park Press.

Feuerstein, R., Rand, Y., Hoffman, M., Hoffman, M., & Miller, R. (1979). Cognitive modifiability in retarded adolescents: Effects of instrumental enrichment. *American Journal of Mental Deficiency, 83,* 539–550.

Feuerstein, R., Rand, Y., Hoffman, M.B., & Miller, R. (1980). *Instrumental Enrichment: An intervention program for cognitive modifiability.* Baltimore: University Park Press.

Feuerstein, R., Rand, Y., Jensen, M., Kaniel, S., Tzuriel, D., Ben, S.N., & Mintzker, Y. (1985). Learning potential assessment. *Special Services in the Schools, 2,* 85–106.

Feuerstein, R., Rand, Y., & Rynders, J.E. (1988). *Don't accept me as I am: Helping "retarded" people to excel.* New York: Plenum.

Fine, M. (1995). The politics of who's "at risk." In B.B. Swadener & S. Lubeck (Eds.), *Children and families "at promise": Deconstructing the discourse of risk* (pp. 76–94). Albany: State University of New York Press.

Fine, M., Burns, A., Payne, Y.A., & Torre, M.E., (2004). Civics lessons: The color and class of betrayal. *Teachers College Record, 106,* 2193–2223.

Finn, C.E., Jr. (1995). For whom it tolls [Review of the book *The bell curve: Intelligence and class structure in American life*]. *Commentary, 99,* 76–80.

Fischer, C.S., Hout, M., Jankowski, M.S., Lucas, S.R., Swidler, A., & Voss, K. (1996). *Inequality by design: Cracking the bell curve myth.* Princeton, NJ: Princeton University Press.

Fletcher, R. (1990). [Review of the book *The Burt affair*]. *Society, 27,* 85–87.

Fletcher, R. (1991). *Science, ideology, and the media: The Cyril Burt scandal.* New Brunswick, NJ: Transaction Books.

Flores, B.B., & Clark, E.R. (1997). High-stakes testing: Barriers for prospective bilingual education teachers. *Bilingual Research Journal, 21,* 334–356.

Flores, M.B., & Evans, G.T. (1972). Some differences in cognitive abilities between selected Canadian and Filipino students. *Multivariate Behavioral Research, 7,* 175–191.

Florida Department of Education. (2008). *Membership in Florida public schools, 2007–08.* Report available online at: *http://www.fldoe.org/eias/eiaspubs/default.asp#student.*

Flynn, J.R. (1980). *Race, IQ, and Jensen.* London: Routledge & Kegan Paul.

Flynn, J.R. (1999). Searching for justice: The discovery of IQ gains over time. *American Psychologist, 54,* 5–20.

Foley, D. (with Mota, C., Post, D., & Lozano, I.). (1988). *From peones to politicos: Class and ethnicity in a South Texas town, 1900–1987.* Austin: University of Texas Press.

Foley, D.E. (1991). Reconsidering anthropological explanations of ethnic school failure. *Anthropology & Education Quarterly, 22,* 60–86.

Foley, D.E. (1997). Deficit thinking models based on culture: The anthropological protest. In R.R. Valencia (Ed.), *The evolution of deficit thinking: Educational thought and practice* (pp. 113–131). The Stanford Series on Education and Public Policy. London: Falmer Press.

Foley, D.E. (2001). Reconceptualizing ethnicity and educational achievement. In N.K. Shimahara, I.Z. Holowinsky, & S. Tomlinson-Clarke (Eds.), *Ethnicity, race, and nationality in education: A global perspective* (pp. 17–35). Mahwah, NJ: Lawrence Erlbaum.

Foley, D.E. (2004). Ogbu's theory of academic disengagement: Its evolution and its critics. *Intercultural Education, 15,* 385–397.

Foley, D.E. (2005). Elusive prey: John Ogbu and the search for a grand theory of academic disengagement. *International Journal of Qualitative Studies in Education, 18,* 643–657.

Foley, D.E., Levinson, B.A., & Hurtig, J. (2000). Anthropology goes inside: The new educational ethnography of ethnicity and gender. *Review of Research in Education, 25,* 37–98.

Foley, D.E., & Moss, K. (2001). Studying U.S. cultural diversity: Some non-essentializing perspectives. In I. Susser & T.C. Patterson (Eds.), *Cultural diversity in the United States: A critical reader* (pp. 343–364). Oxford: Blackwell Publishing.

Foster, M. (2000). School practice and community life: Cultural congruence, conflict, and discontinuity [Introduction to section]. In B.A.U. Levinson (Ed.), with K.M. Borman, M. Eisenhart, M. Foster, A.E. Fox, & M. Sutton, *Schooling the symbolic animal: Social and cultural dimensions of education* (pp. 159–168). Lanham, MD: Rowman & Littlefield.

Foster, M., Lewis, J., & Onafowora, L. (2003). Anthropology, culture, and research on teaching and learning: Applying what we have learned to improve practice. *Teachers College Record, 105,* 261–277.

Franklin, W. (2000). Students at promise and resilient: A historical look at risk. In M.G. Sanders (Ed.), *Schooling students placed at risk: Research, policy, and practice in the education of poor and minority students* (pp. 3–16). Mahwah, NJ: Lawrence Erlbaum.

Fraser, S. (Ed.). (1995). *The bell curve wars: Race, intelligence, and the future of America.* New York: Basic Books.

Frattura, E.M., & Capper, C.A. (2007). *Leading for social justice: Transforming schools for all learners.* Thousand Oaks, CA: Corwin Press.

Fries, C.C. (1952). *The structure of English: An introduction to the construction of English.* New York: Harcourt, Brace.

Frost, J.F., & Hawkes, G.R. (Eds.). (1966). *The disadvantaged child: Issues and innovations.* New York: Houghton Mifflin.

Frymier, J., & Gansneder, B. (1989). The Phi Delta Kappa Study of Students at Risk. *Phi Delta Kappan, 71,* 142–146.

Fuentes, M.A. (2006). Keeping our children in high school. In J. Castellanos, A.M. Gloria, & M.A. Kamimura (Eds.), *The Latina/o pathway to the Ph.D.: Abriendo caminos* (pp. 19–34). Sterling, VA: Stylus.

Fuller, E.J., Carpenter, B., & Fuller, G. (2008). *Teacher quality & school improvement in Texas secondary schools.* Austin: Association of Texas Professional Educators. Retrieved March 17, 2009, from: *http://www.atpe.org/Advocacy/Issues/teacherqualitystudy.asp.*

Fussell, P. (1983). *Class: A guide through the American status system.* New York: Summit Books.

Gage, N.L. (1972a). IQ heritability, race differences, and educational research. *Phi Delta Kappan, 53,* 308–312.

Gage, N.L. (1972b). Replies to Shockley, Page, and Kaplan: The causes of race differences in IQ. *Phi Delta Kappan, 53,* 422–427.

Gale, T., & Densmore, K. (2000). *Just schooling: Explorations in the cultural politics of teaching.* Buckingham, England: Open University Press.

Gamoran, A. (Ed.). (2007). *Standards-based reform and the poverty gap: Lessons for No Child Left Behind.* Washington, DC: Brookings Institution Press.

Gans, H.J. (1995). *The war against the poor.* New York: Basic Books.

Gardner, H. (1995). Cracking open the IQ box. In S. Fraser (Ed.), *The bell curve wars: Race, intelligence, and the future of America* (pp. 23–35). New York: Basic Books.

Garrett, H.E. (1945). Comparison of Negro and White recruits on the Army tests given in 1917–18. *American Journal of Psychology, 58,* 480–495.

Garrett, H.E. (1951). *Great experiments in psychology* (3rd ed.). New York: Appleton-Century-Crofts.

Garrett, H.E. (1958). Foreword. In A.M. Shuey, *The testing of Negro intelligence* (pp. vii–viii). Lynchburg, VA: J.P. Bell.

Garrett, H.E. (1960). Klineberg's chapter on race and psychology: A review. *Mankind Quarterly, 1,* 15–22.

Garrett, H.E. (1961). The equalitarian dogma. *Mankind Quarterly, 1,* 253–257.

Garrett, H.E. (1962, May). Rejoinder by Garrett. *SPSSI Newsletter,* pp. 1–2. (Society for the Psychological Study of Social Issues).

Garrett, H.E. (1973). *IQ and racial differences.* Cape Canaveral, FL: Howard Allen Press.

Garrett, H.E. (n.d.). *Breeding down.* Richmond, VA: Patrick Henry Press.

Gates, R. R. (1946). *Human genetics.* New York: Macmillan.

Gay, L.R. (1994). *Educational research: Competencies for analysis and application* (4th ed.). New York: Merrill.

Gee, J.P. (2004). Discourse analysis: What makes it critical? In R. Rogers (Ed.), *An introduction to critical discourse analysis in education* (pp. 19–50). Mahwah, NJ: Lawrence Erlbaum.

George, W.C. (1955). *The race problem from the standpoint of one who is concerned with the evils of miscegenation.* Birmingham, AL: American States Rights Association.

George, W.C. (1962). *The biology of the race problem.* Report prepared by commission of the Governor of Alabama. Richmond, VA: Patrick Henry Press.

Gewirtz, S. (1998). Conceptualizing social justice in education: Mapping the territory. *Journal of Education Policy, 13,* 469–484.

Gilbert, D. (2003). *The American class structure in an age of growing inequality.* Belmont, CA: Wadsworth/Thompson Learning.

Gilmore, P., & Glatthorn, A. (Eds.). (1982). *Children in and out of school.* Washington, DC: Center for Applied Statistics.

Giroux, H.A., & Searls, S. (1996). *The bell curve* debate and the crisis of public intellectuals. In J.L. Kinchloe, S.R. Steinberg, & A.D. Gresson (Eds.), *Measured lies: The bell curve examined* (pp. 71–90). New York: St. Martin's Press.

Gitlin, A., Margonis, F., & Brunjes, H. (1993). In the shadow of the excellence reports: School restructuring for at-risk students. In R. Donmoyer & R. Kos (Eds.), *At-risk students: Portraits, policies, programs, and practices* (pp. 265–290). Albany: State University of New York Press.

Gladwin, T. (1967). *Poverty U.S.A.* Boston: Little, Brown.

Gladwin, T. (1969). [Review of the book *Culture and poverty: Critique and counter-proposals*]. *Current Anthropology, 10,* 185.

Glick, M. (1998). A developmental approach to psychopathology in people with mild mental retardation. In J.A. Burack, R.M. Hodapp, & E. Zigler (Eds.), *Handbook of mental retardation and development* (pp. 563–580). New York: Cambridge University Press.

Godina, E. (2005). [Review of the book *IQ and the wealth of nations*]. *Journal of Biosocial Science, 37,* 783–785.

Goldberg, D., McLaughlin, M., Grossi, M., Tytun, A., & Blum, S. (1992). Which newborns in New York City are at risk for special education placement? *American Journal of Public Health, 82,* 438–440.

Golden, M., & Bridger, W. (1969). A refutation of Jensen's position on intelligence, race, social class, and heredity. *Mental Hygiene, 53,* 648–653.

Goldfarb, K.P., & Grinberg, J. (2002). Leadership for social justice: Authentic participation in the case of a community center in Caracas, Venezuela. *Journal of School Leadership, 12,* 157–173.

González, G.G. (1990). *Chicano education in the era of segregation.* Philadelphia: Balch Institute Press.

González, N. (2004). Disciplining the discipline: Anthropology and the pursuit of quality education. *Educational Researcher, 33*, 17–25.

González, N. (2005). Beyond culture: The hybridity of funds of knowledge. In N. González, L.C. Moll, & C. Amanti (Eds.), *Funds of knowledge: Theorizing practices in households, communities, and classrooms* (pp. 29–46). Mahwah, NJ: Lawrence Erlbaum.

González, N., Moll, L.C., Tenery, M.F., Rivera, A., Rendon, R., Gonzales, R., & Amanti, C. (2005). Funds of knowledge for teaching in Latino households. In N. González, L.C. Moll, & C. Amanti (Eds.), *Funds of knowledge: Theorizing practices in households, communities, and classrooms* (pp. 89–118). Mahwah, NJ: Lawrence Erlbaum.

Goode, J. (2001). Let's get our act together: How racial discourses disrupt neighborhood activism. In J. Goode & J. Maskovsky (Eds.), *New poverty studies: The ethnography of politics, policy and impoverished people in the U.S.* (pp. 364–398). New York: New York University Press.

Goode, J. (2002). How urban ethnography counters myths about the poor. In G. Gmelch & W.P. Zenner (Eds.), *Urban life: Readings in the anthropology of the city* (4th ed., pp. 279–295). Prospect Heights, IL: Waveland Press.

Goodenough, F.L. (1926). *Measurement of intelligence by drawings.* Yonkers-on-the-Hudson, NY: World Book.

Goodenough, F.L., & Harris, D.B. (1950). Studies in the psychology of children's drawings: II. 1928–1949. *Psychological Bulletin, 49*, 369–433.

Gordon, H.L. (1934). Amentia in the East African. *Eugenics Review, 25*, 223–235.

Gorski, P.C. (2005). *Savage unrealities: Uncovering classism in Ruby Payne's Framework.* Unpublished manuscript, Hamline University, St. Paul, MN. Retrieved May 27, 2007, from: *www.edchange.org/publications/Savage_Unrealities.pdf.*

Gorski, P.C. (2006a, February 9). The classist underpinnings of Ruby Payne's *Framework. Teachers College Record.* Retrieved May 27, 2007, from: *http://www.tcrecord.org/content.asp?contentid = 12322.*

Gorski, P.C. (2006b, Winter). Savage unrealities: Classism and racism abound in Ruby Payne's *Framework. Rethinking Schools Online, 21*(2). Available online at: *http://www. rethinkingschools.org/archive/21_02/sava212.shtml.*

Gorski, P.C. (2008). Peddling poverty for profit: Elements of oppression in Ruby Payne's *Framework. Equity & Excellence in Education, 41*, 130–148.

Gould, B. (1932). *Methods of teaching Mexicans.* Unpublished master's thesis, University of Southern California, Los Angeles.

Gould, M. (1999). Race and theory: Culture, poverty, and adaptation to discrimination in Wilson and Ogbu. *Sociological Theory, 17*, 171–200.

Gould, S.J. (1996). *The mismeasure of man* (rev. and expanded). New York: W.W. Norton.

Grassie, J. (Writer). (1995, December 1). *Dateline.* New York: National Broadcasting Corporation.

Graves, J.L., Jr. (1993). Evolutionary biology and human variation: Biological determinism and the mythology of race. *Race Relations Abstracts, 18*, 4–34.

Graves, J.L., Jr. (2001). *The emperor's new clothes: Biological theories of race at the new millennium.* New Brunswick, NJ: Rutgers University Press.

Graves, J.L., Jr. (2002). The misuse of life history theory: J.P. Rushton and the pseudoscience of racial hierarchy. In J.M. Fish (Ed.), *Race and intelligence: Separating science from myth* (pp. 57–94). Mahwah, NJ: Lawrence Erlbaum.

Gray, J.P. (1991). *The race science of J. Philippe Rushton: Professors, protests, and the press.* Unpublished master's thesis, Burnaby, B.C., Canada.

Grebler, L., Moore, J.W., & Guzmán, R.C. (1970). *The Mexican-American people: The nation's second largest minority.* New York: Free Press.

Gronlund, N.E. (1985). *Measurement and evaluation in teaching* (5th ed.). New York: Macmillan.

Grubb, W.N., Goe, L., & Huerta, L.A. (2004). The unending search for equity: California policy, the "improved school finance," and the *Williams* case. *Teachers College Record, 106*, 2081–2101.

Guajardo, M.A., & Guajardo, F.J. (2002). Critical ethnography and community change. In Y. Zou & E.T. Trueba (Eds.), *Ethnography and schools: Qualitative approaches to the study of education* (pp. 281–304). Lanham, MD: Rowman & Littlefield.

Guajardo, M.A., Guajardo, F.J., & del Carmen Casaperalta, E. (2008). Transformative education: Chronicling a pedagogy for social change. *Anthropology & Education Quarterly, 39*, 3–22.

Gunzerhauser, M.G. (2003). High-stakes testing and the default of education. *Theory into Practice, 42*, 51–58.

Gutiérrez, K.D. (2002). Studying cultural practices in urban learning communities. *Human Development, 45,* 312–321.

Gutiérrez, K.D., & Rogoff, B. (2003). Cultural ways of learning: Individual traits or repertoires of practice. *Educational Researcher, 32,* 19–25.

Hale, J.E. (1986). Black *children: Their roots, culture, and learning styles* (rev. ed.). Baltimore: Johns Hopkins University Press.

Hale, J.E. (2001). *Learning while Black: Creating educational excellence for African American children.* Baltimore: Johns Hopkins University Press.

Hale-Benson, J.E. (1986). *Black children: Their roots, culture, and learning styles* (rev. ed.). Baltimore: Johns Hopkins University Press.

Hall, E.R. (1946). The zoological subspecies of man. *Journal of Mammalogy, 27,* 358–364.

Hamilton, D.L., & Trolier, T.K. (1986). Stereotypes and stereotyping: An overview of the cognitive approach. In J.F. Dovidio & S.L. Gaertner (Eds.), *Prejudice, discrimination, and racism* (pp. 127–163). Orlando, FL: Academic Press.

Haney, W.M. (2002). The myth of the Texas miracle in education. *Education Policy Analysis Archives, 8*(41). Available at: *http://epaa.asu.edu/epaa/v8n41/.*

Hannerz, U. (1969). [Review of the book *Culture and poverty: Critique and counter-proposals*]. *Current Anthropology, 10,* 185–186.

Harrington, M. (1962). *The other America: Poverty in the United States.* New York: Macmillan.

Harrington, M. (1981). *The other America: Poverty in the United States* (rev. ed.). New York: Penguin Books.

Harrington, M. (1984). *The new American poverty.* New York: Holt, Rinehart, and Winston.

Harris, A.M., Reynolds, M.A., & Koegel, H.M. (1996). Nonverbal assessment: Multicultural perspectives. In L.A. Suzuki, P.J. Meller, & J.G. Ponterotto (Eds.), *Handbook of multicultural assessment: Clinical, psychological, and educational applications* (pp. 223–252). San Francisco: Jossey-Bass.

Harry, B., & Klingner, J.K. (2006). *Why are so many minority students in special education? Understanding race and disability in schools.* New York: Teachers College Press.

Hauser, M.E., & Thompson, C. (1995). Creating a classroom culture of promise: Lessons from a first grade. In B.B. Swadener & S. Lubeck (Eds.), *Children and families "at promise": Deconstructing the discourse of risk* (pp. 210–223). Albany: State University of New York Press.

Hauser, R.M. (1995). [Review of the book *The bell curve: Intelligence and class structure in American life*]. *Contemporary Sociology–A Journal of Reviews, 24,* 149–153.

Hearnshaw, L.S. (1979). *Cyril Burt, psychologist.* Ithaca, NY: Cornell University Press.

Heath, S.B. (1983). *Ways with words: Language, life and work in communities and classrooms.* New York: Cambridge University Press.

Hellmuth, J. (Ed.). (1967). *Disadvantaged child* (Vol. 1). New York: Brunner/Mazel.

Henderson, A., & Berla, N. (Eds.). (1994). *A new generation of evidence: The family is critical to student achievement.* Columbia, MD: National Committee for Citizens in Education.

Hendricksen, R.M. (1996). *The bell curve,* affirmative action, and the quest for equality. In J.L. Kinchloe, S.R. Steinberg & A.D. Gresson (Eds.), *Measured lies: The bell curve examined* (pp. 351–365). New York: St. Martin's Press.

Hengest, D. (2008, January). Diversity in the Army: A thin veneer covers serious trouble. *American Renaissance, 19.* Available online at: *http://www.amren.com/ar/2008/01/index.html.*

Hergenhahn, B.R. (1992). *An introduction to the history of psychology* (2nd ed.). Belmont, CA: Wadsworth.

Hernández, D. (1970). *Mexican American challenge to a sacred cow* (Monograph No. 1). Los Angeles: Mexican American Cultural Center, University of California.

Herrnstein, R.J. (1971, September). I.Q. *The Atlantic Monthly, 228,* 43–64.

Herrnstein, R.J. (1973). *I.Q. in the meritocracy.* Boston: Little, Brown.

Herrnstein, R.J., & Murray, C. (1994). *The bell curve: Intelligence and class structure in American life.* New York: Free Press.

Hess, R.D. (1970). The transmission of cognitive strategies in poor families: The socialization of apathy and underachievement. In V.L. Allen (Ed.), *Psychological factors in poverty* (pp. 73–92). Chicago: Markham.

Hess, R.D., & Shipman, V. (1965). Early experience and the socialization of cognitive modes in children. *Child Development, 36,* 869–886.

Heubert, J.P., & Hauser, R.M. (Eds.). (1999). *High stakes: Testing for tracking, promotion, and graduation.* Committee on Appropriate Test Use, Board on Testing and Assessment, Commission on Behavioral and Social Sciences and Education, National Research Council. Washington, DC: National Academy Press.

Heyneman, S.P., & Jamison, D.T. (1980). Student learning in Uganda: Textbook availability and other factors. *Comparative Education Review, 24*, 206–220.

Hicks, R.A., & Pellegrini, R.J. (1966). The meaningfulness of Negro–White differences in intelligence test performance. *Psychological Record, 16*, 43–46.

Hill, G.N., & Hill, K.T. (1995). *Real life dictionary of the law: Taking the mystery out of legal language.* Los Angeles: General Publishing Group. Search engine available online at: *http:// dictionary.law.com/.*

Hollingshead, A.B., & Redlich, F.C. (1958). *Social class and mental illness.* New York: Wiley.

Horn, C. (2003). High-stakes testing and students: Stopping or perpetuating a cycle of failure. *Theory into Practice, 42*, 30–41.

Horn, M. (1993). Inventing the problem child: "At risk" children in the child guidance movement of the 1920s and 1930s. In R. Wollons (Ed.), *Children at risk in America: History, concepts, and public policy* (pp. 141–153). New York: State University of New York Press.

Horowitz, I.L. (1995). The Rushton file. In R.J. Jacoby & N. Glauberman (Eds.), *The bell curve debate: History, documents, opinions* (pp. 179–200). New York: Times Books.

Horton, J., & Pacifici, L. (2003). Expanding pre-service teachers' notions of literacy and diversity. In W. Trathen (Ed.), *American Reading Forum Online Yearbook, Volume XXIII: Reading at the Crossroads.* Retrieved June 15, 2007, from: *http://www.americanreadingforum.org/ 03_yearbook/html/Horton.htm.*

Huberty, T.J. (1990). Reducing academic related anxiety. In L.J. Kruger (Ed.), *Promoting success with at-risk students: Emerging perspectives and practical approaches* (pp. 261–276). New York: Haworth Press.

Hunt, J. McV. (1961). *Intelligence and experience.* New York: Ronald Press.

Hunter, H. (2000). *Poverty and inner city education: Community economic development at the local school level.* Unpublished doctoral dissertation, University of Manitoba, Winnipeg, Canada.

Hursch, D. (2007). Assessing No Child Left Behind and the rise of neoliberal education policies. *British Educational Research Journal, 44*, 493–518.

Hymes, D., & Gumperz, J. (Eds.). (1964). The ethnography of communication [Special issue]. *American Anthropologist, 66* (6, Part 2) (186 pps.).

Illinois State Board of Education. (2008). *2007–08 district summary.* Report available online at: *http://www.isbe.state.il.us/research/htmls/fall_housing.htm.*

Irvine, J.J. (1990). *Black students and school failure: Policies, practices, and prescriptions.* New York: Greenwood Press.

Irvine, J.J., & York, D.E. (1995). Learning styles and culturally diverse students: A literature review. In J.A. Banks & C.A. McGee Banks (Eds.), *Handbook of research on multicultural education* (pp. 484–497). New York: Macmillan.

Isserman, M. (2000). *The other American: The life of Michael Harrington.* New York: PublicAffairs.

Itzkoff, S.W. (1994). *The decline of intelligence in America: A strategy for national renewal.* Westport, CT: Praeger.

Jackson, J.P., Jr. (2001). *Social scientists for social justice: Making the case against segregation.* Critical America Series. New York: New York University Press.

Jackson, J.P., Jr. (2004). The scientific attack on Brown v. Board of Education, 1954–64. *American Psychologist, 59*, 530–537.

Jackson, J.P., Jr. (2005). *Race, law, and the case against Brown v. Board of Education.* Critical America Series. New York: New York University Press.

Jackson, J.P., Jr., & Weidman, N.M. (2004). *Race, racism, and science: Social impact and interaction.* New Brunswick, NJ: Rutgers University Press.

Jackson, K., & Remillard, J. (2005). Rethinking parent involvement: African American mothers construct their roles in the mathematics education of their children. *The School Community Journal, 15*, 51–73.

Jackson, T. (1997, April). The descent of man. *American Renaissance, 8*, 7–9.

Jackson, T. (2006, March). The fight against integration: Segregation did not fall without a fight. *American Renaissance, 17.* Available online at: *http://www.amren.com/mtnews/archives/2008/ 01/the_fight_again.php.*

Jacoby, R., & Glauberman, N. (Eds.). (1995). *The bell curve debate: History, documents, opinions.* New York: Times Books.

Jargowsky, P.A. (1996). Take the money and run: Economic segregation in U.S. metropolitan areas. *American Sociological Review, 41*, 30–49.

Jensen, A.R. (1969). How much can we boost IQ and scholastic achievement? *Harvard Educational Review, 39*, 1–123.

Jensen, A.R. (1972). *Genetics and education*. London: Methuen.

Jensen, A.R. (1973). *Educability and group differences*. New York: Harper & Row.

Jensen, A.R. (1980). *Bias in mental testing*. New York: Free Press.

Jensen, A.R. (1981). *Straight talk about mental tests*. New York: Free Press.

Jensen, A.R. (1998). *The g factor: The science of mental ability*. Westport, CT: Praeger.

Jensen, E. (1998). How Julie's brain learns. *Educational Leadership, 56*, 41–45.

Jerald, C.D. (2002). *All talk, no action: Putting an end to out-of-field teaching*. Washington, DC: The Education Trust. Retrieved March 17, 2009, from: *http://www2.edtrust.org/NR/rdonlyres/ 8DE64524-592E-4C83-A13A-6B1DF1CF8D3E/0/AllTalk.pdf*.

Jessor, R. (1958). The problem of reductionism in psychology. *Psychological Review, 65*, 170–178.

Jeynes, W.H. (2003). A meta-analysis—The effects of parental involvement on minority children's academic achievement. *Education and Urban Society, 35*, 202–218.

Jeynes, W.H. (2005). A meta-analysis of the relation of parental involvement to urban elementary school achievement. *Urban Education, 40*, 237–269.

Johnson, K.A. (2000). *Uplifting the women and the race: The educational philosophies, and social activism of Anna Julia Cooper and Nannie Helen Burroughs*. New York: Garland Publishing.

Johnson, K.R. (1996). *Proposition 187: The nativist campaign, the impact on the Latino community, and the future*. JSRI Research Report No. 15. East Lansing: Julian Samora Research Institute, Michigan State University. Available online at: *http://www.jsri.msu.edu/RandS/research/irr/ rr15.html*.

Joint Center for Political Studies (U.S.), & Franklin, J.H. (1989). *Visions of a better way: A Black appraisal of public schooling*. Washington, DC: Joint Center for Political Studies Press.

Jones, D.J. (1993). The culture of achievement among the poor: The case of mothers and children in a Head Start program. *Critique of Anthropology, 13*, 247–266.

Jones, J. (1995). Back to the future with *The bell curve*: Jim Crow, slavery and G. In S. Fraser (Ed.), *The bell curve wars: Race, intelligence, and the future of America* (pp. 80–93). New York: Basic Books.

Jones, R.K., & Luo, Y. (1999). The culture of poverty and African-American culture: An empirical assessment. *Sociological Perspectives, 42*, 439–458.

Joos, M. (1967). *The five clocks: A linguistic excursion into the five styles of English usage*. New York: Harcourt Brace Jovanovich.

Joynson, R.B. (1989). *The Burt affair*. New York: Academic Press.

Juel-Nielsen, N. (1965). Individual and environment: A psychiatric-psychological investigation of monozygous twins reared apart. *Acta Psychiatrica et Neurologia Scandinavica*, Monograph Supplement 183.

Kagan, D.M. (1990). How schools alienate students at risk: A model for examining proximal classroom variables. *Educational Psychologist, 25*, 105–125.

Kamin, L.J. (1974). *The science and politics of I.Q.* Potomac, MD: Lawrence Erlbaum.

Kamin, L.J. (1995). Lies, damned lies, and statistics. In R.J. Jacoby & N. Glauberman (Eds.), *The bell curve debate: History, documents, opinions* (pp. 81–105). New York: Times Books.

Karweit, N.L. (1989a). Effective preschool programs for students at risk. In R.E. Slavin, N.L. Karweit, & N.A. Madden (Eds.), *Effective programs for students at risk* (pp. 75–102). Boston: Allyn and Bacon.

Karweit, N.L. (1989b). Effective kindergarten programs and practices for students at risk. In R.E. Slavin, N.L. Karweit, & N.A. Madden (Eds.), *Effective programs for students at risk* (pp. 103–142). Boston: Allyn and Bacon.

Katz, D., & Stotland, E. (1959). A preliminary statement to a theory of attitude and change. In S. Koch (Ed.), *Psychology: A study of science: Vol. 3, Formulations of the person and the social context* (pp. 423–475). New York: McGraw-Hill.

Katz, M.B. (1986). *In the shadow of the poorhouse: A social history of welfare in America*. New York: Basic Books.

Katz, M.B. (1989). *The undeserving poor: From the war on poverty to the war on welfare*. New York: Pantheon Books.

Katz, M.B. (1995). *Improving poor people: The welfare state, the "underclass," and urban schools as history*. Princeton, NJ: Princeton University Press.

Kaufman, A.S., & Kaufman, N.L. (1977). *Clinical evaluation of young children with the McCarthy Scales*. New York: Grune & Stratton.

Kells, M.H. (2002). Linguistic contact zones in the college writing classroom: An examination of ethnolinguistic identity and language attitudes. *Written Communication, 19,* 5–43.

Kells, M.H. (2004). Understanding the rhetorical value of Tejano codeswitching. In M.H. Kells, V. Balester, & V. Villanueva (Eds.), *Latino/a discourses: On language, identity, and literacy education* (pp. 24–39). Portsmouth, NH: Heinemann-Boynton/Cook.

Kells, M.H. (2006). Tex Mex, metalingual discourse, and teaching college writing. In S.J. Nero (Ed.), *Dialects, Englishes, creoles, and education* (pp. 185–201). Mahwah, NJ: Lawrence Erlbaum.

Kelves, D.J. (1985). *In the name of eugenics: Genetics and the uses of human heredity*. New York: Alfred A. Knopf.

Kempthorne, O. (1978). Logical, epistemological and statistical aspects of the nature–nurture data interpretation. *Biometrics, 34,* 1–23.

Kenny, M.G. (2002). Toward a racial abyss: Eugenics, Wickliffe Draper, and the origins of the Pioneer Fund. *Journal of History of the Behavioral Sciences, 38,* 259–283.

Keogh, B.K., & Jones, R.L. (1986). Special education research on mildly handicapped learners. In M.C. Wittrock (Ed.), *Handbook of research on teaching* (3rd ed., pp. 688–726). New York: Macmillan.

Kinchloe, J.L., & Steinberg, S.R. (1996). Who said it can't happen here? In J.L. Kinchloe, S.R. Steinberg, & A.D. Gresson (Eds.), *Measured lies: The bell curve examined* (pp. 3–47). New York: St. Martin's Press.

Kinchloe, J.L., Steinberg, S.R., & Gresson, A.D. (Eds.). (1996). *Measured lies: The bell curve examined*. New York: St. Martin's Press.

King, K.L., Houston, I.S., & Middleton, R.A. (2001). An explanation for school failure: Moving beyond Black inferiority and alienation as a policy-making agenda. *British Journal of Educational Studies, 49,* 428–445.

Klarman, M.J. (2004). *From Jim Crow to civil rights: The Supreme Court and the struggle for racial equality*. New York: Oxford University Press.

Klineberg, O. (1935). *Race differences*. New York: Harper.

Kluegel, J.R., & Smith, E.R. (1986). *Beliefs about inequality: Americans' views of what is and what ought to be*. New York: Aldine de Gruyter.

Kluger, R. (2004). *Simple justice: The history of Brown v. Board of Education and Black America's struggle for equality*. New York: Vintage Books.

Knapp, T.R. (1977). The unit of analysis problems in applications of simple correlational analysis to educational research. *Journal of Educational Statistics, 2,* 171–186.

Kochar, V.K. (1969). [Review of the book *Culture and poverty: Critique and counter-proposals*]. *Current Anthropology, 10,* 186–188.

Koh, T., Abbatiello, A., & McLoughlin, C.S. (1984). Cultural bias in WISC subtest items: A response to Judge Grady's suggestion in relation to the *PASE* case. *School Psychology Review, 13,* 89–94.

Koschoreck, J.W. (2001). Accountability and educational equity in the transformation of an urban district. *Education and Urban Society, 33,* 284–304.

Koski, W.S., & Weis, H.S. (2004) What educational resources do students need to meet California's educational content standards? A textual analysis of California's educational content standards and their implications for basic educational conditions and resources. *Teachers College Record, 106,* 1907–1935.

Kozol, J. (1991). *Savage inequalities: Children in America's schools*. New York: Crown.

Kretzmann, J., & McKnight, J.P. (1996). Assets-based community development. *National Civic Review, 85,* 23–30.

Kruger, L.J. (Ed.). (1990a). *Promoting success with at-risk students: Emerging perspectives and practical approaches*. New York: Haworth Press.

Kruger, L.J. (1990b). The individualized contingency contract for students: A collaborative approach. In L.J. Kruger (Ed.), *Promoting success with at-risk students: Emerging perspectives and practical approaches* (pp. 65–87). New York: Haworth Press.

Kunjufu, J. (2006). *An African centered response to Ruby Payne's poverty theory*. Chicago: African American Images.

Labaree, D.F. (1997). Public goods, private goods: The American struggle over educational goals. *American Educational Research Journal, 34,* 39–81.

Labov, W. (1970). The logic of nonstandard English. In F. Williams (Ed.), *Language and poverty* (pp. 153–187). Chicago: Markham Press.

Labov, W. (1972). *Language in the inner city: Studies in the Black English vernacular*. Philadelphia: University of Pennsylvania Press.

Ladson-Billings, G. (1994). *The dreamkeepers: Successful teachers of African American children*. San Francisco: Jossey-Bass.

Lam, Y., & Peake, R. (1997). Triad conference: Is it a more effective way of involving parents and students? *McGill Journal of Education, 32,* 249–262.

Lamb, K. (1997). Intelligence and fertility. *Mankind Quarterly, 37,* 335–339.

Land, D., & Legters, N. (2002). The extent and consequences of risk in U.S. education. In S. Stringfield & D. Land (Eds.), *Educating at-risk students: One hundred-first yearbook of the National Society for the Study of Education, Part II* (pp. 1–28). Chicago: National Society for the Study of Education.

Lane, C. (1995). Tainted sources. In R. Jacoby & N. Glauberman (Eds.), *The bell curve debate: History, documents, opinions* (pp. 125–139). New York: Times Books.

Langone, J. (1996). Mild mental retardation. In P.J. McLaughlin & P. Wehman (Eds.), *Mental retardation and developmental disabilities* (2nd ed., pp. 113–129). Austin, TX: PRO-ED.

Lankford, H., Loeb, S., & Wyckoff, J. (2002). Teacher sorting and the plight of urban schools: A descriptive analysis. *Educational Evaluation and Policy Analysis, 24,* 37–72.

Laosa, L.M. (1984). Social policies toward children of diverse ethnic, racial, and language groups in the United States. In H.W. Stevenson & A.E. Siegel (Eds.), *Child development research and social policy* (Vol. 1, pp. 1–109). Chicago: University of Chicago Press.

Larry P. v. Riles, 343 F. Supp. 1306 (N.D. Cal. 1972).

Leacock, E. (1969). [Review of the book *Culture and poverty: Critique and counter-proposals*]. *Current Anthropology, 10,* 188–189.

Lee, J. (2007). *The testing gap: Scientific trials of test-driven school accountability systems for excellence and equity*. Charlotte, NC: Information Age Publishing.

Leeds, A. (1971). The concept of the "culture of poverty": Conceptual, logical, and empirical problems, with perspectives from Brazil and Peru. In E.B. Leacock (Ed.), *The culture of poverty: A critique* (pp. 226–284). New York: Simon and Schuster.

Levin, H. (1992). At-risk students in a yuppie age. *Educational Policy, 4,* 283–295.

Levin, M. (1997). *Why race matters: Race differences and what they mean*. Westport, CT: Praeger.

Levinson, B.A., & Holland, D.C. (1996). The cultural production of the educated person: An introduction. In B.A. Levinson, D.E. Foley, & D.C. Holland (Eds.), *The cultural production of the educated person: Critical ethnographies of schooling and local practice* (pp. 1–54). Albany: State University of New York Press.

Lewis, O. (1959). *Five families: Mexican case studies in the culture of poverty*. New York: Basic Books.

Lewis, O. (1961). *The children of Sánchez: Autobiography of a Mexican family*. New York: Random House.

Lewis, O. (1966a). *La Vida: A Puerto Rican family in the culture of poverty—San Juan and New York*. New York: Random House.

Lewis, O. (1966b). The culture of poverty. *Scientific American, 215,* 19–25.

Lewis, O. (1968). *A study of slum culture: Backgrounds for La Vida*. New York: Random House.

Lewis, O. (1969). [Review of the book *Culture and poverty: Critique and counter-proposals*]. *Current Anthropology, 10,* 189–192.

Lewis, O. (1971). The culture of poverty. In E. Penchef (Ed.), *Four horsemen: Pollution, poverty, famine, violence* (pp. 135–141). San Francisco: Canfield Press.

Lewontin, R.C. (1970). Race and intelligence. *Bulletin of the Atomic Scientists, 26,* 2–8.

Lewontin, R.C. (1973). Race and intelligence. In C. Senna (Ed.), *The fallacy of I.Q.* (pp. 1–17). New York: Joseph Okpatu.

Lewontin, R.C. (1975). Genetic aspects of intelligence. *Annual Review of Genetics, 9,* 387–405.

Lewontin, R.C. (1976). Race and intelligence. In N.J. Block & G. Dworkin (Eds.), *The IQ controversy: Critical readings* (pp. 78–92). New York: Pantheon Books.

Lewontin, R.C. (1996). Of genes and genitals [Review of the book *Race, evolution, and behavior*]. *Transition, 69,* 178–183.

Lidz, C.S. (Ed.). (1987). *Dynamic assessment: An interactional approach to evaluating learning potential*. New York: Guilford.

Lidz, C.S. (1991). *Practitioner's guide to dynamic assessment*. New York: Guilford.

Lidz, C.S. (2001). Multicultural issues and dynamic assessment. In L.A. Suzuki, J.G. Ponterotto, & P.J. Meller (Eds.), *Handbook of multicultural assessment: Clinical, psychological, and educational applications* (pp. 523–539). San Francisco: Jossey-Bass.

Lidz, C.S., & Macrine, S.L. (2001). An alternative approach to the identification of gifted culturally and linguistically diverse learners: The contribution of dynamic assessment. *School Psychology International, 22*, 74–96.

Lieberman, L. (2001). How "Caucasoids" got such big crania and why they shrank: From Morton to Rushton. *Current Anthropology, 42*, 69–80.

Loehlin, J.C. (2007). [Review of the book *Race differences in intelligence: An evolutionary analysis*]. *Intelligence, 35*, 93–94.

Loehlin, J.C., Lindzey, G., & Spuhler, J.N. (1975). *Race differences in intelligence*. San Francisco: Freeman.

Lombardo, P.A. (2002). "The American breed": Nazi eugenics and the origins of the Pioneer Fund. *Albany Law Review, 65*, 743–830.

Lombardo, P.A. (2003). Pioneer's big lie. *Albany Law Review, 66*, 1125–1143.

Lomotey, K. (Ed.). (1990). *Going to school: The African-American experience*. Albany: State University of New York Press.

Long, H.H. (1925). On mental tests and race psychology—a critique. *Opportunity, 3*, 134–138.

López, G.R., Scribner, J.D., & Mahitivanichcha, K. (2001). Redefining parental involvement: Lessons from high-performing migrant-impacted schools. *American Educational Research Journal, 38*, 253–288.

López, M.P. (2005). *Reflections on educating Latino and Latina undocumented children: Beyond Plyler v. Doe. Seton Hall Law Review, 35*, 1373–1406.

Lott, B. (2003). Recognizing and welcoming the standpoint of low-income parents in the public schools. *Journal of Educational & Psychological Consultation, 14*, 91–104.

Lubeck, S. (1995). Mothers at risk. In B.B. Swadener & S. Lubeck (Eds.), *Children and families "at promise": Deconstructing the discourse of risk* (pp. 50–75). Albany: State University of New York Press.

Lugg, C.A. (1996). Social darwinism as public policy. In J.L. Kinchloe, S.R. Steinberg, & A.D. Gresson (Eds.), *Measured lies: The bell curve examined* (pp. 367–378). New York: St. Martin's Press.

Luthar, S.S. (1991). Vulnerability and resilience: A study of high-risk adolescents. *Child Development, 62*, 600–616.

Lynn, R. (1996). *Dysgenics: Genetic deterioration in modern populations*. Westport, CT: Praeger.

Lynn, R. (2001). *The science of human diversity: A history of the Pioneer Fund*. Lanham, MD: University Press of America.

Lynn, R. (2006). *Race differences in intelligence: An evolutionary analysis*. Augusta, GA: Washington Summit Publishers.

Lynn, R. (2008). *The global bell curve: Race, IQ, and inequality worldwide*. Augusta, GA: Washington Summit Publishers.

Lynn, R., & Van Court, M. (2004). New evidence of dysgenic fertility for intelligence in the United States. *Intelligence, 32*, 193–201.

Lynn, R., & Vanhanen, T. (2002). *IQ and the wealth of nations*. Westport, CT: Praeger.

Lynn, R., & Vanhanen, T. (2006). *IQ and global inequality*. Augusta, GA: Washington Summit Publishers.

Lyon, L.L. (1933). *Investigation of the program for the adjustment of Mexican girls to the high schools of the San Fernando Valley*. Unpublished master's thesis, University of Southern California, Los Angeles.

Lytle, J.H. (1990). Reforming urban education: A review of recent reports and legislation. *The Urban Review, 22*, 199–220.

Mace, F.C., & Shea, M.C. (1990). Behavioral self-management with at-risk children. In L.J. Kruger (Ed.), *Promoting success with at-risk students: Emerging perspectives and practical approaches* (pp. 43–64). New York: Haworth Press.

Macedo, D. (2000). The colonialism of the English only movement. *Educational Researcher, 29*, 15–24.

Mackenzie, B. (1984). Explaining race differences in IQ: The logic, the methodology, and the evidence. *American Psychologist, 39*, 1214–1233.

Mackintosh, N.J. (Ed.). (1995). *Cyril Burt: Framed or fraud?* Oxford: Oxford University Press.

Mackintosh, N.J. (2002). [Review of the book *Dysgenics: Genetic deterioration in modern populations*]. *Journal of Biosocial Science, 34,* 283–288.

Mackintosh, N.J. (2007). [Review of the book *Race differences in intelligence: An evolutionary analysis*]. *Intelligence, 35,* 94–96.

MacMillan, D., Siperstein, G., & Leffert, J. (2006). Children with mild mental retardation: A challenge for classification practices—revised. In H.N. Switzky & S. Greenspan (Eds.), *What is mental retardation: Ideas for an evolving disability in the 21st century* (Rev. and updated ed., pp. 197–220). Washington, DC: American Association on Mental Retardation.

Macpherson, C.B. (1977). *The life and times of liberal democracy.* New York: Oxford University Press.

Madaus, G.F. (1988). The influence of testing on the curriculum. In L. Tanner (Ed.), *Critical issues in curriculum: 87th yearbook of the National Society for the Study of Education, Part I* (pp. 83–121). Chicago: University of Chicago Press.

Madden, N.A., & Slavin, R.E. (1989). Effective pullout programs for students at risk. In R.E. Slavin, N.L. Karweit, & N.A. Madden (Eds.), *Effective programs for students at risk* (pp. 52–72). Boston: Allyn and Bacon.

Mangaliman, J., Rodríguez, J., & Gonzales, S. (2006, April, 11). 25,000 march downtown. *San Jose Mercury News,* pp. A1, A15.

Mangin, W. (1969). [Review of the book *Culture and poverty: Critique and counter-proposals*]. *Current Anthropology, 10,* 192.

Marans, A.E., & Lourie, R. (1967). Hypotheses regarding the effects of child-rearing patterns on the disadvantaged child. In J. Hellmuth (Ed.), *Disadvantaged child* (Vol. 1, pp. 17–41). New York: Brunner/Mazel.

Margonis, F. (1992). The cooptation of "at risk": Paradoxes of policy criticism. *Teachers College Record, 94,* 343–364.

Martin, D.H. (1997, September 12). Remarks raise lawmakers' ire. *Daily Texan,* pp. 1–2.

Martínez, G.A. (1994). Legal indeterminacy, judicial discretion and the Mexican-American litigation experience: 1930–80. *U.C. Davis Law Review, 27,* 555–618.

Marx, K., & Engels, F. (1845). *Die deutsche Ideologie: Kritik der neuesten deutschen Philosophie in ihren Repräsentanten, Feuerbach, B. Bauer und Stirner, und des deutschen Sozialismus in seinen verschiedenen Propheten 1845–1846 [The German ideology: Criticism of the newest German philosophy in its representative, Feuerbach, B. Bauer and Stirner, and German socialism in its different prophets]* (Published in 1932 from original 1845 manuscript). Berlin: Marx-Engels-Verlag.

Marx, S. (2001). *Turning a blind eye to racism no more: Naming whiteness and racism with pre-service teachers working with English language learners of color.* Unpublished doctoral dissertation, The University of Texas at Austin.

Marx, S. (2003). Entanglements of altruism, whiteness, and deficit thinking: White preservice teachers working with urban Latinos. *Educators for Urban Minorities, 2,* 41–56.

Marx, S. (2004a). Exploring and challenging whiteness and White racism with White preservice teachers. In V. Lea & J. Helfand (Eds.), *Identifying race and transforming whiteness in the classroom* (pp. 132–152). New York: Peter Lang.

Marx, S. (2004b). Regarding whiteness: Exploring and intervening in the effects of White racism in teacher education. *Equity & Excellence in Education, 37,* 31–43.

Marx, S. (2006). *Revealing the invisible: Confronting passive racism in teacher education.* New York: Routledge.

Marx, S., & Pennington, J. (2003). Pedagogies of critical race theory: Experimentations with White preservice teachers. *International Journal of Qualitative Studies in Education, 16,* 91–110.

Matza, D. (1969). [Review of the book *Culture and poverty: Critique and counter-proposals*]. *Current Anthropology, 10,* 192–194.

Mayer, D.P., Mullins, J.E., & Moore, M.T. (2000). *Monitoring school quality: An indicators report.* Washington, DC: National Center for Education Statistics. Retrieved March 17, 2009, from: *http://nces.ed.gov/pubs2001/2001030.pdf.*

Mayer, S.E. (1997). *What money can't buy: Family income and children's life chances.* Cambridge, MA: Harvard University Press.

McCarthy, C. (1998). *The uses of culture: Education and the limits of ethnic affiliation.* New York: Routledge.

McCarthy, D. (1972). *Manual for the McCarthy Scales of Children's Abilities.* New York: Psychological Corporation.

McCulloch, R. (1995, February). Separation for preservation: Another perspective on the need for separation. *American Renaissance, 6.* Available online at: *http://www.amren.com/ar/1995/02/index.html.*

McDaniel, G. (Ed.). (2003). *A race against time: Racial heresies for the 21st century.* Oakton, VA: New Century Foundation.

McDougall, W. (1921). *Is America safe for democracy?* New York: Scribner.

McGurk, F.C.J. (1956, September 21). A scientist's report on race differences. *U.S. News and World Report,* pp. 92–96.

McGurk, F.C.J. (1961). Psychological test score differences and the "cultural hypothesis." *Mankind Quarterly, 1,* 165–175.

McIntyre, A. (1997). *Making meaning of whiteness: Exploring racial identity with White teachers.* Albany: State University of New York Press.

McKenzie, K.B., & Scheurich, J.J. (2004). Equity traps: A useful construct for preparing principals to lead schools that are successful with racially diverse students. *Educational Administration Quarterly, 40,* 601–632.

McKenzie, K.B., & Scheurich, J.J. (2007). King Elementary: A new principal plans how to transform a diverse urban school. *Journal of Cases in Educational Leadership, 10,* 19–27.

McKenzie, K.B., Skrla, L., & Scheurich, J.J. (2006). Preparing instructional leaders for social justice. *Journal of School Leadership, 16,* 158–170.

McLanahan, S.S. (1997). Parent absence or poverty: Which matters more? In G.J. Duncan & J. Brooks-Gunn (Eds.), *Consequences of growing up poor* (pp. 35–48). New York: Russell Sage Foundation.

McNeil, (2000). *Contradictions of reform: The educational costs of standardization.* New York: Routledge.

McWayne, C., Hampton, V., Fantuzzo, J., Cohen, H.L., & Sekino, Y. (2004). A multivariate examination of parental involvement and the social and academic competencies of urban kindergarten children. *Psychology in the Schools, 41,* 363–377.

Mead, M. (1969). [Review of the book *Culture and poverty: Critique and counter-proposals*]. *Current Anthropology, 10,* 194.

Meece, J.L., & Kurtz-Costes, B. (2001). Introduction: The schooling of ethnic minority children and youth. *Educational Psychologist, 36,* 1–7.

Meier, D. (2002). *In schools we trust.* Boston, MA: Beacon Press.

Meier, D., & Wood, G. (Eds.). (2004). *Many children left behind: How the No Child Left Behind Act is damaging our children and our schools.* Boston, MA: Beacon Press.

Meisenberg, G. (2006). [Review of the book *Race differences in intelligence: An evolutionary analysis*]. *Annals of Human Biology, 33,* 648–650.

Menchaca, M. (1997). Early racist discourses: Roots of deficit thinking. In R.R. Valencia (Ed.), *The evolution of deficit thinking: Educational thought and practice* (pp. 13–40). The Stanford Series on Education and Public Policy. London: Falmer Press.

Menchaca, M. (2000). History and anthropology: Conducting Chicano research. In R. Rochín & D. Valdés (Eds.), *Toward a new Chicano history* (pp. 167–181). East Lansing: Michigan State University Press.

Menchaca, M., & Valencia, R.R. (1990). Anglo-Saxon ideologies and their impact on the segregation of Mexican students in California, the 1920s–1930s. *Anthropology & Education Quarterly, 21,* 222–249.

Menchaca, V.D. (2003). Ensuring success for Latino migrant students. In V.I. Kloosterman (Ed.), *Latino students in American schools: Historical and contemporary views* (pp. 129–138). Westport, CT: Praeger.

Mercer, J.R., & Brown, W.C. (1973). Racial differences in IQ: Fact or fiction? In C. Sienna (Ed.), *The fallacy of IQ* (pp. 56–113). New York: Joseph Okpatu.

Michaels, S. (1981). "Sharing time": Children's narrative styles and differentials access to literacy. *Language in Society, 10,* 423–442.

Miele, F. (1979). Cultural bias in the WISC. *Intelligence, 3,* 149–164.

Miller, E.M. (2002). Differential intelligence and national income [Review of the book *IQ and the wealth of nations*]. *Journal of Social, Political and Economic Studies, 27,* 513–522.

Miller, L.S. (1995). The origins of the presumption of Black stupidity. *The Journal of Blacks in Higher Education, 9,* 78–82.

Miller, W.B. (1969). [Review of the book *Culture and poverty: Critique and counter-proposals*]. *Current Anthropology, 10,* 194–196.

Milliken, W.G. (1970). Making the school system accountable. *Compact, 4,* 17–18.

Mintrop, H. (2004). High-stakes accountability, state oversight, and educational equity. *Teachers College Record, 106*, 2128–2145.

Mirman, J.A., Swartz, R.J., & Barell, J. (1988). Strategies to help teachers empower at-risk students. In B.Z. Presseisen (Ed.), *At-risk students and thinking: Perspectives from research* (pp. 138–152). Washington, DC: National Education Association.

Missiuna, C., & Samuels, M. (1988). Dynamic assessment: Review and critique. *Special Services in the Schools, 5*, 1–22.

Modgil, S., & Modgil, C. (Eds.). (1987). *Arthur Jensen: Consensus and controversy.* New York: Falmer Press.

Montagu, A. (1974). *Man's most dangerous myth: The fallacy of race.* Oxford: Oxford University Press.

Montagu, M.F.A. (1945). Intelligence of northern Negroes and southern Whites in the First World War. *American Journal of Psychology, 58*, 161–188.

Montaño, T., & Metcalfe, E.L. (2003). Triumphs and tragedies: The urban schooling of Latino students. In V.I. Kloosterman (Ed.), *Latino students in American schools: Historical and contemporary views* (pp. 139–151). Westport, CT: Praeger.

Montaño-Harmon, M.R. (1991). Discourse features of written Mexican Spanish: Current research in contrastive rhetoric. *Hispania, 74*, 417–425.

Moore, E.G.J. (1986). Family socialization and the IQ test performance of traditional and trans-racially adopted Black children. *Developmental Psychology, 22*, 317–326.

Moreno, J.F. (Ed.) (1999). *The elusive quest for equality: 150 years of Chicano/Chicana education.* Cambridge, MA: Harvard Educational Review.

Moreno, R.P., & Valencia, R.R. (2002). Chicano families and schools: Myths, knowledge, and future directions for understanding. In R.R. Valencia (Ed.), *Chicano school failure and success: Past, present, and future* (2nd ed., pp. 227–249). London: RoutledgeFalmer.

Morris, M. (1989). From the culture of poverty to the underclass: An analysis of a shift in public language. *American Sociologist, 20*, 123–133.

Moynihan, D.P. (1965). *The Negro family: A case for national action.* Washington, DC: U.S. Department of Labor.

Moynihan, D.P. (1969). [Review of the book *Culture and poverty: Critique and counter-proposals*]. *Current Anthropology, 10*, 196–197.

Munter, J.H. (2004). Tomorrow's teachers re-envisioning the roles of parents in schools: Lessons learned on the U.S./Mexico border. *Thresholds in Education, 30*, 19–29.

Murray, C. (1988). The coming of custodial democracy. *Commentary, 86*, 9–14.

Murray, C. (1995, May). *The Bell Curve* and its critics. *Commentary, 99*, 23–30.

Myrdal, G. (1970). *The challenge of world poverty: A world anti-poverty program in outline.* New York: Pantheon Books.

Nagge, J.W. (1932). Regarding the law of parsimony. *Journal of Genetic Psychology, 41*, 492–494.

Naples, N.A. (1991). Contradictions in the gender subtext of the War on Poverty: The community work and resistance of women from low income communities. *Social Problems, 38*, 316–322.

Naples, N.A. (1998). *Grassroots warriors: Activist mothering, community work and the War on Poverty.* New York: Routledge.

National Coalition of Advocates for Students. (1985). *Barriers to excellence: Our children at risk.* Boston: National Coalition of Advocates for Students.

National Commission on Excellence in Education. (1983). *A nation at risk: The imperative for educational reform.* Washington, DC: U.S. Government Printing Office.

National Commission on Teaching and America's Future. (2007). *Policy brief: The high cost of teacher turnover.* Washington, DC: Author. Retrieved March 17, 2009, from: http://www.nctaf.org/resources/demonstration_projects/turnover/TeacherTurnoverCostStudy.htm.

Nechyba, T.J. (2004). [Review of the book *IQ and the wealth of nations*]. *Journal of Economic Literature, 42*, 220–221.

Nei, M., & Livshits, G. (1989). Genetic relationships of Europeans, Asian, and Africans and the origin of modern Homo sapiens. *Human Heredity, 39*, 276–281.

Neisser, U., Boodoo, G., Bouchard, T.J., Jr., Boykin, W.A., Brody, N., Ceci, S.J., Halpern, D.F., Loehlin, J.C., Perloff, R., Sternberg, R.J., & Urbina, S. (1996). Intelligence: Knowns and unknowns. *American Psychologist, 51*, 77–101.

Newby, I.A. (1967). *Challenge to the court: Social scientists and the defense of segregation, 1954–1966.* Baton Rouge: Louisiana State University Press.

Newman, H.H., Freeman, F.N., & Holzinger, K.J. (1937). *Twins: A study of heredity and environment.* Chicago: University of Chicago Press.

Ng, J.C., & Rury, J.L. (2006, July 18). Poverty and education: A critical analysis of the Ruby Payne phenomenon. *Teachers College Record.* Retrieved May 27, 2007, from *http://www.tcrecord.org/content.asp?contentid = 12596.*

Nichols, P.L. (1970). *The effects of heredity and environment on intelligence test performance in 4 and 7 year old White and Negro sibling pairs.* Doctoral dissertation, University of Michigan. Ann Arbor, MI: University Microfilms, No. 71–18, 874.

Nichols, S.L., & Berliner, D.C. (2007). *Collateral damage: How high-stakes testing corrupts America's schools.* Cambridge, MA: Harvard Education Press.

Nichols, S.L., Glass, G.V., & Berliner, D.C. (2005). *High-stakes testing and student achievement: Problems for the No Child Left Behind Act.* Education Policy Studies Laboratory, Education Policy Research Unit, Arizona State University, Tempe. Available at: *http://www.asu.edu/educ/epsl/EPRU/epru_2005_Research_Writing.htm.*

Nisbett, R.E. (1998). Race, genetics, and IQ. In C. Jencks & M. Phillips (Eds.), *The Black-White test score gap* (pp. 86–102). Washington, DC: Brookings Institution Press.

No Child Left Behind Act, Pub. L. No. (107–110), 115 Stat. 1425 (2002).

Noguera, P.A. (2004). Racial isolation, poverty, and the limits of local control in Oakland. *Teachers College Record, 106,* 2146–2170.

Nuenke, M. (2007). [Review of the books *Future human evolution: Eugenics in the twenty-first century* and *IQ and global inequality*]. *The Occidental Quarterly, 7.* Available online at: *http://www.theoccidentalquarterly.com/archives/vol7no2/index.html.*

Nyberg, D. (1976). Skill school v. education school: An essay on Carl Bereiter's pedagogics. *Educational Theory, 26,* 214–222.

O'Connor, A. (2001). *Poverty knowledge: Social science, social policy, and the poor in twentieth-century U.S. history.* Princeton, NJ: Princeton University Press.

Oakes, J. (1985). *Keeping track: How schools structure inequality.* New Haven, CT: Yale University Press.

Oakes, J. (2002). *Education inadequacy, inequality, and failed state policy: A synthesis of expert reports prepared for Williams v. State of California.* Retrieved March 17, 2009, from: *http://www.decentschools.com/expert_reports/oakes_report.pdf.*

Oakes, J. (2004). Investigating the claims in *Williams v. State of California*: An unconstitutional denial of education's basic tools? *Teachers College Record, 106,* 1889–1906.

Oakes, J., & Lipton, M. (2004). Schools that shock the conscience: *Williams v. California* and the struggle for education on equal terms fifty years after *Brown. Berkeley La Raza Law Journal, 15,* 234–258.

Oakes, J., & Saunders, M. (2004). Education's most basic tools: Access to textbooks and instructional materials in California's public schools. *Teachers College Record, 106,* 1967–1988.

Ochoa, A.M. (2003). The struggle of access: The achievement trends of Latino youth in middle and high school. In V.I. Kloosterman (Ed.), *Latino students in American schools: Historical and contemporary views* (pp. 47–61). Westport, CT: Praeger.

Ogbu, J.U. (1978). *Minority education and caste: The American system in cross-cultural perspective.* New York: Academic Press.

Ogbu, J.U. (1986). The consequences of the American caste system. In U. Neisser (Ed.), *The school achievement of minority children* (pp. 19–56). Hillsdale, NJ: Lawrence Erlbaum.

Ogbu, J.U. (1987). Variability in minority responses to schooling: Nonimmigrants vs. immigrants. In G. Spindler & L. Spindler (Eds.), *Interpretive ethnography of education: At home and abroad* (pp. 255–278). Hillsdale, NJ: Lawrence Erlbaum.

Ogbu, J.U. (1990). Minority education in comparative perspective. *Journal of Negro Education, 59,* 45–57.

Ogbu, J.U. (1991). Immigrant and involuntary minorities in comparative perspective. In M.A. Gibson & J.U. Ogbu (Eds.), *Minority status and schooling: A comparative study of immigrant and involuntary minorities* (pp. 3–33). New York: Garland.

Ogbu, J.U. (1994). Culture and intelligence. In R.J. Sternberg (Ed.), *Encyclopedia of human intelligence* (Vol. 2, pp. 328–338). New York: Macmillan.

Ogletree, C.J., Jr. (2004). *All deliberate speed: Reflections on the first half century of Brown v. Board of Education.* New York: W.W. Norton.

Orfield, G., & Kornhaber, M.L. (2001). *Raising standards or raising barriers? Inequality and high-stakes testing in public education.* New York: Century Foundation Press.

Ortiz, F.I. (2004). Essential learning conditions for California youth: Educational facilities. *Teachers College Record, 106,* 2015–2031.

Osborne, R.T. (1960). Racial difference in mental growth and school achievement: A longitudinal study. *Psychological Reports, 7,* 233–239.

Osborne, R.T. (1961). School achievement of White and Negro children of the same mental and chronological ages. *Mankind Quarterly, 2,* 26–29.

Osborne, R.T. (1962). *Racial difference in school achievement.* Mankind Monographs, 3. Edinburgh: Mankind Quarterly.

Osborne, R.T. (1980). *Twins: Black and White.* Athens, GA: Foundation for Human Understanding.

Osborne, R.T., & Gregor, A.J. (1968). Racial differences in heritability estimates for tests of spatial ability. *Perceptual and Motor Skills, 27,* 735–739.

Osborne, R.T., & McGurk, F.C.J. (Eds.). (1982a). *The testing of Negro intelligence* (Vol. 2). Athens, GA: Foundation for Human Understanding.

Osborne, R.T., & McGurk, F.C.J. (1982b). Summary and conclusions. In R.T. Osborne & F.C.J. McGurk (Eds.), *The testing of Negro intelligence* (Vol. 2, pp. 290–297). Athens, GA: Foundation for Human Understanding.

Osborne, R.T., & Miele, F. (1969). Racial differences in environmental influences on numerical ability as determined by heritability estimates. *Perceptual and Motor Skills, 28,* 533–538.

Osei-Kofi, N. (2005). Pathologizing the poor: A framework for understanding Ruby Payne's work. *Equity & Excellence in Education, 38,* 367–375.

Padrón, Y.N., Waxman, H.C., & Rivera, H.H. (2002). Issues in educating Hispanic students. In S. Stringfield & D. Land (Eds.), *Educating at-risk students: One hundred-first yearbook of the National Society for the Study of Education, Part II* (pp. 66–88). Chicago: National Society for the Study of Education.

Palairet, M. (2004). IQ and economic development [Review of the book *IQ and the wealth of nations*]. *Heredity, 92,* 361–362.

Pardo, M.S. (1998). *Mexican American women activists: Identity and resistance in two Los Angeles communities.* Philadelphia: Temple University Press.

Patall, E.A., Cooper, H., & Robinson, J.C. (2008). Parent involvement in homework: A research synthesis. *Review of Educational Research, 78,* 1039–1101.

Payne, R.K. (2002). *Understanding learning: The how, the why, the what.* Highlands, TX: aha! Process.

Payne, R.K. (2005). *A framework for understanding poverty* (4th rev. ed.). Highlands, TX: aha! Process.

Payne, R.K. (2006a). *Working with students: Discipline strategies for the classroom.* Highlands, TX: aha! Process.

Payne, R.K. (2006b). *Working with parents: Building relationships for student success.* Highlands, TX: aha! Process.

Payne, R.K. (2009, May 17). Using the lens of economic class to help teachers understand and teach students from poverty: A response. *Teachers College Record.* Retrieved June 2, 2009, from: *http://www.tcrecord.org/content.asp?contentid* = 15629.

Payne, R.K., DeVol, P.E., & Smith, T.D. (2006). *Bridges out of poverty: Strategies for professionals and communities.* Highlands, TX: aha! Process.

Payne, R.K., & Krabill, D.L. (2002). *Hidden rules of class at work.* Highlands, TX: aha! Process.

Pearl, A. (1991). Systemic and institutional factors in Chicano school failure. In R.R. Valencia (Ed.), *Chicano school failure and success: Research and policy agendas for the 1990s* (pp. 273–320). The Stanford Series on Education and Public Policy. London: Falmer Press.

Pearl, A. (1997a). Democratic education as an alternative to deficit thinking. In R.R. Valencia (Ed.), *The evolution of deficit thinking: Educational thought and practice* (pp. 211–241). The Stanford Series on Education and Public Policy. London: Falmer Press.

Pearl, A. (1997b). Cultural and accumulated environmental deficit models. In R.R. Valencia (Ed.), *The evolution of deficit thinking: Educational thought and practice* (pp. 132–159). The Stanford Series on Education and Public Policy. London: Falmer Press.

Pearl, A. (2002). The big picture: Systemic and institutional factors in Chicano school failure and success. In R.R. Valencia (Ed.), *Chicano school failure and success: Past, present, and future* (2nd ed., pp. 335–364). London: RoutledgeFalmer.

Pearl, A., & Knight, T. (1999). *The democratic classroom: Theory to inform practice.* Cresskill, NJ: Hampton Press.

Pearl, A., & Pryor, C.R. (Eds.). (2005). *Democratic practices in education: Implications for teacher education*. Lanham, MD: Rowman & Littlefield Education.

Pearl, R. (1934). The weight of the Negro brain. *Science, 80*, 431–434.

Pearson, R. (1991). *Race, intelligence and bias in academe*. Washington, DC: Scott-Townsend.

Peattie, L. (1968). *The view from the barrio*. Ann Arbor: University of Michigan Press.

Pedersen, N.L., Plomin, R., Nesselroade, J.R., & McClearn, G.E. (1992). A quantitative genetic analysis of cognitive abilities during the second half of the life span. *Psychological Science, 3*, 346–353.

Peña, E.D. (1996). Dynamic assessment: The model and its language applications. In K.N. Cole, P.S. Dale, & D.J. Thal (Eds.), *Assessment of communication and language* (pp. 281–307). Baltimore: Paul H. Brookes.

Peña, E.D., Iglesias, A., & Lidz, C.S. (2001). Reducing test bias through dynamic assessment of children's word learning ability. *American Journal of Speech-Language Pathology, 10*, 138–154.

Penchef, E. (Ed.). (1971). *Four horsemen: Pollution, poverty, famine, violence*. San Francisco: Canfield Press.

Perea, J.F. (2003). A brief history of race and the U.S.-Mexican border: Tracing the trajectories of conquest. *UCLA Law Review, 51*, 283–312.

Peske, H.G., Crawford, C., & Pick, B. (2006). *Missing the mark: An Education Trust analysis of teacher equity plans*. Washington, DC: The Education Trust. Retrieved March 17, 2009, from: *http://www2.edtrust.org/NR/rdonlyres/5E2815C9-F765–4821–828F–66F4D156713A/ 0/TeacherEquityPlans.pdf*.

Peske, H.G., & Haycock, K. (2006). *Teaching inequality: How poor and minority students are short-changed on teacher quality*. Washington, DC: The Education Trust. Retrieved March 17, 2009, from: *http://eric.ed.gov/ERICWebPortal/recordDetail?accno* = ED494820.

Peters, M. (1995). [Review of the book *Race, evolution, and behavior: A life history perspective*]. *Aggressive Behavior, 21*, 463–468.

Pettigrew, T.F. (1964). Negro American intelligence: A new look at an old controversy. *Journal of Negro Education, 33*, 6–25.

Pfarr, J.R. (2009). *Tactical communication: Law enforcement tools for successful encounters with people from poverty, middle class, and wealth*. Highlands, TX: aha! Process.

Phillips, D.C., & Kelley, M.C. (1975). Hierarchical theories of development in education and psychology. *Harvard Educational Review, 45*, 351–375.

Philips, S.U. (1983). *Invisible culture: Communication in classroom and community on the Warm Springs Indian Reservation*. New York: Longman.

Phillips, S.E. (2000). GI Forum v. Texas Education Agency: Psychometric evidence. *Applied Measurement in Education, 13*, 343–385.

Piaget, J. (1963). *Origins of intelligence in children*. New York: W.W. Norton.

Piersel, W.C., & Lee, S.W. (1990). Individualized education and applied behavior analysis. In L.J. Kruger (Ed.), *Promoting success with at-risk students: Emerging perspectives and practical approaches* (pp. 89–107). New York: Haworth Press.

Pipho, C. (1986). States move reform closer to reality. *Phi Delta Kappan, 68*, K1–K8.

Piven, F.F., & Cloward, R. (1971). *Regulating the poor: The functions of public welfare*. New York: Pantheon Books.

Piven, F.F., & Cloward, R. (1979). *Poor people's movements: Why they succeed and how they fail*. New York: Vintage Books.

Plessy v. Ferguson, 163 U.S. 537 (1896).

Plomin, R., & DeFries, J.C. (1980). Genetics and intelligence: Recent data. *Intelligence, 4*, 15–24.

Plomin, R., DeFries, J.C., McClearn, G.E., & Rutter, M. (1997). *Behavioral genetics* (3rd ed.). New York: W.H. Freeman.

Prasse, D.P., & Reschly, D.J. (1986). *Larry P.*: A case of segregation, testing, or program efficacy? *Exceptional Children, 52*, 333–346.

Presseisen, B.Z. (Ed.). (1988a). *At-risk students and thinking: Perspectives from research*. Washington, DC: National Education Association.

Presseisen, B.Z. (1988b). Teaching thinking and at-risk students: Defining a population. In B.Z. Presseisen (Ed.), *At-risk students and thinking: Perspectives from research* (pp. 19–37). Washington, DC: National Education Association.

Prins, E., & Schafft, K.A. (2009). Individual and structural attributions for poverty and persistence in family literacy programs: The resurgence of the culture of poverty. *Teachers College*

Record. Retrieved November 18, 2008, from *http://www.tcrecord.org/content.asp?contentid =* 15396.

Purcell-Gates, V. (1995). *Other people's words: The cycle of low literacy.* Cambridge, MA: Harvard University Press.

Putnam, C. (1961). *Race and reason: A Yankee view.* Washington, DC: Public Affairs Press.

Quartz, K.H., & TEP Research Group. (2003). "Too angry to leave": Supporting new teachers' commitment to transform urban schools. *Journal of Teacher Education, 54,* 99–111.

Quijada, P.D., & Álvarez, L. (2006). Cultivando semillas educacionales (Cultivating educational seeds): Understanding the experiences of K–8 Latina/o students. In J. Castellanos, A.M. Gloria, & M.A. Kamimura (Eds.), *The Latina/o pathway to the Ph.D.: Abriendo caminos* (pp. 3–18). Sterling, VA: Stylus.

Quintero, E., & Rummel, M.K. (1995). Voice unaltered: Marginalized young writers speak. In B.B. Swadener & S. Lubeck (Eds.), *Children and families "at promise": Deconstructing the discourse of risk* (pp. 97–117). Albany: State University of New York Press.

Ramírez, M., III, & Castañeda, A. (1974). *Cultural democracy, bicognitive development, and education.* New York: Academic Press.

Rand, Y., Tannenbaum, A.J., & Feuerstein, R. (1988). *Don't accept me as I am: Helping retarded people to excel* (Appendix D). New York: Plenum.

Rank, M.R. (2004). *One nation, underprivileged: Why American poverty affects us all.* New York: Oxford University Press.

Read, F.T. (1977). Judicial evolution of the law of school integration since *Brown v. Board of Education.* In B. Levin & W.D. Hawley (Eds.), *The courts, social science, and school desegregation* (pp. 7–49). New Brunswick, NJ: Transaction Books.

Ready, D.D., Lee, V.E., & Welner, K.G. (2004). Educational equity and school structure: School size, overcrowding, and schools-within-schools. *Teachers College Record, 106,* 1989–2014.

Rebell, M.A., & Wolff, J.R. (2008). *Moving every child ahead: From NCLB hype to meaningful educational opportunity.* New York: Teachers College Press.

Reed, A.R., Jr. (1992). The underclass as myth and symbol: The poverty of discourse about poverty. *Radical America, 24,* 21–40.

Reed, A.R., Jr. (1994). Looking backward [Review of the book *The bell curve: Intelligence and class structure in American life*]. *The Nation, 259,* 654–662.

Reed, T.E. (1969). Caucasian genes in American Negroes. *Science, 165,* 762–768.

Relethford, J.H. (1995). [Review of the book *Race, evolution, and behavior: A life history perspective*]. *Journal of Physical Anthropology, 98,* 91–94.

Reschly, D.J. (1988). Minority MMR overrepresentation and special education reform. *Exceptional Children, 54,* 316–323.

Reyes, A. (2005). Reculturing principals as leaders for cultural and linguistic diversity. In K. Téllez & H.C. Waxman (Eds.), *Preparing quality educators for English language learners: Research, policy, and practice* (pp. 145–165). Mahwah, NJ: Lawrence Erlbaum.

Reyes, P., Scribner, J., & Scribner, A.P. (Eds.). (1999). *Lessons from high-performing Hispanic schools: Creating learning communities.* New York: Teachers College Press.

Reyes, P., & Valencia, R.R. (1993). Educational policy and the growing Latino student population: Problems and prospects. *Hispanic Journal of Behavioral Sciences, 15,* 258–283.

Reyes, P., & Wagstaff, L. (2005). How does leadership promote successful teaching and learning for diverse students? In W.A. Firestone & C. Riehl (Eds.), *A new agenda for research in educational leadership* (pp. 101–118). New York: Teachers College Press.

Ricci, B. (2000). How about parent-teacher student conferences? *Principal, 79,* 53–54.

Rice, J.K. (2003). *Teacher quality: Understanding the effectiveness of teacher attributes.* Washington, DC: Economic Policy Institute.

Richards, M. (2002). [Review of the book *IQ and the wealth of nations*]. *Intelligence, 30,* 574–576.

Richards, M., & Sacker, A. (2003). Lifetime antecedents of cognitive reserve. *Journal of Clinical and Experimental Neuropsychology, 25,* 614–624.

Richardson, K. (2004). [Review of the book *IQ and the wealth of nations*]. *Heredity, 92,* 359–360.

Richardson, V., Casanova, U., Placier, P., & Guilfoyle, K. (1989). *School children at-risk.* New York: Falmer Press.

Rife, D.C. (1959). *Heredity and human nature.* New York: Vantage Press.

Rivin, S.G., Hanushek, E.A., & Kain, J.F. (2005). Teachers, schools, and academic achievement. *Econometrica, 73,* 417–458.

Roberts, S. (2004). *Who we are now: The changing face of America in the twenty-first century*. New York: Times Books.

Robinson, W.S. (1950). Ecological correlations and the behavior of individuals. *American Sociological Review, 15*, 351–357.

Rodriguez v. San Antonio Independent School District, 337 F. Supp. 280 (W.D. Tex. 1971), *prob. juris. noted*, 406 U.S. 966 (1972), *rev'd sub nom* San Antonio Independent School District v. Rodriguez, 411 U.S. 1 (1973) (Marshall, J., dissenting).

Rodríguez, L.J. (1993). *Always running: La vida loca: Gang days in L.A.* Willimantic, CT: Curbstone Press.

Rogers, J.S. (2004). Creating a public accountability for California schools. *Teachers College Record, 106*, 2171–2192.

Romano-V, O.I. (1968). The anthropology and sociology of the Mexican-Americans: The distortion of Mexican-American history. *El Grito, 2*, 13–26.

Ronda, M.A., & Valencia, R.R. (1994). "At-risk" Chicano students: The institutional and communicative life of a category. *Hispanic Journal of Behavioral Sciences, 16*, 363–395.

Rosenthal, S.J. (1995). The Pioneer Fund: Financier of fascist research. *American Behavioral Scientist, 39*, 44–61.

Roser, M.A., & Tanamachi, C. (1997, September 17). Jackson urges UT to fight racism. *Austin American-Statesman*, pp. A1, A10.

Rumberger, R.W., & Gándara, P. (2004). Seeking equity in the education of California's English learners. *Teachers College Record, 106*, 2032–2056.

Rumberger, R.W., & Rodríguez, G.M. (2002). Chicano dropouts: An update of research and policy issues. In R.R. Valencia (Ed.), *Chicano school failure and success: Past, present, and future* (2nd ed., pp. 114–146). London: RoutledgeFalmer.

Rushton, J.P. (1994). The equalitarian dogma revisited. *Intelligence, 19*, 263–280.

Rushton, J.P. (1995). *Race, evolution, and behavior: A life history perspective*. New Brunswick, NJ: Transaction Publishers.

Rushton, J.P. (1997). *Race, evolution, and behavior: A life history perspective* (2nd ed.). New Brunswick, NJ: Transaction Publishers.

Rushton, J.P. (1999). *Race, evolution, and behavior* (special abridged edition). New Brunswick, NJ: Transaction Publishers.

Rushton, J.P. (2000). *Race, evolution, and behavior: A life history perspective* (3rd ed.). Port Huron, MI: Charles Darwin Research Institute.

Rushton, J.P. (2002). The Pioneer Fund and the scientific study of human differences. *Albany Law Review, 66*, 207–262.

Rushton, J.P. (2003). The bigger *Bell Curve*: Intelligence, national achievement, and the global economy [Review of the book *IQ and the wealth of nations*]. *Personality and Individual Differences, 34*, 367–372.

Rushton, J.P. (2006a). [Review of the book *IQ and global inequality*]. *Personality and Individual Differences, 41*, 983–985.

Rushton, J.P. (2006b). [Review of the book *Race differences in intelligence: An evolutionary analysis*]. *Personality and Individual Differences, 40*, 853–855.

Rushton, J.P. (2008). [Review of the book *The global bell curve: Race, IQ, and inequality worldwide*]. *Personality and Individual Differences, 45*, 113–114.

Russell, B. (1927). Education. *Selected papers of Bertrand Russell* (pp. 87–110). New York: The Modern Library.

Russell, G. (1977, August 29). The American underclass: Destitute and desperate in the land of plenty. *Time, 110*, 14–18, 21–22, 27.

Russell, M., Higgins, J., & Raczek, A. (2004). Accountability, California style: Counting or accounting? *Teachers College Record, 106*, 2102–2127.

Ryan, W. (1971). *Blaming the victim*. New York: Random House.

San Miguel, G., Jr. (1987). *"Let all of them take heed": Mexican Americans and the campaign for educational equality in Texas, 1910–1981*. Austin: University of Texas Press.

San Miguel, G., Jr., & Valencia, R.R. (1998). From the Treaty of Guadalupe Hidalgo to *Hopwood*: The educational plight and struggle of Mexican Americans in the Southwest. *Harvard Educational Review, 68*, 353–412.

Sanders, M.G. (Ed.). (2000). *Schooling students placed at risk: Research, policy, and practice in the education of poor and minority students*. Mahwah, NJ: Lawrence Erlbaum.

Sarich, V., & Miele, F. (2004). *Race: The reality of human differences*. Boulder, CO: Westview Press.

Scarr, S., Pakstis, A.J., Katz, S.H., & Barker, W.B. (1977). Absence of a relationship between degree of White ancestry and intellectual skills within a Black population. *Human Genetics, 39,* 69–86.

Scarr, S., & Weinberg, R.A. (1976). IQ test performance of Black children adopted by White parents. *American Psychologist, 31,* 726–739.

Scarr, S., & Weinberg, R.A. (1977). Intellectual similarities within families of both adopted and biological children. *Intelligence, 1,* 170–191.

Scarr, S., Weinberg, R.A., & Waldman, I.D. (1993). IQ correlations in transracial adoptive families. *Intelligence, 17,* 541–555.

Scarr-Salapatek, S. (1971). Race, social class, and IQ. *Science, 174,* 1285–1295.

Schlossman, S., & Turner, S. (1993). Status offenders, criminal offenders, and children "at risk" in early twentieth century juvenile court. In R. Wollons (Ed.), *Children at risk in America: History, concepts, and public policy* (pp. 32–57). New York: State University of New York Press.

Schönemann, P.H. (1994). Heritability. In R.J. Sternberg (Ed.), *Encyclopedia of human intelligence* (pp. 528–536). New York: Macmillan.

Scott, D.M. (1994). Cognitive conceit [Review of the book *The bell curve: Intelligence and class structure in American life*]. *Social Policy, 25,* 50–59.

Scribner, J.D., Young, M.D., & Pedroza, A. (1999). Building collaborative relationships with parents. In P. Reyes, J.D. Scribner, & A.P. Scribner (Eds.), *Lessons from high-performing Hispanic schools: Creating learning communities* (pp. 36–60). New York: Teachers College Press.

Seefeldt, C., Denton, K., Galper, A., & Younoszai, T. (1998). Former Head Start parents' characteristics, perceptions of school climate, and involvement in their children's education. *Elementary School Journal, 98,* 339–349.

Seligman, B.B. (1968). *Permanent poverty: An American syndrome.* Chicago: Quadrangle Books.

Sennett, R., & Cobb, J. (1972). *The hidden injuries of class.* New York: Alfred A. Knopf.

Sequeria, J.H. (1932). The brain of the East African native. *British Medical Journal, 1*(3761), 581.

Sernau, S. (1997). Economies of exclusion: Economic change and the global underclass. In J.E. Behar & A.G. Cuzán (Eds.), *At the crossroads of development: Transnational challenges to developed and developing societies* (pp. 38–51). Leiden: Brill.

Serrano v. Priest, Civil Action No. 938254, Superior Court, Los Angeles County, California January 8, 1969, *aff'd,* 89 Cal. Rptr. 345, 10 Cal. App.3d 1110 (Ct. App. 1970), *rev'd and rem'd,* 5 Cal.3d 584, 96 Cal. Rptr. 601, 487 P.2d 1241 (Cal. 1971), *aff'd,* 18 Cal.3d 728, 135 Cal. Rptr. 345, 557 P.2d 929 (Cal. 1976), *aff'd,* 226 Cal. Rptr. 584, 200 Cal. App.3d 897 (Ct. App. 1986).

Sharff, J. (1987). The underground economy of a poor neighborhood. In L. Mullings (Ed.), *Cities of the United States: Studies in urban anthropology* (pp. 19–50). New York: Columbia University Press.

Sharff, J. (1998). *King Kong on 4th Street: Families and the violence of poverty on the Lower East Side.* Boulder, CO: Westview Press.

Sheehy, D. (2006). *Fighting immigration anarchy: American patriots battle to save the nation.* Bloomington, IN: Rooftop Publishing.

Sheldon, S.B. (2003). Linking school-family-community partnerships in urban elementary schools to student achievement on state tests. *The Urban Review, 35,* 149–165.

Shields, C.M. (2006). Creating spaces for value-based conversations: The role of school leaders in the 21st century. *International Studies in Educational Administration, 34,* 62–81.

Shields, J. (1962). *Monozygotic twins brought up apart and brought up together.* London: Oxford University Press.

Shuey, A.M. (1958). *The testing of Negro intelligence.* Lynchburg, VA: J.P. Bell.

Shuey, A.M. (1966). *The testing of Negro intelligence* (2nd ed.). New York: Social Science Press.

Simonton, D.K. (1995). Behavioral laws in histories of psychology: Psychological science, meta-science, and the psychology of science. *Psychological Inquiry, 6,* 89–114.

Skrabanek, P. (1989). The mismeasure of Burt [Review of the book *The Burt affair*]. *Lancet, 8667,* 856–857.

Skrla, L., & Scheurich, J.J. (2001). Displacing deficit thinking in school district leadership. *Education and Urban Society, 33,* 235–259.

Skrla, L., & Scheurich, J.J. (Eds.). (2004). *Educational equity and accountability: Paradigms, policies, and politics.* New York: RoutledgeFalmer.

Skrla, L., Erlandson, D.A., Reed, E.M., & Wilson, A.P. (2001). *The emerging principalship.* Larchmont, NY: Eye on Education.

Skrla, L., Scheurich, J.J., García, J., & Nolly, G. (2004). Equity audits: A practical leadership tool for developing equitable and excellent schools. *Educational Administration Quarterly, 40,* 133–161.

Slavin, R.E. (1989). Students at risk of school failure: The problem and its dimensions. In R.E. Slavin, N.L. Karweit, & N.A. Madden (Eds.), *Effective programs for students at risk* (pp. 3–19). Boston: Allyn and Bacon.

Slavin, R.E., Karweit, N.L., & Madden, N.A. (Eds.). (1989). *Effective programs for students at risk.* Boston: Allyn and Bacon.

Slocumb, P.D., & Payne, R.K. (2000). *Removing the mask: Giftedness in poverty.* Highlands, TX: aha! Process.

Smiley, A.D., & Helfenbein, R.J. (in press). Becoming teachers: The Payne effect. *Multicultural Perspectives.*

Smith, M.S., & Bissell, J.S. (1970). Report analysis: The impact of Head Start. *Harvard Educational Review, 40,* 51–104.

Smith, R.C., & Lincoln, C.A. (1988). *America's shame, America's hope: Twelve million youth at risk.* Chapel Hill, NC: MDC, Inc.

Snider, W. (1990, April 18). Outcry follows Cavazos comments on the values of Hispanic parents. *Education Week,* pp. 1–2.

Snyderman, M., & Rothman, S. (1988). *The IQ controversy: The media and public policy.* New Brunswick, NJ: Transaction Books.

Solberg, V.S.H., Carlstrom, A.H., Howard, K.A.S., & Jones, J.E. (2007). Classifying at-risk high school youth: The influence of community violence and protective factors on academic and health outcomes. *Career Development Quarterly, 55,* 313–327.

Sowell, T. (1981). *Ethnic America: A history.* New York: Basic Books.

Sowell, T. (1995). Ethnicity and IQ. In S. Fraser (Ed.), *The bell curve wars: Race, intelligence, and the future of America* (pp. 70–79). New York: Basic Books.

Spearman, C. (1927). *The abilities of man.* New York: Macmillan.

Spence, J.T., Underwood, B.J., Duncan, C.P., & Cotton, J.W. (1968). *Elementary statistics* (2nd ed.). New York: Appleton-Century Crofts.

Stack, C. (1974). *All our kin.* New York: Harper & Row.

Stedman, L.C., & Smith, M.S. (1983). Recent reform proposals for American schools. *Contemporary Education Review, 2,* 85–104.

Steen, R.G. (1996). *DNA and destiny: Nature and nurture in human behavior.* New York: Plenum.

Steinberg, S. (2001). *The ethnic myth: Race, ethnicity, and class in America* (3rd ed.). Boston: Beacon Press.

Stell v. Savannah-Chatham County Bd. of Education, order directing trial ct., 318 F.2d 425 (5th Cir. 1963), *prelim inj. denied,* 220 F. Supp. 667 (S.D. Ga. 1963), *rev'd in part, aff'd in part,* 333 F.2d 55 (5th Cir. 1964), 255 F. Supp. 83 (S.D. Ga. 1965), *plan modified,* 255 F. Supp. 88 (S.D. Ga. 1966), *rev'd and rem'd,* 387 F.2d 486 (5th Cir. 1967), *vac'd and rem'd,* 446 F.2d 904 (5th Cir. 1971), *aff'd,* 450 F.2d 880 (5th Cir. 1971), 334 F. Supp. 909 (S.D. Ga. 1971).

Stephan, W. (1999). *Reducing prejudice and stereotyping in schools.* New York: Teachers College Press.

Stringfield, S., & Land, D. (Eds.). (2002). *Educating at-risk students: One hundred-first yearbook of the National Society for the Study of Education, Part II.* Chicago: National Society for the Study of Education.

Sutterby, J.A., Rubin, R., & Abrego, M. (2007). Amistades: The development of relationships between preservice teachers and Latino families. *The School Community Journal, 17,* 77–94.

Swadener, B.B. (1995). Children and families "at promise": Deconstructing the discourse of risk. In B.B. Swadener & S. Lubeck (Eds.), *Children and families "at promise": Deconstructing the discourse of risk* (pp. 17–49). Albany: State University of New York Press.

Swadener, B.B., & Lubeck, S. (Eds.). (1995a). *Children and families "at promise": Deconstructing the discourse of risk.* Albany: State University of New York Press.

Swadener, B.B., & Lubeck, S. (1995b). The social construction of children and families "at risk": An introduction. In B.B. Swadener & S. Lubeck (Eds.), *Children and families "at promise": Deconstructing the discourse of risk* (pp. 1–14). Albany: State University of New York Press.

Swadener, E.B. (1990). Children and families "at risk": Etiology, critique, and alternative paradigms. *Educational Foundations, 4,* 17–39.

Swanson, M.S. (1991). *At-risk students in elementary education: Effective schools for disadvantaged learners.* Springfield, IL: Charles C Thomas.

Tabachnick, B.R., & Bloch, M.N. (1995). Learning in and out of school: Critical perspectives on the theory of cultural compatibility. In B.B. Swadener & S. Lubeck (Eds.), *Children and families "at promise": Deconstructing the discourse of risk* (pp. 187–209). Albany: State University of New York Press.

Tanur, J.M., Mosteller, F., Kruskal, W.H., Lehmann, E.L., Link, R.F., Pieters, R.S., & Rising, G.R. (1989). *Statistics: A guide to the unknown* (3rd ed.). Pacific Grove, CA: Wadsworth & Brooks/Cole.

Taylor, H.F. (1980). *The IQ game: A methodological inquiry into the heredity-environment controversy.* New Brunswick, NJ: Rutgers University Press.

Taylor, H.F. (1992). Intelligence. In E.F. Borgatta & M.L. Borgatta (Eds.), *Encyclopedia of sociology* (pp. 941–949). New York: Macmillan.

Taylor, L.J., & Skanes, G.R. (1976). Level I and Level II intelligence in Inuit and White children from similar environments. *Journal of Cross-Cultural Psychology, 7*, 157–168.

Taylor, M.C. (1927). *Retardation of Mexican children in the Albuquerque schools.* Unpublished master's thesis, Leland Stanford Junior University, Stanford, CA.

Templeton, A.R. (2002). The genetic and evolutionary significance of human races. In J.M. Fish (Ed.), *Race and intelligence: Separating science from myth* (pp. 31–56). Mahwah, NJ: Lawrence Erlbaum.

Teranishi, R., Allen, W.R., & Solórzano, D.G. (2004). Opportunity at the crossroads: Racial inequality, school segregation, and higher education in California. *Teachers College Record, 106*, 2224–2245.

Terman, L.M. (1916). *The measurement of intelligence.* Boston: Houghton Mifflin.

Texas Education Agency. (2006). *Technical digest for the academic year 2006–2007.* Retrieved March 17, 2009, from: *http://ritter.tea.state.tx.us/student.assessment/resources/techdig07/index.html.*

Texas Education Agency. (2008a). *State report, 2007–2008.* Report available online from Texas Education Agency's Academic Excellence Indicator System at: *http://ritter.tea.state.tx.us/perfreport/aeis/2008/index.html.*

Texas Education Agency. (2008b). *2007–08 Houston ISD district performance report.* Report available online from Texas Education Agency's Academic Excellence Indicator System at: *http://ritter.tea.state.tx.us/perfreport/aeis/2008/district.srch.html.*

Theoharis, G. (2004a, November). Toward a theory of social justice educational leadership. In D.C. Thompson & F.E. Crampton (Eds.), *UCEA Conference Proceedings for Convention 2004: The Changing Face(s) of Educational Leadership: UCEA at the Crossroads,* Kansas City, MO. Retrieved June 15, 2007, from: *http://coe.ksu.edu/ucea/byauthor04.htm.*

Theoharis, G. (2004b, November). The rough road to justice: A meta-analysis of the barriers to teaching and leading for social justice. In D.C. Thompson & F.E. Crampton (Eds.), *UCEA Conference Proceedings for Convention 2004: The Changing Face(s) of Educational Leadership: UCEA at the Crossroads,* Kansas City, MO. Retrieved June 15, 2007, from: *http://coe.ksu.edu/ucea/byauthor04.htm.*

Theoharis, G. (2004c). *At no small cost: Social justice leaders and their response to resistance.* Unpublished doctoral dissertation, University of Wisconsin-Madison.

Theoharis, G. (2007a). Social justice educational leaders and resistance: Toward a theory of social justice leadership. *Educational Administration Quarterly, 43*, 221–258.

Theoharis, G. (2007b). Navigating rough waters: A synthesis of the countervailing pressures against leading for social justice. *Journal of School Leadership, 17*, 4–27.

Thomas, R.M., & Sjah, A. (1961). The Draw-a-Man test in Indonesia. *Journal of Educational Psychology, 52*, 232–235.

Thomas, W.B. (1982). Black intellectuals' critiques of early mental testing: A little known saga of the 1920s. *American Journal of Education, 90*, 258–292.

Thompson, G.L. (2004). *Through ebony eyes: What teachers need to know but are afraid to ask about African American students.* San Francisco: Jossey-Bass.

Thurstone, L.L. (1941). *Factorial studies of intelligence.* Chicago: University of Chicago Press.

Thurstone, L.L., & Thurstone, T.G. (1962). *Primary mental abilities* (Rev. ed.). Chicago: Science Research Associates.

Timar, T.B. (2004). School governance and oversight in California: Shaping the landscape of equity and adequacy. *Teachers College Record, 106*, 2057–2080.

Tinker v. Des Moines Independent Community School District, 393 U.S. 503 (1969).

Tough, P. (2007, June 10). The class-consciousness raiser. *New York Times Magazine*. Available online at: *http://www.nytimes.com/2007/06/10/magazine/10payne-t.html?scp* = 1&sq = %22class+consciousness+raiser%22&st = nyt.

Tropea, J.L. (1993). Structuring risks: The making of urban school order. In R. Wollons (Ed.), *Children at risk in America: History, concepts, and public policy* (pp. 58–88). New York: State University of New York Press.

Tropman, J.E. (1998). *Does America hate the poor?: The other American dilemma: Lessons for the 21st century from the 1960s and 1970s.* Westport, CT: Praeger.

Trueba, H.T. (1991). From failure to success: The roles of culture and cultural conflict in the academic achievement of Chicano students. In R.R. Valencia (Ed.), *Chicano school failure and success: Research and policy agendas for the 1990s* (pp. 151–163). The Stanford Series on Education and Public Policy. London: Falmer Press.

Tucker, W.H. (1994). *The science and politics of racial research.* Urbana: University of Illinois Press.

Tucker, W.H. (2001). Bankrolling racism: "Science" and the Pioneer Fund. *Race & Society, 4,* 195–205.

Tucker, W.H. (2002). *The funding of scientific racism: Wickliffe Draper and the Pioneer Fund.* Urbana: University of Illinois Press.

Tucker, W.H. (2003). A closer look at the Pioneer Fund: Response to Rushton. *Albany Law Review, 66,* 1145–1159.

Tyler, K.M., Uqdah, A.L., Dillihunt, M.L., Beatty-Hazelbaker, R., Conner, T., Gadson, N., Henchy, A., Hughes, T., Mulder, S., Owens, E., Roan-Belle, C., Smith, L., & Stevens, R. (2008). Cultural discontinuity: Toward a quantitative investigation of a major hypothesis in education. *Educational Researcher, 37,* 280–297.

Tymchuk, A., Lakin, K., & Luckasson, R. (2001). *The forgotten generation: The status and challenges of adults with mild cognitive limitations.* Baltimore: Paul H. Brookes.

Tzuriel, D., & Klein, P.S. (1987). Assessing the young child: Children's analogical thinking modifiability. In C.S. Lidz (Ed.), *Dynamic assessment: An interactional approach to evaluating learning potential* (pp. 268–287). New York: Guilford.

Uzzell, D. (1975). The interaction of population and locality in the development of squatter settlements in Lima. In W. Cornelius & F. Trueblood (Eds.), *Latin American urban research* (Vol. 4, pp. 113–134). Beverly Hills, CA: Sage.

Valencia, R.R. (1988). The McCarthy Scales and Hispanic children: A review of psychometric research. *Hispanic Journal of Behavioral Sciences, 10,* 81–104.

Valencia, R.R. (1990). Clinical assessment of young children with the McCarthy Scales. In C.R. Reynolds & R.W. Kamphaus (Eds.), *Handbook of psychological and educational assessment of children: Intelligence and achievement* (pp. 209–258). New York: Guilford.

Valencia, R.R. (Ed.). (1991). *Chicano school failure and success: Research and policy agendas for the 1990s.* The Stanford Series on Education and Public Policy. London: Falmer Press.

Valencia, R.R. (Ed.). (1997a). *The evolution of deficit thinking: Educational thought and practice.* The Stanford Series on Education and Public Policy. London: Falmer Press.

Valencia, R.R. (1997b). Introduction. In R.R. Valencia (Ed.), *The evolution of deficit thinking: Educational thought and practice* (pp. ix–xvii). The Stanford Series on Education and Public Policy. London: Falmer Press.

Valencia, R.R. (1997c). Conceptualizing the notion of deficit thinking. In R.R. Valencia (Ed.), *The evolution of deficit thinking: Educational thought and practice* (pp. 1–12). The Stanford Series on Education and Public Policy. London: Falmer Press.

Valencia, R.R. (1997d). Genetic pathology model of deficit thinking. In R.R. Valencia (Ed.), *The evolution of deficit thinking: Educational thought and practice* (pp. 41–112). The Stanford Series on Education and Public Policy. London: Falmer Press.

Valencia, R.R. (2002). The plight of Chicano students: An overview of schooling conditions and outcomes. In R.R. Valencia (Ed.), *Chicano school failure and success: Past, present, and future* (2nd ed., pp. 3–51). London: RoutledgeFalmer.

Valencia, R.R. (2005). The Mexican American struggle for equal educational opportunity in *Mendez v. Westminster*: Helping to pave the way for *Brown v. Board of Education. Teachers College Record, 107,* 389–423.

Valencia, R.R. (2008). *Chicano students and the courts: The Mexican American legal struggle for educational equality.* Critical America Series. New York: New York University Press.

Valencia, R.R. (2009, June 25). A response to Ruby Payne's claim that the deficit thinking model has no scholarly utility. *Teachers College Record.* Retrieved June 29, 2009, from: *http:// www.tcrecord.org/Content.asp?ContentId* = 15691.

Valencia, R.R., & Aburto, S. (1991). The uses and abuses of educational testing: Chicanos as a case in point. In R.R. Valencia (Ed.), *Chicano school failure and success: Research and policy agendas for the 1990s* (pp. 203–251). The Stanford Series on Education and Public Policy. London: Falmer Press.

Valencia, R.R., & Bernal, E.M. (Eds.). (2000). The Texas Assessment of Academic Skills (TAAS) case: Perspectives of plaintiffs' experts [Special issue]. *Hispanic Journal of Behavioral Sciences, 22*(4).

Valencia, R.R., & Black, M.S. (2002)."Mexican Americans don't value education!"—On the basis of the myth, mythmaking, and debunking. *Journal of Latinos and Education, 1,* 81–103.

Valencia, R.R., & Guadarrama, I.N. (1996). High-stakes testing and its impact on racial and ethnic minority students. In L.A. Suzuki, P.J. Meller, & J.G. Ponterotto (Eds.), *Multicultural assessment: Clinical, psychological, and educational applications* (pp. 561–610). San Francisco: Jossey-Bass.

Valencia, R.R., Menchaca, M., & Donato, R. (2002). Segregation, desegregation, and integration of Chicano students: Old and new realities. In R.R. Valencia (Ed.), *Chicano school failure and success: Past, present, and future* (2nd ed., pp. 70–113). London: RoutledgeFalmer.

Valencia, R.R., Menchaca, M., & Valenzuela, A. (1993). The educational future of Chicanos: A call for affirmative diversity. *The Journal of the Association of Mexican American Educators,* 5–13.

Valencia, R.R., & Rankin, R.J. (1985). Evidence of content bias on the McCarthy Scales with Mexican American children: Implications for test translation and nonbiased assessment. *Journal of Educational Psychology, 77,* 197–207.

Valencia, R.R., & Solórzano, D.G. (1997). Contemporary deficit thinking. In R.R. Valencia (Ed.), *The evolution of deficit thinking: Educational thought and practice* (pp. 160–210). The Stanford Series on Education and Public Policy. London: Falmer Press.

Valencia, R.R., & Suzuki, L.A. (2001). *Intelligence testing and minority students: Foundations, performance factors, and assessment issues.* Series on Racial and Ethnic Minority Psychology. Thousand Oaks, CA: Sage.

Valencia, R.R., Valenzuela, A., Sloan, K., & Foley, D.E. (2001). At odds—Let's treat the cause, not the symptoms: Equity and accountability in Texas revisited. *Phi Delta Kappan, 83,* 318–321, 326.

Valencia, R.R., & Villarreal, B.J. (2003). Improving students' reading performance via standards-based school reform: A critique. *The Reading Teacher, 56,* 612–621.

Valencia, R.R., Villarreal, B.J., & Salinas, M.F. (2002). Educational testing and Chicano students: Issues, consequences, and prospects for reform. In R.R. Valencia (Ed.), *Chicano school failure and success: Past, present, and future* (2nd ed., pp. 253–309). London: RoutledgeFalmer.

Valentine, B. (1978). *Hustling and other hard work.* New York: Free Press.

Valentine, C.A. (1968). *Culture and poverty: Critique and counter-proposals.* Chicago: University of Chicago Press.

Valentine, C.A. (1969). Reply. *Current Anthropology, 10,* 197–201.

Valentine, C.A. (1971). Deficit, difference, and bicultural models of Afro-American behavior. *Harvard Educational Review, 41,* 137–157.

Valenzuela, A. (Ed.). (2005). *Leaving children behind: How "Texas-style" accountability fails Latino youth.* Albany: State University of New York Press.

Van Court, M. (1998). [Review of the book *Dysgenics: Genetic deterioration in modern populations*]. *Journal of Social, Political, and Economic Studies, 23,* 223–228.

van den Haag, E. (1960). Social science testimony in the desegregation cases—A reply to Kenneth Clark. *Villanova Law Review, 6,* 69–79.

Vandenberg, S.G. (1969). A twin study of spatial ability. *Multivariate Behavioral Research, 4,* 273–294.

Vandenberg, S.G. (1970). A comparison of heritability estimates of U.S. Negro and White high schools students. *Acta Geneticae Medicae et Gemellologiae, 19,* 280–284.

Vega, W.A., Zimmerman, R.S., Warheit, G.J., Apospori, E., & Gil, A.G. (1993). Risk factors for early adolescent drug use in four ethnic and racial groups. *American Journal of Public Health, 83,* 185–189.

Villenas, S., & Foley, D.E. (2002). Chicano/Latino critical ethnography of education: Cultural productions from *la frontera.* In R.R. Valencia (Ed.), *Chicano school failure and success: Past, present, and future* (2nd ed., pp. 195–226). London: RoutledgeFalmer.

Vint, F.W. (1934). The brain of the Kenya native. *Journal of Anatomy, 68,* 216–223.

Volken, T. (2003). [Review of the book *IQ and the wealth of nations*]. *European Sociological Review*, *19*, 411–412.

Vygotsky, L.S. (1978). *Mind in society: The development of higher psychological processes*. Cambridge, MA: Harvard University Press.

Wade, N. (1976). IQ and heredity: Suspicion of fraud beclouds classic experiment. *Science*, *194*, 916–919.

Wahlsten, D. (1990). Insensitivity of the analysis of variance to heredity-environment interaction. *Behavioral and Brain Sciences*, *13*, 109–161.

Wahlsten, D. (1995). [Review of the book *Race, evolution, and behavior: A life history perspective*]. *Canadian Journal of Sociology*, *20*, 129–133.

Wallace, B. (1975). Genetics and the great IQ controversy. *American Biology Teacher*, *37*, 12–18, 50.

Washington, G. (1797). *Farewell address*. Available online from the University of Virginia collection, "The Papers of George Washington," at: *http://gwpapers.virginia.edu/documents/farewell/intro.html*.

Watson-Gegeo, K. (1992). Thick explanations in the ethnographic study of child socialization: A longitudinal study of the problem of schooling for Kwara'ae (Solomon Islands) children. *Directions for Child Development*, *58*, 51–66.

Waxman, H.C. (1992). Reversing the cycle of educational failure for students in at-risk school environments. In H.C. Waxman, J. Walker de Felix, J. Anderson, & H.P. Baptiste, Jr. (Eds.), *Students at risk in at-risk schools: Improving environments for learning* (pp. 1–9). Newbury Park, CA: Sage.

Wayne, A.J., & Youngs, P. (2003). Teacher characteristics and student achievement gains: A review. *Review of Educational Research*, *73*, 89–122.

Webster, Y.O. (1992). *The racialization of America*. New York: St. Martin's Press.

Wechsler, D. (1949). *Manual for the Wechsler Intelligence Scale for Children*. New York: Psychological Corporation.

Weinberg, M. (1977). *A chance to learn: The history of race and education in the United States*. New York: Cambridge University Press.

Weinberg, R.A., Scarr, S., & Waldman, I.D. (1992). The Minnesota Transracial Adoption Study: A follow-up of IQ performance at adolescence. *Intelligence*, *16*, 117–135.

West, C. (1993). *Race matters*. Boston, MA: Beacon Press.

Weyher, H.F. (1998). Contributions to the history of psychology: CXII. Intelligence, behavioral genetics, and the Pioneer Fund. *Psychological Reports*, *82*, 1347–1374.

Weyher, H.F. (1999a). The Pioneer Fund, the behavioral sciences, and the media's false stories. *Intelligence*, *26*, 319–336.

Weyher, H.F. (1999b). Reply to Tucker: Defending early IQ researchers. *Psychological Reports*, *84*, 485–487.

Weyl, N. (1960). *The Negro in American civilization*. Washington, DC: Public Affairs Press.

Whetzel, D.A., & McDaniel, M.A. (2006). Prediction of national wealth. *Intelligence*, *34*, 449–458.

White, C.J. (1995). Native Americans at promise: Travel in borderlands. In B.B. Swadener & S. Lubeck (Eds.), *Children and families "at promise": Deconstructing the discourse of risk* (pp. 163–184). Albany: State University of New York Press.

White, K.R. (1982). The relation between socioeconomic status and academic achievement. *Psychological Bulletin*, *91*, 461–481.

White, R.K., & Lippitt, R. (1960). *Autocracy and democracy: An experimental inquiry*. New York: Harper.

Whitney, G. (1998). [Review of the book *Dysgenics: Genetic deterioration in modern populations*]. *Journal of Social and Evolutionary Systems*, *21*, 343–355.

Wiersma, W., & Jurs, S.G. (2005). *Research methods in education: An introduction* (8th ed.). Boston: Allyn and Bacon.

Williams v. California, Civil Action No. 312236 (Superior Court, San Francisco County, California March 23, 2005).

Williams, M. (1981). *On the street where I live*. New York: Holt, Rinehart, and Winston.

Willie, C.V. (1976). *A new look at Black families*. New York: General Hall.

Wilmoth, J.R. (1997). [Review of the book *Dysgenics: Genetic deterioration in modern populations*]. *Population and Development Review*, *23*, 664–666.

Winston, A.S. (1998). Science in the service of the far right: Henry E. Garrett, the IAAEE, and the Liberty Lobby. *Journal of Social Issues*, *54*, 179–210.

Wollenberg, C. (1978). *All deliberate speed: Segregation and exclusion in California schools, 1855–1975.* Berkeley: University of California Press.

Wollons, R. (1993). Introduction. In R. Wollons (Ed.), *Children at risk in America: History, concepts, and public policy* (pp. ix–xxv). New York: State University of New York Press.

Worthen, A. (1995). Has there been a cognitive revolution in America? The flawed sociology of *The bell curve.* In S. Fraser (Ed.), *The bell curve wars: Race, intelligence, and the future of America* (pp. 109–123). New York: Basic Books.

Worthen, B.R., Borg, W.R., & White, K.R. (1993). *Measurement and evaluation in the schools.* New York: Longman.

Wright, S.E. (1993). Blaming the victim, blaming society or blaming the discipline: Fixing responsibility for poverty and homelessness. *The Sociological Quarterly, 34,* 1–16.

Wright, S.P., Horn, S.P., & Sanders, W.L. (1997). Teacher and classroom context effects on student achievement: Implications for teacher evaluation. *Journal of Personnel Evaluation in Education, 11,* 57–67.

Young, P.A. (2007). Thinking outside the box: Fostering racial and ethnic discourses in urban teacher education. In R.P. Solomon & D. Sekayi (Eds.), *Urban teacher education and teaching: Innovative practices for diversity and social justice* (pp. 109–128). Mahwah, NJ: Lawrence Erlbaum.

Zenderland, L. (1990). Burt again [Review of the book *The Burt affair*]. *Science, 248,* 884–886.

Index

Made in the USA
San Bernardino, CA
21 January 2015